Lecture Notes in Computer Science 16466

The series Lecture Notes in Computer Science (LNCS), including its subseries Lecture Notes in Artificial Intelligence (LNAI) and Lecture Notes in Bioinformatics (LNBI), has established itself as a medium for the publication of new developments in computer science and information technology research, teaching, and education.

LNCS enjoys close cooperation with the computer science R & D community, the series counts many renowned academics among its volume editors and paper authors, and collaborates with prestigious societies. Its mission is to serve this international community by providing an invaluable service, mainly focused on the publication of conference and workshop proceedings and postproceedings. LNCS commenced publication in 1973.

Henrich C. Pöhls · Chris J. Mitchell
Editors

Security Standardisation Research

10th International Conference, SSR 2025
Passau, Germany, December 4–5, 2025
Proceedings

Editors
Henrich C. Pöhls
University of Passau
Passau, Germany

Chris J. Mitchell
University of London
Egham, UK

ISSN 0302-9743 ISSN 1611-3349 (electronic)
Lecture Notes in Computer Science
ISBN 978-3-032-19566-1 ISBN 978-3-032-19567-8 (eBook)
https://doi.org/10.1007/978-3-032-19567-8

This Springer imprint is published by the registered company Springer Nature Switzerland AG
The registered company address is: Gewerbestrasse 11, 6330 Cham, Switzerland

Preface

The Security Standardization Research (SSR) Conference 2025 was the 10th iteration of the SSR conference series, launched in 2014. SSR 2025 was held in Passau, Germany, on December 4th and 5th, 2025.

Over the past two decades, cybersecurity standards have advanced significantly and many of them have become very widely used. Despite their widespread use, it is essential to continually revise existing standards and develop new standards to cover emerging domains, such as post-quantum cryptography, fully homomorphic encryption, 6G and artificial intelligence. The purpose of the 2024 SSR conference was to discuss the numerous research challenges arising from studies of existing standards, the development of revisions to these standards, and the exploration of entirely new areas of standardization. Many security standards bodies are only beginning to address the issue of transparency, ensuring that the process of selecting security techniques for standardization is as scientific and unbiased as possible.

The SSR conference series covers the full spectrum of research on security standardization, including, but not restricted to, work on cryptographic techniques, security management, security evaluation criteria, security policy, network security, privacy and identity management, smart cards and RFID tags, biometrics, security modules and industry-specific security standards (e.g. those produced by the payments, telecommunications and computing industries for such things as payment protocols, mobile telephony and trusted computing). Through these discussions and research presentations, the conference series aims to advance the field of security standardization, fostering a collaborative environment for both revising existing standards and developing new ones to address the evolving challenges in cybersecurity. We are pleased to say that the SSR 2025 programme reflected our goal of achieving a broad coverage of the area.

We received a total of 25 high-quality submissions to SSR 2025 via the EasyChair conference management system, which allowed us to appropriately manage the reviewing process where there were potential conflicts of interest, for example ensuring that papers co-authored by members of the programme committee were handled in an appropriate and confidential way. The Programme Chairs interacted with the invited speaker to ensure that the extended abstract was of appropriate quality. We observed a continuation of the pleasing increase in numbers submitted to recent iterations of the event. Each submission was reviewed by at least three members of the programme committee in a mutually anonymous way. After a period of discussion, we chose to accept only 10 (i.e. 40%) of the submissions for presentation at the conference. We are very grateful to the 28 excellent members of the programme committee for proving detailed reviews in a prompt way.

We were delighted to have a distinguished invited (keynote) speaker who contributed their expertise and perspectives from both academia and the standardization community to the SSR 2025 programme.

- Amelie Leipprand from DIN, the Deutsches Institut für Normung e. V.

We would like to sincerely thank everyone who contributed to the success of SSR 2025. First and foremost, we must thank all the authors for submitting their work to the conference, and the speakers at the conference for making such a valuable contribution to the conference programme. We are, of course, heavily indebted to the programme committee, which, as we already mentioned, did a great job in the interactive discussion and by providing thorough reviews — it was a pleasure to work with you. We would like to thank the Team of the Centre for IT Security at the University of Passau for their unstinting support. Finally, we must thank all attendees of SSR 2025.

December 2025

Henrich C. Pöhls
Chris J. Mitchell

Organization

General Chair

Henrich C. Pöhls	University of Passau, Germany

Program Committee Chairs

Henrich C. Pöhls	University of Passau, Germany
Chris J. Mitchell	Royal Holloway, University of London, UK

Steering Committee

Liqun Chen	University of Surrey, UK
Shin'Ichiro Matsuo	Georgetown University, USA
Bart Preneel	Katholieke Universiteit Leuven, Belgium

Program Committee

Aysajan Abidin	Katholieke Universiteit Leuven, Belgium
Joppe Bos	NXP Semiconductors
Sofía Celi	Brave
Lily Chen	NIST, USA
Zhaohui Cheng	Olym Info Sec Inc., China
Jihoon Cho	Samsung SDS, South Korea
Benjamin R. Curtis	Zama
Orr Dunkelman	University of Haifa, Israel and Technische Universität Berlin, Germany
Scott Fluhrer	Cisco Systems
Matt Henricksen	Huawei International Pte Ltd., Singapore
John Kelsey	NIST, USA and Katholieke Universiteit Leuven, Belgium
Stephan Krenn	AIT Austrian Institute of Technology, Austria
Thalia Laing	HP Inc.
Shin'Ichiro Matsuo	Georgetown University, USA
Elisabeth Oswald	University of Birmingham, UK

Additional Reviewers

Invited Keynote Talk

Shedding Light on Standardization (Extended Abstract)

Amelie Leipprand

DIN, Deutsches Institut für Normung e. V., Am DIN-Platz, Burggrafenstrasse 6, 10787 Berlin
Amelie.Leipprand@din.de

The word "standard" is not standardized. Industry standards arise when a company either has the only solution to a problem and thus dominates the market, or when a company is particularly successful in establishing its solution in the market and therefore controls it. In sociology, we speak of societal norms. In the application of legal texts, we speak of legal norms. In the IT context, the word standard is used for interfaces, protocols or sometimes program code. That produces confusion when talking about technical standards.

It is important to be aware of this ambiguity of terminology, as disagreements often arise precisely from it[1]. Therefore, the term deserves explanation.

What is Technical Standardization?

Standardization is the process by which documents are developed. Often surprisingly, standards are not set by DIN but rather developed in committees at DIN. In this process, different viewpoints are brought forward, and a consensus is reached.

What is Consensus?

Consensus is not the lowest common denominator or the foulest of compromises, but rather a different way of communicating with one another. Instead of a destructive approach of attacking each other, a constructive search for common ground is needed. Every perspective is equally important: environmental protection just as much as manufacturing, consumer protection just as much as logistics, occupational safety just as much as certification. Every stakeholder connected to the topic of the committee is invited. The need to work out a consensus together and on equal terms cultivates a skill that seems to be becoming rare: speaking in order to be understood and listening in order to understand.

---

[1] See also the textbook "A world built on standards" by DS (Danish Standards), available for free at: https://www.ds.dk/media/px5jhney/a-world-built-on-standards.pdf?srsltid=AfmBOorrM-9MxkY0ffi10Hezi0TRw-dMTL7AcRF3PdqP5ZrY4SJokIoq.

What are Standards?

They are often mistaken for a kind of technical law. However, they are voluntary. They only become binding when a legally binding document (e.g., a contract, a law) refers to them. Standards can even be mandated. In this case, the legislator issues a mandate to the standards organizations to technically define a specific topic. One example is the European AI Act[2].

Only 20% of all standards are referenced in laws, and here a sensible division of labor applies between societal rule-making (called politics), which establishes the fundamental direction and enacts corresponding laws, and technical rule-making (called standardization), which makes technical proposals on how these can be implemented. Adherence to standards makes life easier because the standardization process answers many questions, clarifies many issues, and addresses many difficulties. Furthermore, a system encompassing certification, training, consulting, manufacturing, etc., is generally more aligned with standards. This usually makes the individual steps more cost-effective. However, it remains permissible to find one's own way. This fosters innovation and takes into account the fact that technological developments sometimes progress faster than the documentation can be adapted.

If the Technical Standardization System Offers so Much Potential, Why Isn't This Known Better?

In Germany and many European Countries, standardization is not a component of higher education curricula. If students learn about it, it's only thanks to dedicated individual professors. This has been recognized as a deficit and is being addressed in the European strategy on standardization[3] in "VI. Ensuring future standardisation expertise — the need for education and skills", further differentiated in High Level Forum[4] Workstream 1 "Education and skills".

Still, a lot of work needs to be done to achieve broad education about standardization, as countries like China or South Korea show us. Many national standardization bodies (NSBs) support education strongly by providing material or offering seminars. If interested, please contact DIN via mailto:durchstarten@din.dedurchstarten@din.de or go to your NSB.

---

[2] More information is available on the DIN webpage https://www.din.de/en/innovation-and-research/artificial-intelligence/ai-act-/ai-act-ai-legislation-906712.

[3] https://ec.europa.eu/docsroom/documents/48598.

[4] https://single-market-economy.ec.europa.eu/single-market/goods/european-standards/standardisation-policy/high-level-forum-european-standardisation_en.

Contents

Contributed Papers

SoK: Anonymous Credentials for Digital Identity Wallets ... 3
Christian Bormann and Anja Lehmann

Making BBS Anonymous Credentials eIDAS 2.0 Compliant ... 26
Nicolas Desmoulins, Antoine Dumanois, Seyni Kane, and Jacques Traoré

VISION: A Modular Framework for Anonymous Credential Systems ... 46
Anja Lehmann, Andrey Sidorenko, and Alexandros Zacharakis

A Threat Model for the W3C Digital Credentials API: An Initial Analysis ... 69
Zahra Ebadi Ansaroudi, Amir Sharif, Giada Sciarretta, Simone Onofri, and Silvio Ranise

Benchmarking of the Amortized Post Quantum Combiner for MLS ... 89
Britta Hale, Xisen Tian, and Lee Wang

QUIC-MLS: Making a Space Security Draft Standard Resilient for Disconnected Environments ... 111
Benjamin Dowling, Britta Hale, Xisen Tian, and Bhagya Wimalasiri

Cryptographic Binding Should Not Be Optional: A Formal-Methods Analysis of FIDO UAF Channel Binding ... 133
Enis Golaszewski, Alan T. Sherman, Edward Zieglar, Jonathan D. Fuchs, and Sophia Hamer

CRA and Cryptography: The Story Thus Far ... 162
Markku-Juhani O. Saarinen

Post-quantum Cryptography in eMRTDs Evaluating PAKE and PKI for Travel Documents ... 181
Nouri Alnahawi, Melissa Azouaoui, Joppe W. Bos, Gareth T. Davies, SeoJeong Moon, Christine van Vredendaal, and Alexander Wiesmaier

Towards Cryptography Bill of Materials Compliance ... 202
Claudio Foroncelli, Pietro De Matteis, Luis Augusto Dias Knob, Luca Piras, Alessandro Tomasi, and Silvio Ranise

Author Index ... 223

Contributed Papers

SoK: Anonymous Credentials for Digital Identity Wallets

Christian Bormann[1(✉)] and Anja Lehmann[1,2]

[1] SPRIN-D - Federal Agency for Breakthrough Innovation, Leipzig, Germany
christian.bormann@eudi.sprind.org
[2] Hasso Plattner Institute, University of Potsdam, Potsdam, Germany
anja.lehmann@hpi.de

Abstract. Digital identity wallets are currently being developed around the globe, aiming to provide user-centric and secure authentication. Realizing this in a privacy-preserving manner is paramount, and even mandated in Europe which is developing the European Digital Identity Wallet with planned release in 2026. Current proposals to build these wallets are based on classic signature schemes such as ECDSA, but would benefit greatly from the use of *anonymous credentials*. Thus, there is currently a strong interest in developing the necessary standards to bring these cryptographic concepts into the real world. This work aims to inform ongoing standardization efforts by providing an overview of the most prominent solutions, and the remaining open challenges. We split our overview among two fundamental architectural approaches: (1) dedicated multi-message signature schemes that allow for efficient ZKPs, and (2) general-purpose ZKPs used on top of legacy ECDSA. We also provide a comprehensive summary of the broad feature set that anonymous credentials can provide for identity wallets, in order to demonstrate that upgrading to these systems is a worthwhile endeavor and help to design standards that can leverage the rich existing body of work.

Keywords: Anonymous Credentials · EUDI · Zero-knowledge Proofs

1 Introduction

Anonymous credentials (AC) enable privacy-preserving and user-centric authentication. Trusted issuers attest the user's attributes in form of cryptographic credentials. The user can then use these credentials to create presentations towards relying parties (RP) that reveal only the minimally necessary subset of the attested information in a verifiable manner. Despite being well-understood in the academic community with research spanning over more than two decades [6,13,24,27,49,89], they have not seen wide-spread adoption yet. However, they are currently enjoying increased attention in the context of several digital identity systems being built around the globe, e.g., in the US [91], Europe [44], Switzerland [88], and the UK [78]. Notably, both the IRTF [63,84] and ISO [56] are currently working on standards for anonymous credentials.

H. C. Pöhls and C. J. Mitchell (Eds.): SSR 2025, LNCS 16466, pp. 3–25, 2026.
https://doi.org/10.1007/978-3-032-19567-8_1

Particularly noteworthy are the efforts in Europe, that aims to roll out a phone-based solution – the European Digital Identity (EUDI) wallet – by the end of 2026. What stands out in these efforts is the strong commitment to *privacy*: the underlying eIDAS regulation mandates several strong privacy properties such as selective disclosure, pseudonymity, untraceability and unlinkability, e.g. stating that "*The technical framework of the European Digital Identity Wallet shall (a) not allow providers of electronic attestations of attributes or any other party [..] to obtain data that allows transactions or user behaviour to be tracked, linked or correlated [..]; (b) enable privacy preserving techniques which ensure unlinkability*" (Article 5a, 16b of eIDAS [45]).

Despite being *the* use case anonymous credentials were invented for, the design currently proposed in the EU Architecture Reference Framework (ARF) [41] instead relies on classical signature schemes such as ECDSA. To achieve a weak form of unlinkability and selective disclosure, it uses batch-issuance of one-time use credentials and salted hashes.

While the proposed solution achieves some of the privacy properties mandated by the regulation, it clearly cannot achieve unlinkability when the issuer and RP collude. Unlinkability across different malicious RPs requires using a fresh one-time credential in every presentation, which imposes a significant load on the issuer's infrastructure and also raises challenges in the user's secure key management. This has been highlighted in the cryptographers' feedback [10] for the ARF, advocating for the use of ACs instead.

Given recent advances and better alignment of constructions with the requirements of eIDAS, the EU is now re-considering the use of anonymous credentials and started gathering requirements for the development of a standard [41]. In fact, a core aspect that hindered the adoption of ACs so far is the lack of a unified standard, and any efforts made in the EU will also largely impact similar deployment endeavors in other areas. Thus, it is important to inform decision makers and standardization bodies on the available solution space, their individual challenges and benefits, such that this seminal step towards the real-world deployment of anonymous credentials is done in the best way possible.

Our Contributions. Our work aims to provide this informational foundation and gives an overview of the two most prominent directions to build identity systems from anonymous credentials: dedicated multi-message signatures with efficient proofs (such as BBS signatures with Schnorr proofs [6]), and general-purpose zero-knowledge (ZKP) systems build on top of ECDSA. We describe their state-of the art, status in terms of standardization and challenges they need to overcome in order to be suitable for digital identity wallets. For the first approach relying on dedicated and mature signatures such as BBS [6], we focus on the most pressing challenges: compatibility with existing user phones for the feature of device binding, as well as the support for pairing-friendly curves. When it comes to general-purpose ZKP systems, the situation is much more open and almost complementary: they can be built on top of any legacy signature scheme and even entire classical credential systems, avoiding the deployment challenges inherent in the BBS-based approach. However, they are still a highly active field of research, with a multitude of options and introduce a level of complexity through their circuit-based design that the ZKProof work [95] aims to tame for almost 8 years already.

Before giving an overview of these technical solutions, we summarize the features of anonymous credentials that we believe are of particular interest in the digital identity context. In fact, the discussion so far focuses solely on the most basic feature of ACs – multi-show unlinkability – but does not consider the bigger picture and feature set they enable. Without being aware of the overall feature set, there is a risk that technical standards are chosen and built in a premature way, hard-coding the design choices to a bare bone solution that will be hard to extend. Apart from being relevant for properly designing the technical standards, they also demonstrate that anonymous credentials will bring significant benefits compared to the existing classical signature approach for digital identity wallets: not only in privacy but also in security and large scale deployability.

The goal to inform the ongoing standardization activities in the EU around ACs gives this SoK a more "executive-level" flavour. A more technical and full-fledged overview of anonymous credentials has been attempted over a decade ago in the ABC4Trust project, and our SoK can be seen as an updated and wallet-centric overview of such technologies [13]. Further, the focus on the use of anonymous credentials for digital identity wallets and the most pressing challenges to overcome is also what separates our work from the more general SoK on anonymous credentials by Kakvi et al. [58].

2 Features of Anonymous Credentials

This section gives an overview of the general privacy and security features that anonymous credentials (ACs) can provide in the context of digital identity systems. We focus mainly on features where they differ from the current approach of batch-issued classic certificates as described in the EU ARF [41]. Note that they not only provide additional privacy properties but also enable better security and scalability than the currently designed system.

Core Features. We start with the fundamental features that are supported by most anonymous credential systems. The systems entails three main entities: issuers, users and relying parties (RP). The issuers attest attributes in form of credentials to the user. The user can then derive presentations based on these credentials to transmit authenticated attribute-based information to the relying party which is able to verify the authenticity of those statements.

Selective Disclosure: With every presentation, the user can choose the subset of attributes they want to selectively disclose towards the RP.

Multi-show Unlinkability: Relying party to relying party unlinkability ensures that different presentations of the same user, that don't reveal any identifying information, cannot be linked. This prevents profiling of users in scenarios where only limited information about their credentials is revealed, e.g., in age proofs or proofs of personhood.

Untraceability: Relying party to issuer unlinkability prevents that a malicious issuer can link the credentials it issued to the derived presentations the user sends to the relying parties. This again aims to prevent any profiling and tracking through malicious relying parties and issuers.

Single Key Binding: Many or even all credentials that belong to the same user can be bound to the same user private key. Such single key binding reduces complexity for the user/device and increases security. When all of the user's credentials are bound to the same key, this disincentivizes the sharing or pooling of credentials through malicious users, and is often referred to as all-or-nothing transferability.

Presentation Freshness: Presentation of a credential never reveals the original credential, but only a proof thereof. The proof can be bound to a particular context, e.g., the session nonce or the RP's identity towards which the presentation is done. From such a presentation, no further presentation for a different context can be derived. This ensures that certified attributes cannot be used in a context other than what was intended by the user.

Certified Pseudonyms: Anonymous credentials do not come with the classical notion of public keys for the user. Instead, they allow to derive verifiable yet unlinkable pseudonyms from a user's secret key embedded in her credentials. From a single key, many unlinkable pseudonyms can be verifiably derived and bound to attested user attributes. Pseudonyms can optionally be context-bound, e.g., realizing a 1-to-1 binding of a user to an RP or enforcing rate-limiting, while keeping her pseudonyms unlinkable across RPs/contexts. This introduces a controlled level of linkability back into the system.

Further Features. Beyond the basic features summarized above, ACs can provide more capabilities that are impossible with classic certificates. Most are designed to further improve privacy and security by minimizing the information that users have to expose during issuance and presentation.

Predicate Proofs: Instead of revealing an exact attribute, the presentation proves that a specific property of or statement about an attribute holds true. A prominent example is the age over 18 proof instead of revealing the date of birth. This feature allows for more flexibility during presentation (issuers do not need to know the concrete requests) and also helps to hide correlation factors, such as expiration date, in a presentation.

Composite Proofs: Composite proofs (presentations) can be constructed over several credentials, also allowing more advanced logic over the different attributes. For instance, a composite proof could demonstrate that a user possesses both, a valid university credential, and a government ID with a matching name, all without revealing the name. Composite proofs also enable to separate between user and device binding: credentials can be bound to a user secret, which is never revealed, but be used to prove that several credentials belong together. When needed, a special device-bound credential that blindly connects the user secret with the device secret can further establish a proof of device-binding. This will allow for a simpler backup and restore, as the attribute credentials are not directly bound to a user device.

Deniable Presentations: Presentations can be bound to a specific relying party, and constructed such that only this RP will be convinced of the correctness of the user's attributes (also called designated verifier proof). If the RP forwards the proof to a third party, this does not provide convincing cryptographic evidence of the validity of the user's attributes. This capability would allow for switching between presentations that offer repudiation or non-repudiation based on use-case and regulatory requirements.

(Partially-)Blind Issuance: Allows for the issuance of data that stays hidden from the issuer. This enables distributed issuance concepts, e.g., for a central issuance authority for academic credentials. The sensitive data, such as students' names and grades, is checked and vouched for by a local university, but remains hidden to the centrally provided issuance infrastructure, which only sees the university and final degree, but signs the whole document.

Issuer Hiding: Creates a presentation that only reveals membership in a certain trust ecosystem instead of revealing a specific issuer. For example, proving that one owns a master's degree from a German university, without revealing the specific university.

Conditional Disclosure: The presentation contains verified but initially protected attributes, which can be discovered by a dedicated party only when needed. For instance, making the personal address only accessible to the postal service, not the online shop, or the credit card number used in a hotel reservation that is can only be revealed in case of a no-show.

Benefits of Anonymous Credentials. Discussions about ACs are often focused solely on the privacy features, but in the case of the EUDI Wallets, they also bring deployment advantages that we summarize next.

Enhanced Privacy and Security. Solutions based on ACs achieve stronger privacy and security guarantees, which can lead to better user acceptance.

(1) Relying on ACs is the only practical way to fully achieve the unlinkability requirement specified in §16 of the eIDAS regulation. Realizing this requirement and incorporating modern cryptography sets a high standard for digital wallets and lessens the risk that users will face and perceive when using the technology. This holds particularly in unregulated use-cases where a certain level of trust in the issuer not acting maliciously cannot be assumed.

(2) Classic certificates reveal the original attribute credential with every presentation, which harms the actual and perceived security of the system. Average users will not understand the difference between a credential with and without a fresh proof-of-possession (PoP), but might consider the system insecure when copies of their credentials can be made easily. This is also an actual risk: RPs might accept credentials without a fresh PoP, e.g., due to false configuration or the intent to act outside of the regulated EUDI ecosystem.

With ACs, every attribute presentation has an implicit freshness proof and cannot be reused outside the original context. Further, to verify the user attributes, the context string must be given as input for verification as well. This typically contains the targeted RP's identity and thus allows for immediate tracing of the faulty or malicious RP that has lost/reused the users' credentials.

Reduced System Complexity. ACs can help to reduce the system's complexity, both for issuers and users, for instance, as follows:

(3) The currently proposed EUDI solution achieves multi-show unlinkability at the cost of system complexity, via single-use credentials. In contrast, this is achieved naturally for ACs, as they allow to derive many unlinkable presentations from the same credential. By getting rid of one-time use credentials, batch issuance, and the need to manage possibly hundreds of device keys, the overall system becomes more robust, and the expected load is reduced significantly.

(4) Composite proofs enable to decouple the device-binding aspect from attribute credentials, which leads to a simpler backup as described above. They also enable an efficient way to handle short-lived credentials [13]: instead of regularly updating all of the user's credentials, they can all be bound to a dedicated revocation credential. Only the revocation credential must get refreshed regularly, and binding is proven in a privacy-preserving way.

(5) Issuance can be outsourced without the risk of leaking data or introducing traceability, e.g., for central – yet partially blind – issuance for use-cases like medical or educational credentials. This has significant benefits for settings where the actual issuance infrastructure is provided by an external service provider.

3 Anonymous Credential Options

Generally, anonymous credentials always follow the same blueprint: (1) at issuance, the user obtains a credential, which is an issuer's signature on a set of attributes; and (2) at presentation, the user proves knowledge (via a ZKP) of such an issuer's signature instead of revealing it directly. The relying party then verifies that the proof is valid for the issuer's public key. The proof system used in the presentation must be *sound* and *zero-knowledge*. Soundness ensures that a malicious prover cannot convince an honest verifier of an incorrect statement; in this context, it guarantees that users can only prove possession of a credential or attested attributes contained in a credential that was genuinely issued, preventing forgery. The zero-knowledge property guarantees that the verifier does not learn anything beyond the validity of the proven statement. For every presentation, the user creates a fresh ZKP of their credential, which yields the desired multi-show unlinkability and untraceability. Concrete protocols for such constructions can be grouped into two categories:

Multi-message signature schemes with efficient proofs: These are digital signature schemes that are designed to natively support selective disclosure and efficient proofs of knowledge of a signature. This is the most simple and efficient way to build anonymous credentials, but requires a dedicated and non-standard signature scheme for the issuers.

General-purpose ZKPs: General-purpose ZKPs are a class of ZKP protocols that allow proving statements over arbitrary computations. The core advantage of anonymous credentials using such ZKPs is that they can be built upon legacy systems and standard signatures. However, they are several orders of magnitude more complex and less efficient than systems built from dedicated signature schemes.

The following section provides an overview of both approaches and the most promising protocols therein. The description focuses on the maturity and security, complexity, and hardware support for secure device binding

3.1 Multi-message Signatures with Efficient Proofs

Multi-message signatures refer to a class of signature schemes with two main properties built-in: (i) the signature scheme allows to sign several messages (i.e., the user attributes) *individually*, which natively enables selective disclosure, and (ii) possess a cryptographic structure that allows to efficiently prove knowledge of a signature through a ZKP (typically by avoiding that messages get hashed).

Currently, the most popular multi-message signature scheme supporting ACs is BBS [17]. Follow-up works from the initial signature scheme have provided formal security proofs, support for multiple attributes, and improved the zero-knowledge proof of a signature [6, 24, 89]. Other multi-message signature schemes are the RSA-based CL-signatures [27], pairing-based CL-signatures [28], and PS signatures [77]. The ZKP used with BBS is essentially a non-interactive Schnorr-proof of the required discrete-logarithm statements, with an efficiency comparable to classical DL-based signature. That is, proof generation and verification take a few milliseconds, and the proofs have a size of several hundred bytes.

Maturity and Security. BBS signatures are currently the most studied and widely used multi-message signature scheme, with more than two decades of research and analysis, and thus were recommended in the cryptographers' feedback to the EU ARF [10]. BBS signatures have already been ISO standardized in ISO/IEC 20008-2:2013 [55] (the amendment from 2023 now also includes PS signatures), and the updated variant is currently undergoing standardization in the IRTF CFRG [63]. All aforementioned features from pseudonyms [60], deniability [38], to partially-blind issuance [59] and conditional disclosure [29] to issuer hiding [16] have already been proposed and are easily compatible and composable through Schnorr-type proof statements [13] – see the paragraph on further features and extendability below. Anonymous credentials have already seen real-world deployment through the TPM DAA and SGX EPID protocols, and the pairing-free version (see discussion below) is used, e.g., by Signal [34], and has recently been considered by Apple [94] and Google [86] to replace batch-issuance based token implementations such as PrivacyPass.

There are two main challenges related to the real-world deployment of BBS: the reliance on **pairing-friendly elliptic curves** and how to use Secure Elements (SE) for **device binding**. We sketch possible solutions for both.

Device Binding. For device binding, the BBS credential includes a device public key, and every presentation must include a fresh proof-of-possession (PoP) under that key. Device binding aims at non-transferability of credentials as the device secret key is stored at a particularly secured hardware component – the Secure Element (SE), and has been raised as the main open challenge to overcome in the response to the cryptographers' feedback [82]. There are different options for how this PoP can be realized, with different trade-offs.

BBS with Native Device Binding: The most established way for native BBS device binding is the Direct Anonymous Attestation (DAA) protocol [21,23], which essentially requires a simple Schnorr signature (in $\mathbb{G}_1$ of the pairing-friendly curve used for BBS) from the SE and only a single exponentiation per presentation. That is, SE does *not* have to compute the full BBS ZKP, but only the PoP part of it, which takes a few milliseconds. The DAA protocol was ISO standardized in 2013 [55], and is supported by the TPM2.0 standard and Intel's SGX attestation [20]. A recent work by Hesse et al. [54] proposes a slightly different solution that requires only a single call – instead of two as in DAA – to the SE, by relying on an additional secret key that is shared by the SE and host. The SE's contribution is again a variation of a Schnorr signature (in $\mathbb{G}_1$). Another alternative is described in the BBS♯ protocol [40], which also requires only a single call to the SE (for either an ECDSA or a Schnorr signature, both in $\mathbb{G}_1$) but does so without a shared secret. The protocol has no formal security analysis yet, though. The most recent work on native device binding for BBS credentials [48] further improves on that, as it requires only access to a plain BLS-signature interface on the SE, i.e., requires only a single call and no state. It is also the first protocol for BBS signatures that does not require trusting the SE for unlinkability and comes with a privacy-preserving variant for cloud-based settings.

While being highly efficient, the main hurdle of such native device binding is that it requires the SE to perform computations in $\mathbb{G}_1$ (or $\mathbb{G}_2$) of a pairing-friendly curve, whereas current SEs only support P-256. While the necessary API for this approach is very simple and lightweight, it *does* require changes in the SEs and proper re-certification, and thus does not work for immediate deployment. However, several countries, e.g., Germany [80], the Netherlands [79], and Sweden [81], aim for a cloud-based solution for device binding for credentials that require a high level of assurance, i.e., the PoP is executed by an external cloud HSM. In this setting, there are fewer limitations regarding the supported cryptography, and native device-binding protocols such as [48] can be integrated with less hurdles.

Note on BBS♯ in the pairing-free setting. If the device binding protocol from BBS♯ is used with the *pairing-free* variant (see discussion below), then their device binding is compatible with existing SEs through a standard ECDSA interface. However, switching to a pairing-free version inherently comes with additional complexity, e.g., in the form of batch-issuance.

BBS + ECDSA: The main challenge with the native device binding is that it is not compatible with existing SEs on the market. Essentially, the only interface available thereon is to create an ECDSA signature over P-256. However, using more advanced cryptography, it is possible to combine a BBS credential (in a pairing-friendly curve) to a standard ECDSA PoP (in P-256). The BBS credential then – in addition to the user's attributes – contains the ECDSA public key dpk as an attribute, encoded through the x/y-coordinates of the public key. The SE holds the standard ECDSA secret key dsk and is used to compute a standard ECDSA signature σ_{PoP} for a fresh session nonce. However, neither the (full) PoP signature nor the device public key get revealed in a presentation. Instead, the client computes a zero-knowledge proof π_{PoP} that the user has a valid ECDSA signature σ_{PoP} for the session nonce and under the public key certified dpk in the BBS credential. The bridging to the BBS credential is done through commitments: the main BBS ZKP proves that it contains a dpk that is only revealed in freshly committed form com_{dpk} and π_{PoP} proves that the user knows a signature under that committed key.

The proof of π_{PoP} can be done through either a dedicated proof protocol such as CDLS [30] (building upon ZKAttest [46]) – relying entirely on classical Schnorr proofs – or an optimized zkSNARK, e.g., based on Google's Longfellow [49], Microsoft's Crescent [74] or the protocol from Woo et al. [93]. A BBS-ECDSA hybrid based on ZKAttest/CDLS has already been implemented by Ubique [2] in the context of an innovation challenge run by the German EUDI project. Their implementation currently takes around 800ms to generate proofs, which have a size of 150KB. Thus, while it is more costly than native device binding, it is practical enough for online authentication.

Comparison to Full-fledged SNARK. Compared to computing a zkSNARK over an ECDSA attribute-credential (and ECDSA-PoP), e.g., [49,74,93] the BBS-ECDSA approach has several advantages: zkSNARKs that are efficient enough for real-world deployment currently require highly-optimized circuits and proof systems. Generic approaches are at least 1–2 magnitudes slower. This makes zkSNARKs in the short/midterm mostly applicable for scenarios where hard-coding the circuit and proof statement does not limit the flexibility and extendability of the system. This is the case here, as the statement to be proven via the zkSNARK is independent of the attribute statements proven on top, which is done via a simple and flexible Schnorr proof. Further, as the ECDSA PoP signature is an *one-time* signature computed for a fresh nonce, the signed message as well as parts of the ECDSA signature (the r value) can be revealed in the zero-knowledge proof, which significantly reduces the size and complexity of the proof. In particular, no statement over a hash function must be proven, which is often the most complex part within the circuit.

Status of Pairings. BBS, as well as all other highly efficient multi-show unlinkable anonymous credential schemes, relies on a pairing-friendly curve (with a type-3 pairing). An exception are the RSA-based CL signatures [27], which are less efficient than their pairing-based variants and thus have seen only little attention since the introduction of pairing-based cryptography in 2001.

A pairing-friendly curve is a special elliptic curve that enables to compute bilinear maps among different groups. While the cryptography is well understood [67], pairing-friendly curves are not widely deployed. Some pairing curves, such as BN254 have been standardized through ISO and the TCG (in the context of DAA), but the currently most popular curve BLS12-381 lacks a formal standard yet. The curve is fully specified through the IRTF drafts [84] and [47] though. There also exists a NIST report from 2015 on pairing-based cryptography [67] providing an overview, application scenarios, and challenges.

Pairing-based cryptography has seen some real-world adoption, mostly in the context of BLS-signatures [18], e.g., by Ethereum and DFINITY. Industry-grade implementations of BLS12-381 are available, e.g., BLST (https://github.com/supranational/blst), arkworks (https://arkworks.rs/), Cloudflare CIRCL (https://github.com/cloudflare/circl).

While BLS12-381 is currently the de facto standard for (roughly) 128-bit security, options for higher security levels exist too, see e.g., [84]. A recent overview of 192-bit pairing-based curves was given by Aranha et al. [3], recommending BLS24-509 as the most efficient curve for that security level.

Pairing-Free Solutions. If supporting a pairing-friendly curve is considered to be infeasible, one can switch to a pairing-free variant of ACs. This essentially trades each computation that requires a pairing with an interaction with the issuer (and computation relying on the issuer's secret key). Thus, while it will provide significant privacy improvements over currently planned solutions, it will not solve the main deployment bottleneck introduced through batch-issuance.

The most prominent solution for pairing-free ACs are *one-time use anonymous credentials* such as U-Prove [75] or Anonymous Credentials Light [8], which are based on blind signatures extended to include attributes. Blind signatures are inherently *single-show* credentials, and thus require batch issuance of credentials for multi-show unlinkability.

Another approach being explored is to rely on *keyed-verification anonymous credentials* (KVAC), which are used for deployments where issuer and verifier are the same entity. KVACs can be seen as symmetric (MAC) variants of ACs, first introduced as CMZ MAC [33,71] (PS signatures are the publicly-verifiable version thereof), and later also being adapted for BBS MAC [9,71]. Such KVACs have already been deployed by Signal [34], and more recently, KVAC-based protocols have been proposed by Apple [94] and Google [86], in order to overcome deployment challenges in systems such as PrivacyPass.

While KVACs themselves are not suitable for user-centric and decentralized identity systems, they have recently been adopted for this application through the introduction of *Server-Aided Anonymous Credentials (SAAC)*. The idea was initially put forward by Desmoulins et al. [40] as BBS♯, and was later refined and formally analyzed by Chairattana-Apirom et al. (SAAC) [31]. The main idea is that all attribute-related statements in a presentation are verified directly by the relying party, and only the one equation that requires the issuer's secret key for validation is checked with the help of the issuer. The underlying observation here is that this extra check does not reveal information about the user's attribute or identity to the issuer. There are two main ways how this can be implemented:

RP-Issuer Interaction: While the relying party verifies the bulk parts of the presentation, it asks the issuer for the verification of a sub-part of every proof. This requires high availability of the issuer, as every relying party relies on the issuer and its secret key based verification.

Batch Issuance: The user gets a batch of one-time use sub-tokens from the issuer in advance, and can spend them independently later on. This would require a similar deployment setting as the current batch issuance of salted hash based credentials with ECDSA, but provide the full feature set of anonymous credentials, and stronger privacy guarantees. In particular, Chairattana-Apirom et al. (SAAC) [31] show how to ensure that the issuer's sub-tokens can be used in an untraceable manner.

Most of the computations in the server-aided anonymous credential schemes based on BBS or PS signatures are equivalent to their pairing-based and multi-show unlinkable versions: the entire ZKP part is identical, only the pairing check gets replaced through a different computation. Thus, a server-aided and pairing-free version can also be used as a migration path towards full-fledged ACs.

Further Features and Extendability. Apart from efficiency, another core advantage of (DL-based) multi-message signature schemes is their simplicity and extendability. The proof system used on top of such signature schemes is simply a Schnorr proof. There exist general descriptions of how credential systems with an extensive feature set can be composed from multi-message signatures and Schnorr proofs [13,26], and adapting this to BBS or PS signatures is straightforward. There are also IETF specifications that extend the BBS core scheme [63], with pseudonyms [60], and blind issuance [59]. A promising approach is the IETF draft on Sigma protocols (which is the core of Schnorr proofs) [73] that would enable a more modular approach to extend DL-based multi-message signature with various Schnorr-based proof statements.

For some features, PS signatures [77] have advantages over BBS signatures, in particular when aiming at features involving the issuer secret key, e.g., credential aggregation [66,85] or distributed issuance [25,87]. If these features are important and cannot be rectified through other means, PS signatures might be the better choice. Note that the Schnorr-based proofs over the user's attributes built on top of the signature proof, as well as the different options for device binding work exactly the same for both BBS and PS, i.e., switching the signature scheme, or using both in parallel, is easily possible.

Quantum-Safeness. The most efficient multi-message schemes currently all rely on assumptions that are *not* quantum-safe, such as the DL or RSA assumption. This only affects unforgeability, privacy can hold perfectly and unconditionally, which implies quantum-safeness. The latter depends on the concrete protocol and feature set, though, e.g., extensions for pseudonyms or conditional disclosure are, so far, often based on the DL assumption too. This is not an inherent limitation, and realizing these extensions in a quantum-safe manner for privacy protection is possible – albeit at higher costs.

Quantum-safe variants for such multi-message signatures with efficient proofs exist as well, e.g., [4,19,43]. As they rely on new number-theoretic lattice assumptions, more time to study the hardness of these problems is desirable.

3.2 General-Purpose Zero-Knowledge Proofs

The second path to construct anonymous credentials is to use general-purpose ZKPs, sometimes also referred to as circuit-based ZKPs. They allow a prover to convince a verifier that it correctly executed a particular algorithm, while possibly hiding all in- and outputs. The construction of most general-purpose ZKPs follow the same blueprint: first, the algorithm or function that the statement shall be proven over is transformed into an *arithmetic circuit*. The proof system then takes the circuit (or rather its translation into a constraint system) as well as private and public input, and proves correct evaluation of that circuit.

The main benefit of general-purpose ZKPs is that they allow to build anonymous credential systems based on *any* signature scheme, and in particular on legacy ECDSA – not only for the device, but also issuer signature. For a long time, these proof systems have been purely of theoretical interest, as their efficiency was far from being practical. This has changed with the introduction of zkSNARKs [14], which stands for *Succinct Non-Interactive Arguments of Knowledge*, which have seen their first practical implementation with Pinocchio [76] in 2013. Technically, zkSNARKs are only a particular type of general-purpose ZKPs, but this term is often used synonymously for the entire class of such ZKPs, and we also use the latter understanding here. The idea of using zkSNARKs to build privacy-preserving authentication on top of legacy systems was first explored in Cinderella by Delignat-Lavaud et al. [39] for the verification of X.509 Certificate Chains, and zk-creds by Rosenberg et al. [83] built the first anonymous credential system upon legacy systems.

The most recent advances entail the protocols by Frigo and Shelat [49], Paquin et al. [74], and Woo et al. [93], all enabling ZKPs over ECDSA-signed data in a few seconds with varying proof sizes. In fact, the work by Frigo and Shelat [49] not only proves knowledge of a plain ECDSA signature, but over a standardized credential format (mdoc), keeping the entire issuance infrastructure unchanged. From a deployment perspective, this approach introduces a separate privacy layer on top of existing standards and implementations, allowing for a clear separation of concerns. Also, device binding is solved naturally, as no changes to the Secure Elements are needed.

The main drawbacks of this approach are its complexity, since the proof systems are several magnitudes more complex than Schnorr proofs over BBS, and its maturity, since it is a field that is still evolving actively. And while our work can not give a comprehensive overview of the state of the art on zkSNARKs and their individual trade-offs (we refer to [62] for such an overview), we want to highlight the main challenges that the adoption of this generic approach in the eID context needs to address and overcome.

Maturity and Security. There has been a significant amount of research in this area over the past decade, with Groth16 [53], Plonk [51], Bulletproofs [22] or Ligero [1] belonging to the most prominent systems. The recent systematization of knowledge paper on zkSNARKs lists over 40 constructions, and several new proof systems with significant performance improvements are published every year [62]. They differ significantly in their design choices, cryptographic assumptions and efficiency – often aiming at particular aspects for efficiency, such as either prover or verifier time, or proof sizes. For instance, schemes from pairings and DL-based assumptions, such as Groth16 [53] and Bulleproofs [22] allow for highly compact proofs, but have modest prover time. Proof systems such as Ligero can be built entirely from hash functions, which are faster and can provide quantum-safeness, but come with much larger proof sizes.

While these proof systems attract a significant amount of implementations and adoption, especially from the blockchain space, this ongoing development hinders a solid security analysis and understanding. It also poses a challenge for standardization, as any standardization effort that is started now will most likely not represent the state of the art by the time it is finished. Further, applications in the blockchain context (e.g., zk-Rollups) often focus on the succinctness property of zkSNARKs and, albeit using the term "zk", do not require or achieve privacy [90]. Thus, the results must be analyzed carefully to evaluate their suitability in the EUDI context, which does require the zero-knowledge property.

Multitude of Instantiations: zkSNARKs is the general term, and many different instantiations of that concept exist. This can be compared to the general concept of multi-message signatures, with BBS signatures being a concrete instantiation that has evolved over time as the most promising candidate (together with PS signatures). Different zkSNARK proof systems result in varying properties in terms of prover speed, verifier speed, proof size, and security assumptions. To the best of our knowledge, there is no consensus in the community yet, which is the best or most promising zkSNARK proof system to date and such an evaluation likely heavily depend on the intended usage of the system. To avoid a lock-in situation, a modular specification that allows to re-use common parts of these protocols is desirable. The ZKProofs community works on a similar approach for more than 7 years already [95], indicating that this is an endeavor requiring significant effort.

Trusted Setup: A particular differentiator among proof systems is whether they require a trusted setup or not. A trusted setup is a ceremony in which one or more parties create a common reference string (CRS) using secret and randomly generated inputs. The random inputs, sometimes also called "toxic waste" [70], must be destroyed afterwards to guarantee the soundness of the protocol. This trusted setup can exist in different forms: (i) a circuit-specific trusted setup, where every change to the circuit requires an update to the trusted setup, or (ii) a universal (and updatable) trusted setup where the CRS can be used by all circuits within certain size boundaries and the setup can be updated by different parties over the time. For the updatable setup, to break soundness an adversary would need to get the inputs of all parties, thus a single party not leaking its input guarantees the soundness of the system. Groth16 is an example that falls in the first category, whereas Plonk requires the relaxed setup of the second category. So-called *transparent* proof systems, or transparent setups do not have that limitation, and the public parameters are derived from public randomness or are not necessary at all. Examples in that category are Bulletproofs, zkSTARKs, and hash-based proof systems such as Ligero [1]. Clearly, systems with transparent setups are easier to deploy than systems that require a trusted setup. However, systems with trusted setups have been successfully deployed in real-world applications, e.g., ZCash [70]. Similar setups are also not uncommon in existing internet infrastructure, with an example being the DNSSEC root signing ceremony that happens every 3 months [36].

Security Assumptions: As previously mentioned, the different proof systems are based on different security assumptions. Generally speaking, pairing-based constructions usually rely on strong non-falsifiable assumptions [69] or idealized models like AGM [50], whereas most transparent constructions make use of the random oracle model (ROM) which in turn can cause some challenges in the analysis and instantiations of security parameters [15]. Further, security is often traded for efficiency, e.g., the scheme Frigo and Shelat [49] achieves practical efficiency with prover time of 1.2 s only for a reduced security level of 86-bit; performance numbers for a higher security level are unknown.

Complexity and Efficiency. The construction and security proofs of general-purpose ZKPs are significantly more complex than those of special-purpose constructions like multi-message signature schemes. For instance, the aforementioned protocol by Frigo et al. runs requires roughly 17.000 lines of code (without unit tests or benchmarks) [49]. Apart from the proof system itself, the complexity and efficiency are determined by the size of the circuit to be proven. The circuit is translated into a constraint system over which the proof is then computed. Small circuits have a few thousand constraints, whereas larger ones reach millions of constraints, and the same function can be represented in different circuits targeting different optimizations. To illustrate, the overview by Liang et al. [62] shows that to prove knowledge of a hash preimage x, such that $\mathsf{SHA256}(x) = y$, the necessary circuit can be represented in 27k to 600k constraints and prover time varies between 0.28 s and 556 s depending on proof system and circuit. Zero-knowledge proofs over ECDSA-signed credentials contain several such subproofs.

This complexity has already led to several attacks on proof systems and their implementations [32,35,61], which allowed malicious users to forge proofs for random statements. In fact, the security review of the Google ZKP also revealed such vulnerabilities, including a "high-severity finding that allows arbitrary forgery of mdoc attribute claims" [42]. Thus, tool support to verify the correctness of the implementation and circuits become an essential part for the security properties of the overarching system. There is on-going work on the formal verification of proof systems, circuits, and implementations [7,37], but more work is necessary to reach a point where formal verification of constructions and implementations for complex systems needed in the context of ACs becomes feasible.

Further attention also needs to be given to optimizing the prover time, and to trade-offs made by tailoring the proof system for efficiency.

Prover performance: Most zkSNARKs have been designed for blockchain use-cases, and often aim at small proof sizes and verifier speed. In the context of digital credential systems, prover time is more important, though. Recent works aim to overcome those prover performance challenges by optimizing the building blocks for ECDSA-based signatures [49] or by splitting the proof generation into a computationally expensive pre-computation step and efficient presentation step [74]. Leveraging the performance gains from these recent advances, implementations on smartphones become feasible. While those novel optimizations build upon established techniques such as Ligero [1] and Groth16 [53], the optimizations themselves are relatively new and their constructions have not yet undergone thorough review by the scientific community.

General-purpose vs. tailored proof systems: While zkSNARKs are general-purpose proof systems by promise, the practical variants of these proof systems typically target a particular application and then develop a tailored protocol for this target. These optimizations usually identify costly parts in circuits and provide optimized components for those subparts/sub-proofs, or even move them out of the circuit as recently proposed by [57,72]. Those optimizations reduce prover time, but introduce additional complexity into the system, which needs to be formally analyzed, and make the protocol suitable only for a specific class of problems or arithmetic structures.

An interesting trend in the context of blockchain applications has been the research on so-called zero-knowledge Virtual Machines (zkVM) that allow for any program compiled with a specific compiler backend (or architecture) to be executed in a specially constructed virtual machine [5,52,92]. However, in contrast to their name, not all of these systems feature zero-knowledge properties, and the focus seems to be often more on verifiable computation and succinctness. The benefit of these constructions is that it simplifies the creation and extension of applications that use zkSNARKs for developers, but adds additional complexity in the proof system and does not provide practical efficiency yet.

Further Features and Extendability. Apart from the compatibility with legacy systems, another theoretical advantage of general-purpose ZKPs is the ability to express *any* logic and policy on the users' attributes in the signed credential. Thus, general-purpose ZKPs can support more expressive statements over attributes than what is possible through plain Schnorr-proofs. The latter is essentially limited to statements that prove the equality, or and/or statements over DL-represented attributes. However, as mentioned above, this general-purpose feature is typically not (fully) achieved by the practical instantiations yet, which achieve the necessary efficiency by hard-coding a particular policy, credential format, and signature scheme into the proof system. This leads to a situation where general-purpose ZKPs can be less extendable than systems based on simple Schnorr proofs: adding practical extensions that go beyond the capabilities of the original protocol often require expert cryptographic knowledge, and significant resources for secure and efficient development.

Quantum-Safeness. The most widely deployed zkSNARKs e.g., Groth16 [53], Plonk [51], and Bulletproofs [22] rely on DL-based assumptions, and thus are not quantum-safe. Similar to BBS, the zero-knowledge property is often unconditional, which implies the quantum-safeness for zero-knowledge. Further, Groth16 and Plonk also rely on pairing-friendly curves, as do BBS signatures. Hash-based proof systems such as FRI [11] and Ligero [1], which is used by Frigo and shelat [49], have the advantage of quantum-resistance for soundness, if sufficiently large hash functions are used. There have also been significant advances in the area of lattice-based proof systems, e.g., [12,64,65], which will be the natural candidate when switching to lattice-based signatures such as ML-DSA.

Finally, it is important to note that while a proof system might provide quantum-safe soundness, this does not extend to the anonymous credentials scheme when it is build on top of classic signatures, such as ECDSA [49]. In fact, the practical efficiency of these proof systems often stems from highly-optimized and scheme-specific circuits. These circuits and techniques cannot be immediately re-used when switching to quantum-safe signature schemes such as ML-DSA, and in fact are likely to require a significant amount of research to develop targeted optimizations (and possibly new proof systems too).

4 Conclusion

Overall, several practical instantiations for a ZKP-based credential system exist that can improve the privacy and security in the EUDI ecosystem. They branch into two main approaches: 1) using a dedicated signature scheme that allows for simple Schnorr-based ZKPs, or 2) using a more powerful general-purpose ZKP system that can be used with any signature scheme, such as ECDSA. Both approaches differ significantly in their maturity, complexity, and legacy aspects.

BBS-based credential systems provide the best efficiency, maturity, and ease of extendability (for a certain set of features), and therefore have been recommended by the Cryptographers' Feedback [10]. However, they require additional support for standardization, depending on the device binding possibly additional hardware support, and the approval of pairing-friendly curves. The latter can be omitted through the use or BBS♯/Server-aided credentials, but this inherently requires additional communication with the issuer, similar to batch-issued credentials. Also, BBS-based signatures will require changes to all issuers, holders, and verifiers that already support ECDSA-based attribute credentials. Device-binding from existing Secure Elements is feasible without any changes though.

In terms of compatibility with legacy systems, specialized general-purpose ZKPs have a compelling advantage as they can be built on top of the existing infrastructure. It will require changes to all holders, and verifiers, but issuers and especially issuer infrastructure can remain (mostly) unchanged. The latter only holds if credential formats are kept the same, whereas specialized formats would allow for much better performance. These protocols are significantly more complex and less efficient than BBS-based credential systems. Practical protocols have only been developed very recently, and thus do not enjoy the same level of scrutiny and maturity when it comes to their security analysis. Further, the complexity of the proof system and the speed with which these proof systems are currently developing will pose a challenge for standardization and formal verification. Currently, efficiency is typically gained by tailoring the proof system to a particular application and instantiation, and extensions that go beyond that initial scope will require significant resources and expert knowledge. In theory, however, general-purpose ZKPs can express arbitrary statements over the user's attributes, whereas Schnorr-proofs are more limited to DL-based statements.

Further, while none of the proposed solutions are fully quantum-safe yet, their further development and integration will provide valuable insights into the concrete constraints and actual feature sets that are needed by the real-world application. These insights then allow a more focused research to re-design such schemes and protocols, e.g., from lattices or hash-based signatures. The research in these areas in the last two years already demonstrates that practical quantum-safe anonymous credential systems are within reach. In terms of upgradeability, we expect similar resources to be required when migrating from either option. Even when parts rely on a quantum-safe proof system, the main work of designing efficient circuits and *practical* anonymous credential systems through tailored optimizations needs to be redone. Finally, we like to stress that the quantum risk for signatures is substantially different than for encryption, for which immediate PQC-transition to prevent harvest-now decrypt-later attacks is adviced. In contrast, anonymous credential schemes with quantum-vulnerable soundness, but perfect/statistical privacy can be used until practical quantum-computers capable of breaking their soundness become a reality, which is in line with the NIST recommendation on the use of quantum-vulnerable algorithms for authentication systems [68].

Acknowledgement. We thank Paul Bastian, Andrey Sidorenko, and Alexandros Zacharakis for their helpful feedback on an earlier draft of this work. The authors are solely responsible for the content of this publication; the positions presented here do not reflect the views of SPRIND.

References

1. Ames, S., Hazay, C., Ishai, Y., Venkitasubramaniam, M.: Ligero: Lightweight sublinear arguments without a trusted setup. In: Thuraisingham, B.M., Evans, D., Malkin, T., Xu, D. (eds.) ACM CCS 2017, pp. 2087–2104. ACM Press (2017). https://doi.org/10.1145/3133956.3134104
2. Amrein, P.: https://github.com/UbiqueInnovation/zkattest-rs (2025)
3. Aranha, D.F., Fotiadis, G., Guillevic, A.: A short-list of pairing-friendly curves resistant to the special TNFS algorithm at the 192-bit security level. CiC **1**(3), 3 (2024). https://doi.org/10.62056/angyl86bm
4. Argo, S., Güneysu, T., Jeudy, C., Land, G., Roux-Langlois, A., Sanders, O.: Practical post-quantum signatures for privacy. In: Luo, B., Liao, X., Xu, J., Kirda, E., Lie, D. (eds.) ACM CCS 2024, pp. 1523–1537. ACM Press (Oct 2024). https://doi.org/10.1145/3658644.3670297
5. Arun, A., Setty, S.T.V., Thaler, J.: Jolt: SNARKs for virtual machines via lookups. In: Joye, M., Leander, G. (eds.) EUROCRYPT 2024, Part VI. LNCS, vol. 14656, pp. 3–33. Springer, Cham (2024). https://doi.org/10.1007/978-3-031-58751-1_1
6. Au, M.H., Susilo, W., Mu, Y.: Constant-size dynamic k-TAA. In: De Prisco, R., Yung, M. (eds.) SCN 06. LNCS, vol. 4116, pp. 111–125. Springer, Berlin, Heidelberg (2006). https://doi.org/10.1007/11832072_8
7. Bailey, B., Miller, A.: Formalizing soundness proofs of SNARKs. Cryptology ePrint Archive, Report 2023/656 (2023). https://eprint.iacr.org/2023/656
8. Baldimtsi, F., Lysyanskaya, A.: Anonymous credentials light. In: Sadeghi, A.R., Gligor, V.D., Yung, M. (eds.) ACM CCS 2013, pp. 1087–1098. ACM Press (2013). https://doi.org/10.1145/2508859.2516687
9. Barki, A., Brunet, S., Desmoulins, N., Traoré, J.: Improved algebraic MACs and practical keyed-verification anonymous credentials. In: Avanzi, R., Heys, H.M. (eds.) SAC 2016. LNCS, vol. 10532, pp. 360–380. Springer, Cham (2016). https://doi.org/10.1007/978-3-319-69453-5_20
10. Baum, et al.: Cryptographers' feedback on the eu digital identity's ARF (2024). https://github.com/eu-digital-identity-wallet/eudi-doc-architecture-and-reference-framework/issues/200
11. Ben-Sasson, E., Bentov, I., Horesh, Y., Riabzev, M.: Fast reed-solomon interactive oracle proofs of proximity. In: Chatzigiannakis, I., Kaklamanis, C., Marx, D., Sannella, D. (eds.) ICALP 2018. LIPIcs, vol. 107, pp. 14:1–14:17. Schloss Dagstuhl (2018). https://doi.org/10.4230/LIPIcs.ICALP.2018.14
12. Beullens, W., Seiler, G.: LaBRADOR: Compact proofs for R1CS from module-SIS. In: Handschuh, H., Lysyanskaya, A. (eds.) CRYPTO 2023, Part V. LNCS, vol. 14085, pp. 518–548. Springer, Cham (2023). https://doi.org/10.1007/978-3-031-38554-4_17
13. Bichsel, P., et al.: D2. 2 architecture for attribute-based credential technologies-final version. ABC4TRUST project deliverable (2014)
14. Bitansky, N., Canetti, R., Chiesa, A., Tromer, E.: From extractable collision resistance to succinct non-interactive arguments of knowledge, and back again. In: Goldwasser, S. (ed.) ITCS 2012, pp. 326–349. ACM (2012). https://doi.org/10.1145/2090236.2090263
15. Block, A.R., Tiwari, P.R.: On the concrete security of non-interactive FRI. In: Galdi, C., Phan, D.H. (eds.) SCN 24, Part I. LNCS, vol. 14973, pp. 275–296. Springer, Cham (2024). https://doi.org/10.1007/978-3-031-71070-4_13

16. Bobolz, J., Eidens, F., Krenn, S., Ramacher, S., Samelin, K.: Issuer-hiding attribute-based credentials. In: Conti, M., Stevens, M., Krenn, S. (eds.) CANS 21. LNCS, vol. 13099, pp. 158–178. Springer, Cham (2021). https://doi.org/10.1007/978-3-030-92548-2_9
17. Boneh, D., Boyen, X., Shacham, H.: Short group signatures. In: Franklin, M. (ed.) CRYPTO 2004. LNCS, vol. 3152, pp. 41–55. Springer, Berlin, Heidelberg (2004). https://doi.org/10.1007/978-3-540-28628-8_3
18. Boneh, D., Lynn, B., Shacham, H.: Short signatures from the Weil pairing. J. Cryptol. **17**(4), 297–319 (2004). https://doi.org/10.1007/s00145-004-0314-9
19. Bootle, J., Lyubashevsky, V., Nguyen, N.K., Sorniotti, A.: A framework for practical anonymous credentials from lattices. In: Handschuh, H., Lysyanskaya, A. (eds.) CRYPTO 2023, Part II. LNCS, vol. 14082, pp. 384–417. Springer, Cham (2023). https://doi.org/10.1007/978-3-031-38545-2_13
20. Brickell, E., Li, J.: Enhanced privacy id from bilinear pairing for hardware authentication and attestation. In: IEEE International Conference on Social Computing (2010)
21. Brickell, E., Li, J.: A pairing-based daa scheme further reducing tpm resources. In: International Conference on Trust and Trustworthy Computing (2010), pp. 181–195. Springer, Cham (2010)
22. Bünz, B., Bootle, J., Boneh, D., Poelstra, A., Wuille, P., Maxwell, G.: Bulletproofs: short proofs for confidential transactions and more. In: 2018 IEEE Symposium on Security and Privacy, pp. 315–334. IEEE Computer Society Press (2018). https://doi.org/10.1109/SP.2018.00020
23. Camenisch, J., Drijvers, M., Lehmann, A.: Anonymous attestation using the strong Diffie Hellman assumption revisited. Cryptology ePrint Archive, Report 2016/663 (2016). https://eprint.iacr.org/2016/663
24. Camenisch, J., Drijvers, M., Lehmann, A.: Universally composable direct anonymous attestation. In: Cheng, C.M., Chung, K.M., Persiano, G., Yang, B.Y. (eds.) PKC 2016, Part II. LNCS, vol. 9615, pp. 234–264. Springer, Berlin (2016). https://doi.org/10.1007/978-3-662-49387-8_10
25. Camenisch, J., Drijvers, M., Lehmann, A., Neven, G., Towa, P.: Short threshold dynamic group signatures. In: Galdi, C., Kolesnikov, V. (eds.) SCN 20. LNCS, vol. 12238, pp. 401–423. Springer, Cham (2020). https://doi.org/10.1007/978-3-030-57990-6_20
26. Camenisch, J., Krenn, S., Lehmann, A., Mikkelsen, G.L., Neven, G., Pedersen, M.Ø.: Formal treatment of privacy-enhancing credential systems. In: Dunkelman, O., Keliher, L. (eds.) SAC 2015. LNCS, vol. 9566, pp. 3–24. Springer, Cham (2016). https://doi.org/10.1007/978-3-319-31301-6_1
27. Camenisch, J., Lysyanskaya, A.: An efficient system for non-transferable anonymous credentials with optional anonymity revocation. In: Pfitzmann, B. (ed.) EUROCRYPT 2001. LNCS, vol. 2045, pp. 93–118. Springer, Cham (2001). https://doi.org/10.1007/3-540-44987-6_7
28. Camenisch, J., Lysyanskaya, A.: Signature schemes and anonymous credentials from bilinear maps. In: Franklin, M. (ed.) CRYPTO 2004. LNCS, vol. 3152, pp. 56–72. Springer, Cham (2004). https://doi.org/10.1007/978-3-540-28628-8_4
29. Camenisch, J., Shoup, V.: Practical verifiable encryption and decryption of discrete logarithms. In: Boneh, D. (ed.) CRYPTO 2003. LNCS, vol. 2729, pp. 126–144. Springer, Cham (2003). https://doi.org/10.1007/978-3-540-45146-4_8
30. Celi, S., Levin, S., Rowell, J.: CDLS: Proving knowledge of committed discrete logarithms with soundness. In: Vaudenay, S., Petit, C. (eds.) AFRICACRYPT 24.

LNCS, vol. 14861, pp. 69–93. Springer, Cham (2024). https://doi.org/10.1007/978-3-031-64381-1_4
31. Chairattana-Apirom, R., Harding, F., Lysyanskaya, A., Tessaro, S.: Server-aided anonymous credentials. Cryptology ePrint Archive, Report 2025/513 (2025). https://eprint.iacr.org/2025/513
32. Chaliasos, S., Ernstberger, J., Theodore, D., Wong, D., Jahanara, M., Livshits, B.: SoK: What don't we know? Understanding security vulnerabilities in SNARKs. In: Balzarotti, D., Xu, W. (eds.) USENIX Security 2024. USENIX Association (2024). https://www.usenix.org/conference/usenixsecurity24/presentation/chaliasos
33. Chase, M., Meiklejohn, S., Zaverucha, G.: Algebraic MACs and keyed-verification anonymous credentials. In: Ahn, G.J., Yung, M., Li, N. (eds.) ACM CCS 2014, pp. 1205–1216. ACM Press (2014). https://doi.org/10.1145/2660267.2660328
34. Chase, M., Perrin, T., Zaverucha, G.: The Signal private group system and anonymous credentials supporting efficient verifiable encryption. In: Ligatti, J., Ou, X., Katz, J., Vigna, G. (eds.) ACM CCS 2020, pp. 1445–1459. ACM Press (2020). https://doi.org/10.1145/3372297.3417887
35. Ciobotaru, O., Peter, M., Velichkov, V.: The last challenge attack: exploiting a vulnerable implementation of the fiat-shamir transform in a KZG-based SNARK. Cryptology ePrint Archive, Report 2024/398 (2024). https://eprint.iacr.org/2024/398
36. cloudflare.com: The dnssec root signing ceremony (2025). https://www.cloudflare.com/en-gb/learning/dns/dnssec/root-signing-ceremony/
37. Coglio, A., McCarthy, E., Smith, E., Chin, C., Gaddamadugu, P., Dellepere, M.: Compositional formal verification of zero-knowledge circuits. Cryptology ePrint Archive, Report 2023/1278 (2023). https://eprint.iacr.org/2023/1278
38. Cramer, R., Damgård, I., Schoenmakers, B.: Proofs of partial knowledge and simplified design of witness hiding protocols. In: Desmedt, Y. (ed.) CRYPTO'94. LNCS, vol. 839, pp. 174–187. Springer, Cham (1994). https://doi.org/10.1007/3-540-48658-5_19
39. Delignat-Lavaud, A., Fournet, C., Kohlweiss, M., Parno, B.: Cinderella: Turning shabby X.509 certificates into elegant anonymous credentials with the magic of verifiable computation. In: 2016 IEEE Symposium on Security and Privacy, pp. 235–254. IEEE Computer Society Press (2016). https://doi.org/10.1109/SP.2016.22
40. Desmoulins, N., Dumanois, A., Kane, S., Traoré, J.: Making BBS anonymous credentials eIDAS 2.0 compliant (2025)
41. DG Connect: The european digital identity wallet architecture and reference framework (2025). Retrieved January, https://github.com/eu-digital-identity-wallet/eudi-doc-architecture-and-reference-framework
42. Doyle, J., Ilunga, M.: Google longfellow security assessment. https://github.com/google/longfellow-zk/blob/main/docs/static/reviews/Longfellow_report_2025_08_18.pdf
43. Dubois, A., Klooß, M., Lai, R.W.F., Woo, I.K.Y.: Lattice-based proof-friendly signatures from vanishing short integer solutions. In: Jager, T., Pan, J. (eds.) PKC 2025, Part I. LNCS, vol. 15674, pp. 452–486. Springer, Cham (2025). https://doi.org/10.1007/978-3-031-91820-9_15
44. European Commission (2024). https://commission.europa.eu/strategy-and-policy/priorities-2019-2024/europe-fit-digital-age/european-digital-identity_en
45. European Commission: Regulation on electronic identification and trust services for electronic transactions (2024). https://eur-lex.europa.eu/eli/reg/2024/1183/oj/eng

46. Faz-Hernández, A., Ladd, W., Maram, D.: ZKAttest: Ring and group signatures for existing ECDSA keys. In: AlTawy, R., Hülsing, A. (eds.) SAC 2021. LNCS, vol. 13203, pp. 68–83. Springer, Cham (2022). https://doi.org/10.1007/978-3-030-99277-4_4
47. Faz-Hernandez, A., Scott, S., Sullivan, N., Wahby, R.S., Wood, C.A.: Hashing to Elliptic Curves. Request for Comments RFC 9380, Internet Engineering Task Force (2023). https://doi.org/10.17487/RFC9380
48. Friedrichs, K., Harding, F., Lehmann, A., Lysyanskaya, A.: Device-bound anonymous credentials with(out) trusted hardware. Cryptology ePrint Archive, Report 2025/1995 (2025). https://eprint.iacr.org/2025/1995
49. Frigo, M., shelat, a.: Anonymous credentials from ECDSA. Cryptology ePrint Archive, Report 2024/2010 (2024). https://eprint.iacr.org/2024/2010
50. Fuchsbauer, G., Kiltz, E., Loss, J.: The algebraic group model and its applications. In: Shacham, H., Boldyreva, A. (eds.) CRYPTO 2018, Part II. LNCS, vol. 10992, pp. 33–62. Springer, Cham (2018). https://doi.org/10.1007/978-3-319-96881-0_2
51. Gabizon, A., Williamson, Z.J., Ciobotaru, O.: PLONK: Permutations over Lagrange-bases for oecumenical noninteractive arguments of knowledge. Cryptology ePrint Archive, Report 2019/953 (2019). https://eprint.iacr.org/2019/953
52. Goldberg, L., Papini, S., Riabzev, M.: Cairo – a Turing-complete STARK-friendly CPU architecture. Cryptology ePrint Archive, Report 2021/1063 (2021). https://eprint.iacr.org/2021/1063
53. Groth, J.: On the size of pairing-based non-interactive arguments. In: Fischlin, M., Coron, J.S. (eds.) EUROCRYPT 2016, Part II. LNCS, vol. 9666, pp. 305–326. Springer, Cham (2016). https://doi.org/10.1007/978-3-662-49896-5_11
54. Hesse, J., Singh, N., Sorniotti, A.: How to bind anonymous credentials to humans. In: Calandrino, J.A., Troncoso, C. (eds.) USENIX Security 2023. pp. 3047–3064. USENIX Association (2023). https://www.usenix.org/conference/usenixsecurity23/presentation/hesse
55. ISO: Iso 20008-2:2013: Information technology - security techniques - anonymous digital signatures - part 2: Mechanisms using a group public key. Standard, International Organization for Standardization, Geneva, CH (2013)
56. ISO: Iso/iec 24843: Information security - attribute-based credentials. Working draft, International Organization for Standardization, Geneva, CH (2025)
57. Kadianakis, G., Maller, M., Novakovic, A.: Sigmabus: binding sigmas in circuits for fast curve operations. Cryptology ePrint Archive, Report 2023/1406 (2023). https://eprint.iacr.org/2023/1406
58. Kakvi, S., Martin, K., Putman, C., Quaglia, E.: Sok: Anonymous credentials. In: SSR 2023. https://doi.org/10.1007/978-3-031-30731-7
59. Kalos, V., Bernstein, G.: Blind bbs signatures. Internet Draft draft-irtf-cfrg-bbs-blind-signatures-01, Internet Research Task Force (2025)
60. Kalos, V., Bernstein, G.M.: Bbs per verifier linkability. Internet Draft draft-irtf-cfrg-bbs-per-verifier-linkability-01, Internet Research Task Force (2025)
61. Khovratovich, D., Rothblum, R.D., Soukhanov, L.: How to prove false statements: Practical attacks on fiat-shamir. Cryptology ePrint Archive, Report 2025/118 (2025). https://eprint.iacr.org/2025/118
62. Liang, J., Hu, D., Wu, P., Yang, Y., Shen, Q., Wu, Z.: SoK: Understanding zk-SNARKs: The gap between research and practice. Cryptology ePrint Archive, Report 2025/172 (2025). https://eprint.iacr.org/2025/172
63. Looker, T., Kalos, V., Whitehead, A., Lodder, M.: The BBS Signature Scheme. Internet Draft draft-irtf-cfrg-bbs-signatures-09, Internet Research Task Force (2025)

64. Lyubashevsky, V., Nguyen, N.K., Plançon, M.: Lattice-based zero-knowledge proofs and applications: Shorter, simpler, and more general. In: Dodis, Y., Shrimpton, T. (eds.) CRYPTO 2022, Part II. LNCS, vol. 13508, pp. 71–101. Springer, Cham (2022). https://doi.org/10.1007/978-3-031-15979-4_3
65. Lyubashevsky, V., Seiler, G., Steuer, P.: The LaZer library: Lattice-based zero knowledge and succinct proofs for quantum-safe privacy. In: Luo, B., Liao, X., Xu, J., Kirda, E., Lie, D. (eds.) ACM CCS 2024, pp. 3125–3137. ACM Press (2024). https://doi.org/10.1145/3658644.3690330
66. Mir, O., Bauer, B., Griffy, S., Lysyanskaya, A., Slamanig, D.: Aggregate signatures with versatile randomization and issuer-hiding multi-authority anonymous credentials. In: Meng, W., Jensen, C.D., Cremers, C., Kirda, E. (eds.) ACM CCS 2023, pp. 30–44. ACM Press (2023). https://doi.org/10.1145/3576915.3623203
67. Moody, D., Peralta, R., Perlner, R., Regenscheid, A., Roginsky, A., Chen, L.: Report on Pairing-based Cryptography. J. Res. Nat. Inst. Stan. Technol. **120**, 11–27 (2015). https://doi.org/10.6028/jres.120.002
68. Moody, D., Perlner, R., Regenscheid, A., Robinson, A., Cooper, D.: Nist ir 8547: Transition to post-quantum cryptography standards (2024)
69. Naor, M.: On cryptographic assumptions and challenges (invited talk). In: Boneh, D. (ed.) CRYPTO 2003. LNCS, vol. 2729, pp. 96–109. Springer, Cham (2003). https://doi.org/10.1007/978-3-540-45146-4_6
70. Nikolaenko, V., Ragsdale, S., Bonneau, J., Boneh, D.: Powers-of-tau to the people: decentralizing setup ceremonies. In: Pöpper, C., Batina, L. (eds.) ACNS 2024, Part III. LNCS, vol. 14585, pp. 105–134. Springer, Cham (2024). https://doi.org/10.1007/978-3-031-54776-8_5
71. Orrù, M.: Revisiting keyed-verification anonymous credentials. Cryptology ePrint Archive, Report 2024/1552 (2024). https://eprint.iacr.org/2024/1552
72. Orrù, M., Kadianakis, G., Maller, M., Zaverucha, G.: Beyond the circuit: how to minimize foreign arithmetic in ZKP circuits. Cryptology ePrint Archive, Report 2024/265 (2024). https://eprint.iacr.org/2024/265
73. Orrù, M., Yun, C.: Sigma protocols. Internet Draft draft-irtf-cfrg-sigma-protocols-01, Internet Research Task Force (2025)
74. Paquin, C., Policharla, G.V., Zaverucha, G.: Crescent: Stronger privacy for existing credentials. Cryptology ePrint Archive, Report 2024/2013 (2024). https://eprint.iacr.org/2024/2013
75. Paquin, C., Zaverucha, G.: U-prove cryptographic specification v1. 1. Technical Report, Microsoft Corporation (2011)
76. Parno, B., Howell, J., Gentry, C., Raykova, M.: Pinocchio: Nearly practical verifiable computation. In: 2013 IEEE Symposium on Security and Privacy, pp. 238–252. IEEE Computer Society Press (2013). https://doi.org/10.1109/SP.2013.47
77. Pointcheval, D., Sanders, O.: Short randomizable signatures. In: Sako, K. (ed.) CT-RSA 2016. LNCS, vol. 9610, pp. 111–126. Springer, Cham (2016). https://doi.org/10.1007/978-3-319-29485-8_7
78. Prime Minister's Office: https://www.gov.uk/government/news/new-digital-id-scheme-to-be-rolled-out-across-uk (2025)
79. Project, D.E.W.: Nl wallet: Software system overview (2025). https://minbzk.github.io/nl-wallet/main/architecture/c4/software-system.html
80. Project, G.E.W.: German national eudi wallet: Architecture documentation (2025). https://bmi.usercontent.opencode.de/eudi-wallet/wallet-development-documentation-public/v0.7.0/architecture-concept/02-decomposition/
81. Project, S.E.W.: Remote pake-protected services protocol (r2ps) (2025). https://expg.eidasweb.se/s/03jK698rE

82. Rosa, P.D.: Response to cryptographer's feedback. https://github.com/eu-digital-identity-wallet/eudi-doc-architecture-and-reference-framework/discussions/211#discussioncomment-9882388
83. Rosenberg, M., White, J.D., Garman, C., Miers, I.: zk-creds: flexible anonymous credentials from zkSNARKs and existing identity infrastructure. In: 2023 IEEE Symposium on Security and Privacy, pp. 790–808. IEEE Computer Society Press (2023). https://doi.org/10.1109/SP46215.2023.10179430
84. Sakemi, Y., Kobayashi, T., Saito, T., Wahby, R.S.: Pairing-Friendly Curves. Internet Draft draft-irtf-cfrg-pairing-friendly-curves-12, Internet Engineering Task Force (2025)
85. Sanders, O., Traoré, J.: Compact issuer-hiding authentication, application to anonymous credential. PoPETs **2024**(3), 645–658 (2024). https://doi.org/10.56553/popets-2024-0097
86. Schlesinger, S., Katz, J.: Anonymous credit tokens. Internet Draft draft-schlesinger-cfrg-act, Internet Engineering Task Force (2025)
87. Sonnino, A., Al-Bassam, M., Bano, S., Meiklejohn, S., Danezis, G.: Coconut: threshold issuance selective disclosure credentials with applications to distributed ledgers. In: NDSS 2019. The Internet Society (2019). https://doi.org/10.14722/ndss.2019.23272
88. Swiss federal authorities: e-id law approved at the ballot box (2025). https://www.eid.admin.ch/en/e-id-gesetz-an-der-urne-angenommen-e
89. Tessaro, S., Zhu, C.: Revisiting BBS signatures. In: Hazay, C., Stam, M. (eds.) EUROCRYPT 2023, Part V. LNCS, vol. 14008, pp. 691–721. Springer, Cham (2023). https://doi.org/10.1007/978-3-031-30589-4_24
90. Tortola, D., Lisi, A., Mori, P., Ricci, L.: Tethering layer 2 solutions to the blockchain: a survey on proving schemes. Comput. Commun. **225**, 289–310 (2024)
91. Transportation Security Administration (2025). https://www.tsa.gov/real-id/real-id-mobile-drivers-license-mdls
92. Wang, R., Hazay, C., Venkitasubramaniam, M.: Ligetron: Lightweight scalable end-to-end zero-knowledge proofs post-quantum ZK-SNARKs on a browser. In: 2024 IEEE Symposium on Security and Privacy, pp. 1760–1776. IEEE Computer Society Press (2024). https://doi.org/10.1109/SP54263.2024.00086
93. Woo, A.P.Y., Ozdemir, A., Sharp, C., Pornin, T., Grubbs, P.: Efficient proofs of possession for legacy signatures. Cryptology ePrint Archive, Report 2025/538 (2025). https://eprint.iacr.org/2025/538
94. Wood, C.A., Yun, C.: Anonymous rate-limited credentials. Internet Draft draft-yun-privacypass-crypto-arc-00, Internet Engineering Task Force (2025)
95. ZKProof.org: Zkproof charter (2018). https://docs.zkproof.org/general

Making BBS Anonymous Credentials eIDAS 2.0 Compliant

Nicolas Desmoulins[1], Antoine Dumanois[1], Seyni Kane[1,2], and Jacques Traoré[1(✉)]

[1] Orange Innovation, Applied Crypto Group, Caen, France
{nicolas.desmoulins,antoine.dumanois,seyni.kane, jacques.traore}@orange.com
[2] Télécom SudParis, Institut Polytechnique de Paris, Palaiseau, France

Abstract. eIDAS 2.0 (electronic IDentification, Authentication and trust Services) is a very ambitious regulation aimed at equipping European citizens with a personal digital identity wallet (EU Digital Identity Wallet) on a mobile phone that not only needs to achieve a high level of security, but also needs to be available as soon as possible for a large number of citizens and respect their privacy (as per GDPR - General Data Protection Regulation).

In this paper, we introduce the foundations of a digital identity wallet solution that could help move closer to this objective by leveraging the proven anonymous credentials system BBS (Eurocrypt 2023), also known as BBS+, but modifying it to avoid the limitations that have hindered its widespread adoption, especially in certified infrastructures requiring trusted hardware implementation.

In particular, the solution we propose, which we call BBS#, does not rely, contrary to BBS/BBS+, on bilinear maps and pairing-friendly curves (which are not supported by existing hardware) and only depends on the hardware implementation of well-known digital signature schemes such as ECDSA (ISO/IEC 14888-3) or ECSDSA (also known as ECSchnorr, ISO/IEC 14888-3) using classical elliptic curves. More precisely, BBS# can be rolled out without requiring any change in existing hardware or the algorithms that hardware supports.

BBS#, which is proven secure in the algebraic group and random oracle models (AGM+ROM), retains the well-known security property (unforgeability of the credentials under the (gap) q-SDH assumption) and anonymity properties (multi-show full unlinkability and statistical anonymity of presentation proofs) of BBS/BBS+.

By implementing BBS# on several smartphones using different secure execution environments, we show that it is possible to achieve eIDAS 2.0 transactions which are not only efficient (around 70 ms on Android StrongBox), secure and certifiable at the highest level but which would also provide strong (optimal) privacy protection for all European ID Wallet users.

H. C. Pöhls and C. J. Mitchell (Eds.): SSR 2025, LNCS 16466, pp. 26–45, 2026.
https://doi.org/10.1007/978-3-032-19567-8_2

1 Introduction

The so-called eIDAS 2.0 European regulation adopted May 20th, 2024, is a very ambitious one, aiming at changing the digital (and physical) life of European citizens and corporations alike by providing them a personal digital identity wallet on a mobile phone to perform transactions on their behalf, not only for eGov services, but also for any daily transaction, including very critical ones, like payments. In order to achieve these ambitious goals, these wallets and the associated architectural framework need to simultaneously ensure security (of the digital credentials issued to users) and privacy (of the usage of these credentials) but also reach (the ability to work for as many users and as many technical environments as possible) and a proper user experience (UX). Given the impacts of the technical choices that will be made on hundreds of millions of individuals, intense discussions continue to determine the best solutions to deploy and standardize to comply with these requirements. Although the security aspect has gathered most of the focus of initial talks by designated experts, privacy and data protection is only recently emerging as a major aspect that still needs to be properly tackled, the goal obviously being to add privacy without relinquishing on any of the other aspects.

To solve the privacy issues raised by the EU Digital Identity Wallet (EUDI Wallet), renowned cryptographers have proposed the use of anonymous credentials.[1] Introduced by David Chaum [13], anonymous credentials systems allow users to obtain a credential from an issuer and then, later, prove possession of this credential, in an unlinkable way, without revealing any additional information [24]. This primitive, which is currently standardized at ISO/IEC SC 27 WG2 (ISO/IEC 24843), has attracted a lot of interest as it complies with data minimization principles that consist in preventing the disclosure of irrelevant and unnecessary information. Typically, an anonymous credentials system is expected to enable users to reveal a subset of the attributes associated with their credentials while keeping the remaining ones hidden (*selective disclosure*). [2] For example, one can prove that they have a driving license, so that they can access sites reserved for adults, without having to reveal their identity or date of birth.

This handset of cryptographers specifically recommended to use the BBS/BBS+ [35] family of anonymous credentials, which are efficient, mathematically proven secure, and are currently the object of a standardization effort [26].

However, the European Commission did not consider this solution mainly because BBS/BBS+ uses bilinear maps and pairing-friendly curves (which are not supported by trusted phone hardware) but also because BBS/BBS+ does not use SOG-IS sanctioned protocols for the implementation of the *holder binding*

---

[1] Cryptographers' Feedback on the EU Digital Identity's ARF.

[2] Current solutions such as ISO mDL (ISO/IEC 18013-5) provide selective disclosure but all credentials presentations remain traceable by colluding issuers and verifiers. Therefore, they do not adequately protect users' privacy.

feature.[3][4] This feature states that only the legitimate holder of a credential shall be able to perform transactions with that credential. In practice, this is achieved by binding that credential to a private key stored in a trusted hardware (or Secure Element) of the credential holder's mobile device and making presentation of such a credential impossible without that private key.

1.1 Related Work on Pairing-Free Anonymous Credentials

One of the most prevalent pairing-free anonymous credentials system is Microsoft's U-Prove [32] which is based on a blind signature scheme due to Brands [7]. It is quite efficient, as it works in prime-order groups, and supports the selective disclosure of attributes. Unfortunately, U-Prove does not provide *multi-show unlinkability* (multiple presentations of the same credential are linkable). Besides, Benhamouda et al. [5] have shown that U-Prove issuance protocol is vulnerable to a parallel attack (*ROS attack*). Specifically, a user simultaneously running a large number (l) of blind issuance sessions with the issuer would be able, after these l sessions, to forge an additional U-Prove credential for the same set of attributes (and thus fraudulently obtain $l + 1$ different U-Prove credentials instead of just l).

Very recently, Orrù et al. [30] provided a variant of the U-Prove issuance protocol that is secure in a concurrent setting.

Baldimsti and Lysyanskaya have proposed a slightly less efficient pairing-free anonymous attribute-based credentials system [1], called Anonymous Credential Light (ACL for short), which is not vulnerable to a ROS attack. However, similarly to U-Prove, this system is *one-show* (i.e. credential presentations are linkable if a credential is used more than once). To solve this issue, the user needs to interact with the issuer to renew their credential, i.e., they need to obtain as many new versions of their credential as the number of intended showings/presentations. This unfortunately introduces a tradeoff between privacy and efficiency: either they need to get as many copies of the ACL credential as a reasonable upper bound on the lifetime use of the credential, or they need to get credentials reissued upon running out of them, revealing the rate of credential use.

IBM's Identity Mixer, commonly known as Idemix [29], is built on Camenisch-Lysyanskaya (CL) signature scheme [8]. Unlike the above cited credentials systems, Idemix provides multi-show unlinkability but at the cost of a less efficient proof of possession. Indeed, the used CL signatures are based on the Strong RSA assumption [2]. This implies large RSA parameters which make Idemix unsuitable for current (constrained) Secure Elements.

Chase et al. [12] have opted for the use of symmetric key primitives, instead of digital signatures, so as to achieve better performances. More precisely, they used algebraic Message Authentication Codes (MACs), which relies on group operations rather than block ciphers or hash functions, as the main building block of

[3] Cryptographers' Feedback on the EU Digital Identity's ARF.
[4] https://www.sogis.eu/.

their credentials system. Their two proposals, denoted $\mathrm{MAC}_{\mathrm{GGM}}$ and $\mathrm{MAC}_{\mathrm{DDH}}$, assume that the credential issuer and the verifier share a secret key. In such a setting, the anonymous credentials system is referred to as Keyed-Verification Anonymous Credentials (KVAC). The main drawback of their pairing-free KVAC systems is that they are tailored to specific settings in which the issuer also acts as verifier, as in the case of e-government or public transportation. They are not suited to the more general setting, envisioned for the EUDI Wallet, in which the issuer and the verifier are two distinct entities that do not necessarily share a secret key.

In [3], Barki et al. proposed a more efficient KVAC based on a different algebraic MAC called $\mathrm{MAC}_{\mathrm{BB}}$. They also shown how to turn their KVAC system into an efficient publicly verifiable anonymous credentials system. Unfortunately, they have to rely on pairings to transform their KVAC into a publicly verifiable anonymous credentials system.

In [31], Orrù improved Barki et al. KVAC by reducing presentation and MAC costs while aligning with standardization efforts [25]. Unfortunately, Orrù's KVAC, called μ_{BBS}, still lacks public verifiability when showing credentials and would therefore not be suitable in the eIDAS context. Moreover μ_{BBS} does not support holder binding as classical SE's cannot handle the computations involved in the issuance and presentation protocols of this KVAC.

In [27], Mirzamohammadi et al. proposed two appealing and highly efficient KVAC constructions that eliminate the need for zero-knowledge proofs during the credential presentation and achieve constant-size presentations. Only their second construction is pairing-free. Unfortunately, it does not provide public verifiability, and it is not clear how this feature could be added to this construction. Both constructions however implement the holder binding feature, called non transferability in [27], which ensures that users will not be able to transfer their credentials, either intentionally or unintentionally. However, current SE's embedded in mobile phones only support classical legacy signatures schemes such as ECDSA, and unfortunately cannot carry out the computations, although simple, involved by their holder binding technique.

In [11], Chairattana-Apirom et al. introduced the concept of Server-Aided Anonymous Credentials (SAAC for short) as an alternative model for multi-show anonymous credentials, in which efficient pairing-free anonymous credentials are possible. In contrast to KVAC, SAAC enable publicly verifiable presentations of credentials. This is achieved by allowing the credential holder to interact anonymously with the issuer (either during the credential showing or ahead of time) to generate additional proofs, that will convince any verifier of the validity of a credential showing. Chairattana-Apirom et al. proposed two constructions satisfying this new model of anonymous credentials. Unfortunately, none of them incorporates the holder binding feature which is one of the main requirements for the EUDI wallet.

Another recent approach [19] to design multi-show anonymous credentials relies on generic zero-knowledge proofs. While promising in theory, this approach requires dynamic design and deployment of custom circuits for each new type of proof statement (e.g. depending on the format or structure of the credential) posing significant challenges for standardization, interoperability, and formal security analysis. The rapid evolution of circuit-based ZKP frameworks further complicates their adoption in industrial settings. Moreover, current solutions are still quite inefficient compared to their KVAC counterparts (two orders of magnitude less efficient both in terms of the size of the credentials and of the time to generate and verify a credential presentation).

1.2 Motivation

In this paper, our objective is to design an efficient anonymous credential (AC) system that meets the requirements put forth in the eIDAS 2.0 regulation. This means that our AC system should be pairing-free, and the holder binding feature should be implementable on certified hardware (typically Secure Elements or Hardware Security Modules) using SOG-IS certified digital signature algorithms (ECDSA or ECSDSA/ECSchnorr).

To this end, we first introduce a new algebraic MAC scheme which is the secret key and pairing-free variant of BBS [35] which we naturally call $\mathrm{MAC}_{\mathrm{BBS}}$.[5] Next, we use it to construct a practical pairing-free KVAC, which is proven secure under classical assumptions.

Next, we show how to turn it into an efficient pairing-free and publicly verifiable anonymous credentials system. To achieve this, we use a recent technique (Oblivious Issuance of Proofs) developed by Orrrù et al. [30].

Finally, we show (to provide the holder binding feature) how to distribute the holder's computations, during the verifiable presentation of their credentials to a verifier, between a mobile application and the Secure Element embedded in their mobile phone. We call the resulting anonymous credential system BBS#.

To demonstrate its efficiency and suitability for the EUDI Wallet, we implemented BBS# on trusted mobile hardware. We found that eIDAS 2.0 transactions can be performed in less than 100 ms when using Android StrongBox SE on the user's smartphone.

1.3 Organization

This paper is structured as follows. Section 2 introduces our main notation and the necessary building blocks. In particular, we introduce our algebraic MAC scheme called $\mathrm{MAC}_{\mathrm{BBS}}$. In Sect. 3, we describe our pairing-free KVAC based on $\mathrm{MAC}_{\mathrm{BBS}}$. Next, in Sect. 4 we explain how our KVAC can be turned into a traditional (pairing-free) public-key anonymous credential system. In Sect. 5, we explain how to distribute the computations on the user's side between a SE and a wallet application on their mobile phone, to provide the holder binding feature. Finally, Sect. 6 presents the efficiency and complexity evaluations, along with

[5] Orrrù recently proposed independently the same algebraic MAC scheme in eprint 2024/1552 but a different KVAC than the one we propose.

the implementation benchmarks of BBS#.[6] We provide formal security proofs of BBS# in the full version [15].

2 Preliminaries

2.1 Notation

We introduce some notation used throughout this document. To state that x is chosen uniformly at random from the set S, we use one of the two following notations $x \overset{R}{\leftarrow} S$ or $x \in_R S$. In addition, $\overrightarrow{m}$ will denote the vector or list $(m_1, m_2, \ldots, m_n)$, also written as $\{m_i\}_{i=1}^n$. λ will denote the security parameter and 1^λ will represent the security parameter in unary form. All algorithms are probabilistic, unless otherwise indicated. By $y \leftarrow \mathcal{A}(x_1, x_2, \ldots, x_n)$, we denote the action of running $\mathcal{A}$ on inputs $(x_1, x_2, \ldots, x_n)$ and assigning the output to y. We write $y \leftarrow \mathcal{A}^{\mathcal{O}}(x_1, x_2, \ldots, x_n)$ to indicate that $\mathcal{A}$ is an algorithm, with oracle access to some algorithm or set of algorithms $\mathcal{O}$, that takes as inputs $(x_1, x_2, \ldots, x_n)$, and assigns the output to y.

We use the term "Experiment" in the context of security definitions and proofs. An experiment will be denoted **Exp**. An experiment **Exp** in which an adversary $\mathcal{A}$ interacts with a challenger $\mathcal{C}$ to break the security property prop of a scheme Schem is denoted by $\mathbf{Exp}_{\mathcal{A}}^{\text{prop}}(1^\lambda)$.

2.2 Zero-Knowledge Proofs (ZKP)

A Zero-Knowledge Proof of Knowledge (ZKPK) [21] is an interactive protocol between a prover $\mathcal{P}$ and a verifier $\mathcal{V}$, where the prover attempts to convince the verifier of the knowledge of some secrets verifying a given statement, without revealing any information about the said secrets. A ZKPK should satisfy three properties, namely (i) *completeness* (*i.e.* a valid prover should be able to convince an honest verifier with overwhelming probability), (ii) *soundness* (*i.e.* a malicious prover should be rejected with overwhelming probability), (ii) *zero-knowledge* (*i.e.* the proof reveals no information about the secret(s)). In our constructions, we use as building blocks non-interactive zero-knowledge proofs of knowledge (or signatures of knowledge, SoK for short), obtained with a heuristic transformation such as Fiat-Shamir [17]. We use the Camenisch-Stadler notation [10], where, for example, $\pi := \text{SoK}\{\alpha, \beta : y = g^\alpha \wedge z = g^\beta\}[m]$ denotes a signature of knowledge of secrets α, β, verifying the statement on the right side of the colon. The signature of knowledge itself is generated on the message m. If the message is empty, we use the following notation to denote this signature of knowledge:

$$\pi := \text{PoK}\{\alpha, \beta : y = g^\alpha \wedge z = g^\beta\}.$$

[6] Obviously, BBS# also works in a pairing-based setting, with pairing-friendly curves. In addition, BBS# is compatible with different data formats, such as ISO mDL (ISO/IEC 18013-5).

In the random oracle model (ROM) [4], one can use the forking lemma [33] to extract the secrets from such a signature of knowledge if correct care is taken that the prover can indeed be efficiently rewound. Moreover, in the ROM one can simulate such signatures of knowledge for unknown secrets [33].

2.3 Oblivious Issuance of Proofs (OIP)

For our (pairing-free) anonymous credentials scheme, we will use a specific ZKPK, namely a *proof of equality of discrete logarithms* [14], denoted π_{DLEQ}, that can be requested *anonymously* and issued *obliviously* [30], i.e., in such a way that it cannot be linked back to the interaction that produced it: $\pi_{\mathrm{DLEQ}} := \mathrm{PoK}\{\alpha : B = A^\alpha \wedge h = g^\alpha\}$, where α is the prover's secret, g and h are two public generators of a cyclic group $\mathbb{G}$ and A and B are two generators of $\mathbb{G}$ satisfying $B = A^\alpha$ but which are unknown (blinded) to the prover.

More precisely, the proof will be issued in such a way that the prover will not be able to link $(A, B, \pi_{\mathrm{DLEQ}})$ to its respective issuance (*obliviousness*) and the verifier will not be able after the issuance of l such proofs, even in a *concurrent manner*, to forge, on its own, a new valid proof (*one-more unforgeability*). The resulting proof is transferable and can be verified non-interactively by anyone.

2.4 Signature Schemes with Key Blinding

To protect their privacy, users in our anonymous credential scheme will make use of specific signature schemes that support *key blinding* a.k.a., *key randomization* [18]. Signature schemes with this property have the advantage that one can randomize or blind the original key pair (sk, pk) to a new random key-pair (sk', pk') and sign a message m with the seemingly unrelated key (sk'). In our context, the user will have to prove (in ZK) that pk' is a randomized version of a public key pk that has been certified by a given issuer. The main goal of this randomization is to ensure that a verifier will not be able to trace a user from the signatures the latter issued. In other words, the former should not be able to distinguish between two signatures using two fresh keys obtained from the randomization of the same long-term key sk and two signatures using two fresh keys but obtained from the randomization of two distinct long-term keys sk and sk^*.

Obviously, the signatures generated by a user should be unforgeable and this should even hold when the adversary is allowed to learn message/signature pairs made with respect to randomized public keys that they have chosen (*unforgeability*).

We propose two concrete signature schemes with key blinding (see Sect. 5): ECSDSA (a.k.a. ECSchnorr) [23] with *additive blinding* and ECDSA [23] with *multiplicative blinding*.

2.5 Assumptions

Computational assumptions are fundamental tools used to establish the security of cryptographic schemes. In this document, we rely on several well-known assumptions, including the Discrete Logarithm (DL) assumption and its variants, to prove the security of our constructions. Specifically, we use the Discrete Logarithm (DL) assumption, Decisional Diffie-Hellman (DDH) assumption, gap Discrete Logarithm (gap DL) assumption, q-Strong Diffie-Hellman (q-SDH) assumption, gap q-Strong Diffie-Hellman (gap q-SDH) assumption, and q-Discrete Logarithm (q-DL) assumption. Due to space constraints, detailed definitions of these assumptions are provided in the full version [15].

2.6 An Algebraic MAC Scheme Based on BBS

An algebraic Message Authentication Code (MAC) uses cyclic groups instead of hash functions or block ciphers for traditional MACs, enabling efficient zero-knowledge proofs. This makes it useful for privacy preserving systems like anonymous credentials. It is a symmetric-key primitive with three algorithms: Setup (which generates the system parameters), KeyGen (which given as input the system parameters produces a secret key), MAC (which given a message, produces a tag on the given message using the secret key), and Verify (which given a tag, and a secret key verifies if that tag was produced on that message using that secret key). An algebraic MAC is secure if it is (strongly) unforgeable under chosen message attacks (sUF-CMVA) [12]. For more details on algebraic MACs, see full version [15].

Our pairing-free KVAC is based on a variant of Barki et al. scheme [3], called $\mathrm{MAC_{BB}}$. We introduce a modified version, $\mathrm{MAC_{BBS}}$, which produces shorter authentication tags than $\mathrm{MAC_{BB}}$. This variant can be viewed as the secret key counterpart of the BBS scheme [35]. The $\mathrm{MAC_{BBS}}$ operates as follows:

- Setup($1^\lambda, n$): creates the system public parameters $pp = (\mathbb{G}, p, \tilde{g}, g_0, g_1, g_2, \ldots, g_n)$ where $\mathbb{G}$ is a cyclic group of prime order p, a λ-bit prime, and $\tilde{g}, g_0, g_1, g_2, \ldots, g_n$ are random generators of $\mathbb{G}$.
- KeyGen(pp): selects a random value $x \in_R \mathbb{Z}_p$ as the issuer's secret key and optionally computes the corresponding public key $pk_I = \tilde{g}^x$.
- MAC($pp, x, \{m_i\}_{i=1}^n$): takes as input a set of n messages $\overrightarrow{m} = \{m_i\}_{i=1}^n$ and computes $A = (g_0 g_1^{m_1} g_2^{m_2} \ldots g_n^{m_n})^{\frac{1}{x+e}}$, where $e \in_R \mathbb{Z}_p$. The MAC on $\overrightarrow{m}$ consists of the pair (A, e).
- Verify($pp, x, \{m_i\}_{i=1}^n, A, e$): checks the validity of the authentication tag $\tau = (A, e)$ with respect to the set of n messages $\{m_i\}_{i=1}^n$. The authentication tag $\tau = (A, e)$ is valid on $\{m_i\}_{i=1}^n$ only if $(g_0 g_1^{m_1} g_2^{m_2} \ldots g_n^{m_n})^{\frac{1}{x+e}} = A$.

Theorem 1. *(Adapted from [35] Theorem 2) In the Algebraic Group Model (AGM) [20]* $\mathrm{MAC_{BBS}}$ *is sUF-CMVA secure under the gap DL and gap q-DL assumptions. More precisely, for every algebraic sUF-CMVA adversary $\mathcal{A}$ issuing at most q requests to* $\mathcal{O}$MAC, *there exist adversaries $\mathcal{B}_1$ and $\mathcal{B}_2$ such that*

$$\mathrm{Adv}_{\mathcal{A}}^{\mathrm{sUF-CMVA}}(1^\lambda) \leq \mathrm{Adv}_{\mathbb{G},\mathcal{B}_1}^{gap\ q-dl}(1^\lambda) + \mathrm{Adv}_{\mathbb{G},\mathcal{B}_2}^{gap\ dl}(1^\lambda) + \frac{1}{p}.$$

The adversaries $\mathcal{B}_1$ and $\mathcal{B}_2$ have running times comparable to $\mathcal{A}$.

Remark 1. The proof of this theorem follows along the lines of Theorem 2 of [35]. The major difference is that the cited theorem holds in the AGM with a pairing. The pairing allows to simulate a DDH oracle for the DL challenge x (the issuer's secret key). In our context, we have no pairings, but a DDH oracle provided by our gap-DL and gap-q-DL challengers. We can therefore easily check that Theorem 2 of [35] also holds in our (pairing-free) context.

MAC_{BBS} can also be proven secure in the standard model, under the gap q-SDH assumption (along the lines of Theorem 1 of [35]). However, the corresponding proof is not tight, as it incurs a multiplicative loss equal to the number of $\mathcal{O}$MAC queries.

Remark 2. A particular feature of MAC_{BBS} is that anyone can verify the validity of a given MAC by himself, i.e. without neither knowing the private key x nor querying the $\mathcal{O}$Verify oracle. In fact, a MAC on $\overrightarrow{m} = \{m_i\}_{i=1}^{n}$ consists of a pair $(A,\ e)$ such that $A = (g_0 g_1^{m_1} g_2^{m_2} \dots g_n^{m_n})^{\frac{1}{x+e}}$. This implies that $A^{x+e} = g_0 g_1^{m_1} g_2^{m_2} \dots g_n^{m_n}$ and hence $B = g_0 g_1^{m_1} g_2^{m_2} \dots g_n^{m_n} A^{-e} = A^x$. Therefore, if the issuer of the MAC $(A,\ e)$ also provides the following ZKPK $\pi_{\text{DLEQ}} := \text{PoK}\{\alpha : B = A^{\alpha} \wedge pk_I = \tilde{g}^{\alpha}\}$, then anyone will be able to check if the MAC is valid.

Remark 3. Our pairing-free (public-key) anonymous credential scheme (Sect. 4) heavily relies on the fact that the above discrete logarithm equality proof π_{DLEQ} can be requested anonymously and issued obliviously on a randomized version (A^l, B^l) of the pair (A, B) ([30]).

3 A Keyed-Verification Anonymous Credentials System Based on MAC_{BBS}

Traditional anonymous credentials schemes rely on public-key primitives (namely, digital signatures), with the issuer and verifier being two distinct entities. KVACs proposed by Chase et al. [12] are the symmetric counterpart of anonymous credentials schemes, using symmetric key primitives (algebraic MACs) and are tailored to settings where the issuer of credentials is also the verifier or more generally where the issuer and the verifier share the private issuance key.

In a KVAC, three parties are involved: the issuer, the user, and the verifier. The issuer is a trusted entity that issues credentials on user's attributes. The user can later prove that their attributes are certified to a verifier who could be the same entity as the issuer or at least who shares the same MAC secret key. The system operates in three phases: a *setup and key-generation phase* (where system parameters and keys are generated), an *issuance phase* (where the user interacts with the issuer to obtain a credential), and a *presentation phase* (where the user reveals some of their attributes required by the verifier and proves possession of a credential on these attributes to the verifier).[7] To better protect their privacy, a user should be able to reveal to a verifier (also called a Relying Party, RP

[7] We will also sometimes call this phase a Verifiable Presentation, VP for short.

for short) only the attributes *strictly necessary* for the requested service. This property is known as *selective disclosure* of attributes.

A KVAC must satisfy *unforgeability* (it is not possible to successfully present to a verifier a credential that was not previously obtained during an interaction with the issuer) and *anonymity* (no information about the user is disclosed beyond the attributes that the user agreed to reveal during the presentation of their credential).

For a comprehensive overview, including the formal definition of KVACs, please refer to the full version [15].

In the following, we present our novel KVAC system, which is built upon $\mathrm{MAC}_{\mathrm{BBS}}$. Our KVAC significantly differs from the ones proposed in [3,27,31], in that all cryptographic algorithms and computations performed on the user's side are supported by current certified secure elements embedded in existing mobile phones.

3.1 Our Construction

Based on the previously introduced $\mathrm{MAC}_{\mathrm{BBS}}$ scheme, we construct a KVAC system involving a user $\mathcal{U}$ (also called a holder), an issuer I and a verifier $\mathcal{V}$ (who holds the issuer's secret key sk_I). We would however like to emphasize that this KVAC system is just a stepping stone to the publicly verifiable anonymous credentials system BBS#.

3.2 Intuition of Our Construction

In our approach, the issuer creates a $\mathrm{MAC}_{\mathrm{BBS}}$ authentication tag σ on the user's public pk (of a signature scheme supporting key blinding / randomization) and on their attributes $\{m_i\}_{i=1}^{n}$. The tag σ represents the user's credential and authenticates both the user's attributes and their public key pk. During a Verifiable Presentation of their attributes (or a subset of them) to the verifier, the user will first randomize their public key pk (either additively if ECSDSA is used on the user's secure cryptographic device or multiplicatively in the case of ECDSA) as well as their verifiable credential σ. We denote by pk_{Blind} and σ_{Blind} respectively, these randomized versions. The user will then first generate a SoK $\pi_{\mathrm{HolderBinding}}$ (π_{HB} for short) of the private key associated to pk_{Blind} on a *nonce* generated by the verifier (to guarantee the freshness of the VP) and then a ZKP π_{Validity} proving knowledge of : (a) two random factors (r, r'), (b) a credential σ and (c) a public pk such that (1) σ_{Blind} is a randomized version of σ under the random factor r, (2) pk_{Blind} is a randomized version of pk under the random factor r', and (3) σ is a valid $\mathrm{MAC}_{\mathrm{BBS}}$ authentication tag on the (disclosed) attributes requested by the verifier. The proof $\pi_{\mathrm{HolderBinding}}$ is, as its name indicates, a proof that the VP comes from the user who truly holds the credential σ (underlying σ_{Blind}), which certifies the attributes disclosed to the verifier (*holder binding*). Our KVAC works as follows:

- Setup$(1^\lambda, n)$: On input a security parameter λ and a bound n on the number of attributes to certify, this algorithm generates the public parameters $pp = (\mathbb{G}, p, g, \tilde{g}, g_0, g_1, g_2, \ldots, g_n, H, F)$, where $\mathbb{G}$ is a cyclic group of prime order p, a λ-bit prime, and $g, \tilde{g}, g_0, g_1, g_2, \ldots, g_n, H, F$ are random generators of $\mathbb{G}$. For $i \in \{1, \ldots, n\}$, g_i is associated with a specific type of attributes (*e.g.*. age, gender, etc.). This will help to differentiate attributes and avoid any ambiguity. Note that, from now on, all computations involving exponents are computed modulo p (i.e., $\bmod p$).
- IssKeyGen(pp): On input the system public parameters pp, this algorithm selects a random value $sk_I \in_R \mathbb{Z}_p$ and computes the corresponding public key $pk_I = \tilde{g}^{sk_I}$ and optionally a ZKPK $\pi_\mathrm{I} := \mathrm{PoK}\{\alpha : pk_I = \tilde{g}^\alpha\}$ proving knowledge of the private key sk_I.
- UserKeygen(pp): To generate a key pair (sk, pk) for a user, this algorithm selects a random value $s \in_R \mathbb{Z}_p$, set $sk = s$ and computes the corresponding public key $pk = g^s$. In practice, the key pair $(sk = s, pk = g^{sk})$ will be managed by the user's cryptographic device (also called WSCD for Wallet Secure Cryptographic Device in the eIDAS 2.0 terminology).
- (Obtain$(sk, pk_I, \{m_i\}_{i=1}^n)$, Issue$(pk, sk_I, \{m_i\}_{i=1}^n)$): To obtain an anonymous credential on a set of attributes $\{m_i\}_{i=1}^n$, the user first sends their public key pk along with a signature of knowledge of sk on a challenge ch, chosen by the Issuer, to guarantee the freshness of this SoK: $\pi_\mathrm{U} = \mathrm{SoK}\{\alpha : pk = g^\alpha\}[ch]$. If this SoK, which can be generated using for example the Schnorr's protocol [34], is correct, then the issuer randomly picks $e \in_R \mathbb{Z}_p$, computes $C_m = g_0 pk \prod_{i=1}^n g_i^{m_i}$ and $A = (C_m)^{\frac{1}{sk_I + e}}$. The issuer may also build a ZKPK $\pi_\mathrm{DLEQ} := \mathrm{PoK}\{\alpha : B = A^\alpha \wedge pk_I = \tilde{g}^\alpha\}$ where $B = C_m A^{-e} = A^{sk_I}$. Then the issuer returns the pair (A, e) along with the proof π_DLEQ to the user. If the proof is valid, the user sets their anonymous credential σ as $\sigma = (A, e)$.
- (Show$(pk_I, sk, \{m_i\}_{i=1}^n, \mathcal{D}, \sigma)$, $Verify(sk_I, \{m_i\}_{i \in \mathcal{D}})$: To anonymously prove that they hold a credential on a subset $\{m_i\}_{i \in \mathcal{D}}$ of their attributes, with $\mathcal{D} \subset [1, n]$, the user engages in an interactive protocol with the verifier $\mathcal{V}$.
  - Show$(pk_I, sk, \{m_i\}_{i=1}^n, \mathcal{D}, \sigma)$. The user will first randomize their public key (so that neither the issuer nor the verifier can trace them from this key). To do this, they will randomly pick an integer r in $\mathbb{Z}_p$ and compute using this value: $pk_\mathrm{Blind} = g^{sk+r}$ and $\pi_\mathrm{HB} := \mathrm{SoK}\{\alpha\colon pk_\mathrm{Blind} = g^\alpha\}[nonce]$, where $nonce \in_R \{0,1\}^\mu$, is a random value sent by the verifier (to guarantee the freshness of the VP). They will then "randomize" their $\mathrm{MAC_{BBS}}$ authentication tag σ, to also prevent the issuer and the verifier from tracing them from this element, and "adapt" it to be on pk_Blind and the $\{m_i\}_{i=1}^n$. To do this, they will choose integers $r_1, r_2 \in_R \mathbb{Z}_p^*$ and compute:
    1. $\overline{A} = A^{r_1 \times r_2}$,
    2. $D = C_m{}^{r_2}$
    3. $\overline{B} = \overline{A}^{-e} D^{r_1} = \overline{A}^{sk_I}$
    4. $r_3 = r_2^{-1} \mod p$

5. $\pi_{\text{validity}} = \text{SoK}\{\alpha, \beta, \gamma, \delta, \{\theta_i\}_{i \notin \mathcal{D}} : \overline{B} = \overline{A}^{\alpha} D^{\beta}$
$\wedge g_0 pk_{\text{Blind}} \prod_{i \in \mathcal{D}} g_i^{m_i} = D^{\gamma} \prod_{i \notin \mathcal{D}} g_i^{\theta_i} g^{\delta}\}[nonce]$
We have the following two equalities, hence the ZKP
π_{validity}: $\overline{B} = \overline{A}^{-e} D^{r_1}$ and $g_0 pk_{\text{Blind}} \prod_{i \in \mathcal{D}} g_i^{m_i} = D^{r_3} \prod_{i \notin \mathcal{D}} g_i^{-m_i} g^r$.
6. The user transmits $VP = (\{m_i\}_{i \in \mathcal{D}}, pk_{\text{Blind}}, \pi_{\text{HB}}, \overline{A}, \overline{B}, D, \pi_{\text{validity}})$ to the verifier.

- Verify($sk_I, \{m_i\}_{i \in \mathcal{D}}$). Upon receipt of $VP = (\{m_i\}_{i \in \mathcal{D}}, pk_{\text{Blind}}, \pi_{\text{HB}}, \overline{A}, \overline{B}, D, \pi_{\text{validity}})$, $\mathcal{V}$ first checks than π_{HB} is a valid SoK on *nonce*, and then verifies that π_{validity} is valid. If so, $\mathcal{V}$ uses sk_I to check whether $\overline{B} = \overline{A}^{sk_I}$. $\mathcal{V}$ is convinced that $\mathcal{U}$ really holds a valid credential on the disclosed attributes $\{m_i\}_{i \subset \mathcal{D}}$ if, and only if, all these checks succeed. We prove this fact in the full version [15]. In other words, we prove that $VP = (\{m_i\}_{i \in \mathcal{D}}, pk_{\text{Blind}}, \pi_{\text{HB}}, \overline{A}, \overline{B}, D, \pi_{\text{validity}})$ constitutes a proof of knowledge of a blinding factor r, a private key sk and of a valid credential, $\sigma = (A, e)$, on the subset $\{m_i\}_{i \in \mathcal{D}}$ and on a public key $pk = pk_{\text{Blind}} g^{-r}$.

4 From KVAC to Pairing-Free Anonymous Credentials

The main drawback of KVAC systems is that they are tailored to specific settings in which the issuer also acts as a verifier, as in the case of e-government or public transportation. They are not suited to the more general setting in which the issuer and the verifier are two distinct entities.

In this section, we explain how to turn our (pairing-free) KVAC system into a (pairing-free) public key anonymous credential system. Thereby, a user will be able to prove possession of a credential to any entity (i.e., without the latter necessarily knowing the issuer's private key).

In BBS/BBS+ based anonymous credentials schemes, pairings are used by the verifier to check whether the following equality $\overline{B} = \overline{A}^{sk_I}$ holds or not, where sk_I is the issuer's private key (see $Verify(sk_I, \{m_i\}_{i \in \mathcal{D}})$, in Sect. 3.1).

We propose below three options to let any verifier perform this check without using pairings.

4.1 Option 1

The first option is to let the verifier ask the issuer to check whether this equality, $\overline{B} = \overline{A}^{sk_I}$, holds or not. As $\overline{A}$ and $\overline{B}$ have been randomized by the user (they consist of the randomization of his credential values A and B), the Issuer cannot trace back the user from these values. Obviously, the issuer should prove to the verifier whether this equality holds or not. This can be done, for example, by using the classical Chaum-Pedersen ZKP of discrete logarithms equality π_{DLEQ} [14] when the equality holds or by using, for example, the proof of the inequality of discrete logarithms of Camenisch and Shoup otherwise [9].

A similar approach has been adopted in the card payment sector to enable a *point-of-sale terminal* to check the validity of a smart card transaction online with the *issuer* (the cardholder's bank).[8]

4.2 Option 2

The second option is to let the user *anonymously* request from the issuer, during the *Show* protocol, a blind proof (a.k.a. an Oblivious Proof [30]), π_{DLEQ}, showing that $\overline{B} = \overline{A}^{sk_I}$ that will be sent, along with the VP, to the Verifier. By blind, we mean that the issuer, although contributing to the generation of this proof (as only they know sk_I), will be unable, given such a proof, to determine for which user it was intended. This proof can be verified by anyone using solely the issuer's public key.

This approach (option 2) is similar to the one used in the context of centralized / federated identity management systems (IMS). In fact, in a federated IMS when a user wants to authenticate at a RP (or prove that they hold the attributes requested by that RP), the user is redirected to their IDP (issuer) in order to obtain a *token* (signed by the issuer), which the user can present to the RP as a proof that they have authenticated to the issuer (or that they hold the requested attributes). However, we would like to point out that, unlike federated IMS or ACL (where users are identified and authenticated during their interactions with the issuer), with Option 2, neither the issuer nor the RP (even if they collude) will be able to track or link the user's activity. Indeed, since the user *anonymously* requests the blind proof π_{DLEQ}, a *time-correlation attack* will not work.

4.3 Option 3

The user generates several pairs ($A_i = A^{l_i}, B_i = B^{l_i}$) and *anonymously* requests from the issuer, in advance, blind proofs π_{DLEQ} showing that $B_i = A_i^{sk_I}$ and stores these blind proofs for future use (and only uses them in the rare cases where both the user and the verifier are offline). The blind proof π_{DLEQ} can be obtained using the Chaum-Pedersen seminal blind signature protocol [14], which is standardized in the ISO/IEC standard 18370-2 ([16], mechanism 4) and which represents the core cryptographic mechanism used in the anonymous credential scheme U-Prove. This blind signature protocol can be seen, in fact, as an Oblivious Issuance of proof (OIP for short), for the proof π_{DLEQ}.

Unfortunately, Benhamouda et al. [5] have shown that this OIP is vulnerable to a parallel attack (ROS attack). Specifically, a user simultaneously running a large number (l) of Chaum-Pedersen blind signatures sessions with the issuer would be able, after these l sessions, to forge an additional valid signature/proof (and thus fraudulently obtain $l + 1$ DL equality proofs instead of just l).

[8] which roughly consists of a MAC computed by the card on the payment data elements such as the transaction amount and transaction date.

We therefore consider for Option 2 and Option 3, the Oblivious Issuance Proof proposed by Orrù et al. [30], which is *one more unforgeable* even in the concurrent setting.[9] This OIP which we have adapted to our context and which we denote Blind π_{DLEQ} is described in [15].[10]

This approach (option 3) is similar to that described in ISO mDL, where a user can obtain several verifiable credentials at once (in batch) to prevent colluding RPs from tracing them. However, option 3 provides *full unlinkability*, unlike the ISO mDL batch credential issuance approach.[11]

In practice, Option 1 will be the preferred one, whereas Option 3 will be used in the rare cases where both the user and the verifier are offline. Option 2 could be used when the verifier is offline, but not the user (who would be online).

5 Distributed Computations on the User's Side

In practice, Secure Elements (SE) are relatively closed devices. Although most of them support common digital signature algorithms such as ECDSA, developers do not have the ability to implement new cryptographic functionalities for security reasons. Therefore, it is difficult to use these SEs for purposes other than what they were originally designed for (such as generating ECDSA signatures). As a result, an SE cannot "randomize" its own public and private keys because it has not been programmed to perform such operations. It cannot carry out these basic operations, even though they may seem straightforward: such as generating a random value r and computing $sk_{\text{Blind}} = sk + r \mod p$, its randomized private key. Similarly, an SE cannot generate the SoK π_{HB}, that is, a signature of knowledge of the discrete logarithm of pk_{Blind} in the base g (which is equal to $sk + r \mod p$).

In the following, we explain how the Secure Element (SE) of the user's mobile device and the associated mobile wallet application (referred to as M-Wallet) can jointly randomize the public key pk_{Blind} and compute the SoK π_{HB}. It is important to note that in practice only the secure hardware (SE) knows the private key sk corresponding to the user's public key pk.

We propose two variants of BBS#: in the first one, we assume that the digital signature algorithm supported by the SE is ECSchnorr [23], while in the second one, we assume that it is ECDSA [23].

---

[9] As shown in [11], to transform a KVAC into a secure SAAC, one should also prove that the underlying OIP does not leak the issuer's private key. We provide such a proof in the full version [15].

[10] In [11], Chairattana-Apirom et al. consider a different OIP for their SAAC which they claim is not required to resist strong attacks such as ROS. However, we believe that such an OIP should resist to these attacks, as it is envisioned in specific use cases to use them for *credential monetization*. In this way, verifiers would contribute financially to the credential ecosystem when they benefit from the use of reliable data (i.e., verifiable credential). Therefore, users or verifiers shoud not be able to forge such OIPs.

[11] A different credential must be used for each new VP.

5.1 Joint Computation of pk_{Blind} and π_{HB} with ECSchnorr

We assume that the SE supports the classical ECSchnorr digital signature algorithm, also known as ECSDSA in ISO/IEC 14888-3 standard. We will use an *additive blinding* of the SE private key sk.[12]

It should be noted that in this standard, the so-called "weak" version of the Fiat-Shamir heuristic is implemented; however, in certain contexts, this version is vulnerable to an attack introduced by Bernhard et al. [6]. Although this attack does not apply to our context, we will nevertheless indicate how to use the so-called Strong version of the Fiat-Shamir heuristic (Strong FS) with ECSDSA (as specified in ISO/IEC 14888-3 standard). The attack by Bernhard et al. [6] does not apply to non-interactive proofs using the Strong version of the Fiat-Shamir heuristic. The joint computation of the

$$\text{SoK}\pi_{\text{HB}} = \text{SoK}\{\alpha : pk_{\text{Blind}} = g^{\alpha}\}[nonce, pk_{\text{Blind}}]$$

could be performed in the following way:

1. The M-Wallet chooses a random value r and computes $pk_{\text{Blind}} = g^{r}pk = g^{sk+r}$ and transmits it to the SE along with the *nonce* sent by the verifier.
2. The SE will first compute a signature of knowledge (denoted π) of the discrete logarithm of pk in the base g (that is, its private key sk): $\pi = \text{SoK}\{\alpha : pk = g^{\alpha}\}[nonce, pk_{\text{Blind}}]$. The algorithm called ECSDSA will be used to compute this signature. This signature of knowledge is computed as follows using the ECSDSA algorithm. The SE generates a random value ω and computes $T = g^{\omega}$, $c = \mathcal{H}(T,\ nonce, pk_{\text{Blind}})$ and $\rho = \omega + csk \mod p$ where $\mathcal{H}$ denotes a cryptographic hash function (e.g., SHA-256). The SoK π consists of the pair $(c,\ \rho)$: $\pi = (c,\ \rho)$. It is valid if $c' = \mathcal{H}\left(g^{\rho}\times pk^{-c},\ nonce, pk_{\text{Blind}}\right) = c$ and invalid otherwise.
3. The SE transmits the SoK to the M-Wallet.
4. The M-Wallet computes $\rho_{Blind} = \rho + c\times r = \omega + c\times sk + c\times r = \omega + c\times(sk+r) \mod p$.

The SoK $\pi_{\text{HB}} = (c,\ \rho_{Blind})$ is a valid ECSDSA signature on $(nonce, pk_{\text{Blind}})$ with respect to the public key pk_{Blind}.

5.2 Security of BBS# with ECSchnorr Splitting

The unforgeability of our KVAC system directly relies on the one of MAC_{BBS} and on the DL assumption. Anonymity holds *statistically/unconditionally*, which means that anonymity is preserved even against possible future quantum adversaries. This is formally stated by the following theorem.

---

[12] We would like to emphasize that the interactive version of ECSchnorr, which would greatly ease the holder binding feature, is currently not deployed on SE's. This also explains why the non transferability/holder binding technique used in [27] would not work in practice.

Theorem 2. *Our KVAC system is unforgeable in the ROM if* $\mathrm{MAC_{BBS}}$ *is sUF-CMVA secure and if the DL assumption holds in* $\mathbb{G}$.
Our KVAC system is anonymous if π_{DLEQ} *is a sound proof system and if* π_{HB} *and* π_{validity} *are zero-knowledge proof systems.*

The proof of Theorem 2 will appear in the full version [15] of this extended abstract.

5.3 Joint Computation of pk_{Blind} and π_{HB} with ECDSA

This time, we will assume that the SE supports the classic digital signature algorithm ECDSA [FIPS186-4, ISO/IEC 14888 3]. We will use this time a multiplicative blinding of the SE private key sk. The joint computation of the ECDSA signature (π_{HB}) on the message $(nonce, pk_{\mathrm{Blind}})$ using the private key $sk_{\mathrm{Blind}} = sk \times r \mod p$, could be performed in the following way (see Fig. 1):

1. The M-Wallet chooses a random value r and computes $pk_{\mathrm{Blind}} = pk^r = g^{sk \times r}$ and $M = r^{-1} \times \mathcal{H}(nonce, pk_{\mathrm{Blind}}) \mod p$ and transmits M to the SE after authenticating itself with the latter.
2. The SE chooses a random value $k \in \mathbb{Z}_p^*$ and calculates $g^k = (i,\ j)$.[13] Let $x = i \mod p$.
3. If $x = 0$ then go back to step 2.
4. The SE calculates $\rho = k^{-1}(M + sk \times x) \mod p$.
5. If $\rho = 0$ go back to step 2. Otherwise, the SE transmits $\sigma_0 = (x,\ \rho)$ to the M-Wallet.
6. The M-Wallet computes
$\rho_{Blind} = r \times \rho = k^{-1}(\mathcal{H}(nonce, pk_{\mathrm{Blind}}) + sk_{\mathrm{Blind}} \times x) \mod p$

The signature $\pi_{\mathrm{HB}} = (x, \rho_{Blind})$ is a valid ECDSA signature on $(nonce, pk_{\mathrm{Blind}})$ with respect to the public key pk_{Blind}.

$$VP = (\{m_i\}_{i \in \mathcal{D}},\ pk_{\mathrm{Blind}}, \pi_{\mathrm{HB}}, \overline{A}, \overline{B}, D,\ \pi_{\mathrm{validity}}).$$

Only the SoK π_{validity} differs when ECDSA is used on the user's side. In the ECDSA case, the proof π_{validity} would be the following:

$$\pi_{\mathrm{validity}} = \mathrm{PoK}\{\alpha, \beta, \gamma, \delta, \{\tau_i\}_{i \notin \mathcal{D}} : \ \overline{B} = \overline{A}^{-\alpha} D^{\beta} \wedge F = pk_{Blind}{}^{\delta} D^{\gamma} \textstyle\prod_{i \notin \mathcal{D}} g_i^{-\tau_i} \mod p\}$$

where, $F = g_0 \prod_{i \in \mathcal{D}} g_i^{m_i}$. We have the following two equalities, hence the validity proof π_{validity}: $\overline{B} = \overline{A}^{-e} D^{r_1}$ and $F = pk_{Blind}{}^{\tilde{r}} D^{r_3} \prod_{i \notin \mathcal{D}} g_i^{-m_i}$ where, $\tilde{r} = -r^{-1} \mod p$ and $r_3 = r_2^{-1} \mod p$.

---

[13] Here, we are abusively using multiplication (instead of addition) to denote the group operation in $\mathbb{G}$. The element g^k is therefore considered (abusively) as a point on the underlying elliptic curve.

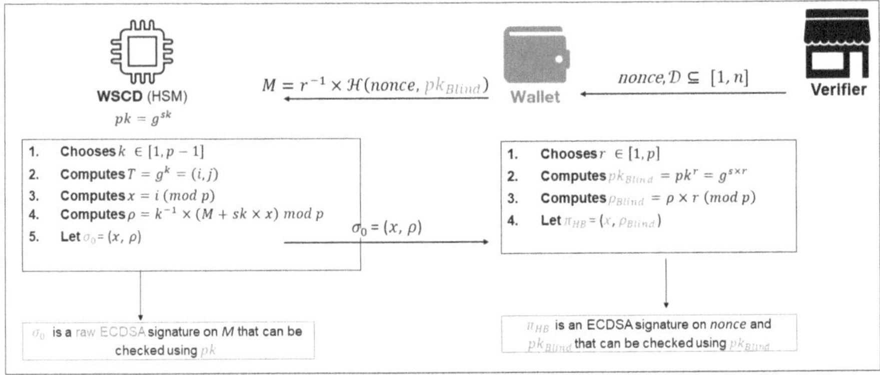

Fig. 1. Joint computation of pk_{Blind} and π_{HB} with ECDSA.

5.4 Security of BBS# with ECDSA Splitting

The particularity of our splitting technique described in Fig. 1 is that it makes use of *raw ECDSA* on the WSCD/SE side (*i.e.*, the signing queries are on $\mathcal{H}(m)$ rather than on plain m) instead of the classical ECDSA (where the signing queries are on plain m). Raw ECDSA is, however, supported by a majority of WSCDs: the iOS/Secure Enclave, Android-/HBK+Strongbox, TPMs, PKCS11 based HSMs for example, all support this functionality.

Another specificity of our splitting technique is that we include pk_{Blind} in the message to be signed by the WSCD (unlike SECDSA [36]). Without pk_{Blind}, our splitting technique would be vulnerable to a simple related-key attack (see for example [28] Sect. 4.2).[14]

The security of our splitting mechanism relies on the security of raw ECDSA (*one-more unforgeability*).[15] By one-more unforgeability, we mean that an attacker after having requested l raw ECDSA signatures on l chosen hash values $H_1, H_2, \cdots, H_l$, will not be able to generate an additional signature on a hash value H that was not requested.

Theorem 3. *Our KVAC system is unforgeable in the elliptic curve GGM and ROM if raw ECDSA is one-more unforgeable and if* MAC_{BBS} *is sUF-CMVA secure.*

The proof of Theorem 3 will appear in the full version [15] of this extended abstract.

6 Performance

To confirm the efficiency and suitability of BBS# for the forthcoming EUDI wallet, we implemented it on several smartphones using different secure execution

[14] Which unfortunately applies to SECDSA [36].

[15] Groth and Shoup have shown that raw ECDSA signatures are one-more unforgeable in the *elliptic curve generic group model* [22].

environments: eIDAS 2.0 transactions can be performed in less than 100 ms when using Android StrongBox SE on the user's smartphone. Due to space constraints, our detailed benchmarks are provided in [15].

7 Conclusion

The EU Digital Identity Wallet (EUDI Wallet), introduced by the eIDAS 2.0 regulation, is a digital identity solution for securely presenting personal identification data (PID) and verifiable credentials (a.k.a., Qualified Electronic Attestations of Attributes, QEAAs for short, in the eIDAS 2.0 terminology). eIDAS 2.0 mandates selective disclosure and unlinkability for privacy protection.

Anonymous credentials, which allow holders to prove statements about their identity in a privacy preserving way, is likely to become the key technology to meet the stringent requirements (no pairing-based cryptography and hardware-based holder binding) put forth in the eIDAS 2.0 regulation. Unfortunately, current efficient anonymous credentials protocols, such as BBS/BBS +, do not meet these requirements: they either make use of bilinear maps and pairing-friendly curves (which are not supported by current certified secure elements) or would require, to be rolled out, changes in these certified hardware or the algorithms they support to implement the holder binding feature.

In this paper, we introduced BBS#, a pairing-free variant of the anonymous credentials scheme BBS, which can be used with 'classic' (non-pairing friendly) elliptic curves, and more importantly with current existing 'Wallet Secure Cryptographic Devices' (WSCD): iOS/Secure Enclave, Android-/HBK+Strongbox, TPMs or PKCS11 based HSMs.

BBS# is provably secure; it inherits the security of BBS, of Oblivious Issuance of Proofs and the security of ECDSA with multiplicative key randomization.

Finally, our implementation results confirm the efficiency and suitability of BBS# for the forthcoming EUDI Wallet.

References

1. Baldimtsi, F., Lysyanskaya, A.: Anonymous credentials light. In: Proceedings of the 2013 ACM SIGSAC Conference on Computer & Communications Security, pp. 1087–1098 (2013)
2. Barić, N., Pfitzmann, B.: Collision-free accumulators and fail-stop signature schemes without trees. In: Fumy, W. (eds.) EUROCRYPT 1997. LNCS, vol. 1233. Springer, Berlin (1997). https://doi.org/10.1007/3-540-69053-0_33
3. Barki, A., Brunet, S., Desmoulins, N., Traoré, J.: Improved algebraic MACs and practical keyed-verification anonymous credentials. In: Avanzi, R., Heys, H. (eds.) Selected Areas in Cryptography – SAC 2016. SAC 2016. LNCS, vol. 10532. Springer, Cham (2017). https://doi.org/10.1007/978-3-319-69453-5_20
4. Bellare, M., Rogaway, P.: Random oracles are practical: a paradigm for designing efficient protocols. In: Proceedings of the 1st ACM Conference on Computer and Communications Security, pp. 62–73 (1993)

5. Benhamouda, F., Lepoint, T., Loss, J., Orrù, M., Raykova, M.: On the (in) security of ros. In: Annual International Conference on the Theory and Applications of Cryptographic Techniques, pp. 33–53. Springer (2021)
6. Bernhard, D., Pereira, O., Warinschi, B.: How not to prove yourself: pitfalls of the fiat-shamir heuristic and applications to helios. In: Wang, X., Sako, K. (eds) ASIACRYPT 2012. LNCS, vol. 7658. Springer, Berlin (2012). https://doi.org/10.1007/978-3-642-34961-4_38
7. Brands, S.A.: An efficient off-line electronic cash system based on the representation problem (1993)
8. Camenisch, J., Lysyanskaya, A.: A signature scheme with efficient protocols. In: Cimato, S., Persiano, G., Galdi, C. (eds.) SCN 2002. LNCS, vol. 2576. Springer, Berlin (2003). https://doi.org/10.1007/3-540-36413-7_20
9. Camenisch, J., Shoup, V.: Practical verifiable encryption and decryption of discrete logarithms. In: Annual International Cryptology Conference.,pp. 126–144. Springer (2003). https://doi.org/10.1007/978-3-540-45146-4_8
10. Camenisch, J., Stadler, M.: Efficient group signature schemes for large groups. In: Annual International Cryptology Conference, pp. 410–424. Springer (1997). https://doi.org/10.1007/BFb0052252
11. Chairattana-Apirom, R., Harding, F., Lysyanskaya, A., Tessaro, S.: Server-aided anonymous credentials. Cryptology ePrint Archive, Paper 2025/513 (2025)
12. Chase, M., Meiklejohn, S., Zaverucha, G.: Algebraic macs and keyed-verification anonymous credentials. In: Proceedings of the 2014 ACM SIGSAC Conference on Computer and Communications Security, pp. 1205–1216 (2014)
13. Chaum, D.: Security without identification: transaction systems to make big brother obsolete. Commun. ACM **28**(10), 1030–1044 (1985)
14. Chaum, D., Pedersen, T.P.: Wallet databases with observers. In: Wallet Databases with Observers. In: Brickell, E.F. (eds.) CRYPTO 1992. LNCS, vol. 740. Springer, Berlin (1993). https://doi.org/10.1007/3-540-48071-4_7
15. Desmoulins, N., Dumanois, A., Kane, S., Traoré, J.: Making BBS anonymous credentials eIDAS 2.0 compliant. Cryptology ePrint Archive, Paper 2025/619 (2025). https://eprint.iacr.org/2025/619
16. Fal', O.: Standardization in information technology security. Cybern. Syst. Anal. **53**, 78–82 (2017)
17. Fiat, A., Shamir, A.: How to prove yourself: practical solutions to identification and signature problems. In: Odlyzko, A.M. (eds.) CRYPTO 1986. LNCS, vol. 263. Springer, Berlin (1986). https://doi.org/10.1007/3-540-47721-7_12
18. Fleischhacker, N., Krupp, J., Malavolta, G., Schneider, J., Schröder, D., Simkin, M.: Efficient unlinkable sanitizable signatures from signatures with re-randomizable keys. Cryptology ePrint Archive. Paper 2015/395 (2015)
19. Frigo, M., abhi shelat: Anonymous credentials from ECDSA. Cryptology ePrint Archive, Paper 2024/2010 (2024). https://eprint.iacr.org/2024/2010
20. Fuchsbauer, G., Kiltz, E., Loss, J.: The algebraic group model and its applications. In: Shacham, H., Boldyreva, A. (eds) CRYPTO 2018. LNCS, vol. 10992. Springer, Cham (2018). https://doi.org/10.1007/978-3-319-96881-0_2
21. Goldwasser, S., Micali, S., Rackoff, C.: The knowledge complexity of interactive proof-systems. In: Providing sound foundations for cryptography: On the work of shafi goldwasser and silvio micali, pp. 203–225 (2019)
22. Groth, J., Shoup, V.: On the security of ECDSA with additive key derivation and presignatures. Cryptology ePrint Archive, Paper 2021/1330 (2021)
23. ISO: Iso/iec 14888-3: 2018 it security techniques-digital signatures with appendix-part 3: discrete logarithm based mechanisms (2018)

24. Kakvi, S.A., Martin, K.M., Putman, C., Quaglia, E.A.: Sok: anonymous credentials. In: International Conference on Research in Security Standardisation, pp. 129–151. Springer (2023). https://doi.org/10.1007/978-3-031-30731-7_6
25. Looker, T., Kalos, V., Whitehead, A., Lodder, M.: The BBS Signature Scheme. Internet-Draft draft-irtf-cfrg-bbs-signatures-08, Internet Engineering Task Force. https://datatracker.ietf.org/doc/draft-irtf-cfrg-bbs-signatures/08/, work in Progress
26. Looker, T., Kalos, V., Whitehead, A., Lodder, M.: The BBS Signature Scheme. Internet-Draft draft-irtf-cfrg-bbs-signatures-05, Internet Engineering Task Force (Dec 2023), work in Progress
27. Mirzamohammadi, O., et al.: Keyed-verification anonymous credentials with highly efficient partial disclosure. Cryptology ePrint Archive, Paper 2025/041 (2025)
28. Morita, H., Schuldt, J.C., Matsuda, T., Hanaoka, G., Iwata, T.: On the security of the schnorr signature scheme and dsa against related-key attacks. In: Kwon, S., Yun, A. (eds.) ICISC 2015. LNCS, vol. 9558. Springer, Cham (2016). https://doi.org/10.1007/978-3-319-30840-1_2
29. Neven, G.: Ibm identity mixer (idemix). In: NIST Meeting on Privacy Enhancing Technology, Zurich, Switzerland, pp. 8–9 (2011)
30. Orrù, M., Tessaro, S., Zaverucha, G., Zhu, C.: Oblivious issuance of proofs. In: Annual International Cryptology Conference, pp. 254–287. Springer (2024). https://doi.org/10.1007/978-3-031-68400-5_8
31. Orrrù, M.: Revisiting keyed-verification anonymous credentials. Cryptology ePrint Archive, Paper 2024/1552 (2024)
32. Paquin, C., Zaverucha, G.: U-prove cryptographic specification v1. 1. Technical Report, Microsoft Corporation (2011)
33. Pointcheval, D., Stern, J.: Security arguments for digital signatures and blind signatures. J. Cryptol. **13**, 361–396 (2000)
34. Schnorr, C.P.: Efficient identification and signatures for smart cards. In: Brassard, G. (eds.) CRYPTO 1989. LNCS, vol. 435. Springer, New York (1990). https://doi.org/10.1007/0-387-34805-0_22
35. Tessaro, S., Zhu, C.: Revisiting bbs signatures. In: Annual International Conference on the Theory and Applications of Cryptographic Techniques, pp. 691–721. Springer (2023). https://doi.org/10.1007/978-3-031-30589-4_24
36. Verheul, E.: SECDSA: Mobile signing and authentication under classical "sole control". Cryptology ePrint Archive, Paper 2021/910 (2021)

Vision: A Modular Framework for Anonymous Credential Systems

Anja Lehmann, Andrey Sidorenko(✉), and Alexandros Zacharakis

Hasso Plattner Institute, University of Potsdam, Potsdam, Germany
{anja.lehmann,andrey.sidorenko,alexandros.zacharakis}@hpi.de

Abstract. Anonymous credentials enable the unlinkable presentation of previously attested information, or even only predicates thereof. They are a versatile tool and currently enjoy attention in various real-world applications, ranging from the European Digital Identity project to Privacy Pass. While each application usually requires their own tailored variant of anonymous credentials, they all share the same common blueprint. So far, this has not been leveraged though, and currently several proposals either targeting monolithic variants of core components such as BBS signatures, or application-specific protocols undergo standardization. This is clearly not optimal, as the same work gets repeated multiple times, while still risking ending up with many slight modifications of the same main idea and protocols. In this work we present our vision to use a modular approach to build anonymous credential systems: they are built from a core component – consisting of a commitment, signature and NIZK scheme – that can be extended with additional commitment-based modules in a plug-and-play manner. We sketch modules for pseudonyms, range proofs and device binding. Importantly, apart from the committed input, all modules are entirely independent of each other. We use this modularity to propose a concrete instantiation that uses BBS signatures for the core component and ECDSA signatures for device binding, addressing the need to bind modern credential schemes to legacy signatures in secure hardware elements.

1 Introduction

Anonymous credentials (AC) are the privacy-preserving version of classical digital certificates. They enable users to obtain attested attributes from a trusted issuer that they can later present towards a third-party verifier. On top of the standard security properties provided by classic certificates, anonymous credentials have several important privacy features built-in, such as selective disclosure of the attested attributes and multi-show unlinkability. Importantly, they guarantee these privacy properties even against corrupt issuers. This makes anonymous credentials the perfect tool for all applications that target or require

---

The full version of this work is available at https://eprint.iacr.org/2025/1981.

H. C. Pöhls and C. J. Mitchell (Eds.): SSR 2025, LNCS 16466, pp. 46–68, 2026.
https://doi.org/10.1007/978-3-032-19567-8_3

privacy-preserving authentication – at least in theory. In the real-world however, anonymous credentials are still not widely deployed, despite major applications demanding exactly their capabilities. Most prominently, the European efforts to build a European Digital Identity Wallet (EUDI) must adhere with strong privacy requirements stated in the eIDAS regulation, which explicitly demands that the system must support pseudonyms, selective disclosure and unlinkable authentications [1,28]. Similarly, Privacy Pass [25], was invented to provide privacy-preserving rate-limiting for online services. Both require multi-show unlinkable presentation of certified information, for which anonymous credentials would have been a natural fit. However, neither application uses ACs, instead they reverted to batch-issuance of one-time tokens. As batch-issuance inherently incurs significant costs and challenges for secure deployment, the interest in "upgrading" to an AC-based solution remains strong.

Lack of Existing Standards. A core reason that hindered real-world adoption of anonymous credentials so far is the lack of suitable standards for the underlying cryptography. Apart from the ISO standards in the context of Direct Anonymous Attestation (DAA) [36], no fully approved standard of these credential schemes exists. The DAA standard is partly outdated, and targets a particular application, which does not fit the requirements e.g., in the EUDI or Privacy Pass. The standard from 2013 already contains a protocol relying on BBS signatures [16] which is also a widely considered candidate for ACs today. While the core BBS signature has not changed since then, the associated zero-knowledge (ZKP) proof has seen significant efficiency improvements in the last decade [13,41,51]. The ISO has also initiated a working draft on a new standard, [2].

Challenges in Standardization. The increased interest in deployment of anonymous credentials has already led to several standardization activities: BBS-based credentials currently undergo standardization in the IETF CFRG [41], including two extensions to support pseudonyms [37] and blind issuance [38]. Concrete protocols for using anonymous credentials in the context of Privacy Pass have been proposed in the respective IETF working group by Apple [53] and Google [50]. Further, a standard on Sigma protocols is being developed too, essentially abstracting the ZKP component therein [45].

As these standards have significant overlaps in the underlying techniques, this has already sparked discussions how to best package and combine these efforts [47]. Standards tailored to a specific application will not only repeat the same work, but might result in various incarnations of the same core concept with minor modifications – resulting in incompatible implementations and duplicated work across projects. Standards that focus on building blocks avoid such a lock-in situation on the application side, but in turn can be too shielded to be extendable and usable. This is in fact a new situation compared to more conventional cryptographic building blocks such as encryption or classic signatures. These classic primitives have monolithic APIs which can be composed on pure in/output behavior. In contrast, anonymous credentials are built from a core signature primitive upon which various statements via a ZKP are proven. While the core part is relatively stable across application, the ZKP part and the exact feature set will vary greatly.

1.1 Modular Framework for Standardization

In this work we formulate our vision to standardize and build anonymous credential systems in a modular manner. We identify re-usable components – which we call *modules* – and design them in a way that makes them compatible via a core module, and allow for flexible extensions. Protocols can be built in a plug-and play manner from these modules, and standardization and security analysis can focus on modules instead of the entire credential system. By abstracting modules we also aim to support a crypto agile design where individual parts can have different instantiations that can be combined and replaced with ease.

Sign, Commit and Prove. Our framework abstracts the common blueprint that underlies *all* anonymous credential systems so far: the core component is a (multi-message) signature scheme used by the issuer to attest the user's attributes. The signature scheme must enable efficient non-interactive ZKPs (NIZK) of knowledge of such a signature on both *revealed* and *committed* attributes (all other attributes remain *hidden*). The commitments serve as the main glue between the main module and further extensions. That is, we define the core module (CD) to be a multi-message signature scheme which allows for such *committed disclosure proofs*. Any capability that goes beyond plain selective disclosure is added through modules that operate on the committed attributes. To exemplify the role of these modules, we sketch how *pseudonyms* and *range proofs* can be expressed therein. Notably, all our modules can come with their individual NIZK proof system, as they prove each module in an isolated way. This allows to use optimized NIZKs for different parts of the system, instead of aiming for a monolithic system that covers all. Further, security can be analyzed on the level of the independent modules and then propagates to the full system.

Explicit Device Binding. A particular focus in our modular framework is on *device-binding*, which is currently not covered by any of the standardization efforts, but is a crucial requirement in the EUDI context [28]. Device-binding aims to provide non-transferability of credentials, i.e., prevent malicious users from copying and sharing their credentials. It assumes that the user's host device includes a secure hardware component– the Secure Element (SE) – that contains cryptographic keys that cannot be extracted and are only accessible through a minimal signature API. The user's credential then includes a device public key as an attribute, and every presentation must include a fresh proof-of-possession (PoP) under that key.

We propose an *explicit device binding* solution that essentially mimics this standard approach in a privacy-preserving way: the SE is still assumed to only output a standard signature under a public key attested in the user's credential. The public key will only be revealed in committed form through the CD module, and the device-binding module adds a NIZK that proves knowledge of a fresh

PoP under that key. Notably, the proof system and signature scheme for this PoP can both be different from the main multi-signature scheme used for the attribute credential.

This approach differs from existing proposals in anonymous credential schemes that design these capabilities directly within the system itself [13,35,36]. These solutions are highly-efficient, but require non-standard APIs from the SEs, typically involving computations over a pairing-friendly group. The reality is much more bleak though, and current SEs merely support ECDSA signatures over P-256 curves. As the development and lifecycle of SEs is extremely static, our explicit device binding enables to add non-transferability to anonymous credential systems in a way that is compatible with these hardware limitations. In fact, we believe that decoupling the aspect of device binding from the core credential component is essential for any short term deployment. While signature schemes for embedded hardware devices will be notoriously hard – or even impossible – to update, signature schemes for the main credential itself do not adhere to such constraints. Our modular approach with explicit device binding caters for these differences, and does not impose that hardware limitations stemming from the SEs are propagated to the entire credential system.

Instantiation: BBS-ECDSA. As a concrete instantiation, we show how to use BBS signatures [8,41] as the multi-message signature while relying on ECDSA for device binding. The NIZK of a BBS signature on committed attributes can be done through simple and lightweight Schnorr proofs, and using Pedersen commitments to bridge to further modules. For computing the PoP NIZK, we employ the Schnorr-based protocol ZKAttest/CDLS [20,30], extended with an additional proof to bridge the underlying elliptic curves, which differ between BBS and ECDSA. This BBS-ECDSA solution has been proposed and implemented by Ubique [4] in the context of an innovation challenge of the German EUDI project, and was further improved by Dock Labs [34]. We believe this BBS-ECDSA combination to be of independent interest: it provides the simplicity and flexibility of BBS credentials, while supporting device-binding with legacy hardware. We provide an overview of this construction and demonstrate how it fits our proposed framework.

Related Work. We stress that none of the building blocks used in our framework are novel, and existing implementations may be used for large parts of the system. The modular approach relying on commitments to bridge and compose different instantiations is not new either, and has been used by Camenisch et al. [15] in the ABC4Trust project [3]. Their framework focused on bridging the two prevalent constructions back in 2015, IBM's Identity Mixer and Microsoft's U-Prove, and showed how they can be combined to yield the same overall credential system. Here we do not believe that *the* credential system exists, but every application will require their own combination of features and modules. Further, our work fully decouples the modules from each other, supporting different proof systems per module which we leverage to capture legacy-compliant device binding.

More generally, our framework follows the Commit-and-Prove approach [19, 39] that underlies many cryptographic protocols. The work by Bobolz et al. [7] is also somewhat similar in spirit as it considers signatures on committed messages as main component, and shows how this yields provably secure anonymous credentials with selective disclosure and group signatures. Our work targets more expressive functionality, but does not aim at a formal study (yet).

Similar to us, various works also rely on commitments as linking component that allows to extend functionality and link different proofs from (potentially) different proving systems. García-Rodríguez et al. [32] use Pedersen commitments as a bridging component to extend a Pointcheval-Sanders multi-message signature [48,49] instantiation with additional functionalities. Crescent [46] functions on a similar spirit, using Groth16 [33] to prove knowledge of (legacy) credentials and outputting Pedersen commitments to attributes which can be fed to other proving systems to prove additional statements. In fact, Crescent can perfectly fit into the design paradigm described in this work. Finally, the implementation of DockNetwork [34] is very close to our work; it implements proofs-of-knowledge of commitment opening consistent with the signed credential and allows proving arbitrary statements over these openings via the techniques of [18].

Vision and Future Work. The idea is to evolve this work in a community driven fashion. We invite the wider community to propose alternative instantiations for the modules presented here and also extend the considered module set – and of course exercise the framework through designing concrete applications from it. On the theoretical side, security models and the study of provably secure composition are obvious next steps. Overall, we hope our work can serve as a foundation for a common architecture for building and using modern anonymous credentials.

2 Preliminaries

Notation. We denote with λ the security parameter. To write the set $\{1,\ldots,m\}$, we use the shorthand $[m]$. For a set S, we denote with S^ℓ its ℓ-fold Cartesian product, namely $S^\ell = \{s_1,\ldots,s_\ell \mid s_j \in S\}$. For vectors, we use bold fonts. Given a vector $\boldsymbol{v} = (v_1,\ldots,v_n)$ we denote with $\boldsymbol{v}[i]$ the element v_i and with $\boldsymbol{v}[S]$ the vector $(v_i)_{i\in S}$. We also denote $x \xleftarrow{\$} S$ to denote sampling an element from S uniformly at random and assigning it to x. For a group $\mathbb{G}$, denote the identity element in $\mathbb{G}$ as $1_\mathbb{G}$. We will use various groups based on Elliptic Curves. We associate each elliptic curve with two fields: the base field, where the elliptic curve point coordinates live, and the scalar field, where scalars lives.

Public (Shared) Parameters. We next define the basic cryptographic primitives we will use in this work. Since some of them will share public parameters, we assume there exists a global Setup algorithm that on input the security parameter 1^λ outputs the public parameters $pp(\lambda)$ (we will omit λ in what follows and simply write pp). These global public parameters are then given as input to instantiate the primitives. In our instantiations, such parameters will include group descriptions and hash functions.

(Multi-message) Signature Scheme. A signature scheme allows a party in possession of a secret key to digitally sign a message m.

Definition 1 ((Multi-message) Signature Scheme). *A signature scheme* Sig *is a tuple of algorithms*

$\mathsf{Sig.Setup}(pp) \rightarrow pp_{\mathsf{Sig}}$*: probabilistically generates parameters* pp_{Sig} *from* pp*,*
$\mathsf{Sig.KeyGen}(pp_{\mathsf{Sig}}) \rightarrow (sk, pk)$*: probabilistically generates a key pair* (sk, pk)*,*
$\mathsf{Sig.Sign}(sk, m) \rightarrow \sigma$*: a probabilistic algorithm that takes as input a secret key* sk *and a message* m[1] *and outputs a signature* σ*,*
$\mathsf{Sig.Vf}(pk, m, \sigma) \rightarrow \{0, 1\}$*: a deterministic algorithm that takes as input a public key* pk*, a message* m *and a signature* σ *and outputs a bit.*

When the message space is a vector of ℓ *elements, namely* $\mathcal{M}^\ell$*, we call the scheme a* ***multi-message*** *signature scheme* MSig.

A signature Sig is secure when it satisfies the standard existential unforgeability under chosen message attacks (EUCMA). We define the notion formally in the full version of this work.

Commitment Schemes. A commitment scheme Com allows a prover to commit to a message that she can later reveal.

Definition 2 (Commitment Scheme). *A commitment scheme with canonical opening* Com = (Setup, Commit) *consists of two algorithms:*

$\mathsf{Com.Setup}(pp) \rightarrow pp_{\mathsf{Com}}$ *: probabilistically generates parameters* pp_{Com} *from* pp*,*
$\mathsf{Com.Commit}(pp_{\mathsf{Com}}, m; \rho) \rightarrow C$ *: probabilistically outputs a commitment* C *from parameters* pp_{Com} *and a message* m *using the explicit randomness* ρ*.*

Verification is canonical, i.e. to verify a commitment C to a message m given the randomness ρ, the verifier asserts that $C \stackrel{?}{=} \mathsf{Com.Commit}(pp_{\mathsf{Com}}, m; \rho)$.

The security guarantees are (1) *binding*, i.e. a commitment can only be opened to a unique message and (2) *hiding*, i.e. the commitment does not reveal any information about the underlying message.

Non-Interactive Zero-Knowledge Proofs. A Non-Interactive Zero-Knowledge NIZK proof for an NP relation $\mathcal{R}$ allows a prover to compute a proof for the validity of a statement x.

Definition 3 (Non-Interactive Zero-Knowledge Proofs).
A Non-Interactive Zero-Knowledge (NIZK) proof system for an NP relation $\mathcal{R}$ *is a tuple of efficient algorithms:*

[1] The message m belongs to some message space $\mathcal{M}$ implicit in pp_{Sig}.

$\mathsf{NIZK.Setup}(pp) \rightarrow pp_{\mathcal{R}}$: *A probabilistic algorithm that on input the global parameters pp outputs parameters* $pp_{\mathcal{R}}$.

$\mathsf{NIZK.P}(pp_{\mathcal{R}}, x, w) \rightarrow \pi$: *A probabilistic algorithm that on input the parameters* $pp_{\mathcal{R}}$ *and a statement/witness pair* (x, w) *belonging to* $\mathcal{R}$ *outputs a proof* π.

$\mathsf{NIZK.V}(pp_{\mathcal{R}}, x, \pi) \rightarrow \{0, 1\}$ *A deterministic algorithm that on input the parameters* $pp_{\mathcal{R}}$, *the statement* x *and a proof* π *outputs a bit.*

It satisfies completeness, stating that an honest prover will always succeed in verifying an accepting proof; knowledge soundness, stating that a convincing proof implies knowledge of a valid witness w; zero knowledge, stating that a proof for statement x reveals nothing but the validity of the statement (i.e. there exists some w s.t. $(x, w) \in \mathcal{R}$). We give a more formal definition in the full version of this work.

We use the Camenisch-Stadler notation [17] to succinctly present the relation to be proven for a NIZK. To denote, e.g., the discrete logarithm relation, we write:

$$\underbrace{DL}_{\text{relation}} = \Big\{ \underbrace{(y)}_{\text{witness}} : \underbrace{Y = y \cdot G}_{\text{statement}} \Big\}$$

Here, G and Y are public values that constitute the statement and y is the witness. Unless otherwise stated, we assume all variables in the statement, which are not part of the witness, to be public, or at least known to the verifier.

In our constructions, we usually need to associate proofs with some context ctx (e.g. some random nonce sent by the verifier). This corresponds to a signature of knowledge [22]. Since all the NIZK used in this work can be turned into signatures of knowledge by including the context in the Fiat-Shamir input, we simply abuse notation and write $\mathsf{P}(pp_{\mathcal{R}}, x, w)[ctx]$ and $\mathsf{V}(pp_{\mathcal{R}}, x, \pi)[ctx]$ when we want to make the context explicit.

3 Modular Framework for Anonymous Credentials

In this section we present our core anonymous credential construction that supports *modular functionality* via the commit-and-prove approach [19,39]. We start by presenting an informal description of the setting and the security properties we aim to achieve and then describe our black box construction. To this end, we first identify the core relation underlying any presentation which we call *committed disclosure*; roughly, this allows proving ownership of a credential while revealing some attributes and committing to some others. We then explain how to achieve modularity by proving statements over the committed attributes. To demonstrate this, we present the black-box construction with one (w.l.o.g.) generic relation $\mathcal{R}$ over the committed attributes, modelling an abstract module. We then give concrete examples of modules, focusing on usual use cases and requirements of anonymous credentials. Concretely, we show how to specialize the construction with modules for proving (1) possession of a device key, (2) range proofs and (3) pseudonyms.

Anonymous Credentials: Functionality and Properties. There are three entities in anonymous credentials: the *issuers*, the *users* and the *verifiers*. Issuers attest attributes in form of a credential to the user. If a user wants to authenticate towards a verifier, she derives a presentation from her credential that reveals the minimal amount of information in a verifiable manner. The presentation convinces the verifier that the presented information is authentic.

We require that the system satisfies *unlinkability*, *credential unforgeability* and *presentation unforgeability*. Informally,

Unlinkability. Captures user privacy needs; it asserts that presentations cannot be traced back to a user and that different presentations of the same credential cannot be linked even when corrupted issuers and verifier collude,

Credential unforgeability. Captures that only the issuer can create valid credentials.

Presentation unforgeability. Captures that during presentation only information attested by the issuer can be accepted, and optionally that the attributes of the credential satisfy additional properties.

Note that presentation unforgeability allows extending the "basic" presentation requirement (committed disclosure) of the system. In particular, we can define one or more relations that capture additional system functionalities. We can then implement a module for each functionality and add it on top of the core construction. The latter property should require that during presentation the additional relations are satisfied by the credential attributes.

We emphasize that we only provide an informal treatment of security and leave defining a formal security model and security proofs as future work.

3.1 Commit-and-Prove Construction

We now present the idea of our modular framework, that yields an anonymous credential scheme.

We present our core black box construction w.r.t. some generic relation $\mathcal{R}$ abstracting the additional functionality added via modules. The core idea is to use a multi-message signature scheme MSig to sign a set of attributes $\boldsymbol{a} \in \mathcal{M}^\ell$ and derive the credential *cred*. During presentation, the prover commits to some attributes (for which it wants to prove additional statements) and reveals some other. Then it proves that it owns a credential that is consistent with the revealed attributes and the commitments (i.e. the credential attributes are the openings of the commitments). We identify the *committed disclosure relation* (CD) that captures the above requirements. Having established a set of commitments whose openings are verifiably part of the credential, we can prove an *additional relation* on the committed values captured by the relation $\mathcal{R}$ in a commit-and-prove fashion. To this end, we employ a NIZK for $\mathcal{R}$. The commitment scheme acts as the glue between the two statements: since in both proofs we present statements about the committed values and since the user can only possibly know a single opening, the proven statement for $\mathcal{R}$ must hold for the attributes contained on the credential *cred*.

The Committed Disclosure Relation. We start by defining the committed disclosure relation CD. Let MSig[2] and Com be a multi-message signature scheme with message space $\mathcal{M}^\ell$ and a commitment scheme[3] with message space $\mathcal{M}$, and two (disjoint) subsets $\mathsf{S}_{\mathsf{Rev}}, \mathsf{S}_{\mathsf{Com}} \subseteq [\ell]$ corresponding to the sets of revealed and committed attributes. These sets also implicitly define the set of hidden attributes $\mathsf{S}_{\mathsf{Hid}} = [\ell] \setminus (\mathsf{S}_{\mathsf{Rev}} \cup \mathsf{S}_{\mathsf{Com}})$. We define the relation CD as:

$$\mathsf{CD}\left\{\begin{pmatrix} \boldsymbol{a} \in \mathcal{M}^\ell, cred, \\ \{\rho_i\}_{i \in \mathsf{S}_{\mathsf{Com}}} \end{pmatrix} : \begin{array}{l} \mathsf{MSig.Vf}(ipk, \boldsymbol{a}, cred) = 1 \\ \forall i \in \mathsf{S}_{\mathsf{Rev}} : a_{\mathsf{Rev},i} = \boldsymbol{a}[i] \\ \forall i \in \mathsf{S}_{\mathsf{Com}} : C_i = \mathsf{Com.Commit}(pp_{\mathsf{Com}}, \boldsymbol{a}[i]; \rho_i) \end{array}\right\}$$

This relation underpins all reasonable AC constructions in the sense that it (1) asserts possession of a credential issued by the issuer due to the $\mathsf{MSig.Vf}$ condition and (2) discloses some of the attributes in a presentation. We also assume an efficient $\mathsf{NIZK}_{\mathsf{CD}}$ for the relation CD.

Additional Functionality Captured by Relations. We next explain how to express additional functionalities by expressing them as NP relations. Let Φ be a predicate capturing the additional functionality that should hold during a presentation. Φ involves some of the credential attributes and possibly additional public and secret inputs x, w (looking ahead, this can for example correspond to a valid signature over some committed public key). We define $\mathcal{R}$ as the relation over the committed attributes that shows that (1) the predicate Φ is satisfied and (2) the inputs to the predicate correspond to the commitments' openings. Formally we have:

$$\mathcal{R}\left\{\left(\boldsymbol{a} \in \mathcal{M}^{|\mathsf{S}_{\mathcal{R}}|}, \{\rho_i\}_{i \in \mathsf{S}_{\mathcal{R}}}, w\right) : \begin{array}{l} \Phi(\boldsymbol{a}, w, x) \\ \forall i \in \mathsf{S}_{\mathcal{R}} : C_i = \mathsf{Com.Commit}(pp_{\mathsf{Com}}, \boldsymbol{a}[i]; \rho_i) \end{array}\right\}$$

We also assume a $\mathsf{NIZK}_{\mathcal{R}}$ for proving statements of the relation $\mathcal{R}$[4] and rely on its properties to prove the added module secure.

Our Construction. We now explain the construction along the four phases of a credential scheme: Setup, $\mathsf{IssueCred}$, $\mathsf{Present}$, and Verify. We present the construction assuming an additional abstract module captured by a relation $\mathcal{R}$. The core building blocks are a multi-message signature MSig scheme with message space $\mathcal{M}^\ell$, a commitment scheme Com with message space $\mathcal{M}$, as well as two NIZK systems, $\mathsf{NIZK}_{\mathsf{CD}}, \mathsf{NIZK}_{\mathcal{R}}$ for proving statements for CD and $\mathcal{R}$ respectively.

Setup. The system setup involves generating global parameters $pp \leftarrow \mathsf{Setup}(1^\lambda)$ and running each primitive's $\mathsf{Setup}(pp)$ algorithm to specialize them,

[2] Aligning with the context of ACs, we refer to a signature of MSig as *cred*.

[3] For ease of presentation, we use one commitment per committed attribute. One can modify the construction to support compact commitments that will give a single commitment for multiple attributes.

[4] One might want to relax the zero knowledge property of this NIZK and allow partial leakage of w (see Remark 1).

namely $pp_{\mathsf{Com}} \leftarrow \mathsf{Com.Setup}(pp)$, $pp_{\mathsf{CD}} \leftarrow \mathsf{NIZK_{CD}.Setup}(pp)$, $pp_{\mathcal{R}} \leftarrow \mathsf{NIZK}_{\mathcal{R}}.\mathsf{Setup}(pp)$. The issuer key generation involves running the multi-message signature scheme's KeyGen to get a key pair, namely, $(isk, ipk) \leftarrow \mathsf{MSig.KeyGen}(pp_{\mathsf{MSig}})$.

IssueCred. Issuance is a protocol run between the issuer and user, at the end of which the user obtains her attested attributes $\boldsymbol{a}$ in form of an issuer-signed credential *cred*. We assume the simplest form of issuance here, and let the issuer sign all attributes through the multi-message signature scheme; concretely, the issuer generates the credential as $cred \leftarrow \mathsf{MSig.Sign}(isk, \boldsymbol{a})$. Extending this to blind issuance is an interesting future extension, in particular as blind issuance is necessary whenever native device binding is needed, where one of the attributes is a device secret key that is not known to the user. Note however that blind issuance is not needed for the explicit device binding feature we introduce later, as we realize device binding through an explicit binding, where the credential contains the device public key, not the secret key (see discussion of native vs. explicit device binding below).

Present. The user starts by preparing some attributes $\boldsymbol{a}_{\mathsf{Rev}}$ to be revealed (corresponding to an index set $\mathsf{S}_{\mathsf{Rev}}$) and computes fresh commitments to the set of attributes $\boldsymbol{a}_{\mathsf{Com}}$ that need to be committed (corresponding to index set $\mathsf{S}_{\mathsf{Com}}$). She then uses $\mathsf{NIZK_{CD}.P}$ to assert these are parts of a credential *cred* under the issuer's key *ipk*. Finally, she invokes $\mathsf{NIZK}_{\mathcal{R}}.\mathsf{P}$ to compute a proof about the statement $\mathcal{R}$ involving a subset of $\boldsymbol{a}_{\mathsf{Com}}$ corresponding to an index set $\mathsf{S}_{\mathcal{R}} \subseteq \mathsf{S}_{\mathsf{Com}}$ and possibly additional statement/witness x, w. For the latter, she uses the same commitments as in the proof of CD. The presentation proof consists of the commitments $\{C_i\}_{i \in \mathsf{S}_{\mathsf{Com}}}$ and the two NIZK proofs $\pi_{\mathsf{CD}}, \pi_{\mathcal{R}}$.

Verify. The verifier takes the presentation proof $\pi = (\{C_i\}_{i \in \mathsf{S}_{\mathsf{Com}}}, \pi_{\mathsf{CD}}, \pi_{\mathcal{R}})$ and invokes the $\mathsf{NIZK_{CD}.V}$ for verifying π_{CD} using these commitments; it then takes the subset of commitments $\{C_i\}_{i \in \mathsf{S}_{\mathcal{R}}}$ and invokes $\mathsf{NIZK}_{\mathcal{R}}.\mathsf{V}$ with these commitments (and additional input x). It accepts if both proof are accepting.

We present the algorithms for Present, Verify in Fig. 1. We emphasize that each relation can have their own optimized NIZK proof, as they are generated and verified in a modular way, only proving their respective sub-statement. This yields a crypto agile and modular design, and in particular caters for the fact that we might have to prove statements over different cryptographic primitives – each having their optimized NIZK.

Remark 1 (Relaxed NIZK). We can relax the properties of the $\mathsf{NIZK}_{\mathcal{R}}$ to achieve better efficiency. In particular, we can relax the perfect/statistical zero knowledge requirement by allowing some "leakage" of the witness w (while still requiring perfect zero knowledge for the $\boldsymbol{a}$ part of the witness which is vital for unlinkability). As an example, in the construction for proof of possession of an ECDSA signature we present in Sect. 4.1, we note that since this is used as a one-time signature, parts of the signature can be revealed without compromising privacy (if the Secure Element is assumed to be trusted) while providing better overall efficiency for the system. We refer the reader to [29, 40] for more details on how to define such relaxed NIZKs and leave the systematic study and analysis of this generalization as future work.

$\underline{\mathsf{Present}(ipk, \mathsf{S_{Rev}}, \mathsf{S_{Com}}, \mathsf{S}_{\mathcal{R}}, \boldsymbol{a}, cred, x, w, ctx_V)}$

Compute commitments $\forall i \in \mathsf{S_{Com}}$: $\mathsf{Com.Commit}(pp_{\mathsf{Com}}, a_i; \rho_i)$
Prepare statements/witnesses for relations CD, $\mathcal{R}$:

$$x_{\mathsf{CD}} \leftarrow (ipk, \mathsf{S_{Rev}}, \mathsf{S_{Com}}, \{a_i\}_{i\in\mathsf{S_{Rev}}}, \{C_i\}_{i\in\mathsf{S_{Com}}}), \quad w_{\mathsf{CD}} \leftarrow (\boldsymbol{a}, cred, \{\rho_i\}_{i\in\mathsf{S_{Rev}}})$$

$$x_{\mathcal{R}} \leftarrow (\mathsf{S}_{\mathcal{R}}, \{C_i\}_{i\in\mathsf{S}_{\mathcal{R}}}, x), \quad w_{\mathcal{R}} \leftarrow (\{a_i, \rho_i\}_{i\in\mathsf{S}_{\mathcal{R}}}, w)$$

Compute $ctx \leftarrow ctx_V||C_1||\cdots||C_\ell$ and output $\pi = (\{C_i\}_{i\in\mathsf{S_{Com}}}, \pi_{\mathsf{CD}}, \pi_{\mathcal{R}})$ where

$$\pi_{\mathsf{CD}} \leftarrow \mathsf{NIZK_{CD}.P}(pp_{\mathsf{CD}}, x_{\mathsf{CD}}, w_{\mathsf{CD}})[ctx], \quad \pi_{\mathcal{R}} \leftarrow \mathsf{NIZK}_{\mathcal{R}}.\mathsf{P}(pp_{\mathcal{R}}, x_{\mathcal{R}}, w_{\mathcal{R}})[ctx]$$

$\underline{\mathsf{Verify}(ipk, \mathsf{S_{Rev}}, \mathsf{S_{Com}}, \mathsf{S}_{\mathcal{R}}, \{C_i\}_{i\in\mathsf{S_{Com}}}, \{a_{\mathsf{Rev},}\}_{i\in\mathsf{S_{Rev}}} x, ctx_V, \pi)}$

Parse $\pi = (\{C_i\}_{i\in\mathsf{S_{Com}}}, \pi_{\mathsf{CD}}, \pi_{\mathcal{R}})$ and prepare the statements for relations CD, $\mathcal{R}$:

$$x_{\mathsf{CD}} \leftarrow (ipk, \mathsf{S_{Rev}}, \mathsf{S_{Com}}, \{a_{\mathsf{Rev},i}\}_{i\in\mathsf{S_{Rev}}}, \{C_i\}_{i\in\mathsf{S_{Com}}}), \quad x_{\mathcal{R}} \leftarrow (\mathsf{S}_{\mathcal{R}}, \{C_i\}_{i\in\mathsf{S}_{\mathcal{R}}}, x),$$

Compute $ctx \leftarrow ctx_V||C_1||\cdots||C_\ell$ and Output $b_{\mathsf{CD}} \wedge b_{\mathcal{R}} \wedge b_{\mathsf{S}}$ where

$$b_{\mathsf{S}} \leftarrow \mathsf{S}_{\mathcal{R}} \overset{?}{\subseteq} \mathsf{S_{Com}} \wedge \mathsf{S_{Com}} \overset{?}{\subseteq} [\ell] \wedge \mathsf{S_{Rev}} \overset{?}{\subseteq} [\ell] \wedge \mathsf{S_{Com}} \cap \mathsf{S_{Rev}} \overset{?}{=} \varnothing$$

$$b_{\mathsf{CD}} \leftarrow \mathsf{NIZK_{CD}.V}(pp_{\mathsf{CD}}, x_{\mathsf{CD}}, \pi_{\mathsf{CD}})[ctx], \quad b_{\mathcal{R}} \leftarrow \mathsf{NIZK}_{\mathcal{R}}.\mathsf{V}(pp_{\mathcal{R}}, x_{\mathcal{R}}, \pi_{\mathcal{R}})[ctx]$$

Fig. 1. The Present and Verify parts of a credential presentation.

Instantiating MSig *and* CD. Natural candidates for the MSig are the BBS and PS signature schemes. Both schemes are build for that purpose, support multi-messages, are efficient, and well understood. Furthermore, they natively support efficient NIZKs for committed disclosure when combined with the Pedersen commitment scheme through standard Schnorr protocols, yielding a highly-efficient instantiation for the core module. Another approach is to use ECDSA for the MSig in combination with a zkSNARK (e.g. [31,46,52]); this has the advantage of supporting legacy credentials, at the cost of an increased complexity for the NIZK. When post-quantum security is needed, one could use a post-quantum signature scheme such as ML-DSA in combination with a lattice based zkSNARK (e.g. [6]) and a hash based commitment scheme; or one of the recent lattice-based multi-message signature schemes [11,27] with a simpler NIZK for committed disclosure.

Remark 2 (Supporting KVAC). We state our framework for publicly-verifiable credentials using multi-message signatures, but this can be easily turned into a variant for keyed-verification anonymous credentials (KVACs) too. KVACs can be seen as the symmetric version of ACs, that were developed to avoid the need for pairing-friendly curves that are required for all efficient multi-message signatures. By assuming the issuer and verifier to be the same entity, and turning verification into a keyed operation, anonymous credential schemes can be run on standard elliptic curves. Essentially, the pairing check in the verification is replaced through a computation using the issuer secret key. Apart from this check, KVACs and ACs are typically equivalent, and, e.g. MAC versions for both BBS and PS exist [23,26,43]. KVACs will only differ in this core module, and can re-use the same extension modules, e.g., for range proofs or pseudonyms.

3.2 Device Binding Module

In the digital identity context, an essential additional functionality is *device binding*, which we can express through an appropriate relation in our framework. This property aims to ensure non-transferability of credentials. To this end, the credential gets bound to a cryptographic device key that is protected through a hardware component, e.g., a Secure Element (SE). The hardware protection ensures that the key cannot be extracted, and any presentation of the credential requires access to that device.

In particular, we consider the case where the user owns a device that stores a secret key of a signature scheme and provides an API to request signatures on messages that are valid under the corresponding public key. The user's credential contains the device public key as an attribute, and credential presentation requires to also prove knowledge of a device signature under that attested (but not revealed) device public key on a random challenge nonce sent by the verifier.

Explicit vs. Native Device Binding. We focus on such *explicit* device binding that essentially follows the classic proof-of-possession paradigm used for conventional certificates. The main benefit of that approach is modularity, as it fully decouples the device part from the main credential and NIZK thereof. In particular, it enables to combine different schemes for the main attribute credential and the device signature, which we exemplify in Sect. 4 with the BBS-ECDSA scheme. An alternative approach is to rely on *native* device-binding which is directly built into the credential scheme. The Direct Anonymous Attestation (DAA) protocol [13,36] is such a variant. Therein, the device *secret* key is embedded through a blind issuance protocol as an attribute in the main credential, and the NIZK is then jointly computed by the device and host. Such native device binding will result in much better performance, both in computational costs and proof sizes, but requires dedicated interfaces from the SE for the credential scheme. Currently, deployed SEs do not provide interfaces that enable native device binding for BBS though, which is why we focus on the explicit device binding option here.

High-Level Idea. We next describe how explicit device binding works. We assume a secure element that stores internally a device secret key dsk of a signature scheme Sig and exposes an API to produce signatures under this key, namely, when queried on some message m, it outputs $\sigma \leftarrow \mathsf{Sig.Sign}(sk, m)$. The user presenting the credential gets some challenge nonce and queries its secure element to produce $\sigma \leftarrow \mathsf{Sig.Sign}(sk, \mathsf{nonce})$. She is then charged to prove knowledge of the (secret) signature σ under the (secret) public key encoded in the attributes.

To achieve this, the user encodes its device public key as a set of attributes which are included in the credential during issuance. During the presentation, the user includes these attributes to the set $\mathsf{S}_{\mathsf{Com}}$ when defining the committed disclosure statement. The task now is reduced to proving knowledge of a signature σ on nonce under the *committed encoding of the device public key.* This can be done with a NIZK for an appropriate relation $\mathcal{R}$ capturing *proof of possession.*

More formally, let $\mathsf{Encode}(pk) \to m \in \mathcal{M}^t$ be an efficient algorithm that allows encoding a public key of Sig as a vector of elements in $\mathcal{M}^t$ for a fixed t, where $\mathcal{M}$ is the space where attributes live. The user needs to prove the following relation:

$$\mathsf{PoP}\left\{ (\{dpk_i, \rho_i\}_{i\in[t]}, \sigma) : \begin{array}{l} \mathsf{Sig.Vf}(dpk, \mathsf{nonce}, \sigma) = 1 \\ \mathsf{Encode}(dpk) = \mathbf{dpk} \\ \forall i \in [t]\ C_i = \mathsf{Com.Commit}(pp_{\mathsf{Com}}, dpk_i; \rho_i) \end{array} \right\}$$

The corresponding predicate Φ in the proof of possession case captures that a vector $\mathbf{dpk}$ encodes some public key dpk and a (secret) signature σ on some (public) message nonce verifies under this key. The credential must contain the encoding $\mathbf{dpk}$ as dedicated attributes.

Instantiating PoP. Due to restrictions imposed by the available secure elements, smartphone-based applications are currently limited to using ECDSA over the P-256 curve. We present in Sect. 4.1 an efficient instantiation for $\mathsf{NIZK}_{\mathsf{PoP}}$ with ECDSA based on existing ideas when the core module is implemented via BBS. We note, however, that in principle any signature scheme could be used when such hardware supports it. A scheme "compatible" with the MSig of the core module would translate to significant efficiency improvements.

3.3 Additional Modules: Range Proofs and Pseudonyms

We next describe the relations and possible instantiations of additional modules to the base construction. In particular, we consider the range proof module, allowing to prove that attributes lie in a range, and the pseudonym module, allowing to deterministically derive pseudonyms from the credential, that yield a form of controlled linkability.

Range Proofs. A typical feature of ACs is allowing to prove that an attribute a lies in some range, namely $l \leqslant a < h$. This can be used for example to achieve credential revocation, proof of non-expiration, or pseudonyms as we will see next. We can add such functionality by simply extending the system with the range proof relation defined next:

$$\mathsf{RP}\left\{(a, \rho) : l \leqslant a < h,\ C = \mathsf{Com.Commit}(pp_{\mathsf{Com}}, a; \rho)\right\}$$

In this case there is no additional secret input and the public input consists of the bounds l, h. We also note that we can run different instances of this relation when multiple attributes need to satisfy some range.

Instantiating RP. Bulletproofs can be easily applied to instantiate range proofs [10,12]. They provide a very small proof size, require no trusted setup, and have been extensively analyzed in academic literature. It is also well-known in the community how to construct zero-knowledge range proofs from polynomial commitments, e.g. as summarized in [9]. Additionally, there is also an ongoing discussion within the IETF [47] where a standard for such range proofs is developed, and detailing a concrete instantiation for RP is an open next step here, too.

Pseudonyms. Pseudonyms allow to introduce a level of controlled linkability. They are identifiers (deterministically) derived from a dedicated high-entropy seed pns embedded in the user's credential. Of particular interest are so called scope-exclusive pseudonyms [3] that ensure that only a unique pseudonym can be derived per scope scp. Pseudonyms across scopes are still fully unlinkable. If the scope encodes the identity of a service, this enables pseudonymous authentication while still guaranteeing that only a single account per user can be generated. A more flexible variant considers a looser upper bound lim and ensures that a user can create up to lim unlinkable pseudonyms per scope. The latter is currently considered for rate-limiting in the anonymous credential variant of Privacy Pass [53].

All existing constructions for such pseudonyms can be expressed through a PRF as $nym = \mathsf{PRF}(pns, scp||ctr)$. The PRF key is an attested high-entropy seed pns in the main credential that must never get revealed, whereas the scope is public. The counter ctr can either be revealed, or just proven to be below a limit lim. We state the more general version and again start from a committed input for pns:

$$\mathsf{NYM}\left\{(pns, \rho, ctr) : \begin{array}{l} nym = \mathsf{PRF}(pns, scp||ctr),\ 1 \leqslant ctr < lim \\ C = \mathsf{Com.Commit}(pp_{\mathsf{Com}}, pns; \rho) \end{array}\right\}$$

Instantiating NYM. The simplest way to instantiate the PRF is to use HashDH leading to $nym = pns \cdot \mathsf{H}(scp||ctr)$, and using a simple Schnorr proof for $\mathsf{NIZK}_{\mathsf{NYM}}$. This pseudonym generation (w/o counter) is standardized as part of DAA by ISO [36] and undergoes standardization in the IETF for BBS credentials [37], and the counter-based variant is suggested for rate-limited credentials based on CMZ MAC [53]. This construction reveals the counter though, which reduces the anonymity set with every presentation. If the counter should remain hidden, one can use the Dodis-Yampolskiy PRF instead [14], which was recently proposed for rate-limited BBS credentials [50]. The drawback of both constructions is that their privacy relies on the DL assumption, which would make the entire credential system susceptible to harvest now – link latter attacks. A construction for pseudonyms that is compatible with DL-based credential schemes, yet has everlasting (and thus PQ) privacy was recently proposed by Chairattana-Apirom et al. [21]. All aforementioned solutions require Schnorr proofs for their NIZKs, and thus are very lightweight. An alternative for post-quantum privacy is to simply rely on AES as PRF, for which highly-optimized zkSNARKs exist [44].

3.4 Discussion of Modularity and Instantiation Choices

Our core motivation is to build anonymous credential schemes in a more modular way, to simplify both the theoretical analysis as well as their implementations and standardization efforts. The price we pay is a slight overhead through the commitment layer: every functionality beyond the core CD is bridged over a commitment and the opening is possibly proven repeatedly in every module. Thus, on paper, it will be slightly less efficient than a targeted construction where the entire statement is proven through a monolithic NIZK. However we believe that this is a reasonable trade-off, and the added costs of a few group elements will not matter in most applications. Further, if many schemes reuse the same components, this will likely lead to optimized implementations that can compensate for these additional steps. In fact, we believe that this modularity will rather lead to better efficiency than a monolithic solution for the following reasons.

Optimal Signatures for CD *vs* PoP. Our device binding approach leverages the observation that the signature schemes for the main credential and the device *do not need to be the same*, which can lead to both better efficiency and simpler systems (and therefore easier to standardize). Concretely, our task is reduced to optimizing NIZKs for CD and PoP. The only limitation is that the NIZKs used for both must be compatible with the commitment scheme Com[5]. Depending on the application requirements and trade-offs, one can use an appropriate instantiation (for example zkSNARKs to optimize proof size or sigma protocols to optimize proving time or even combinations of them).

This separation also allows to address hardware or legacy limitation in parts of the system, without imposing this on all modules. As mentioned, device binding is currently restricted to using ECDSA. However, we do have flexibility on choosing the MSig of the issuer for which dedicated schemes such as BBS or PS provide significant advances in terms of simplicity and efficiency. The same design pattern can be applied when migrating to post-quantum solutions. While future device binding will most likely again be restricted to standard signatures, i.e., ML-DSA, the multi-message signature schemes can rather be an optimized variant that natively supports NIZKs, e.g., [11,27]. In fact, in the transition

[5] In fact, this limitation is even weaker since one can use different commitment schemes and additionally prove they commit to the same values.

time even mixed settings are plausible, where only the main credential should be quantum-safe, but device binding is still done via ECDSA[6].

In Fig. 2 we present a table with possibilities for instantiating anonymous credentials with device binding support. Not listed here is the commitment construction, which, of course, can be instantiated as needed. All the possible choices for a building block "suite" for a credential can be compared regarding their efficiency, quantum-readiness, proof size, and other aspects.

MSig	$\mathsf{NIZK}_{\mathsf{CD}}$
BBS	Schnorr proof
PS	Schnorr proof
ECDSA	zkSNARK (various)
PQC-MSig [11,27]	native NIZK [42]
ML-DSA	LaBRADOR [6]

+

Sig	$\mathsf{NIZK}_{\mathsf{PoP}}$
ECDSA	Schnorr proof (CDLS)
ECDSA	zkSNARK, e.g. [31,46,52]
Schnorr	Schnorr proof
ML-DSA	LaBRADOR [6]

Fig. 2. Examples for MSig, Sig, and proof primitive combinations.

Taming the Complexity of zkSNARKs. Our modular approach can also help to address a significant barrier for zkSNARK-based solutions: it is notoriously complex to properly design secure "circuits" for concrete computations. This affects also standardization; in fact, despite significant efforts, it seems we are still far from having standards for zkSNARKs (see for example the current status in [54]). With our modular approach, this complexity can be partially alleviated since one would now need to design and optimize smaller and simpler circuits. For example, one could adapt "full-fledged" zkSNARK solutions to prove knowledge of ECDSA-based credentials such as [31, 46, 52] to merely instantiate the core and device binding modules, essentially translating the ECDSA-attested information into a Pedersen commitment. Then, for all further relations that need to be proven on the user's attributes one can use simple Schnorr proofs.

4 BBS Credentials with ECDSA Device Binding

Here we present an instantiation of our black box construction with proof-of-possession functionality based on modules from Fig. 2, specifically BBS as the

[6] Note that this makes sense for two reasons. First, assuming a high cost to quantum-break a signature scheme, the consequences of doing that on the issuer level is catastrophic compared to compromising individual users' keys. Second, whereas issuer signatures can be replaced upon a quantum-threat, upgrading secure elements in already shipped phones appears impossible. Thus, for device binding, ECDSA might still be the only available option during such a transition time.

multi-message signature and ECDSA (over P-256) for device binding. This is based on the BBS-ECDSA idea that has been proposed and implemented by Ubique [4]. More concretely, we instantiate the primitives of Sect. 3 as follows:

MSig. We choose BBS for implementing the issuer side MSig, since it is the most mature multi-message signature scheme, with native support for efficient selective disclosure (which can be easily fine-tuned for committed disclosure). It is also currently undergoing standardization [41], and we can use the main operations KeyGen, Sign, Vf from this draft without any modifications. BBS requires a pairing-friendly group with $\mathbb{G}_1, \mathbb{G}_2, \mathbb{G}_T$ of order q, e.g., BLS12-381[7].

$\mathsf{NIZK}_{\mathsf{CD}}$. To prove the committed disclosure relation, BBS natively supports efficient NIZK proofs via Schnorr proofs [51]. Note that here our core module *deviates from the BBS draft* which only considers selective disclosure, whereas we need to also prove equivalence over committed inputs. Including this capability requires little effort, and yields a more versatile BBS standard.

Sig. We use ECDSA for the PoP signature scheme. While ECDSA can work with any group $\mathbb{G}$, secure element support is currently limited to NIST P-256. Crucially, we use a group different from the one of BBS.

Com. We use the Pedersen commitments Ped over the group $\mathbb{G}_1$ of BBS.

$\mathsf{NIZK}_{\mathsf{PoP}}$. We use a combination of a sigma protocol based approach using the techniques of [20, 30] for proving knowledge of a signature in combination with techniques from [24, 44] for showing that two Pedersen commitments over different groups admit the same opening.

We formally state the standard building blocks for ECDSA and Pedersen commitments in the full version of this work. In the remainder of this section we focus on the most challenging part which is bridging the ECDSA signature to a BBS credential.

4.1 Proof-of-Possession of ECDSA Signature

The main challenge towards an efficient implementation of a NIZK for ECDSA proof-of-possession is the need for foreign field arithmetic, that is, proving statements over a field different than the one the statements are about. In particular, verifying an ECDSA signature is a computation over $\mathbb{Z}_t$, the base field of P-256 while the committed public key lives in $\mathbb{Z}_q$, the scalar field of BLS12-381.

Our approach to mitigate the efficiency issues that rise from this is to "transfer" the committed public key to a different curve, amenable to efficient computations over $\mathbb{Z}_t$. Concretely, the prover first presents *fresh* commitments to the (encoded) device public key *dpk* over a curve with scalar field $\mathbb{Z}_t$. She then shows that the new commitment indeed encodes the same public key as the one presented in the committed attributes. Finally, she proves knowledge of a signature of a challenge nonce over the *committed* public key. Note that the last step is now a native computation. This corresponds to expressing the relation PoP as a conjunction of two relations as follows:

[7] Other curves, such as those from [5] may be used, in particular when a higher security level is required.

$$\mathsf{ECDSA}\left\{(dpk, \sigma, \{\rho_i\}_{i\in[t]}) : \forall i \in [t]\ \begin{array}{c}\mathsf{ECDSA.Vf}(dpk, \mathsf{nonce}, \sigma) = 1 \\ C_i = \mathsf{Ped}_t.\mathsf{Commit}(pp_t, dpk_i; \rho_i) \\ \mathsf{Encode}(dpk) = (dpk_1, \dots, dpk_t)\end{array}\right\}$$

$$\mathsf{EQ}_t\left\{\left(\{dpk_i, \rho_i, \rho_i'\}_{i\in[t]}\right) : \forall i \in [t]\ \begin{array}{l}C_i = \mathsf{Ped}_t.\mathsf{Commit}(pp_t, dpk_i; \rho_i) \\ C_i' = \mathsf{Ped}_q.\mathsf{Commit}(pp_q, dpk_i; \rho_i')\end{array}\right\}$$

In the above, we use the subscripts t, q for the Pedersen commitments over $\mathbb{Z}_t$ (the base field of P-256) and $\mathbb{Z}_q$ (the scalar field of BLS12-381) respectively. We also treat the witness elements dpk_i as integers. Note that while similar, the relation for ECDSA is different from the generic PoP relation since it involves a commitment scheme for a different domain. The EQ_t relation is used to show consistency between the two sets of commitments.

Next, we give an overview of an instantiation for each of the above proofs based on sigma protocols. We emphasize however that *any* instantiation works; one could for example use SNARKs for proving the ECDSA relation with smaller proof size and slower proving time[8].

Tom Curve. As mentioned, our proof of knowledge of an ECDSA signature needs to be defined as a computation over $\mathbb{Z}_t$ – the base field of P-256. When working on elliptic curves, however, the native computation is defined over the *scalar field* of the curve. We therefore need an elliptic curve whose scalar field is the base field of P-256. Such a curve is the Tom curve T-256 introduced in [30]. Our proof for the relation ECDSA will be defined over this curve and the proof EQ will show that pairs of commitments over T-256 and BLS12-381 respectively open to the same value (as integers). Therefore, our full construction involves three curves: P-256, T-256 and BLS12-381. To avoid confusion about field notation we present in Table 1 the symbols we use for the fields of each curve (when needed).

We also use the notation Ped_q with parameters pp_q to denote the Pedersen commitment over the curve with scalar field $\mathbb{Z}_q$ (and similarly for $\mathbb{Z}_p, \mathbb{Z}_t$). Finally, given a point $P = (x, y)$ we denote its affine coordinates as $(x, y) = (P.x, P.y)$.

Table 1. Notation for base and scalar fields for the Elliptic Curves used in the manuscript.

Curve	Scalar Field	Base Field
P-256	$\mathbb{Z}_p$	$\mathbb{Z}_t$
T-256	$\mathbb{Z}_t$	
BLS12-381	$\mathbb{Z}_q$	

[8] There are some limitation on the families of SNARKs that can be (natively) used due to the properties of the field $\mathbb{Z}_t$. In particular, one should use a SNARK that is efficient in curves that are not "FFT-friendly".

PoKs for Equality Across Different Groups. To prove that the opening of two commitments over different groups are equal, we employ the techniques of [24, 44]. There, a simple protocol is presented for the relation EQ_1.

Note the "promise" $x < 2^b$. Due to technical reasons, the protocol requires a bound on the committed value x. The concrete choice of the value b affects the efficiency metrics of the protocol[9]. We must therefore handle the two following issues:

1. the coordinates of the ECDSA key *dpk* are longer than the supported bound,
2. the verifier must be convinced that the promise is satisfied.

For the first, we can do a "limb decomposition" of x as suggested in [24, 44]. Concretely, we decompose x as $x = \sum x_i 2^{ib}$ with $x_i \in [0, 2^b)$. We then run a proof of equality for all limbs x_i. The second issue is handled during issuance. In particular, the user presents to the issuer the coordinates of the point corresponding to the ECDSA public key and its encoding in 64-bit limbs and the issuer asserts that (1) it corresponds to a valid point and (2) the limbs lie in the correct range. Since the promise is guaranteed to hold a priori, to implement the EQ_8 proof, we simply provide the 8 proofs for the statement EQ of each limb. We present the construction in the full version of this work.

PoKs for ECDSA *Verification.* Having transferred the commitments to T-256, proving knowledge of an ECDSA signature is now (mostly) a native computation. To create a proof, we follow the techniques of [20,30]. Roughly, we can reduce the verification of a signature to two claims: (1) proving that three committed (in affine form) points satisfy $P_1 + P_2 = P_3$ over P-256, and (2) proving that a scalar multiplication equation of the form $P_1 = sP_2$ holds where the points and the scalar are committed in T-256 and P-256 respectively. The former is a native computation and can be proven with standard sigma protocols. The latter is more involved due the two fields involved; nevertheless sigma protocol techniques can still be applied, albeit with some additional efficiency overhead. We also take advantage of the fact that the signed nonce is public and that parts of the signature can be revealed without compromising user privacy (if the secure element is assumed to trusted). We present the details in the full version of this work.

Putting It All Together. We next give a high level overview of the NIZK for PoP by combining the above building blocks. We encode the ECDSA public key $dpk = (x, y) \in$ P-256 as 8 attributes corresponding to 64-bit limbs of the coordinates x, y. These are included in the BBS credential *cred*. To make a presentation, the user starts by providing commitments to these attributes *over both* BLS12-381 and T-256 and uses $\mathsf{NIZK}_{\mathsf{EQ}}$ to create proofs $\{\pi_{x,i}, \pi_{y,i}\}_{i=1}^{4}$ that they correspond to the same value. Then, she creates two T-256 commitments

[9] We will use the bound $b = 64$ and therefore a point $Q = (x, y)$ can be represented as 8 64-bit values, 4 for each of the coordinates. This is used by current implementations. We expect, however, that using 2 limbs of 128 bits and encoding only coordinate x would result in a more efficient construction.

C_x, C_y to the coordinates (x, y) by homomorphically combining the corresponding commitments and proves that she knows a valid signature on nonce w.r.t. to the committed key C_x, C_y. The latter is done by invoking $\mathsf{NIZK}_{\mathsf{ECDSA}}$. We defer details to the full version of this work. We plan to provide a full description of the approach and formally analyze its security in future work.

Acknowledgement. We thank Patrick Amrein and Fabian Aggeler from Ubique for many fruitful discussions on their BBS-ECDSA idea that has been captured in this work. We further thank Andrea Flamini for helpful feedback on an earlier draft of this work. This research was partially funded by the HPI Research School on Systems Design and by SPRIND, the Federal Agency for Breakthrough Innovation. The authors are solely responsible for the content of this publication; the positions presented here do not reflect the views of SPRIND.

References

1. Regulation (EU) 2024/1183 of the European parliament and of the council of 11 April 2024 amending regulation (EU) no 910/2014 as regards establishing the European digital identity framework (2014). https://eur-lex.europa.eu/legal-content/EN/TXT/?uri=CELEX:32014R0910. Accessed 18 Oct 2024
2. ISO/IEC WD 24843: Information security—attribute-based credentials. Working Draft ISO/IEC WD 24843, International Organization for Standardization, 2025. Under development. A working group has prepared a draft
3. EU FP7 Trust & Security Program ABC4TRUST. Attribute-based credentials for trust. ABC4TRUST project (2014). https://abc4trust.eu/
4. Amrein, P. (2025). https://github.com/UbiqueInnovation/zkattest-rs
5. Aranha, D.F., Fotiadis, G., Guillevic, A.: A short-list of pairing-friendly curves resistant to the special TNFS algorithm at the 192-bit security level. CiC **1**(3), 3 (2024)
6. Beullens, W., Seiler, G.: LaBRADOR: compact proofs for R1CS from module-SIS. In: Handschuh, H., Lysyanskaya, A. (eds.) CRYPTO 2023, Part V. LNCS, vol. 14085, pp. 518–548. Springer, Cham (2023). https://doi.org/10.1007/978-3-031-38554-4_17
7. Bobolz, J., Diaz, J., Kohlweiss, M.: Foundations of anonymous signatures: formal definitions, simplified requirements, and a construction based on general assumptions. In: Clark, J., Shi, E. (eds.) FC 2024, Part II. LNCS, vol. 14745, pp. 121–139. Springer, Cham (2024). https://doi.org/10.1007/978-3-031-78679-2_7
8. Boneh, D., Boyen, X., Shacham, H.: Short group signatures. In: Franklin, M. (ed.) CRYPTO 2004. LNCS, vol. 3152, pp. 41–55. Springer, Berlin, Heidelberg (2004). https://doi.org/10.1007/978-3-540-28628-8_3
9. Boneh, D., Fisch, B., Gabizon, A., Williamson, Z.: A simple range proof from polynomial commitments. Technical report (2020). Accessed 12 Sept 2025
10. Bootle, J., Cerulli, A., Chaidos, P., Groth, J., Petit, C.: Efficient zero-knowledge arguments for arithmetic circuits in the discrete log setting. In: Fischlin, M., Coron, J.-S. (eds.) EUROCRYPT 2016, Part II. LNCS, vol. 9666, pp. 327–357. Springer, Berlin, Heidelberg (2016). https://doi.org/10.1007/978-3-662-49896-5_12

11. Bootle, J., Lyubashevsky, V., Nguyen, N.K., Sorniotti, A.: A framework for practical anonymous credentials from lattices. In: Handschuh, H., Lysyanskaya, A. (eds.) CRYPTO 2023, Part II. LNCS, vol. 14082, pp. 384–417. Springer, Cham (2023). https://doi.org/10.1007/978-3-031-38545-2_13
12. Bünz, B., Bootle, J., Boneh, D., Poelstra, A., Wuille, P., Maxwell, G.: Bulletproofs: short proofs for confidential transactions and more. In: 2018 IEEE Symposium on Security and Privacy, pp. 315–334. IEEE Computer Society Press (2018)
13. Camenisch, J., Drijvers, M., Lehmann, A.: Anonymous attestation using the strong Diffie Hellman assumption revisited. In: Franz, M., Papadimitratos, P. (eds.) Trust 2016. LNCS, vol. 9824, pp. 1–20. Springer, Cham (2016). https://doi.org/10.1007/978-3-319-45572-3_1
14. Camenisch, J., Hohenberger, S., Kohlweiss, M., Lysyanskaya, A., Meyerovich, M.: How to win the clonewars: efficient periodic n-times anonymous authentication. In: Proceedings of the 13th ACM Conference on Computer and Communications Security. CCS '06, pp. 201–210. Association for Computing Machinery, New York, NY, USA (2006)
15. Camenisch, J., Krenn, S., Lehmann, A., Mikkelsen, G.L., Neven, G., Pedersen, M.Ø.: Formal treatment of privacy-enhancing credential systems. In: Dunkelman, O., Keliher, L. (eds.) SAC 2015. LNCS, vol. 9566, pp. 3–24. Springer, Cham (2016). https://doi.org/10.1007/978-3-319-31301-6_1
16. Camenisch, J., Lysyanskaya, A.: Signature schemes and anonymous credentials from bilinear maps. In: Franklin, M. (ed.) CRYPTO 2004. LNCS, vol. 3152, pp. 56–72. Springer, Heidelberg (2004). https://doi.org/10.1007/978-3-540-28628-8_4
17. Camenisch, J., Stadler, M.: Efficient group signature schemes for large groups (extended abstract). In: Kaliski, B.S. (ed.) CRYPTO 1997. LNCS, vol. 1294, pp. 410–424. Springer, Heidelberg (1997). https://doi.org/10.1007/BFb0052252
18. Campanelli, M., Fiore, D., Querol, A.: LegoSNARK: modular design and composition of succinct zero-knowledge proofs. In: Cavallaro, L., Kinder, J., Wang, X., Katz, J. (eds.) ACM CCS 2019, pp. 2075–2092. ACM Press (2019)
19. Canetti, R., Lindell, Y., Ostrovsky, R., Sahai, A.: Universally composable two-party and multi-party secure computation. In: 34th ACM STOC, pp. 494–503. ACM Press (2002)
20. Celi, S., Levin, S., Rowell, J.: CDLS: proving knowledge of committed discrete logarithms with soundness. In: Vaudenay, S., Petit, C. (eds.) AFRICACRYPT 24. LNCS, vol. 14861, pp. 69–93. Springer, Cham (2024). https://doi.org/10.1007/978-3-031-64381-1_4
21. Chairattana-Apirom, R., Döttling, N., Lysyanskaya, A., Tessaro, S.: Everlasting anonymous rate-limited tokens. Cryptology ePrint Archive, Paper 2025/1030 (2025)
22. Chase, M., Lysyanskaya, A.: On signatures of knowledge. In: Dwork, C. (ed.) CRYPTO 2006. LNCS, vol. 4117, pp. 78–96. Springer, Heidelberg (2006). https://doi.org/10.1007/11818175_5
23. Chase, M., Meiklejohn, S., Zaverucha, G.: Algebraic MACs and keyed-verification anonymous credentials. In: Ahn, G.-J., Yung, M., Li, N. (eds.) ACM CCS 2014, pp. 1205–1216. ACM Press (2014)
24. Chase, M., Orrù, M., Perrin, T., Zaverucha, G.: Proofs of discrete logarithm equality across groups. Cryptology ePrint Archive, Report 2022/1593 (2022)
25. Davidson, A., Iyengar, J., Wood, C.A.: The Privacy Pass Architecture. RFC 9576 (2024)
26. Desmoulins, N., Dumanois, A., Kane, S., Traoré, J.: Making BBS anonymous credentials eIDAS 2.0 compliant (2025). https://eprint.iacr.org/2025/619

27. Dubois, A., Klooß, M., Lai, R.W.F., Woo, I.K.Y.: Lattice-based proof-friendly signatures from vanishing short integer solutions. Cryptology ePrint Archive, Paper 2025/356 (2025)
28. European Commission: EU digital identity wallet home (n.d.). https://ec.europa.eu/digital-building-blocks/sites/spaces/EUDIGITALIDENTITYWALLET/pages/694487738/EU+Digital+Identity+Wallet+Home. Accessed 07 Oct 2025
29. Faonio, A., Fiore, D., Kohlweiss, M., Russo, L., Zajac, M.: From polynomial IOP and commitments to non-malleable zkSNARKs. In: Rothblum, G., Wee, H. (eds.) TCC 2023, Part III. LNCS, vol. 14371, pp. 455–485. Springer, Cham (2023). https://doi.org/10.1007/978-3-031-48621-0_16
30. Faz-Hernández, A., Ladd, W., Maram, D.: ZkAttest: ring and group signatures on top of existing ECDSA keys. Cryptology ePrint Archive, Report 2021/1183 (2021)
31. Frigo, M., shelat, A.: Anonymous credentials from ECDSA. Cryptology ePrint Archive, Report 2024/2010 (2024)
32. García-Rodríguez, J., Krenn, S., Bernabe, J.B., Skarmeta, A.: Beyond selective disclosure: extending distributed p-abc implementations by commit-and-prove techniques. Comput. Netw. **248**, 110498 (2024)
33. Groth, J.: On the size of pairing-based non-interactive arguments. In: Fischlin, M., Coron, J.-S. (eds.) EUROCRYPT 2016, Part II. LNCS, vol. 9666, pp. 305–326. Springer, Heidelberg (2016). https://doi.org/10.1007/978-3-662-49896-5_11
34. Harchandani, L. (2025). https://github.com/docknetwork/crypto/tree/main/equality_across_groups
35. Hesse, J., Singh, N., Sorniotti, A.: How to bind anonymous credentials to humans. In: 32nd USENIX Security Symposium (USENIX Security 23), pp. 3047–3064. USENIX Association, Anaheim, CA (2023)
36. ISO. Iso 20008-2:2013: Information technology - security techniques - anonymous digital signatures - part 2: mechanisms using a group public key. Standard, International Organization for Standardization, Geneva, CH (2013)
37. Kalos, V., Bernstein, G.M.: Bbs per verifier linkability. Internet Draft draft-irtf-cfrg-bbs-per-verifier-linkability-02, Internet Research Task Force, September 2025
38. Kalos, V., Bernstein, G.M.: Blind bbs signatures. Internet Draft draft-irtf-cfrg-bbs-blind-signatures-01, Internet Research Task Force, March 2025
39. Kilian, J.: Uses of Randomness in Algorithms and Protocols. MIT Press (1990)
40. Lehmann, A., Özbay, C.: Commit-and-prove system for vectors and applications to threshold signing. In: Jager, T., Pan, J. (eds.) PKC 2025, Part III. LNCS, vol. 15676, pp. 200–232. Springer, Cham (2025). https://doi.org/10.1007/978-3-031-91826-1_7
41. Looker, T., Kalos, V., Whitehead, A., Lodder, M.: The BBS Signature Scheme. Internet-Draft draft-irtf-cfrg-bbs-signatures-09, Internet Engineering Task Force, July 2025. Work in Progress
42. Lyubashevsky, V., Nguyen, N.K., Plançon, M.: Lattice-based zero-knowledge proofs and applications: shorter, simpler, and more general. In: Dodis, Y., Shrimpton, T. (eds.) CRYPTO 2022, Part II. LNCS, vol. 13508, pp. 71–101. Springer, Cham (2022). https://doi.org/10.1007/978-3-031-15979-4_3
43. Orrù, M.: Revisiting keyed-verification anonymous credentials. Cryptology ePrint Archive, Report 2024/1552 (2024)
44. Orrù, M., Kadianakis, G., Maller, M., Zaverucha, G.: Beyond the circuit: how to minimize foreign arithmetic in ZKP circuits. CiC **2**(1), 23 (2025)
45. Orrù, M.: Sigma protocols. Internet Draft draft-orru-zkproof-sigma-protocols-00, February 2025

46. Paquin, C., Policharla, G.-V., Zaverucha, G.: Crescent: stronger privacy for existing credentials. Cryptology ePrint Archive, Report 2024/2013 (2024)
47. Patton, C.: [privacy-pass] arc, acs: dividing the work with CFRG (2025). https://mailarchive.ietf.org/arch/msg/privacy-pass/AgLCkR1I_DdP1Q9eSALbDGmkkVM/. Mailing list post. Accessed 02 Apr 2026
48. Pointcheval, D., Sanders, O.: Short randomizable signatures. In: Sako, K. (ed.) CT-RSA 2016. LNCS, vol. 9610, pp. 111–126. Springer, Cham (2016). https://doi.org/10.1007/978-3-319-29485-8_7
49. Pointcheval, D., Sanders, O.: Reassessing security of randomizable signatures. In: Smart, N.P. (ed.) CT-RSA 2018. LNCS, vol. 10808, pp. 319–338. Springer, Cham (2018). https://doi.org/10.1007/978-3-319-76953-0_17
50. Schlesinger, S., Katz, J.: Anonymous credit tokens. Internet-Draft draft-schlesinger-cfrg-act-00, Internet Engineering Task Force, August 2025. Work in Progress
51. Tessaro, S., Zhu, C.: Revisiting BBS signatures. In: Hazay, C., Stam, M. (eds.) EUROCRYPT 2023. LNCS, vol. 14008, pp. 691–721. Springer, Cham (2023). https://doi.org/10.1007/978-3-031-30589-4_24
52. Woo, A.P.Y., Ozdemir, A., Sharp, C., Pornin, T., Grubbs, P.: Efficient proofs of possession for legacy signatures. In: Blanton, M., Enck, W., Nita-Rotaru, C. (eds.) 2025 IEEE Symposium on Security and Privacy, pp. 3291–3308. IEEE Computer Society Press (2025)
53. Yun, C., Wood, C.A.: Anonymous rate-limited credentials. Internet-Draft draft-yun-cfrg-arc-01, Internet Engineering Task Force, August 2025. Work in Progress
54. ZKProof Standards Committee: Plan for 2024/2025 - zkproof standards (2024). https://docs.zkproof.org/standards#plan-for-20242025. Accessed 10 Oct 2025

A Threat Model for the W3C Digital Credentials API: An Initial Analysis

Zahra Ebadi Ansaroudi[1(✉)], Amir Sharif[1(✉)], Giada Sciarretta[1], Simone Onofri[3], and Silvio Ranise[1,2]

[1] Center for Cybersecurity, FBK, Trento, Italy
{zebadiansaroudi,asharif,g.sciarretta,ranise}@fbk.eu
[2] Department of Mathematics, University of Trento, Trento, Italy
[3] World Wide Web Consortium (W3C), Delaware, USA

Abstract. Accessing online services requires users to choose from a growing set of identity providers, including social logins (e.g., Google), national eID providers (e.g., CIE), and recently, under the revised electronic Identification, Authentication and Trust Services regulation (eIDAS 2.0), "Log in with Digital Wallet". In self sovereign identity settings, this choice worsens the "NASCAR problem": users must select among many wallets, while relying parties face significant integration and maintenance costs. The W3C Digital Credentials API shifts selection from the wallet to the specific credential required by the relying parties, enabling a simpler and more interoperable user journey. To achieve this, the API mediates requests and responses through both web and operating system interfaces. Yet this multi-party, cross layer architecture, which spans user agents, operating systems, and wallets, expands the attack surface. This paper presents a preliminary threat model for the Digital Credentials API to identify and mitigate potential threats, thereby supporting a secure, privacy preserving, and interoperable self sovereign identity ecosystem.

Keywords: W3C Digital Credentials API · Threat Modeling · Identity Wallet

1 Introduction

In centralized identity architectures, an identity provider (IdP) mediates user access to multiple Relying Parties (RPs). Centralized models maintain credentials and profile data within a single provider-controlled repository, reducing repeated registrations but creating a high-value breach target and limiting user agency over data sharing [19]. Centralized models delegate authentication to external IdPs, lowering friction while concentrating control in a small set of providers, increasing cross-site correlation and tracking risk, and introducing ecosystem-wide failure modes (e.g., outages, policy shifts) and potential provider lock-in.

H. C. Pöhls and C. J. Mitchell (Eds.): SSR 2025, LNCS 16466, pp. 69–88, 2026.
https://doi.org/10.1007/978-3-032-19567-8_4

Self-sovereign identity (SSI) approaches aim to solve these concerns by giving users direct control over their data. This shift is architecturally realized through the three-party model, a foundational pattern in the W3C Verifiable Credentials ecosystem [6,21,29]. This model involves three core roles: the Issuer that creates, signs and manages status of the credentials; the Holder (a.k.a User) who stores these credentials in a digital wallet; and the RP (a.k.a Verifier) who requests proof from the Holder to grant access. In this user-centric design, data is stored, managed, and presented by Holders, mitigating the privacy concerns of centralized systems. However, while elegant in theory, the practical interaction between the Holder and RP—the presentation phase—has been hampered by wallet-specific integrations and an inconsistent user experience (UX). Many sites expose a grid of wallet or social login buttons—the "NASCAR problem"—which forces RPs to build and maintain bespoke integrations with multiple IdPs and wallets [8]. This fragments deployments, inflates maintenance costs, and yields a fragile path from user click to verified presentation, with security and privacy guarantees that vary across browsers and operating systems (OSs) [29].

To address this problem, the World Wide Web Consortium (W3C) introduces the Digital Credentials API (DC API) [28]. DC API solves this issue by making presentation credential-centric rather than wallet-centric. Through a standardized web interface, a site issues a single request, while the browser (a.k.a User Agent (UA)) mediates discovery and selection of matching credentials via the operating system's Credential Manager (CM) [20,28]. This architecture improves interoperability and reduces RP–wallet coupling, but it also concentrates sensitive interactions at the UA–OS boundary and introduces new trust assumptions. When high-value credentials (e.g., government IDs) are involved, these concentrations may create new attack surfaces and privacy risks that warrant careful mediation and verification.

In this paper, we present a foundational threat model to support the secure deployment and safe adoption of the DC API. Our model focuses on the DC API interaction model and is scoped to the *presentation flow* initiated via the DC API call and the paths it induces across the UA, the CM, and the wallet in both same-device and cross-device modes. To make the DC API flow concrete, we provide limited illustrative details (wallet UX, CM behavior, cross-device relay); these examples are non-normative and out of scope for the DC API specification. Furthermore, we exclude threats arising from a fully compromised OS or device-level malware. Based on this model, we provide a roadmap for a resilient SSI ecosystem [28,29], and make the following contributions:

- **A systematic overview** of the DC API's architecture and core presentation workflow in simple terms.
- **A threat model** for the DC API, derived using a systematic, question-driven methodology. This model decomposes the workflow into distinct analysis zones to systematically identify threats, which are then mapped to affected assets and categorized using the well-known STRIDE [14] and LINDDUN [11] categories [2,22].

- **A corresponding catalog** of security and privacy controls designed to mitigate the identified threats.

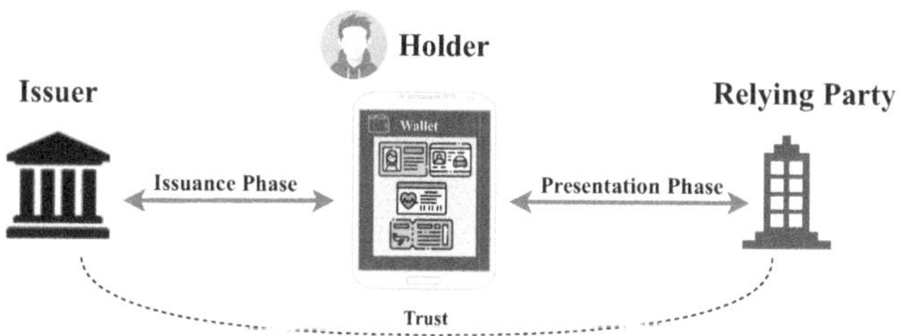

Fig. 1. Three Party Model.

Paper Structure. The remainder of this paper is structured as follows. Section 2 provides the background necessary to help the reader understand the paper. Section 3 details the DC API architecture and the DC API–mediated presentation flow. Section 4 describes our question-driven threat modeling methodology. Section 5 discusses the findings and presents the lessons learned. Finally, Sect. 6 concludes and outlines directions for future work.

2 Background

This section provides the main concepts to make the paper self-contained.

2.1 Three-Party Model

The W3C Verifiable Credentials (VC) ecosystem is architecturally defined by a three-party model—often called the *trust triangle*—that decouples credential issuance from presentation [6,13]. The roles, as depicted in Fig. 1, are:

Issuer: An entity that creates a VC bound to a key provided by a subject during the issuance phase using issuance protocols (e.g., OpenID4VCI [26]). The VC contains one or more claims about the subject and is signed by the Issuer to ensure authenticity [6];

Holder: An entity (often, but not necessarily, the subject) that receives and stores VCs in a wallet and, later, in the presentation phase, generates a Verifiable Presentation (VP) in response to a request using presentation protocols (e.g., OpenID4VP [15]). The Holder controls disclosure and may use selective disclosure mechanisms [6];

Verifier (RP): An entity that requests evidence for a claim in a VP and evaluates the VP by checking cryptographic validity, determining trust in the Issuer, and confirming that the VP is bound to the legitimate Holder (Holder binding) [6,15].

In this model, the Issuer (e.g., an educational institution) issues VCs (e.g., a Diploma) to the Holder during the issuance phase using issuance protocols [26]. The Holder can store VCs in their wallet applications. The wallet is typically provided as a mobile application on the Holder's smartphone. Subsequently, during the presentation phase, the Holder provides a VP to an RP's service. The Holder, using presentation protocols, can potentially selectively disclose the claims required by the RP [6,15].

In the rest of this paper, we focus on the presentation phase, specifically, the presentation flow mediated by the DC API. This API offers a protocol-agnostic solution that enables RPs to request VCs from a Holder's wallet. To understand how this API works in practice as explained in Sect. 3, the following section introduces the two building blocks upon which this API is established.

2.2 W3C Credential Management Level 1

The W3C Credential Management Level 1 [20] enables a website to create, store, and retrieve credentials within the UA on the user's device. Supported credential types include username–password credentials, federated identity credentials, and public-key credentials (via Web Authentication). This API provides the following advantages: (*i*) it reduces friction in sign-in flows; (*ii*) it enables one-tap sign-in with an account chooser; and (*iii*) it stores credentials within the UA. The first feature enables users to be automatically signed back in to a website even if their session has expired or if they saved credentials on another device; the second provides a native account chooser; and the third enables (optional) credential syncing across a user's devices via the UA.

2.3 FIDO Client to Authenticator Protocol 2.2

The FIDO Client to Authenticator Protocol (CTAP) specifies an application-layer protocol for communication between an authenticator (e.g., a security key) and a client platform, as well as bindings of this protocol to multiple transport protocols (e.g., Bluetooth Low Energy, BLE) across different physical media. CTAP 2.2 is the latest specification and supports a cross-device authentication mode, called "hybrid", which enables an external device (such as a phone or tablet) to act as a roaming authenticator for signing in on a primary device (such as a personal computer) [4]. This is commonly referred to as FIDO cross-device authentication.

When a user authenticates with a mobile device (roaming authenticator) for the first time, the authenticator must be linked to the primary device by scanning a QR code. The QR code conveys a public key and a shared secret. The public key is used to authenticate the primary device to the smartphone, while possession of the shared secret authenticates the roaming authenticator (mobile device) to the primary device. After scanning, the mobile device sends an encrypted BLE advertisement containing keying material and a tunnel identifier. Keying material from the encrypted BLE payload, together with the pre-shared secret, is used to derive a symmetric key that the primary device and the authenticator use to establish a secure tunnel via a web service, after which the normal CTAP exchange proceeds. If the user chooses to keep the authenticator linked to the primary device, the QR code step is not required on subsequent use; the user instead receives a push notification on the authenticator.

3 W3C Digital Credentials API: Architecture and Workflows

The *DC API* is a web-platform interface that enables RPs to request *VCs* from a user's wallet through a single, protocol-agnostic call [28].

```
navigator.credentials.get({ digital: { requests: [{ protocol:
                    "...", data: {...} }] } }).
```

This API extends the *Credential Management Level 1 API*, which already supports multiple sign-in methods such as passwords, passkeys, and federated sign-in solutions [20]. In the context of SSI, its role is to provide a unified interface for credential presentation across different protocols (e.g., OpenID4VP, ISO 18013-5). At a high level, the DC API enables applications to register as wallets for storing and presenting VCs. It acts as an intermediary, communicating with registered wallets to identify VCs that meet a specific request, which is initiated by the RP. The UA then presents the Holder with a list of matching VCs, eliminating the need to integrate with individual wallets. Therefore, the DC API delivers a consistent and intuitive UX by focusing on selecting the VCs that can satisfy a presentation request rather than selecting a wallet.

When the call succeeds, the UA resolves the promise with a `DigitalCredential` object. Its structure includes:

- `protocol` – the protocol identifier used (e.g., `"openid4vp"`).
- `data`—a protocol-defined JSON object that encapsulates an opaque presentation (typically encrypted or otherwise unreadable to page scripts).
- Internal slots:

  `[[type]]` – denotes that this object is a digital credential (defined as the constant `"digital"`).

  `[[discovery]]` – indicates how the credential was discovered (defined as the constant `"remote"`).

The `protocol` and `data` fields in the response correspond to the request parameters, while the internal slots are maintained by the UA to enforce type safety and transport policies. A non-normative example of a `DigitalCredential` response object is shown below:

```
{
  "protocol": "openid4vp",
  "data": {
    "vp_token": {
```

```
    "cred1": "
    o2d2ZXJzaW9uYzEuMGlkb2N1bW9yZyxLm1ETGxpc3N1ZXJTaWduZWSiam5hbWVT...
    uNS4xgdgYWFSwC"
}}}
```


3.1 Modes of Operation

The DC API supports two operational modes for presentation flow as illustrated by Figs. 2 and 3:

- **Same-device.** The UA, CM, wallet, and RP page all run on the same physical device. The UA delivers the request to the CM through inter-process communication (IPC). The wallet response is returned directly.
- **Cross-device.** The UA runs on one device (e.g., desktop) and the wallet on another (e.g., phone). A *local CM* (desktop) receives the request as same-device mode and then communicates with a *remote CM* (phone) over a secure channel established via the CTAP 2.2 hybrid transport [4]. Using this mechanism, the local CM encodes a compact bootstrap bundle (an identity key, a short `qrSecret`, and tunnel hints) in the form of a `FIDO:/...` URI, passes it to the UA, which renders it as a QR code, and the UA displays it for the user to scan. The remote CM establishes a BLE "Just-Works" link, using the `qrSecret` as an out-of-band pairing value, announcing a BLE advertisement that the local CM trial-decrypts to recover a proximity nonce and routing information. Then both sides select and connect to an appropriate tunnel service and perform an authenticated, forward-secure handshake over that connection which derives session keys.

  Implementations may persist opaque linking or pairing metadata so that subsequent interactions between the same devices can reconnect without re-displaying the QR; such cached state is an implementation detail and should be governed by appropriate lifecycle controls (unlinking, expiry, server-side invalidation). The response traverses the same path back to the UA.

CTAP 2.2 defines a QR+BLE+tunnel-service for cross-device relay; some reference implementations (e.g., Chrome) realize this with a WebSocket rendezvous/tunnel [12,15]. The DC API itself is transport-agnostic and does not mandate any specific bootstrap or relay.

3.2 Presentation Flow

Preconditions (configured setup)

- **Wallet registration.** Wallet applications have registered their credential metadata and matcher logic with the CM, including a declaration of the credential-exchange protocols they support (e.g., OpenID4VP, ISO 18013-5).
- **CM integration.** The CM is configured to interoperate with the DC API client (UA), enabling secure discovery and aggregation of credentials across registered wallets.

- **Credential issuance.** The user has previously obtained one or more VCs from trusted Issuers, which are stored in a wallet and available for discovery via the CM.

The unified DC API presentation flow proceeds as follows (with step references to Figs. 2 and 3, where the flows differ):

- **Invocation & preconditions (WebIDL dispatch).** The RP page calls:

  `navigator.credentials.get({ digital: { requests:[...] }}).`

  The UA requires a *secure context* (HTTPS) and a *transient user activation* (e.g., click/tap) to enter the DC API path. Calls that lack either precondition are rejected before DC API processing.
- **Discovery hook.** The UA invokes `[[DiscoverFromExternalSource]]`, *consumes* the user activation, and validates the request:
  (*i*) *request shape*—`options.digital.requests` exists, is non-empty, and each entry is well-formed (has `protocol` and `data`);
  (*ii*) *context/policy*—either `sameOriginWithAncestors` holds (Permissions Policy default allowlist `"self"`), or permission policy has been explicitly delegated to a cross-origin embedded inline frame (iframe) via the `digital-credentials-get`.
  Invalid or unsupported requests fail *before* any wallet is contacted.
- **UA permission.** The UA presents a trusted, non-spoofable permission dialog that summarizes the RP origin and high-level purpose of the request. If the user denies, the call fails with a coarse error and no wallet is contacted; if allowed, the UA proceeds to delivery.
- **Request delivery to CM.** If permission is granted, the UA forwards the request to the CM.
  - **Same-device:** delivered directly via native IPC (Fig. 2, Step 4).
  - **Cross-device:** first delivered to the local CM (desktop) and then relayed to the remote CM (phone) over a secure channel (Fig. 3, Step 4–9).
- **Credential enumeration.** The CM queries all registered wallets for credentials matching the request. Responses are aggregated and duplicates removed.
- **System picker.** The CM shows a trusted, non-spoofable system dialog listing candidate credentials, and the user selects one.
- **Wallet invocation & presentation.** The CM invokes the wallet holding the selected credential. The wallet authenticates the user (PIN/biometric), obtains user consent, and builds the requested presentation (e.g., VP-JWT, SD-JWT, mdoc-CBOR).
  - **Same-device:** The CM returns the presentation directly to the UA (Fig. 2, Step 13).
  - **Cross-device:** the remote CM sends the presentation to the local CM via the secure tunnel established after QR bootstrap (Fig. 3, Steps 18–19).
- **Response & resolution.** The UA wraps the presentation in a `Digital Credential` object and resolves the associated `navigator.credentials.get()` promise. The RP page receives the object and forwards the credential `data` to its backend for cryptographic verification.

4 Methodology

To conduct a systematic threat analysis of the DC API mediated presentation flow, we adapt the question-driven methodology proposed by Shostack in his influential work, "Threat Modeling: Designing for Security" [24]. This framework is structured around four guiding questions: (1) What are we working on? (2) What can go wrong? (3) What are we going to do about it? and (4) Did we do a good job? In this paper, we address the first three questions to establish a foundational threat model for the DC API, while leaving the fourth—empirical evaluation of the model and mitigations—for future work.

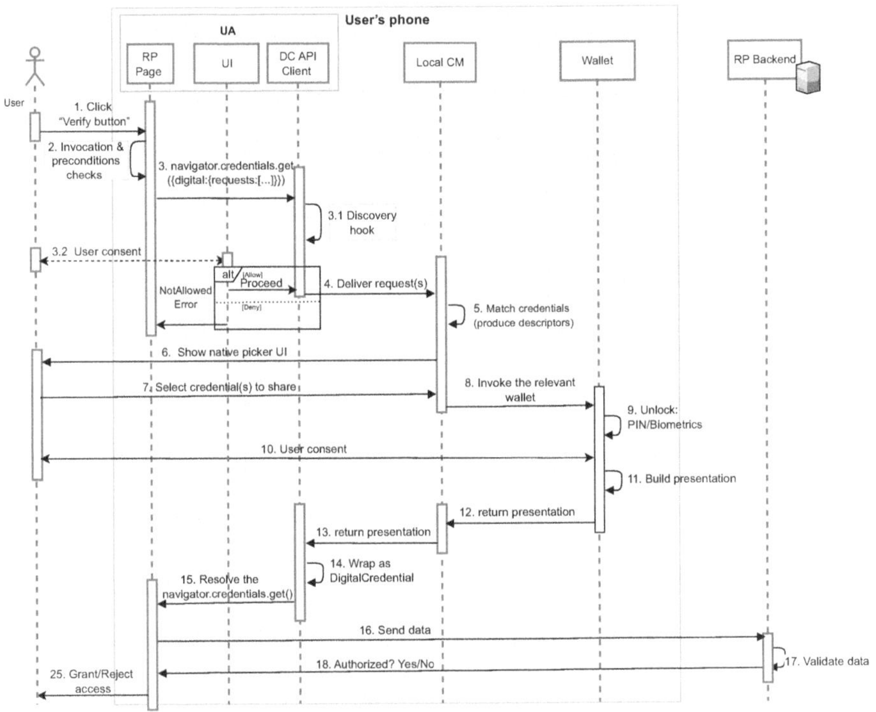

Fig. 2. Same-device presentation via the DC API.

4.1 What Are We Working On? (System Modeling)

To answer Shostack's first question, "What are we working on?", we constructed a detailed system model of the DC API. This model is based on the architecture presented in Sect. 3, and establishes the context and scope for our analysis by formally defining the system's components, actors, and data flows.

Entities. We identify the following entities; concrete components/actors in our model:

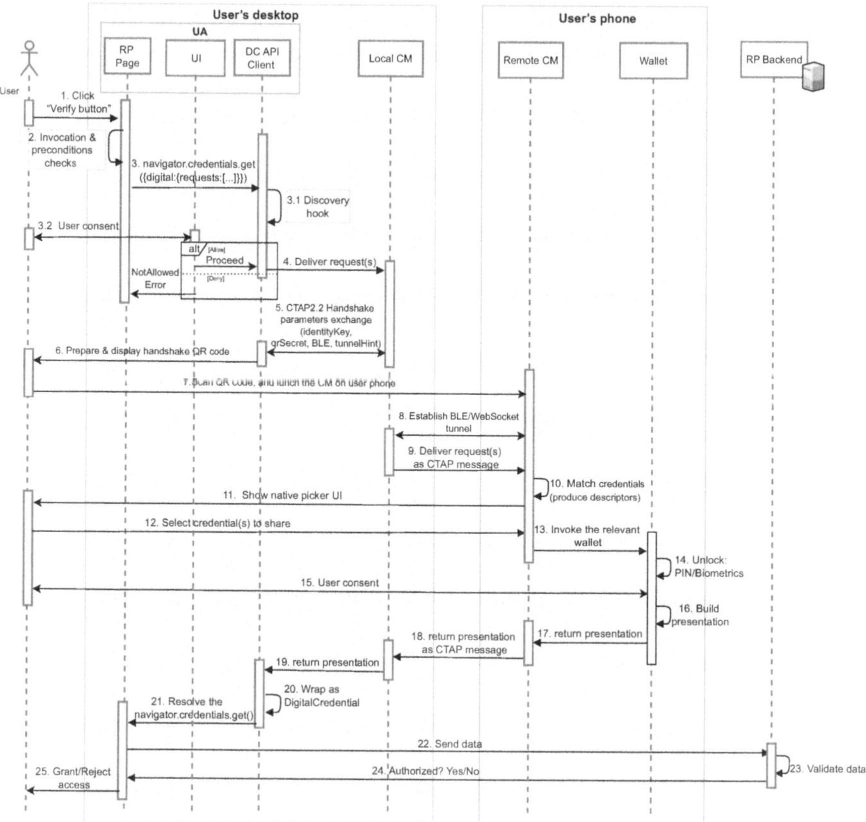

Fig. 3. Cross-device presentation via the DC API (desktop ↔ phone).

- **UA.** Browser/WebView that executes the RP page and implements the DC API; enforces web preconditions, invokes the CM, and resolves the API call back to the RP page [20,28].
- **CM.** Platform/OS component(s) that aggregates Wallet capabilities, runs their matcher, provides the system picker, and relays requests/responses. We distinguish a *local CM* (UA device) and a *remote CM* (Wallet device).
- **Wallet.** Holder software that stores credentials, authenticates the user, and constructs presentations.
- **RP.** Includes the RP page that invokes the API and the backend that verifies presentations.
- **Relay service (cross-device).** Provides CM↔CM tunneling after QR bootstrap [4].
- **Issuer services.** Supply key distribution and status/revocation endpoints for RP checks.

Data Flows and Modes. For threat modeling, we abstract the DC API into two operational modes, described in terms of high-level steps rather than full protocol details.

- **Same-device.** The UA, CM, and Wallet run on the same device; requests and responses are exchanged via local IPC (Fig. 2).
- **Cross-device.** The UA runs on user's desktop, while the Wallet runs on the user's phone. The local CM on desktop relays the request to the remote CM on phone over a proximity-checked, mutually authenticated secure channel established via QR bootstrap and CTAP 2.2 primitives (e.g., BLE plus a rendezvous/WebSocket tunnel) [4]. Responses follow the same channel back (Fig. 3).

Assumptions. We identify threats under the following *assumptions*:

- **A1 (UA mediation).** The UA enforces DC API preconditions and Permissions Policy checks, and mediates request dispatch to and response delivery from the CM without altering protocol payloads [20, 28]. Requests may still be modified *before invocation* by RP page scripts or DOM-level (page-context) browser extensions; such pre-invocation modifications are in scope and are analyzed as origin-level tampering.
- **A2 (CM mediation).** The CM performs credential matching, renders a non-spoofable system picker, and returns the selected Wallet's response to the UA.
- **A3 (UA↔CM channel).** The UA↔CM channel—via same-device IPC or cross-device CTAP 2.2 relay—is assumed to provide endpoint authentication, confidentiality, integrity, forward secrecy, and replay resistance when correctly implemented.
- **A4 (Transport and endpoint authenticity).** All other transport legs used by the DC API (UA↔RP page, CM↔relay service rendezvous, relay↔RP callbacks, and inter-server control channels) are assumed to use authenticated and integrity-protected transports (e.g., TLS or secure WebSocket) with correct endpoint validation and downgrade prevention.

Threats that require full compromise of the UA, the OS or device, the CM, or the Wallet are out of scope. DOM-level/content-script browser extensions are modeled as origin-level adversaries (in scope), whereas extensions with elevated browser privileges are treated as equivalent to a compromised UA (out of scope).

4.2 What Can Go Wrong? (Threat Identification)

With a clear system model established, we now ask: "What can go wrong?" We first define the analysis granularity (Analysis Zones) and the assets we care about, and then enumerate threats against those assets based on our assumptions. While assets are formally part of system modeling, we restate them in this section to highlight their mapping to analysis zones, which provides a clearer basis for enumerating threats.

Table 1. Assets by analysis zones and responsible entities.

Zone	Name	Type	Assets	Primary Entities
Z1	Discovery & Matching	D	Request object (`digital.requests`)	**RP**
			Origin and same-origin-with-ancestors state	**UA**
			Permission outcome	**UA**
			Match summary (capability buckets); *post-permission only*	**LCM / RCM**
		S	Preconditions & discovery (secure context, activation, validity)	**UA**
			API invocation (`navigator.credentials.get()`)	**RP**
		I	System credential picker	**LCM / RCM**
			UA→CM delivery	**UA+LCM / (UA+LCM+RCM)**
Z2	Cross-Device Tunnel	D	Handshake bundle (QR payload, key material)	**UA+LCM**
			Ephemeral channel state (nonces, binding)	**LCM+RCM**
		S	Pairing & CM→CM secure tunnel setup / relay lifecycle	**LCM+RCM**
		I	QR display UI	**UA**
			QR scan UI	**Wallet**
Z3	Consent & Authentication	D	Approved-claims set	**Wallet**
			Local consent record	**Wallet**
			Holder-auth context (presence/time)	**Wallet**
		S	Wallet consent/policy engine (least-disclosure, auth gate)	**Wallet**
		I	Wallet consent UI (attribute preview, toggles)	**Wallet**
			Local authentication prompt	**Wallet+OS**
Z4	Presentation Binding	D	Presentation artifact (VP token, SD–JWT, mdoc)	**Wallet**
			Audience / nonce / binding data	**Wallet+RP**
		S	Proof-of-possession signing & presentation construction	**Wallet+OS**
		I	DC API result channel (Promise resolution)	**UA**
			CM→UA return path	**UA+LCM / (UA+LCM+RCM)**
			RP backend submission	**RP backend**

Notation: A/B = entity differs by mode (A in same-device, B in cross-device). A+B = joint responsibility.

Analysis Zones. We partition the DC API mediated presentation flow into four *Zones*: contiguous segments in which control and responsibilities are stable, and where the dominant technical concerns are internally consistent. We choose these zones because each marks a natural control boundary where the responsible entities and attacker capabilities change. Each zone is defined relative to the presentation flow in Sect. 3.2 and covers steps as below.

Z1—Discovery & Matching covers *invocation & precondition checks, discovery hook, UA permission, request delivery (same-device path), credential enumeration, system picker.*
Z2—Cross-Device Tunnel covers the cross-device *request delivery* (QR bootstrap, CM↔CM tunnel setup, *request relay* to the remote CM) and *response relay* (protected return of the opaque result over the CM↔CM tunnel).
Z3—Consent & Authentication covers *Wallet-side user consent and local authentication.*

Z4—Presentation Binding covers *presentation construction and binding* and *response & resolution.*

Cross-cutting: cancellation, timeout, and error paths are handled within the same zone in which they occur (e.g., permission denial in Z1, tunnel failure in Z2, user cancel in Z3, verification errors in Z4).

Assets. Table 1 lists the *assets* present in each zone (Z#), grouped as:

- **Data (D).** Information that is stored or exchanged and has security/privacy value (e.g., the `digital.requests` object).
- **Service (S).** Components that apply rules or decisions over time to data (e.g., mediation/validation and matching orchestration).
- **Interface (I).** Touchpoints where users or code interact with the system (APIs, UI screens, or tunnel endpoints).

Primary Entities. For each asset, the primary entity (or entities) is indicated as the entity (or entities) responsible for its correct implementation (e.g., the Wallet for consent assets).

Threat Enumeration. To keep the threat catalog consistent and comparable, we document each threat using a uniform "threat card" format inspired by selected elements of the NIST threat modeling ontology. Shostack provides the analytical structure, whereas the NIST-inspired format provides a consistent set of fields for reporting each threat [25].

Therefore, for each identified threat, we report four entries, as illustrated in Table 2:

- **Threat Categories (TC).** Each threat is assigned to one or more categories based on the STRIDE [14] and LINDDUN [11] frameworks. STRIDE (Microsoft) groups security threats into Spoofing (SP), Tampering (TA), Repudiation (RE), Information Disclosure (ID), Denial of Service (DS), and Elevation of Privileges (EP). LINDDUN, a privacy-focused framework, covers Linkability (LN), Identifiability (IF), Non-Repudiation (NR), Detectability (DT), Data Disclosure (DD), Unawareness/Unintervenability (UU), and Non-Compliance (NC). These frameworks are widely recognized in the literature [1,17], ensuring comprehensive coverage of both security and privacy threats.
- **Attack Scenarios.** We report concrete methods or strategies that an attacker may use to exploit the threat in the DC API context.
- **Affected Assets.** The specific data, service, or interface exposed to the threat, reported as *Z#·Asset type* (optionally annotated with facets such as `Z1·I (permission prompt)`). The corresponding primary entities responsible for each asset is provided in Table 1. Note that while these entities are designated as responsible, threats to an asset may also impact other entities.
- **Mitigations.** References to one or more mitigation measures from Table 3, which specify how the identified threats can be addressed.

Table 2. Threat catalog

Threat
T1—Presentation request modification ***Categories:*** TA ***Affected Assets:*** Z1·D, Z1·I, Z1·S ***Description:*** An attacker alters `digital.requests` *before* UA discovery/validation, changing attributes, protocol identifiers, or policy parameters prior to any CM receiving the request. ***Attack Scenarios:*** (1) *Cross-Site Scripting (XSS) on the RP page:* injected script edits `digital.requests` just before `navigator.credentials.get()`; (2) *DOM-level browser extension:* a user-installed content script manipulates the request object or call arguments prior to invocation. ***Mitigations:*** M1 (enforce secure context), M2 (keep request objects inspectable by the UA prior to permission), M5 (provide a non-spoofable UA permission prompt that clearly displays the requested attributes).
T2—Malicious browser extension ***Categories:*** TA, DD ***Affected Assets:*** Z1·I, Z1·S, Z4·I ***Description:*** An extension with page-level privileges tampers with the request flow or exfiltrates results. ***Attack Scenarios:*** (1) *DOM-level request mutation:* a content-script extension edits `digital.requests` just before invocation; (2) *UI redressing:* the page shows look-alike prompts or modals before or after the real CM system picker to nudge the user to cancel or change course; the OS picker itself remains unmodified [3,7]; (3) *Result exfiltration from page context:* after promise resolution, a content-script reads the result available to the RP page and re-sends it (or derived data) via page-level network APIs [9]. ***Mitigations:*** M4 (apply origin and frame-tree constraints), M8 (predictable prompt sequencing), M12 (ensure Wallet-produced presentations remain opaque to page scripts), M13 (protocol-level session binding).
T3—API Flooding ***Categories:*** DS ***Affected Assets:*** Z1·S, Z1·I ***Description:*** An abusive RP origin floods the DC API with requests to exhaust system resources or lock the API execution slot, preventing legitimate usage. Consequences include prompt fatigue and UI freezing. ***Attack Scenarios:*** (1) *Parallel invocation:* the RP fires multiple asynchronous calls on a single user interaction, exploiting timing gaps to bypass the activation lock and instantiate multiple parallel request jobs; (2) *Gesture farming:* the RP uses deceptive UI (e.g., fake buttons) to harvest multiple valid activation tokens, feeding a continuous queue of API invocations; (3) *Cross-origin iframe abuse:* an embedded iframe utilizes delegated permissions to aggressively invoke the API, creating a race for the single active request slot and effectively blocking the top-level page from initiating its own credentials flow. ***Mitigations:*** M15 (transient activation consumption), M3 (restrict DC API use to permitted origins/frames), M7 (enforce single in-flight API invocation per origin plus strict cooldown timers).
T4—CM side-channel attack ***Categories:*** ID, DT, DD ***Affected Assets:*** Z1·S, Z1·I, Z1·D ***Description:*** Timing or outcome signals observable by the RP page leak whether the user is likely to hold certain credentials or satisfy specific attribute predicates. ***Attack Scenarios:*** The RP repeatedly probes the DC API (e.g., via per-page multi-invocation or cross-context probing) and applies oracle techniques over many samples: (1) *Timing oracle:* the RP varies requested predicates (e.g., `age` $\geq$ `18` vs. `age` $\geq$ `65`) and compares response latencies to infer the existence of matching credentials or attributes; (2) *Outcome oracle:* the RP distinguishes promise outcomes or error classes (e.g., “no match” vs. “user cancel”) to infer whether credentials were likely present and shown in the system picker.

continued

Table 2. continued

Threat
Mitigations: M6 (minimize UA-visible signals and avoid fine-grained outcome distinctions), M7 (rate-limit repeated invocations to reduce probing effectiveness).
T5—Improper RP authorization ***Categories:*** UU, NC, DD ***Affected Assets:*** Z1·I, Z3·I, Z3·S ***Description:*** Sensitive attributes are requested by an RP that is not authorized/entitled to receive them, or the Wallet/UA cannot surface authorization status clearly. ***Attack Scenarios:*** (1) *No entitlement policy:* any origin can request high-sensitivity attributes; (2) *Weak authorization signal:* Wallet/UA do not display RP authorization. ***Mitigations:*** M5 (provide a non-spoofable UA permission prompt displaying the RP origin), M9 (enforce selective disclosure and data minimization), M10 (provide a trusted consent interface displaying the RP origin), M11 (require RP authorization).
T6—Cross-origin abuse ***Categories:*** SP, DT ***Affected Assets:*** Z1·I, Z1·S ***Description:*** A malicious third-party iframe embedded in the page initiates DC API requests under confusing context due to lack of or misconfigured permissions policy. ***Attack Scenarios:*** (1) *Policy mis-scope:* top-level origin inadvertently allows DC API use to third-party frames; (2) *Clickjacking/redress:* embedded UI drives the flow under misleading origin/frame tree [7,18]. ***Mitigations:*** M3 (enforce permissions policy scoping), M4 (apply origin and frame-tree constraints), M5 (provide a non-spoofable UA permission prompt).
T7—RP spoofing ***Categories:*** SP ***Affected Assets:*** Z1·I, Z4·D ***Description:*** Attacker induces user to complete a presentation under an attacker-controlled origin and forwards the resulting artifact to a legitimate RP, causing the RP to accept an action the user did not intend. ***Attack Scenarios:*** (1) *Phishing with relayed challenge:* the attacker hosts or relays a genuine RP request on an attacker-controlled page. The user consents there, and the attacker forwards the resulting presentation to the legitimate RP; the attack succeeds only if the RP fails to enforce correct nonce/audience/origin binding. ***Mitigations:*** M5 (non-spoofable permission prompt that surfaces true origin and request purpose), M7 (prompt-rate limits and mandatory user gestures), M10 (trusted consent UI with explicit user approval), M13 (protocol-level session binding).
T8—Presentation response tampering and leakage ***Categories:*** TA, DD ***Affected Assets:*** Z4·I, Z4·D ***Description:*** An attacker attempts to alter or exfiltrate the Wallet-produced presentation after construction on the UA→page path. ***Attack Scenarios:*** (1) *Page-level substitution:* malicious page/extension ignores the opaque result and submits a fake payload; (2) *Presentation leakage from page context:* a DOM-level extension observes the opaque result after promise resolution or during RP-page forwarding and exfiltrates it via page-level network calls. ***Mitigations:*** M12 (ensure Wallet-produced presentations remain opaque to page scripts), M13 (protocol-level session binding), M14 (backend verification of presentation for their integrity).

4.3 What Are We Going to Do About It? (Mitigations)

Finally, we address the third question, "What are we going to do about it?", by identifying and mapping controls to the threats discovered in the previous section. Our threat catalog (Table 2) provides a direct mapping of each threat to a set of mitigation IDs. These IDs correspond to the detailed descriptions in our mitigation catalog (Table 3), pairing DC API requirements/guidance with protocol-level and implementation-level recommendations. This structure provides a clear and direct link between a specific threat and the controls designed to counter it.

Table 3. Mitigations for threats to the DC API presentation.

ID	Mitigation
M1	Enforce secure context (HTTPS) [20, 28].
M2	Keep request objects inspectable by the UA to enable validation and risk analysis [28].
M3	Enforce permissions policy via *digital-credentials-get* (*self*) [28].
M4	Apply origin and frame-tree constraints (e.g., *sameOriginWithAncestors*) and enforce the *digital-credentials-get* Permissions Policy: same-origin by default; cross-origin iframes only when explicitly delegated (e.g., via *allow*) [20, 28].
M5	Provide a non-spoofable UA permission prompt that clearly displays the RP origin, requested attributes and request purpose before contacting the CM or any Wallet. The dialog must be non-injectable and visually distinct from page content.
M6	Provide a non-spoofable platform system picker (CM/OS-rendered prompt) for credential selection, and minimize disclosure in that UI (e.g., no unnecessary logos, counts, or metadata) until explicit user action. In addition minimize RP-observable side-channels at the JS boundary by reducing timing variance and normalizing promise outcomes (e.g., coarse, unified errors and bounded/constant settlement behavior).
M7	Implement abuse controls against prompt spam, including one-call-per-activation (at most one outstanding `get()` per RP origin while a flow is active), apply per-origin cross-context cooldowns after settlement, and suppress or merge prompts to prevent UI stacking.
M8	Ensure UA and OS prompts are shown in a clear, consistent sequence, avoiding overlapping or redundant dialogs [5, 28].
M9	Enforce selective disclosure and data minimization, ensuring that Wallets only release attributes strictly required by the RP [15, 28].
M10	Provide a trusted consent interface that clearly displays the RP origin, the shared attributes by the Wallet, ensuring user awareness before approval [28].
M11	Require RP authorization before access to high-value credentials (e.g., government IDs), and reflect the authorization status in the permission interface [15].
M12	Ensure that Wallet-produced presentations remain opaque to RP page scripts and other web content, including DOM-level/content-script extensions. Only the RP backend may decrypt and verify the presentation, preventing client-side tampering or disclosure [15, 28].
M13	Bind presentation requests and responses to the intended RP (e.g., via *expected_origins*, *aud*), and include session nonces to prevent replay [15].
M14	Verify credential authenticity, freshness, and ensure returned attributes satisfy the requested constraints.
M15	transient activation consumption [20, 28]

5 Discussion and Lessons Learned

Our analysis highlights several insights about where risks concentrate in the DC API mediated presentation flow and how they differ from more traditional credential presentation models. *First*, the majority of threats arise at the *early stages of the flow (Zone 1: Discovery & Matching)*, where the RP, UA, and CM first interact. This aligns with the bulk of early-stage threats (T1–T6), all of which arise in Zone 1, including request modification, malicious extensions, API flooding, CM leakage, and improper RP authorization. These issues are less about broken cryptography and more about exposure at the UA boundary, which mediates between untrusted web content and platform components that contact the wallet.

Second, comparing DC API with traditional invocation methods—*custom URL schemes* (deep links into a wallet application [23]) and *QR-based flows* (an RP-rendered challenge scanned by the wallet)—shows that risk *shifts* rather than disappears. In existing methods, dominant issues include (i) *scheme hijacking* and *handler ambiguity* for URL schemes (a malicious or later-installed app registers the same scheme, or multiple apps claim it, making OS routing nondeterministic and attacker-steerable [23]); and (ii) *QR/code swapping* and scan-path phishing, where users scan attacker-controlled codes and lose any reliable origin signal [10,16]. Under DC API, these specific problems are mitigated: scheme hijacking and handler ambiguity are reduced by UA mediation, and QR-based origin confusion is replaced by an authenticated Web origin that the UA can surface both to the user and to the Wallet. However, these gains come with new risks concentrated at the UA mediation boundary in Zone 1, where malicious page scripts and DOM-level extensions can influence request construction and observe coarse-grained outcomes. In this sense, DC API does not remove risk so much as reconfigure it: it strengthens origin assurance and permission mediation, while making the UA boundary the primary locus of abuse.

Third, our findings point to an open question of *trust between the UA and the wallet*. In the DC API model, the UA must trust the wallet to construct a correct presentation and enforce user consent, while the wallet must trust the UA to present accurate RP context, origin, and purpose. Neither component is inherently dominant; both are necessary for the integrity of the overall flow. In practice, this suggests a "trust but verify" posture: the UA relies on the wallet to build the presentation, but still enforces origin and permissions policy, and the integrity of the DC API call/response flow before handing the presentation back to the RP, while the wallet relies on UA-provided origin information but can still apply its own policy checks before releasing data. This dual dependence is a departure from traditional methods where wallets operate more independently (e.g., QR flows). Ongoing discussions in the DC API working group also raise the question of whether the UA should treat the wallet as a fully trusted party, or whether additional safeguards are required to mitigate misbehavior [27]. This underscores the need for clear specifications of what information is shared across the UA–wallet boundary and how much each side should validate or constrain the other.

Taken together, these lessons show that DC API's contribution is not simply to add a new invocation or mediation model, but to *reconfigure where trust and exposure reside*. Concentration of threats in Zone 1 highlights the need for hardened mediation at the UA. The comparison with QR codes and custom schemes illustrates that risks shift but persist in different guises, while the UA–wallet trust boundary emphasizes that security and privacy guarantees cannot be achieved by one side alone. These insights provide guidance for implementers and standardization bodies on where to focus assurance efforts and where additional security properties may be required in future iterations of the specification.

6 Conclusion and Future Work

The DC API represents a significant shift in web credential presentation by moving from bespoke wallet integrations to a UA-mediated, credential-centric flow. This design provides gains in interoperability and usability, while concentrating critical logic at the boundary between the UA and OS, thereby altering trust assumptions and reshaping the attack surface. In this paper, we developed a preliminary threat model guided by Shostack's methodology, decomposing the credential presentation workflow into coherent analysis zones, identifying the assets involved, and classifying threats with STRIDE and LINDDUN. From this analysis we derived a set of mitigations aligned with the API's design intent.

Our findings show that risks cluster at the early stages of the flow, underscoring the need for robust mediation at the UA boundary. Compared with traditional approaches, the DC API reconfigures rather than eliminates risks: it strengthens origin binding and permission mediation, but expands the UA surface and creates a new interdependence between UA and wallet, making security and privacy contingent on both working in concert. A credential-centric web remains feasible and desirable if its protective measures reinforce one another, and our model provides a structured basis that the working group can refine as the specification evolves. Future work should broaden the threat set, conduct systematic risk assessment, empirically evaluate the effectiveness of mitigations, and extend the analysis to the *issuance* flow, which introduces distinct challenges such as malicious wallet binding, and policy enforcement during credential issuance.

Acknowledgments. This work has been supported in part by a joint laboratory between FBK and the Italian Government Printing Office and Mint, by the project SERICS (PE00000014) under the MUR National Recovery and Resilience Plan funded by the European Union – Next Generation EU, and by the Ministero delle Imprese e del Made in Italy (IPCEI Cloud DM 27 giugno 2022 – IPCEI-CL-0000007) and European Union (Next Generation EU).

Appendix

Abbreviation	Definition
API	Application Programming Interface
BLE	Bluetooth Low Energy
CM	Credential Manager
CTAP	Client to Authenticator Protocol
DC API	Digital Credentials API (W3C)
eIDAS 2.0	Electronic Identification, Authentication and Trust Services Regulation
FIDO	Fast IDentity Online
HTTPS	Hypertext Transfer Protocol Secure
IdP	Identity Provider
IPC	Inter-Process Communication
JSON	JavaScript Object Notation
LINDDUN	Linkability, Identifiability, Non-Repudiation, Detectability, Data Disclosure, Unawareness/Unintervenability, Non-Compliance (privacy threat model)
OS	Operating System
QR	Quick Response (Code)
RP	Relying Party
SSI	Self-Sovereign Identity
STRIDE	Spoofing, Tampering, Repudiation, Information Disclosure, Denial of Service, Elevation of Privilege (security threat model)
TLS	Transport Layer Security
UA	User Agent (typically the browser)
UI	User Interface
URL	Uniform Resource Locator
UX	User Experience
VC	Verifiable Credential
VDC	Verifiable Digital Credential
VP	Verifiable Presentation
W3C	World Wide Web Consortium
XSS	Cross-Site Scripting—a web vulnerability where malicious scripts are injected into trusted websites.

References

1. Bisztray, T., Gruschka, N.: Privacy impact assessment: comparing methodologies with a focus on practicality. In: Nordic Conference on Secure IT Systems. Springer (2019)
2. Ansaroudi, Z.E., Sharif, A., Sciarretta, G., Marino, F.A., Ranise, S.: Secure and reliable digital wallets: a threat model for secure storage in eIDAS 2.0. In: IFIP Annual Conference on Data and Applications Security and Privacy, pp. 271–289. Springer (2025)
3. Elbitar, Y., et al.: Permission rationales in the web ecosystem: an exploration of rationale text and design patterns. In: Proceedings of the 2025 CHI Conference on Human Factors in Computing Systems, pp. 1–25 (2025)
4. FIDO Alliance. Client to Authenticator Protocol (CTAP) v2.2. Proposed standard (2025)

5. Harbach, M., et al.: Don't interrupt me-a large-scale study of on-device permission prompt quieting in chrome. In: 31st Annual Network and Distributed System Security Symposium (NDSS'24) (2024)
6. Herman, I., Jones, M., Sporny, M., et al.: Verifiable credentials data model v2.0. W3C recommendation, World Wide Web Consortium (W3C) (2025)
7. Huang, L.-S., Moshchuk, A., Wang, H.J., Schecter, S., Jackson, C.: Clickjacking: attacks and defenses. In: 21st USENIX Security Symposium (USENIX Security 12), pp. 413–428 (2012)
8. Indie Web. NASCAR problem (2024)
9. Kapravelos, A., Grier, C., Chachra, N., Kruegel, C., Vigna, G., Paxson, V.: Hulk: eliciting malicious behavior in browser extensions. In: 23rd USENIX Security Symposium (USENIX Security 14), pp. 641–654 (2014)
10. Kasselman, P., Fett, D., Skokan, F.: Cross Device Flows: Security Best Current Practice. Internet-Draft, Internet Engineering Task Force (2025)
11. LINDDUN. LINDDUN privacy threat modeling framework
12. Markoborodova, N., Zapata, J.L.: Digital Credentials API: Secure and private identity on the web (2025)
13. Mazzocca, C., Acar, A., Uluagac, S., Montanari, R., Bellavista, P., Conti, M.: A survey on decentralized identifiers and verifiable credentials. IEEE Commun. Surv. Tutorials (2025)
14. Microsoft. STRIDE threat modeling framework
15. OpenID Foundation. OpenID for verifiable presentations (OID4VP) 1.0 (2025)
16. Pernpruner, M., Pasquini, C., Sciarretta, G., Ranise, S.: Beyond screens: investigating identity proofing for the metaverse through cross-device flows. In: 2024 2nd International Conference on Intelligent Metaverse Technologies & Applications (iMETA), pp. 056–064. IEEE (2024)
17. Pöhn, D., et al.: Modeling the threats to self-sovereign identities. Gesellschaft für Informatik eV (2023)
18. Rydstedt, G., Bursztein, E., Boneh, D., Jackson, C.: Busting frame busting: a study of clickjacking vulnerabilities at popular sites. IEEE Oakland Web **2**(6), 24 (2010)
19. Sassetti, G., Sharif, A., Sciarretta, G., Carbone, R., Ranise, S.: Assurance, consent and access control for privacy-aware OIDC deployments. In: IFIP Annual Conference on Data and Applications Security and Privacy, pp. 203–222. Springer (2023)
20. Satragno, N., Caceres, M.: Credential management level 1. W3C working draft, World Wide Web Consortium (W3C) (2024)
21. Schardong, F., Custódio, R.: Self-sovereign identity: a systematic review, mapping and taxonomy. Sensors **22**(15), 5641 (2022)
22. Sharif, A., et al.: Protecting digital identity wallet: a threat model in the age of eIDAS 2.0. In: International Conference on Risks and Security of Internet and Systems, pp. 89–106. Springer (2024)
23. Sharif, A., Carbone, R., Ranise, S., Sciarretta, G., et al.: A wizard-based approach for secure code generation of single sign-on and access delegation solutions for mobile native apps. In: Proceedings of the 16th International Joint Conference on e-Business and Telecommunications-Volume 2: SECRYPT, vol. 2, pp. 268–275 (2019)
24. Shostack, A.: Threat Modeling: Designing for Security. John Wiley & Sons (2014)
25. Souppaya, M., Scarfone, K.: Guide to data-centric system threat modeling. NIST Special Publication 800-154, National Institute of Standards and Technology (NIST) (2016)

26. Terbu, O., Lodderstedt, T., Yasuda, K., Fett, D., Heenan, J.: OpenID for verifiable credential issuance 1.0. Technical report, OpenID Foundation (2025)
27. W3C Credentials Community Group. Digital Credentials API: Question on trust between browser and wallet (2025)
28. W3C Federated Identity Working Group. Digital credentials. W3C working draft, World Wide Web Consortium (W3C) (2025)
29. W3C Threat Modeling Community Group. Threat modeling for decentralized identities (2024). Community group report

Benchmarking of the Amortized Post Quantum Combiner for MLS

Britta Hale[1], Xisen Tian[1(✉)], and Lee Wang[2]

[1] Naval Postgraduate School, Monterey, USA
{britta.hale,xisen.tian1}@nps.edu

[2] Defense Language Institute, Monterey, USA
lee.wang@dliflc.edu

Abstract. Overhead costs associated with post quantum (PQ) algorithms, especially digital signatures, create a significant barrier to incorporation and adoption of post quantum cryptographic protocols in various settings. To counter this, the working group for the Messaging Layer Security (MLS) protocol under the Internet Engineering Task Force has proposed an approach where traditional and PQ sessions of the protocol are strategically combined in such a way as to amortize PQ-associated overhead, i.e., an Amortized Post Quantum (APQ) combiner. In this work, we implement and benchmark APQ using standardized NIST algorithms (ML-KEM and ML-DSA) integrated into OpenMLS with native Rust cryptographic libraries, presenting the first comprehensive performance evaluation of APQ to include PQ authenticity. Our evaluation encompasses execution run-time, message size, and memory consumption across various security levels and amortization ratios to compare and contrast MLS with traditional-only, APQ confidentiality-only, APQ confidentiality+authenticity, and an alternative hybrid ciphersuite. We demonstrate that APQ achieves exponential improvements in message size and memory efficiency as amortization traditional:PQ ratios decrease from 1:1 to 1:100, with optimal performance observed around 1:50 ratios. These findings establish APQ as a practical solution for deploying post quantum security in resource constrained settings.

Keywords: Post Quantum · Messaging Layer Security · Amortized PQC

1 Introduction

The rapid advancements in quantum computing pose an imminent threat to the cryptographic foundations that secure modern digital communications. While practical quantum computers capable of executing Shor's Algorithm at scale remain under development, the cryptography community has proactively developed post quantum (PQ) cryptography, which is based on alternative, quantum-resistant hardness assumptions. Standardized PQ algorithms, under National Institute of Standards and Technology (NIST), exist [11] and integration into

H. C. Pöhls and C. J. Mitchell (Eds.): SSR 2025, LNCS 16466, pp. 89–110, 2026.
https://doi.org/10.1007/978-3-032-19567-8_5

various protocols is ongoing [3,20,22]. Among these, early efforts in PQ migration have been focused on *hybrid* approaches, which aim to attain PQ security while integrating PQ and traditional asymmetric cryptographic algorithms. Because PQ algorithms are relatively nascent and fledging, the hybrid approach allows adopters to maintain classical security even if the PQ algorithm is broken, e.g., [6,8].

Notably, the incorporation PQ cryptographic algorithms is not without challenges. Post quantum key encapsulation and signature operations incur significantly higher computational and bandwidth costs compared to their classical counterparts. For example, according to prior work [21] on TLS, Dilithium (ML-DSA) signature sizes are approximately forty times larger (48B vs 2044B) than ECDSA with private key sizes nearly sixty times larger (48B vs 2800B) than ECDSA. For KEMs, slowdown factors of 1.05 to 2.55 are also to be anticipated in TLS [1] when using PQ KEMs versus ECDHE and ciphertext sizes can be eleven times larger (64B for ECDH vs 736B for ML-KEM512) [18]. These increased costs can be prohibitive for resource-constrained devices with limited compute, power, or bandwidth, creating a challenge even under the necessity for PQ. Use of hybrid approaches further exacerbates this overhead.

Recognizing the different risk tolerance levels of adopters, the Internet Engineering Task Force (IETF), under the Messaging Layer Security (MLS) Working Group, has considered two distinct approaches for integrating quantum resistance, both providing variant hybrid guarantees: 1) use of direct hybrid ciphersuites and 2) strategic integration of traditional and PQ sessions to *amortize* the PQ overhead. The first approach follows a typical hybrid process, namely the combination of traditional and PQ key encapsulation mechanisms (KEMs) for every key update [16]. Meanwhile, the second approach combines two parallel sessions, one with PQ ciphersuites and one with traditional ciphersuites, where randomness from the PQ session is injected in the traditional session at controllable intervals. This is called the Amortized Post Quantum (APQ) combiner method [23]. The APQ approach aims to reduce the overall frequency of PQ operations, and therefore bandwidth overhead, while offering PQ confidentiality and optionally PQ authenticity as well. While much work has looked at the performance of PQ protocols using hybrid ciphersuites such as in (1), in this work, we provide the first comprehensive benchmarking of performance across amortized alternatives, comparing various ciphersuites, modes of operation for the APQ combiner (including PQ confidentiality-only and PQ confidentiality+authenticity), and show comparison vs. other normalized hybrid approaches (e.g., X-Wing [12]) and simple PQ ciphersuites. We cross-compare APQ for amortization ratios of traditional:PQ from 1:1 to 1:100 with metrics for message size, memory efficiency, and time. This work demonstrates the feasibility of achieving not only PQ-confidentiality but also PQ authenticity even on resource constrained devices.

Contributions. This work provides a comprehensive benchmarking of the APQ combiner for MLS from [23] using NIST-standardized algorithms. Our contributions include:

1. **Amortized Post Quantum Combiner Analysis:** We conduct benchmarking of the APQ combiner for time (in seconds), random access memory (RAM) usage (in bytes), and message output size (in bytes) in its two modes (PQ Confidentiality-Only and PQ Confidentiality+Authenticity) and provide analysis of amortization strategies overall protocol performance.
2. **Amortized Combiner vs Hybrid Combiner** We provide the first benchmarking of the APQ combiner in its two modes against the hybrid KEM combiner, X-Wing.

The remainder of this paper is organized as follows. Section 2 provides background on the MLS protocol and related work, hybridization approaches in MLS, and details on the APQ combiner. Section 3 details the implementation approach, ciphersuites used, and metrics considered. Section 4 presents performance results for time, memory usage, and message size. Finally, Sect. 5 concludes the paper with implications for PQ MLS deployment.

2 The Messaging Layer Security Protocol, Hybrids, and the APQ Combiner

Messaging Layer Security. MLS provides end-to-end encryption to communicating parties. It is a type of Continuous Key Agreement (CKA), which also encompasses Signal [10] and other ratcheted protocols. Unlike its predecessors, MLS is built to be extensible to groups of larger sizes than typical 1:1 channels while also achieving lower scaling overhead. While we provide a general introduction to MLS here, inclusive of the group scenario, the functional design of the protocol provides scaling performance improvements relative to the number of participants. Consequently, our testing focuses on the simple two-party case to demonstrate the overhead cost-savings of the flexible hybrid combiner even under the worst case scenario.

CKAs "ratchet" or update keys throughout the lifetime of communications. In MLS, this is facilitated by a subfunctionality called TreeKEM [2] which manages keys as a binary tree that is updated via a series of KEM operations. The root of the tree is used to compute the shared secret from which data encryption keys are derived. To evolve the state (or add/remove communication parties), members update keys through a propose-and-commit sequence. Proposals, which can be made by any member, are suggestions to modify the ratchet tree through adding, removing, or updating of nodes. A commit message is sent by a group member to ratify the proposal(s) and enter a new *epoch*. An *empty* commit, is when a member updates their own representative binary tree leaf node and unilaterally commits to it. All proposals and commits are authenticated through the use of digital signature algorithm (DSA) operations.

As a result of the CKA construct and epochal key evolution, the protocol achieves forward secrecy (FS) and post compromise security (PCS). FS ensures past communications remain secure upon compromise of security keys while PCS allows security to be regained after a compromise using fresh keys. Crucial for APQ, entropy can be added to or exported from the cryptographic state via pre-shared keys (PSK). When evolving the state, a proposal can include a PSK identifier, indicating that it should be included into the next commit. Thus, a PSK can be added to the key derivation function (KDF) along with the new shared secret to derive keys. PSKs can be derived to be exported from the shared secret as an *exporter key*. The PSK functionality and optional inclusion in proposals and commits will become useful in the APQ combiner mechanism, described later.

A variety of MLS implementations exist across major programming languages [9]. Relevant to this work, this includes a Rust version called OpenMLS that offers memory safety features and integrates with widely available PQ libraries. We use OpenMLS due to its clear and thorough documentation [19].

MLS Hybrids. X-Wing has been proposed to the IETF as a hybrid KEM combiner [4]. It provides indcca security based on the indcca of its component KEMs, MLKEM and X25519. The IETF MLS working group has adopted X-Wing as a post quantum security option among the set of new PQ ciphersuites in [17]. As an example of a typical hybridization approach, we include X-Wing for cross-comparison with the APQ combiner.

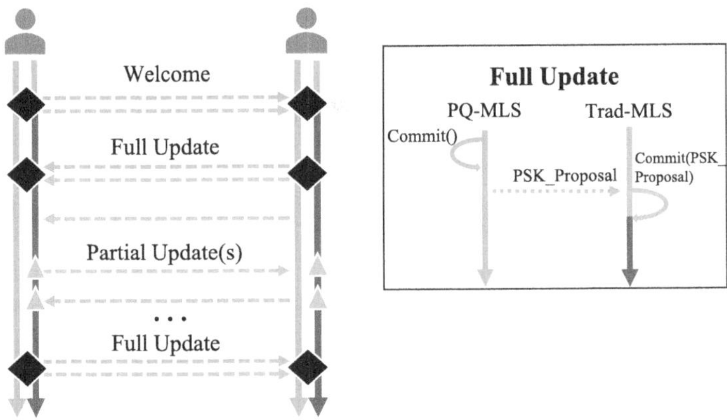

Fig. 1. Overview of the APQ protocol using PQ and traditional MLS sessions (solid lines). Left user adds right user via Welcome messages sent in both sessions (thick dashed lines). ♦ underscores the state changes in both sessions via Full Commits while ▲ highlights state change in just one session via Partial Commits. After a Full Commit, the traditional session is imbued with **PQ entropy** (solid line). MLS Welcome and Commit mechanics are detailed in [5]. APQ PSK_Proposal generation is defined in [23].

APQ Combiner. The APQ combiner [23], illustrated in Fig. 1, combines two MLS sessions, one with PQ algorithms, A, and the other with traditional algorithms, B. These two sessions run in parallel, with the same set of communication participants.

The traditional session B operates according to normal MLS functionality: updates to the shared keying material are proposed and *committed*, effectively ratcheting the state forward. These are performed using a traditional KEM (e.g., DHKEM), and signed with a traditional signature. We call such traditional-only commits *Partial Commits*, and the overall key update performed a *Partial Update*. The new state is used to derive data encryption keys. Application messages are then encrypted with one of a selection of Authenticated Encryption with Associated Data (AEAD) schemes, and also signed to ensure uniqueness and non-repudiation inside the session.

The PQ session A operates in two possible ways, dependent on the combiner mode selected, PQ/T Confidentiality-Only or PQ/T Confidentiality+Authenticity:

- **PQ/T Confidentiality Only Mode:** Within the PQ session, updates to the shared keying material are performed using PQ KEM algorithm but signed with a traditional signature algorithm. No application messages are sent in the PQ session. Rather, it is used for maintaining and updating a PQ key schedule.
  From A's PQ key schedule an exporter secret can be derived using an established label. The PQ PSK is then injected in B using a PSK proposal message that is committed to yield a new B state. As this mixes the PQ PSK into the traditional session B state using a KDF within the MLS key schedule, the resultant B key schedule is also PQ. Thus when data encryption keys are derived within B, they provide for PQ confidentiality. When a proposal-commit sequence in the traditional session B uses the PQ PSK in as described here, we call the overall commit a *Full Commit* and the overall key update a *Full Update*.
- **PQ/T Confidentiality+Authenticity Mode:** This mode follows that of the PQ/T Confidentiality-Only mode, with the exception that key updates in the PQ session are signed with a PQ digital signature algorithm.

Thus, session A uses PQ KEM in the PQ/T Confidentiality-Only (PQ-Conf) mode and a combination of PQ KEM and PQ DSA in the PQ/T Confidentiality+Authenticity (Conf+Auth) mode. Session B uses traditional KEM and DSAs in both modes.

Full Commits can be interspersed or scheduled on a less frequent basis than Partial Commits, thus spreading the associated overhead over a longer period, i.e., amortizing the cost of A operations. Note that Partial Commits update the keying state (which is already PQ, based on the last Full Commit). Thus, a quantum attack on the Partial Commit does not lead to leakage of the session secrets, but only reduces the relative window of PQ key update to that of a Full Commit, i.e., PQ PCS is determined by Full Commits. Meanwhile, PQ FS is still achieved under Partial Commits.

The overall security depends on the frequency of the Full Commits and the mode of operation. In the PT/T Confidentiality+Authenticity Mode, the fact that PQ signatures are used to sign key updates in A enforces PQ authenticity on the overall PQ/T key schedule, which is then used to derive AEAD keys, resulting in PQ authenticity on application data sent in B.[1] The full APQ description and additional bookkeeping mechanisms for signaling Full or Partial updates (to curtail running the two sessions independently, e.g., using the APQMLSInfo object) can be found in [23].

Amortization is a key feature of the APQ combiner and is accomplished through interspersing *Full* key updates with one or more *Partial* key updates. In our testing, we denote amortization with ratios $i : j$ to refer to i number of Full Updates for every j number of Partial Updates.

Other Related Work. Prior work provided a proof of concept implementation and initial metrics for the APQ combiner [13], focusing on the PQ Confidentiality-Only Mode across various group sizes. In contrast, we provide cross comparison with other hybrid options as well as accounting for efficiency under the combined PQ confidentiality and authentication (PQ-Conf-Auth) mode.

Simultaneous to our implementation is that of PheonixIM [15], which also implemented the amortized combiner from [23]. While that work focused on meeting the specifications of the proposed standard in the context of interoperability with OpenMLS, we provide formal benchmarking of performance.

3 Implementation

Our implementation, extending that of [13], is available publicly on GitHub.[2] It is written in Rust, utilizing and modifying open-source Rust crates OpenMLS, hpke, and RustCrypto. OpenMLS implements MLS as promulgated by RFC9240. The cryptographic operations used by MLS (encryption, signing, etc.) are incorporated in a modular fashion using *crypto-providers* like OpenMLS-RustCrypto and OpenMLS-LibcruxCrypto. Crypto-providers are modular interfaces of underlying cryptographic libraries that specify how those libraries interact with OpenMLS. We chose to use OpenMLS-RustCrypto because RustCrypto, as a cryptographic library, is more widely used and does not require more modern x86 and amd64 CPUs [19]. like the high-assurance Libcrux-Crypto library. In total, we utilized three additional cryptographic libraries: the RustCrypto MLDSA crate, RustCrypto MLKEM, and the HPKE crate (which generally implements KEMs). Tests were completed on a MacBook Pro with M2 Max (ARM CPU/GPU Combo), 64GB RAM, and macOS Ventura.

While ML-DSA is incorporated via RustCrypto's MLDSA and OpenMLS traits, support for ML-KEM required further customization of the HPKE library

[1] Digital signatures over the AEAD inside the B session are still traditional, meaning that there is no session-internal non-repudiation. An inside attacker that possesses a quantum computer and wishes to frame another session participant can forge the requisite traditional signature. This is, however, a niche threat model, and unrelated to the PQ authenticity provided against external quantum adversaries.

[2] https://github.com/lwerrors/SSR2025-Tian-APQ-MLS.

used by RustCrypto. Following the structure of the existing KEM implementation in hpke, we created a ml-kem handler to interface with the generic RustCrypto ML-KEM crate.

After incorporation of all levels of ML-DSA and ML-KEM, we implemented the APQ combiner and tested it in sessions with two parties to measure performance across various amortization strategies. Generally, by varying the frequency of full-commits, the cost of PQ operations can be spread across the lifespan of a group session. Concretely, we tested with full-commits in occurring every 10, 50, and 100 commits to gain a sense of amortization effects. Moreover these tests were conducted across the two modes operation, PQ Confidentiality-Only and PQ Confidentiality+Authentication. To establish a baseline of comparison, we measured the performance costs of standard MLS (i.e. individual session) with all levels and appropriate combinations of PQ and traditional ciphersuites as specified by [5,17], respectively. Finally, we measured the performance of an MLS session running the X-Wing hybrid KEM to provide a comparison against hybridization strategies. In those tests, we compare across Full:Partial commit ratios of 1:1, 1:2, 1:5, 1:10, 1:50, and 1:100 to provide more granular comparisons against X-Wing.

3.1 Ciphersuites Tested

We detail which ciphersuites were selected for testing and provide rationale for their selection in this section.

Notation. Table 1 shows the ciphersuites used in our tests. For readability purposes, we assign aliases to the ciphersuites. Each alias begins with a prefix letter denoting which ciphersuite category they belong to: T for traditional, PQ for post quantum, and H for combinations thereof. Within the traditional category, the second prefix represents the underlying curves used (i.e. EC for P256 and P384 and Ed for Ed25519 and Ed448) and the third prefix is an abbreviation of the authenticated encryption algorithm (i.e. AES vs CHACHA20POLY1305). For readability, we give all of the ciphersuites suffixes based on the roughly associated security level (i.e., **L**ow, **M**edium, **H**igh).

Rationale. We chose ciphersuites for benchmarking based on the existing list of supported traditional ciphersuites from [5] as well as the list of proposed PQ ciphersuites from [17]. Following the guidance from [23], we selected to implement 'pure PQ' ciphersuites out of the proposed ciphersuites from [17] which also included PQ and Traditional combined KEMs that redundant in the APQ context. Absent from [17] is support for the lowest security levels of ML-KEM and ML-DSA: ML-KEM512 and ML-DSA44, due to lack of demand. For completeness, we constructed additional ciphersuites (listed in orange in Table 1). As there were no corresponding PQ ciphersuite which uses P521, we rejected the traditional counterpart from testing.

Table 1. Selected standardized traditional ciphersuites [5], draft standard PQ ciphersuites [17], and additional ciphersuites (notated in orange) for comparison. The various hybrid combinations used in APQ testing are indicated on the left side, with ~ representing the component combinations for comparison with X-Wing.

H-C-L	H-C-M	H-C-H	H-CA-L	H-CA-M	H-CA-H	X-Wing	H-C-X	H-CA-X	Alias	Ciphersuite
									Traditional	
*	*								T-EC-AES-L	MLS_128_DHKEMP256_AES128GCM_SHA256_P256
		*							T-EC-AES-H	MLS_256_DHKEMP384_AES256GCM_SHA384_P384
			*						T-Ed-AES-L	MLS_128_DHKEMX25519_AES128GCM_SHA256_Ed25519
				*	*				T-Ed-AES-H	MLS_256_DHKEMX448_AES256GCM_SHA512_Ed448
						~	*	*	T-Ed-Cha-L	MLS_128_DHKEMX25519_CHACHA20POLY1305_SHA256_Ed25519
										PQ Conf-only
*									PQ-C-L	MLS_128_ML-KEM512_AES128GCM_SHA256_P256
	*								PQ-C-M	MLS_128_ML-KEM768_AES256GCM_SHA384_P256
		*							PQ-C-H	MLS_192_ML-KEM1024_AES256GCM_SHA384_P384
						~	*		PQ-C-X	MLS_192_ML-KEM768_CHACHA20POLY1305_SHA256_Ed25519
										PQ Conf+Auth
			*						PQ-CA-L	MLS_128_ML-KEM512_AES128GCM_SHA256_MLDSA44
				*					PQ-CA-M	MLS_192_ML-KEM768_AES256GCM_SHA384_MLDSA65
					*				PQ-CA-H	MLS_256_ML-KEM1024_AES256GCM_SHA512_MLDSA87
								*	PQ-CA-X	MLS_192_ML-KEM768_CHACHA20POLY1305_SHA384_MLDSA65
										Hybrid KEM-Combiner
						*			X-Wing	MLS_256_XWING_CHACHA20POLY1305_SHA256_Ed25519

For a fair comparison with X-Wing, we add traditional and PQ ciphersuites (also in orange) that correspond to the existing X-Wing ciphersuite, as supported by OpenMLS (T-Ed-Cha-L and PQ-C-X in Table 1). To test X-Wing against APQ in the PQ Confidentiality+Authenticity mode, we added an additional PQ ciphersuite with comparable security level components (PQ-CA-X in Table 1).

To establish baselines of comparison, we test single (uncombined) MLS sessions across the traditional (T) and post quantum (PQ) ciphersuite classes in Table 1. For ciphersuite choices for APQ, we pair sessions based on their approximate security level and ciphersuites from each class as also shown in Table 1.

For selection of appropriate traditional ciphersuites to pair with a PQ counterpart, we generally defer to the security levels of the PQ ciphersuite components and selected a traditional to match. Since PQ Confidentiality-Only ciphersuites use ECDSA signature algorithms for signing in the PQ session, we also choose the matching ECDSA counterpart in the traditional ciphersuite category. For the full PQ (confidentiality and authenticity) ciphersuites which uses SUF-CMA DSAs (stipulated by NIST [11]), we select classical ciphersuites that have EdDSA (which is known to be SUF-CMA [7]) and the appropriate parameter-sets (e.g. Curve25519, Curve448). For the H-C-X combiner we create PQ and traditional ciphersuites based on the ML-KEM768 and EdDSAs used in X-Wing. These combinations are summarized in Table 1.

3.2 Performance Metrics

Tests are conducted using a two-participant session size across 500 epochs which are updated via empty commits (one commit per epoch) from a single party.[3] Amortization was tested by varying the ratio of Full to Partial APQ updates.

Time is a direct usability metric that is especially relevant for delay sensitive applications (e.g., secure messaging, media streaming, VoIP). Our time measurements are composed solely of the overhead of cryptographic operations (we do not send packets across a network). Most importantly, our time measurements provide insight into the cost of certain classical ciphersuites that had cascading effects in usage in APQ that would not be revealed by message size and memory usage alone. We measure the total time for 500 epochs, based on an average of 10 samples (i.e., 500 epochs are run 10 times, with the average taken across the 10). This is to mitigate for an spurious interference on time from background processes. Time values are derived using the Rust Criterion [14] microbenching tool which runs 10 iterations of the 500 epoch test and outputs the expected (average) total time for a single 500-epoch sample. As opposed to a single sample, the average of 10 iterations mitigates the effects of background processes effects on timing.

[3] For clarity and simplicity of measurement, all commits are performed by a single party. In normal operation, commits are performed by the various parties in the session.

Message sizes offer another perspective in examining the impacts of implementing PQ algorithms. It is well established that PQ signatures and ciphertexts can be several orders of magnitude higher than their traditional counterparts [21]. For use of PQ in bandwidth limited settings, amortization effects of APQ on cumulative message sizes over time are especially important. MLS message sizes were calculated as a byte summation of the total PSK proposals, Welcome messages, and Commit messages sent between the two parties over 500 epochs.

Peak memory (RAM) consumption helps to determine the minimum RAM requirements for deployment of the various ciphersuites. Total memory measurements across the session run enables fair comparative analysis between the ciphersuites and the amortization ratios due to the clarity provided by the sizes of their overall memory footprint. Memory considerations are relevant for embedded systems and other resource constrained devices that are especially impacted by memory usage. Memory (RAM) usage was measured using the Rust Hotpath [24] process profiling tool which calculates granular peak RAM usage during certain function calls (e.g. encrypt, sign, verify, etc.) as well as the total memory footprint of a program. We measure memory usage as a total across 500 epochs.

3.3 Limitations

Our APQ implementation achieves the core functionality of the combiner (e.g., two MLS sessions tied together via use of an exported/injected PSK via the full commit mechanism from [23]). Our implementation does not include the APQInfo structure and the related bookkeeping mechanisms of Extensions Specification from [23]. Furthermore, our exported PSK uses the `export_secret` as opposed to the `epoch_secret` which is not accessible via the OpenMLS API. These limitations and deviations ultimately have negligible effects to our performance measurements: the APQInfo is a small fixed length byte string that gets added to encryption and signing operations and the secret used for PSK generation are the same sizes. As Github and mailing list discussion on the APQ draft is on-going as of the time of this writing, we leave high fidelity testing using a fully compliant APQ implementation to future work.

4 Results

To establish baselines, we first compare the performance of individual MLS sessions using the traditional, PQ Confidentiality, and PQ Conf+Auth ciphersuites from Table 1. Then we compare the performance of the two modes of APQ across various Full:Partial update ratios to observe the effects of amortization. Finally, we compare hybrid combiners with the X-Wing KEM combiner and our APQ combiner.

In all cases we provide performance metrics as totals across the 500 epochs to clearly illustrate the differences in overall performance. Supplemental tables for per-epoch averages of commit message sizes can be found in Table 3, Table 4, and data summary in Table 5 of Appendix A.

4.1 Baseline Testing

In terms of cumulative total run time, base-line comparisons in Fig. 2 show that MLS sessions using PQ ciphersuites may perform no worse than comparable traditional ciphersuites. Our results indicate that at low security levels, Edwards Curve based DSA and KEM ciphersuites (T-Ed-AES and T-Ed-Cha) are faster than the lowest security level PQ ciphersuites. At high (256-bit) security levels, shown in red in Fig. 2, both classes of PQ ciphersuites (PQ-C-H and PQ-CA-H) outperformed their traditional counterparts.

There is also high variation *within* traditional and PQ ciphersuite classes. Within the traditional class of ciphersuites, MLS sessions using ECDSA and ECDHKEM based ciphersuite were about four times as slow as the Edwards Curve ciphersuites. Additionally, at the high security level, the MLS session using a fully PQ ciphersuite (PQ-CA-H) ran 23% faster than the PQ confidentiality-only ciphersuite (PQ-C-H).

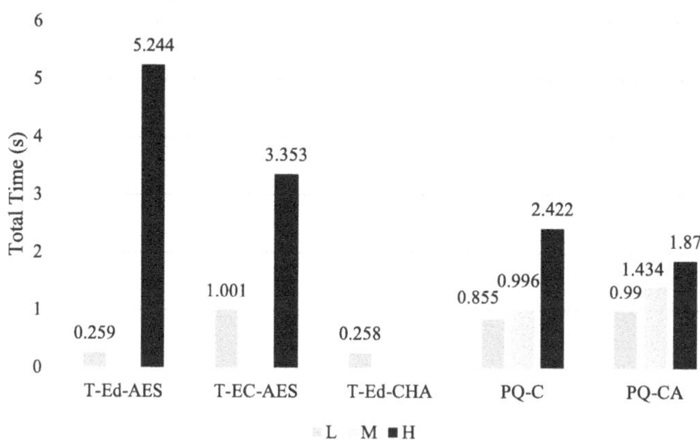

Fig. 2. Total time comparison of individual MLS sessions (group size of 2) across 500 epochs (via empty commits). Clusters (Green-Yellow-Red) based on respective security level (Low, Medium, and High). Absence of a color in a cluster corresponds to a ciphersuite that was not included in testing. Calculations are based on an average of ten 500-epoch samples. (Color figure online)

In terms of message sizes, our baseline results shown in Fig. 3 indicate that comparative PQ ciphersuites are several orders of magnitude higher than their traditional counterparts. This is consistent with the stated outputs on the ciphertext sizes of ML-KEM and signature sizes of ML-DSA from prior research [21] [18] as well as empirical analysis [25]. It is worth noting that out of the class of traditional ciphersuites the ECDSA and ECDHKEM based ciphersuite has the largest ciphertext sizes.

We measure memory allocation by recording the peak RAM consumption (see Table 2) as well as total (cumulative across all 500 epochs) RAM consumption (see Fig. 4). Peak memory usage reveals that classical ciphersuites across all security levels and DSA/KEM types have a ceiling of 1.2MB of peak memory usage. Meanwhile, the PQ ciphersuites increase in peak memory usage with the

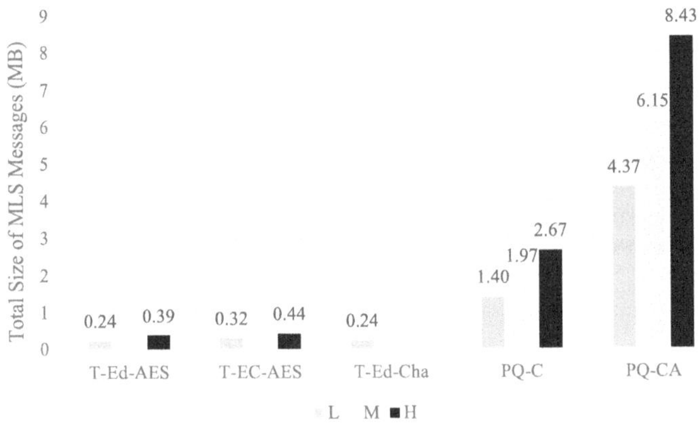

Fig. 3. **Total message size** comparison of individual MLS sessions (group size of 2) for various traditional-only or PQ-only key update methods, totaled across 500 epochs (via empty commits). Clusters (Green-Yellow-Red) based on respective security level (Low, Medium, and High). Absence of a color in a cluster corresponds to a ciphersuite that was not included in testing. (Color figure online)

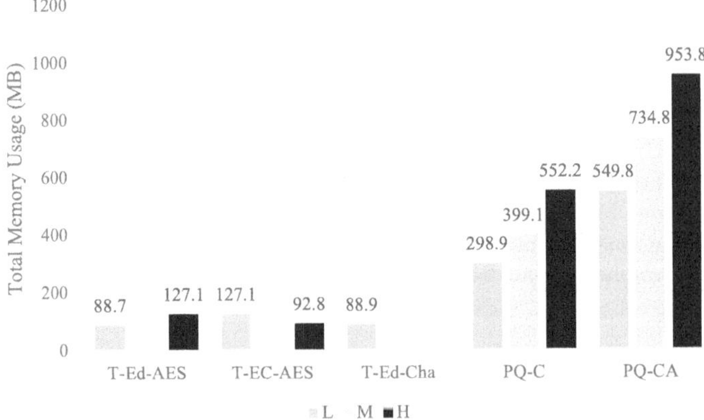

Fig. 4. Total memory (RAM) comparison of individual MLS sessions (group size of 2) for various traditional-only or PQ-only key update methods, totaled across 500 epochs (via empty commits). Clusters (Green-Yellow-Red) based on respective security level (Low, Medium, and High). Absence of a color in a cluster corresponds to a ciphersuite that was not included in testing. (Color figure online)

incorporation of larger KEMs and DSAs, as expected. These impacts are exacerbated when examined using total memory measurements collected across 500 MLS epochs. They reveal that PQ ciphersuites can be several orders of magnitude higher than their traditional counterparts. The difference is smaller for low security level ciphersuites (i.e. only 235% difference between T-EC-AES and PQ-C-L) than high security level ciphersuites (i.e., 750% difference between T-Ed-AES and PQ-CA-L). We expect these differences to increase further with larger group sizes and more epochs.

4.2 Amortization Testing Using APQ

Results from amortization tests show that as the ratio of Full Updates to Partial Updates decreases, total run time, message size, and memory usage decreases which is consistent with amortization claims made in [23]. However, across all APQ modes and ratio, we observe diminishing returns of efficiency gains as the ratio goes beyond 1:50 with a limit based on the less performant component ciphersuite.

In all except H-CA-L and H-C-X, the total runtime exhibited by APQ is generally higher than just running the respective component PQ sessions solo – even at the lowest Full:Partial amortization ratios. This contradicts the intuition of APQ reducing the PQ costs over singular PQ sessions. However, the amortization effect of APQ is working as intended. Because partial updates are applied to the traditional session resulting in far more calls to the traditional ciphersuite components, the amortization effects of APQ likely skew toward the performance of the those traditional ciphersuites. The medium and high security APQ (in both C and CA modes) utilize the slower high security elliptic curve based KEM (X448 and P384) and DSAs (Ed448 and P384), so they set a floor for amortization that is higher than the PQ component alone. On the other hand, low security APQ (in both modes) used traditional KEM and DSAs that were faster than their PQ counterparts so the run-time performances for H-CA-L and H-C-X likely trended toward their traditional ciphersuite performance levels. In summary, because results from our solo session baselines showed PQ sessions performing faster than some of their traditional session counterparts, the APQ combiner also had mixed but correlated results. We leave testing alternative implementations of traditional ciphersuites across alternative crypto-providers and crypto-libraries to address the discrepancies to future work (Fig. 5).

For both message size and memory usage, shown in Fig. 6 and Fig. 7, respectively, the effects of amortization are as expected. For message size, using the worst amortization strategy (1:1) results in producing a total bandwidth roughly equal to the sum of running the individual sessions separately. However, we observe an exponential decrease in message size and memory usage in all APQ modes as we decrease the frequency of Full:Partial commits to 1:10 which are on par with the solo traditional sessions in magnitude. At higher ratios beyond 1:50 Full:Partial commit ratios, this equates to a 94% cumulative message size reduction in comparison to a singular MLS session running the same PQ ciphersuite. This is similarly so for the total memory usage which sees up to an 85% reduction.

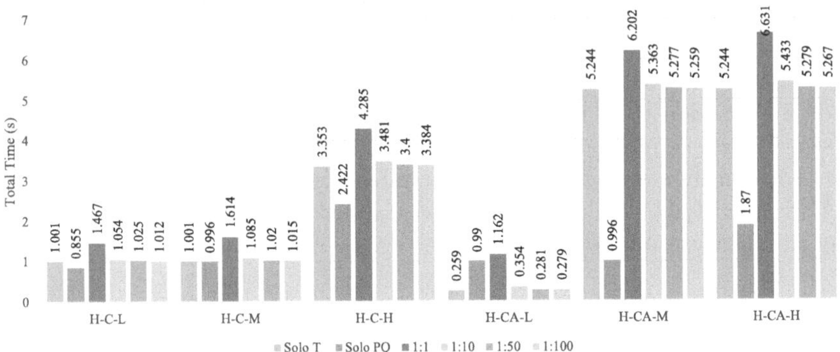

Fig. 5. Total time comparison of APQ for Confidentiality-Only and Confidentiality+Authenticity at various security levels (Low, Medium, and High) across 500-epochs. Full:Partial key update ratios shown at variants of 1:1, 1:10, 1:50, and 1:100. Solo T and Solo PQ refer to individual components of the APQ mode and security level (see Table 1) that are ran in a non-combined configuration (e.g. the sky blue bar in H-C-L refers to T-EC-AES-L but the sky blue bar in H-CA-L refers to T-Ed-AES-L). Calculations are based on an average of ten 500-epoch samples. (Color figure online)

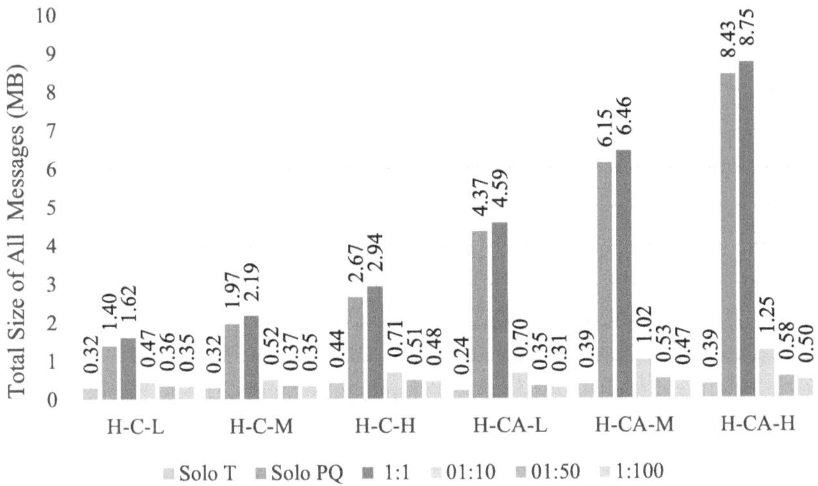

Fig. 6. Total message size of all APQ messages for Confidentiality-Only and Confidentiality+Authenticity at various security levels (Low, Medium, and High), totaled across 500 epochs. Full:Partial key update ratios shown at variants of 1:1, 1:10, 1:50, and 1:100. Solo T and Solo PQ refer to individual components of APQ that are ran in a non-combined configuration.

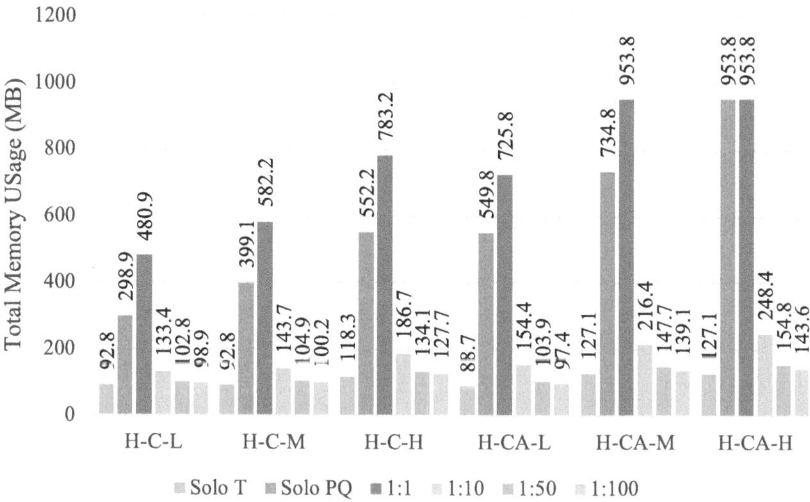

Fig. 7. Total memory (RAM) comparison of APQ for Confidentiality-Only and Confidentiality+Authenticity at various security levels (Low, Medium, and High), totaled across 500 epochs. Full:Partial key update ratios shown at variants of 1:1, 1:10, 1:50, and 1:100. Solo T and Solo PQ refer to individual components of APQ that are ran in a non-combined configuration.

The peak RAM usage for Solo T, Solo PQ, and APQ combined MLS sessions, across the full 500-epoch test, are shown in Table 2. Results indicate consistent peak memory usage across all individual traditional ciphersuites. For the PQ sessions, peak memory usage generally increased with security level. This carries over to the amortized sessions, where results start high for the 1:1 Full:Partial update ratio but trend down toward their Solo PQ component peak memory measurements at lower ratios.

Table 2. Peak Memory (RAM) usage across the 500 epoch test for solo traditional, solo PQ, and APQ for PQ Confidentiality-Only and PQ Confidentiality+Authenticity at various security levels (Low, Medium, and High). Full:Partial key update ratios shown at variants of 1:1, 1:10, 1:50, and 1:100.

Solo Traditional		Solo PQ		Combined (H-C/H-CA)				
Ciphersuite	Peak Mem (MB)	Ciphersuite	Peak Mem (MB)	Ciphersuite	Peak Mem (MB)			
					1:1	1:10	1:50	1:100
T-Ed-AES-L	1.2	PQ-C-L	1.3	H-C-L	1.9	1.3	1.3	1.3
T-Ed-AES-H	1.2	PQ-C-M	1.3	H-C-M	1.9	1.4	1.4	1.4
T-EC-AES-L	1.2	PQ-C-H	1.4	H-C-H	2.1	1.4	1.4	1.4
T-EC-AES-H	1.2	PQ-CA-L	1.5	H-CA-L	2.0	1.5	1.5	1.5
T-Ed-Cha-L	1.2	PQ-CA-M	1.6	H-CA-M	2.5	1.6	1.6	1.6
		PQ-CA-H	1.8	H-CA-H	2.6	1.8	1.8	1.8

4.3 Hybrid Combiners Comparison

In a head-on comparison between X-Wing and H-C-X (see **purple** and teal bars in Fig. 8), which both offer PQ Confidentiality only, the APQ amortization quickly outpaces X-Wing which must call on ML-KEM768 operations for every commit (e.g. a 1:1 ratio using our terminology). As seen in Fig. 8, at Full to Partial Update ratios smaller than 1:2, the APQ speed-ups exhibited over X-Wing range from 26% improvement at a 1:5 ratio to upwards of 50% (diminishing) speed-ups after further reductions past 1:50. Both message size and total memory metrics follow a similar trend as shown in Figs. 9 and 10, respectively.

When X-Wing run-time is compared with H-CA-X APQ variant (see **purple** and **dark-orange** bars in Fig. 8), which has additional PQ-Authenticity with use of ML-DSA65, APQ is slower to outpace X-Wing. The eclipse in run-time performance over X-Wing occurs at 1:5 Full:Partial commit ratio for H-CA-X instead of the 1:2 ratio for H-C-X. This is notable as the APQ combiner at 1:5 outperforms X-Wing even with PQ authenticity included, which X-Wing does not provide. The run-time floor of H-CA-X is, as expected, approaching the solo run-time of T-Ed-Cha (see Fig. 2), which provides the approximate floor for amortization.

As shown in Figs. 9 and 10, APQ becomes drastically more efficient than X-Wing in terms of message size and compute cost (total RAM usage) starting at Full:Partial commit ratios of 1:2 for H-C-X and at 1:5 for H-CA-X. The latter point is particularly significant. These results show that not only can APQ use the same ciphersuite security level as hybrids such as X-Wing (albeit with larger windows between PQ updates) for less 'bytes on the wire' and lower compute

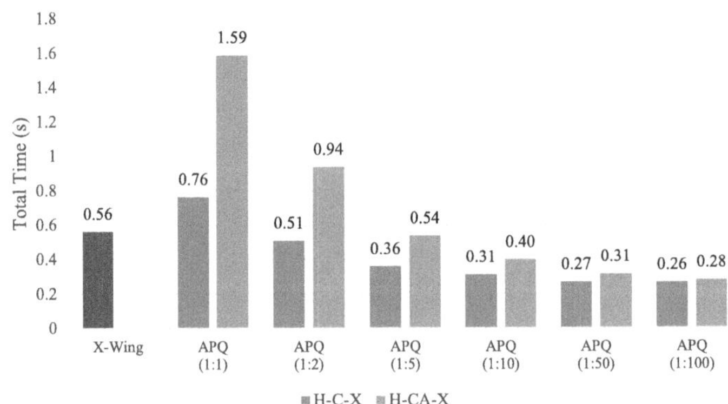

Fig. 8. Total execution time comparison of Confidentiality-Only APQ vs X-Wing, at similar security levels, across 500 epochs. Full:Partial key update ratios shown at variants of 1:1, 1:10, 1:2, 1:5, 1:50, and 1:100. Calculations are based on an average of ten 500-epoch samples. (Color figure online)

costs, but it can also provide support PQ-authenticity under such performance advantages. In fact, the message size and memory costs decrease exponentially toward a floor limit imposed by the classical ciphersuite component performance in each metric.

Although the amortization metrics shown in Figs. 9 and 10 with performance advantages over X-Wing style hybrids use larger windows between PQ commits, they maintains an identical traditional key update frequency. In practice, this provides for a great deal of flexibility for system developers and owners, especially as the needed frequency of quantum resistant key rotation may not be the same as for traditional in all cases. For resource constrained settings, this notably provides options for achieving quantum resistance which can still be tailored according to device constraints.

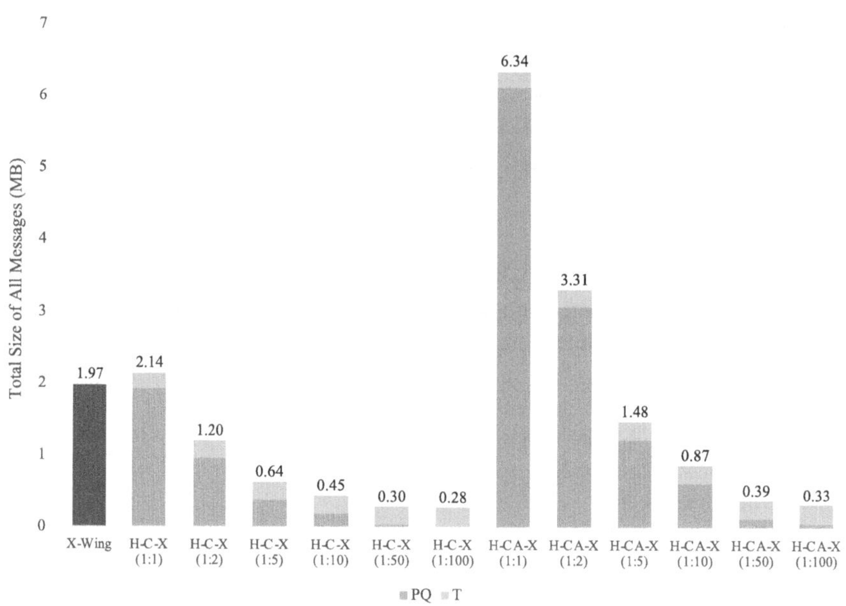

Fig. 9. Total size of all APQ messages for Confidentiality-Only and Confidentiality+Authenticity APQ vs X-Wing, at similar security levels, across 500 epochs. Full:Partial key update ratios shown at variants of 1:1, 1:2, 1:5, 1:10, 1:50, and 1:100, totaled across 500 epochs. Component contributions (stacked) are shown in pink for PQ messages and blue for traditional messages. (Color figure online)

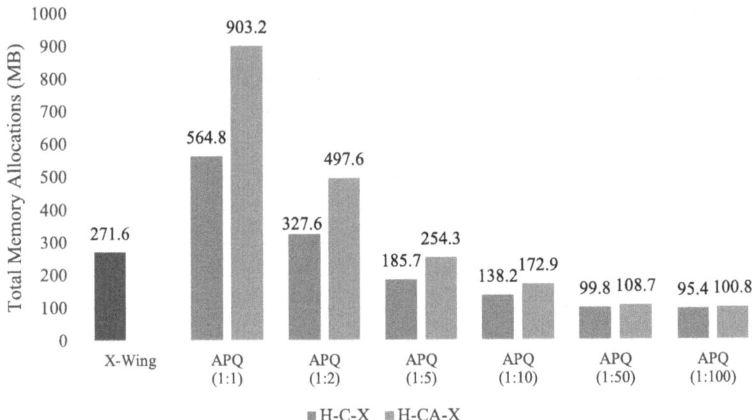

Fig. 10. Total memory (RAM) comparison of Confidentiality-Only APQ vs X-Wing, at similar security levels, totaled across 500 epochs. Full:Partial key update ratios shown at variants of 1:1, 1:2, 1:5, 1:10, 1:50, and 1:100.

5 Conclusion

Our comprehensive benchmark evaluation of the APQ combiner demonstrates the effects of ciphersuite and amortization ratio selection on the protocol performance across time, bandwidth, and memory usage, including significant performance enhancements. Notably our results show that hybrid protocol combiner approaches for overhead amortization can, if strategically defined, substantially outperform simple PQ and hybrid KEM approaches alike. Moreover, this work points a way forward for achieving both PQ confidentiality and authenticity in resource limited use cases.

A Summary Data Tables

We provide additional summary tables corresponding to our graphs here.

Table 3. Average per-epoch commit message size (in bytes) across 500 epochs. This is the averaged number of bytes per epoch specifically for commit messages.

Ciphersuite	Avg Commit Size (B)
T-Ed-AES-L	484
T-EC-AES-L	634
T-Ed-Cha-L	484
T-Ed-AES-H	780
T-EC-AES-H	875
PQ-C-X	3,847
PQ-C-L	2,807
PQ-C-M	3,944
PQ-C-H	5,338
PQ-CA-L	8,752
PQ-CA-M	12,307
PQ-CA-H	16,883
X-wing	3,943

Table 4. Average per-epoch commit message size (in bytes) for all APQ PQ and T ciphersuite combinations across 500 epochs. This is the averaged number of bytes per epoch specifically for commit messages.

Ciphersuite Pair	Avg PQ Commit Size (B)						Avg T Commit Size (B)					
	1:1	1:2	1:5	1:10	1:50	1:100	1:1	1:2	1:5	1:10	1:50	1:100
PQ Confidentiality Only												
H-C-L	2,809	2,809	2,808	2,809	2,808	2,808	220	444	579	624	660	664
H-C-M	3,945	3,946	3,946	3,946	3,946	3,946	220	444	579	624	660	664
H-C-H	5,340	5,339	5,340	5,340	5,339	5,341	284	596	784	847	897	903
H-C-X	3,849	3,849	3,849	3,849	3,849	3,849	213	366	458	488	513	516
PQ Confidentiality + Authentication												
H-CA-L	8,754	8,754	8,754	8,754	8,754	8,754	213	366	458	488	513	516
H-CA-M	12,309	12,309	12,309	12,309	12,309	12,309	330	572	718	766	805	810
H-CA-H	16,885	16,885	16,885	16,885	16,885	16,885	330	572	718	766	805	810
H-CA-X	12,260	12,260	12,260	12,260	12,260	12,260	213	366	458	488	513	516

Table 5. Performance metrics by ciphersuite, totaled across 500 epochs. Data summary from Figs. 2 to 10.

Ciphersuite	Time (s)	RAM Allocations (MB)	Message Size (B)
T			
T-Ed-AES-L	0.259	88.7	241,894
T-EC-AES-L	1.001	92.8	316,789
T-Ed-Cha-L	0.258	88.9	241,894
T-Ed-AES-H	5.244	92.8	389,870
T-EC-AES-H	3.353	118.3	437,216
PQ Confidentiality Only			
PQ-C-X	0.567	388.4	1,921,088
PQ-C-L	0.855	298.9	1,401,817
PQ-C-M	0.996	399.1	1,969,631
PQ-C-H	2.422	552.2	2,665,805
PQ Confidentiality + Authentication			
PQ-CA-L	0.990	549.8	4,370,719
PQ-CA-M	1.434	734.8	6,145,969
PQ-CA-H	1.870	953.8	8,431,293
Hybrid and APQ Combiner			
X-wing	0.563	271.6	1,969,024
H-C-X (1:1)	0.764	564.8	2,135,464
H-C-X (1:2)	0.510	327.6	1,200,989
H-C-X (1:5)	0.359	185.7	637,739
H-C-X (1:10)	0.310	138.2	449,989
H-C-X (1:50)	0.267	99.8	299,789
H-C-X (1:100)	0.263	95.4	281,014
H-CA-X (1:1)	1.588	903.2	6,335,798
H-CA-X (1:2)	0.936	497.6	3,306,984
H-CA-X (1:5)	0.538	254.3	1,482,084
H-CA-X (1:10)	0.399	172.9	873,784
H-CA-X (1:50)	0.313	108.7	387,144
H-CA-X (1:100)	0.279	100.8	326,314

References

1. Alnahawi, N., Müller, J., Oupický, J., Wiesmaier, A.: A comprehensive survey on post-quantum TLS. IACR Communications in Cryptology **1**(2) (2024). https://doi.org/10.62056/ahee0iuc

2. Alwen, J., Coretti, S., Dodis, Y., Tselekounis, Y.: Security analysis and improvements for the IETF MLS standard for group messaging. In: Advances in Cryptology – CRYPTO 2020, pp. 248–277. Springer-Verlag (2020). https://doi.org/10.1007/978-3-030-56784-2_9
3. Banerjee, A., Reddy.K, T., Schoinianakis, D., Hollebeek, T., Ounsworth, M.: Post-quantum cryptography for engineers. Internet-Draft draft-IETF-PQUIP-PQC-engineers-14, Internet engineering task force (2025). https://datatracker.ietf.org/doc/draft-ietf-pquip-pqc-engineers/14/
4. Barbosa, M., et al.: X-wing: the hybrid KEM you've been looking for. Cryptology ePrint Archive, Paper 2024/039 (2024). https://doi.org/10.62056/a3qj89n4e, https://eprint.iacr.org/2024/039
5. Barnes, R., Beurdouche, B., Robert, R., Millican, J., Omara, E., Cohn-Gordon, K.: The Messaging Layer Security (MLS) protocol. RFC 9420 (2023). https://doi.org/10.17487/RFC9420, https://www.rfc-editor.org/info/rfc9420
6. Beullens, W.: Breaking rainbow takes a weekend on a laptop. In: Advances in Cryptology – CRYPTO 2022, pp. 464–479. Springer-Verlag (2022). https://doi.org/10.1007/978-3-031-15979-4_16
7. Brendel, J., Cremers, C., Jackson, D., Zhao, M.: The provable security of ed25519: theory and practice. Cryptology ePrint Archive, Paper 2020/823 (2020). https://eprint.iacr.org/2020/823
8. Castryck, W., Decru, T.: An efficient key recovery attack on SIDH. In: Advances in Cryptology – EUROCRYPT 2023, pp. 423–447. Springer-Verlag (2023). https://doi.org/10.1007/978-3-031-30589-4_15
9. Cohn-Gordon, K., Beurdouche, B., Robert, R.: MLS implementations (2024). https://github.com/mlswg/mls-implementations
10. Cohn-Gordon, K., Cremers, C., Dowling, B., Garratt, L., Stebila, D.: A formal security analysis of the signal messaging protocol. J. Cryptol. **33**, 1914–1983 (2020)
11. Computer Security Division, I.T.L.: Post-quantum cryptography FIPS approved | CSRC (2024). https://csrc.nist.gov/News/2024/postquantum-cryptography-fips-approved
12. Connolly, D., Schwabe, P., Westerbaan, B.: X-wing: general-purpose hybrid post-quantum KEM. Internet-Draft draft-connolly-CFRG-XWING-KEM-09, Internet engineering task force (2025). https://datatracker.ietf.org/doc/draft-connolly-cfrg-xwing-kem/09/
13. Greene, N., Hale, B.: Making post quantum key exchange efficient: An implementation with the MLS protocol. Cryptology ePrint Archive, Paper 2025/1881 (2025). https://eprint.iacr.org/2025/1881
14. Heisler, B.: BHEISLER/CRITERON. https://github.com/bheisler/criterion.rs
15. Kohbrok, K.: PHNX-IM/HPQMLS. https://github.com/phnx-im/hpqmls
16. Mahy, R.: Messaging layer security ciphersuite using XWing key exchange mechanism. Internet Draft draft-MAHY-MLS-XWING-00, Internet engineering task force (2024). https://datatracker.ietf.org/doc/draft-mahy-mls-xwing/00/
17. Mahy, R., Barnes, R.: ML-KEM and hybrid cipher suites for messaging layer security. Internet-Draft draft-IETF-MLS-PQ-ciphersuites-00, Internet engineering task force (2025). https://datatracker.ietf.org/doc/draft-ietf-mls-pq-ciphersuites/00/
18. Paquin, C., Stebila, D., Tamvada, G.: Benchmarking post-quantum cryptography in TLS. In: International Conference on Post-Quantum Cryptography, pp. 72–91. Springer (2020). https://doi.org/10.1007/978-3-030-44223-1_5
19. R&D, P., Cryspen: OpenMLS Book. https://book.openmls.tech/

20. Reddy.K, T., Wing, D., S, B., Kwiatkowski, K.: Adapting constrained devices for post-quantum cryptography. Internet-Draft draft-IETF-PQUIP-PQC-HSM-constrained-01, Internet Engineering Task Force (2025). https://datatracker.ietf.org/doc/draft-ietf-pquip-pqc-hsm-constrained/01/
21. Sikeridis, D., Kampanakis, P., Devetsikiotis, M.: Post-quantum authentication in TLS 1.3: a performance study. In: Network and Distributed Systems Security (NDSS) Symposium 2020 (2020). https://doi.org/10.14722/ndss.2020.24203
22. Stebila, D., Fluhrer, S., Gueron, S.: Hybrid key exchange in TLS 1.3. Internet-Draft draft-IETF-TLS-hybrid-design-16, Internet Engineering Task Force (2025). https://datatracker.ietf.org/doc/draft-ietf-tls-hybrid-design/16/
23. Tian, X., Hale, B., Mularczyk, M., Joël: Amortized PQ MLS combiner. Internet-Draft draft-IETF-MLS-combiner-02, Internet Engineering Task Force (2025). https://datatracker.ietf.org/doc/draft-ietf-mls-combiner/02/, work in Progress
24. Urbanek, P.: PAWURB/HOTPATH. https://github.com/pawurb/hotpath
25. Westerbaan, B., Valenta, L.: A look at the latest post-quantum signature standardization candidates. https://blog.cloudflare.com/another-look-at-pq-signatures/ (2024)

QUIC-MLS: Making a Space Security Draft Standard Resilient for Disconnected Environments

Benjamin Dowling[1], Britta Hale[2], Xisen Tian[2], and Bhagya Wimalasiri[1](✉)

[1] King's College London, London, UK
{benjamin.dowling,bhagya.wimalasiri}@kcl.ac.uk
[2] Naval Postgraduate School, Monterey, USA
{britta.hale,xisen.tian1}@nps.edu

Abstract. Among standardization efforts for space and interplanetary network security, the Internet Engineering Task Force (IETF) is driving work on space network security, accounting for the unique properties of space environments that make space communication challenging. This includes long, variable-length delays, packet loss, and intermittent end-to-end connectivity. Within these efforts, there is a focus on using IP-based protocols for security, and in particular the use of the QUIC protocol. This is unsurprising given QUIC's growing popularity and offer of optimization intended for reducing latency. However, QUIC uses the Transport Layer Security (TLS) key exchange handshake protocol, which was originally designed for 'connect and forget' style Internet connections at scale. It is also session-based, where protocol participants require reestablishment of the session for each reconnection – a costly maneuver in the space setting. Furthermore, TLS by default does not achieve strong post-compromise security properties within sessions, exhibiting a risk under long-lived connections, and need for synchronous handshakes to counteract this are in functional contrast to the space environment, which has intermittent end-to-end connectivity.

We address both drawbacks of QUIC by introducing QUIC-MLS: a variant of QUIC which replaces the session-based, synchronous TLS handshake with the standardized continuous key agreement protocol, Messaging Layer Security (MLS), which achieves asynchronous forward secrecy and post-compromise security. In addition to the design itself, we implement our design and provide benchmarks, and analyze our new construction in a formal cryptographic model.

1 Introduction

Space may be a vacuum, but humans are helping fill it up. According to the United Nations Office for Outer Space Affairs [1], humans have sent more than 2,500 objects into space in 2024, a trend that continues to increase. Since many of these objects are unmanned, they require communication protocols to enable control systems on Earth to make mission-critical adjustments.

H. C. Pöhls and C. J. Mitchell (Eds.): SSR 2025, LNCS 16466, pp. 111–132, 2026.
https://doi.org/10.1007/978-3-032-19567-8_6

However, secure communication protocols used in the terrestrial setting are not generally appropriate as-is for use in space. One can see this in the Internet Engineering Task Force (IETF) where the Taking IP to Other Planets (TIPTOP) working group has been outlining characteristics and use case requirements for space, that deployed protocols must address, including challenges such as "variable delays", "frequent and long interruptions of communications" and "one-way/unidirectional links". Within the same working group, the first and primary focus for deployable secure IP-based protocols for space networking is the QUIC protocol [2,3].

The internet-wide adoption of the QUIC protocol is contributing to its use IP-based space communications [4–6], delay tolerant networks [7], and vehicular adhoc mobile networks [8]. In internet usage, generic QUIC traffic held the #3 spot for total volume and accounted for 6–8% of global internet traffic in 2023 [9]. An arguable driver in the use of QUIC over more traditional protocols such as TLS 1.3 is the efficiency gains and latency reductions from its integrated approach across network layers. While Transport Layer Security (TLS) version 1.3 must be combined with some transport protocol, and therefore is not optimized for combination with any particular one, QUIC has the benefit of optimized integration of transport and security protocol aspects. Multiplexing capabilities are another benefit of the QUIC protocol. However, QUIC has some characteristics that make it difficult to support a deepspace use-case.

QUIC inherited the legacy key establishment characteristics of its predecessor, TLS 1.3, specifically for key exchange (KEX). QUIC uses the TLS 1.3 KEX, which incurs at least one full round trip (RTT) even with the QUIC optimizations [3]. The 0-RTT TLS mode could intuitively be considered as a solution to this inefficiency, but has known weaknesses [10,11]. This leads to a tension between security and the QUIC goals of reducing latency. Within terrestrial uses these issues are not prominent, but within space settings, where transmission delays can take minutes or even hours, the both latency and security risks become more prominent. We highlight that the core functionality of the TLS 1.3 KEX is negatively impacted by the challenges of the deepspace setting. A 1 round trip time (RTT) synchronous handshake requires bidirectional, synchronous communication in order to achieve forward secrecy.

However, a fundamental review of the core challenges reveals a path forward. The TLS 1.3 KEX is a session-based key agreement mechanism, meaning that parties are not assumed to maintain state between sessions. This is an artifact of TLS's original design for use on the Internet, where tens of thousands of new and changing connections make it undesirable to maintain state between instances of client connections. In contrast, in uses such as space settings, where the set of communication parties is usually small and can even be static, state can be maintained between communications. This obviates the need for the original session-based design and opens the aperture for lower latency together with improved security through use of continuous session protocols. Moreover, given that the use of TLS KEX within QUIC is itself a selected handshake option, a such more appropriate handshake alternative could likewise replace it.

Continuous session protocols, a.k.a. continuous key agreement or ratcheted protocols, are stateful protocols that enable key rotation on demand, perhaps according to a schedule, which removes the need for session handshakes at the start of every connection and therefore reduces RTT. This does not necessarily come at the cost of security; in fact, continuous session protocols have been shown to achieve properties that were unattainable under traditional TLS [12]. Normal TLS sessions provide forward secrecy (FS), where *past* communications remain secure if the current session is compromised. In contrast, a continuous session protocol can achieve both FS and post-compromise security (PCS), thus "self-healing" and locking out adversarial access *after* a key compromise [13].

TLS and QUIC have slowly been moving towards a continuous setting, namely with additions for session resumption. Yet these session-based protocols have never been analyzed as continuous session protocols nor fundamentally designed for those goals, and even recent work on session resumption is still synchronous in nature, contrary to the functional needs of space communications. Thus, in this work we show how to leverage another standardized, yet continuous key agreement protocol, Messaging Layer Security (MLS) [14], as an alternative KEX within QUIC in order to create a continuous session protocol QUIC variant. This reduces the latency and security issues of QUIC within space that were previously noted [10,11], supports PCS, and still maintains the networking functionality optimizations of QUIC. Furthermore, it opens up potential for moving uses of QUIC beyond the client-server setting [4,8]. As an added benefit, since MLS was designed for scalable asynchronous group key agreement [14], our solution introduces options beyond pairwise QUIC, namely reducing the overhead of key updates in QUIC for larger multi-device configurations, bringing it down from $\mathcal{O}\left(n^2\right)$ to $\mathcal{O}\left(n \cdot log(n)\right)$ for groups of size n [15]. This benefit is optional, as even 1-to-1 (group size of 2) settings obtain the other benefits of the construction.

In this work we provide a cryptographic design for using the MLS KEX with QUIC, a security model and computational analysis of QUIC-MLS, and benchmark testing of the solution. For generality we model and analyze for the more complex multi-party case, where group key agreement resulting in a shared secure QUIC data channel. This is fully extensible to the 1-to-1 communication scenario where QUIC-MLS is used in a typical pair-wise case, e.g., client-to-server or client-to-client. Our QUIC-MLS variant turns QUIC from a stateless session based protocol to a stateful continuous protocol opening doors for wider adoptions beyond the traditional web applications, and is suitable for the challenges highlighted by the IETF.

2 Preliminaries

Here we describe the abstract models used to capture key establishment methods such as TLS, QUIC, and MLS.

2.1 Secure Channel Establishment

Session-based key establishment and continuous key agreement (CKA) represent two distinct paradigms for establishing a secure channel. Session-based key exchange protocols like TLS or Internet Key Exchange (IKE) execute so-called handshakes to negotiate cryptographic parameters and perform cryptographic operations to derive an ephemeral session key used between two parties that wish to securely communicate. In particular, handshakes are executed independently, with certificates transmitted at each establishment to authenticate the new connection. This approach is used for one-to-one sessions that are short-lived and benefit from statelessness between sessions.

In contrast, CKA protocols, such as the Signal protocol, have often been used as the cryptographic core of secure messaging: they establish a shared cryptographic state between communicating parties and allow for new keys to be generated and updated incrementally and asynchronously (i.e. *without* additional handshakes upon re-connection). This allows for asynchronous key updates, granular control over key lifetime between refresh and update, and recovery from adversarial state compromise. For systems that can afford to manage and store cryptographic states, CKA protocols offer additional security guarantees—such as post-compromise security—compared to their session-based counterparts. CKAs are extended to the multi-user setting as Continuous Group Key Agreement (CGKA), enabling groups of users to establish a series of shared keys consistently. The TreeKEM sub-protocol of the MLS protocol [14] is a prime example of a deployed CGKA. Here we provide the formal definition of a CGKA.

Definition 1 (CGKA from [16]). *A continuous group key-agreement (CGKA) scheme* $\mathsf{CGKA} = (\mathsf{KGen}, \mathsf{Create}, \mathsf{Add}, \mathsf{Join}, \mathsf{Upd}, \mathsf{Rem}, \mathsf{Commit}, \mathsf{Process}, \mathsf{Key})$ *consists of the following algorithms:*

- ***Key Generation:*** $(\mathrm{pk}, \mathrm{sk}) \leftarrow \mathsf{KGen}()$ *samples a fresh public/secret key pair.*
- ***Group creation:*** $\gamma \leftarrow \mathsf{Create}()$ *takes no input and returns a fresh group state* γ *containing only the party running the algorithm. This represents the first* epoch *of a new session.*
- ***Add:*** $(\gamma', \mathrm{p}) \leftarrow \mathsf{Add}(\gamma, \mathsf{id}_t, \mathrm{pk}_t)$ *proposes adding a new member to the group. On input a protocol state* γ*, identity of the new member* id_t *and their public key (generated by* KGen*), it outputs an updated state* γ' *and an* add proposal message p.
- ***Remove:*** $(\gamma', \mathrm{p}) \leftarrow \mathsf{Rem}(\gamma, \mathsf{id}_t)$ *proposes removing a member from the group. On input a protocol state* γ *and identity* id_t*, it outputs an updated state* γ' *and* remove proposal message p.
- ***Update:*** $(\gamma', \mathrm{p}) \leftarrow \mathsf{Upd}(\gamma)$ *proposes updating the member's key material. It outputs an updated state* γ' *and an* update proposal message p.
- ***Commit:*** $(\gamma', \mathrm{commit}, \mathrm{welc}) \leftarrow \mathsf{Commit}(\gamma, \overrightarrow{\mathrm{p}})$ *applies (aka* commits*) a vector of proposals to a group. The output consists of an updated protocol state* γ', commit message *and a (potentially empty)* welcome message *(depending on if any add proposal messages were included in* $\overrightarrow{\mathrm{p}}$*).*
- ***Join:*** $(\gamma', \overrightarrow{\mathsf{G}}, \mathsf{id}_i) \leftarrow \mathsf{Join}(\mathrm{sk}, \mathrm{welc})$ *allows a party with secret key* sk *(generated by* KGen*) to join a group with a welcome message* welc*. The outputs are: an updated protocol state* γ'*, a group* roster $\overrightarrow{\mathsf{G}}$ *(i.e. a set of IDs listing the group members), an epoch ID, and the ID of the inviter (i.e. the party that created the welcome message).*

- ***Process:*** $(\gamma', \text{info}) \leftarrow \mathsf{Process}(\gamma, \text{commit}, \overrightarrow{\text{p}})$ *processes an incoming commit message and the corresponding proposals to output a* commit info message info *and an updated group state* γ' *which represents a new epoch in the ongoing CGKA session. The commit info message captures the semantics of the processed commit and has the form:* info $= (\mathsf{id}, (\text{propSem}_1, \ldots, \text{propSem}_z))$ *where* id *is the ID of the sender of the commit message the* propSem*vector conveys the semantics of the committed add and remove via triples of the form* propSem $= (\mathsf{id}_s, \mathsf{op}, \mathsf{id}_t)$. *Here,* id_s *denotes the identity of the proposal's sender* $\mathsf{op} \in \{\text{"addP"}, \text{"remP"}\}$ *is the proposal's type and* id_t *is the identity of the proposal's target (i.e. the party being added or removed).*
- ***Get Group Key:*** $(\gamma', K) \leftarrow \mathsf{Key}(\gamma)$ *outputs the current group key for use by a higher-level application and deletes it from the state*

We next cover the TLS, QUIC, and MLS standards of the of the IETF, and how their components fit together.

2.2 Transport Layer Security

As a session based protocol, main goal of TLS [17] has always been to establish a secure communications channel across an untrusted network (the Internet). In what began with Secure Socket Layer (SSL) protocol created by Netscape, the TLS protocol has been upgraded multiple times by the IETF, resulting in the current iteration of TLS 1.3 (hereto simply referred as TLS) [17]. TLS itself is comprised of sub-protocols: the handshake protocol which establishes keys (TLS-HS), the record layer protocol (TLS-RL) which uses those keys to provide a secure channel for data transmission using authenticated encryption with associated data (AEAD) and an alert protocol. TLS supports session resumption using an established secret for faster establishment of future sessions with the same client (e.g. 0RTT).

2.3 QUIC

QUIC was first developed by Google in 2012 and later adopted and refined as an internet standard by the IETF [3]. Because QUIC uses TLS-HS for security key establishment [18], its evolution has been tied to TLS's evolution. For analysis purposes, we will also use a similar break down in reference to QUIC, namely as having a handshake component (QUIC-HS $\approx$ TLS-HS) for key agreement and a record layer (QUIC-RL) component. Unlike TLS, once a session key is established in QUIC (i.e., after QUIC-HS), it can be updated using a key-phase bit which is flipped between parties to indicate the use of a new key from a key derivation function (KDF) applied to the old key. This is a symmetric key ratchet, and should not be interpreted as introducing new randomness or achieving PCS. Furthermore, QUIC offers a 0-RTT connection mode for previously connected clients through relying on a server-signed configuration file stored and presented by the client; this is based on the TLS 0-RTT mode.

2.4 Messaging Layer Security (MLS) Protocol

The MLS (RFC 9420) [14] standard was designed for end-to-end encryption, providing users with secure and scalable communications. Similarly to QUIC, MLS can be broken down into key exchange and security channel/*record layer* phases; however, as it was originally intended for application messages, the *record layer* phase is at the application layer. Notably, as with TLS and QUIC, the networking layer use of the overall protocol is determined by the *record layer* protocol definition—the key exchange portion of MLS is not tied to a particular networking layer use. This allows us to modularly change the QUIC-HS from TLS-HS to MLS, as shown in Fig. 1.

Instead of session-based handshake negotiation for key exchange, MLS and similar CKAs establish the cryptographic session state once and then update keys as needed or as scheduled (potentially asynchronously) without additional round-trip negotiations. Such key updates are also what enables PCS. MLS allows for a notable differentiation from prior pair-wise CKA protocols in that it supports *groups*, meaning that not only is it a CKA, but a *continuous group key agreement* (CGKA). Group members can efficiently perform the CGKA with entity authentication and key indistinguishability security guarantees [19]. Group members/clients can also be added or removed, enabling adaption.

3 Related Works

MLS has undergone extensive computational analysis as a CGKA [16,20] resulting in major changes to the protocol by the IETF. Similarly, symbolic analysis (in the Dolev-Yao model) has been used to analyze MLS [21]; such symbolic analysis abstracts cryptographic primitives as "black boxes". In this work, we use the computational analysis approach to analyze and prove security QUIC-MLS, leveraging existing models from work on CGKAs.

Work on CKAs include analyses on the Signal protocol. While there is extensive work in this domain [22–26], we opt to use MLS as it is already standardized. This fits with the overall theme of shifting out one standardized key establishment (TLS-HS) with another (MLS) within the QUIC protocol.

Other related works include analyses of QUIC, especially the work done on record layer analysis [27,28] and TLS vs. QUIC [29]. As noted before, prior work has raised concerns on use of the TLS 0-RTT option [10,30].

4 Protocol Design and Mechanics

In this section we provide a high level overview of how MLS can be incorporated into QUIC in terms of requirements analysis and protocol construction. QUIC combines key agreement and secure channel management into one protocol: for analysis purposes we break these out as Handshake (QUIC-HS) and Record Layer (QUIC-RL) responsibilities, respectively, to reflect the TLS 1.3 components that they are derived from (i.e. TLS Handshake and Record Layers). Low level details such as wire formatting are out of scope for this work.

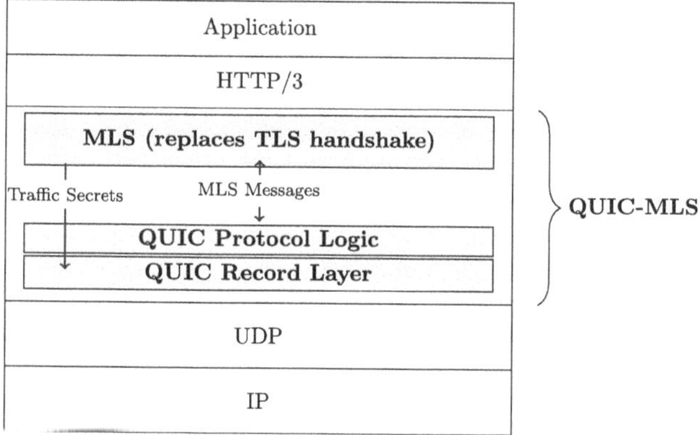

Fig. 1. High level overview of QUIC-MLS, showing slot-in replacement of TLS-HS with MLS.

4.1 General Requirements

QUIC has three general requirements of its handshake component: 1) authenticated key exchange, 2) transport parameter authentication, and 3) authenticated application protocol negotiation [3]. MLS can be used as a drop-in replacement for TLS from the perspective of QUIC-RL, as MLS meets the minimal requirements to be an authenticated key agreement protocol. With minimal additions to the MLS `GroupInfo` to specify transport parameters and application protocols the other requirements are met with MLS as well (see Sect. 4.4).

In satisfying the QUIC requirements, MLS has remaining requirements of its own to function properly. Specifically, to facilitate client communication, MLS relies on two abstract services: an Authentication Service (AS) and a Delivery Service (DS). The AS, as previously mentioned, attests to the bindings of identifier to public key material which can be adapted from existing PKI network services. For our analysis purposes, we assume that the AS functions as it currently does through existing PKI as used by TLS. The DS receives and distributes messages between group members and ensures the ordered delivery of MLS handshake messages [31]. A *strongly consistent* DS ensures messages arrive in order and that all members agree on that order. In web applications, for example, a strongly consistent DS can be enforced through reliable and order enforcing transport protocols or via a centralized server. An *eventually consistent* DS only guarantees that messages arrive (eventually) to all members but makes no guarantees on their ordering, leaving clients responsible for reconciliation. An eventually consistent DS is endemic to decentralized, peer-to-peer, or hop-by-hop networks.

While a protocol designed for an eventually consistent DS can be streamlined for an strongly consistent DS, the reverse is not true. Thus, we design QUIC-MLS for an eventually consistent DS with tunable parameters to fit the reality of the underlying network up to a strongly consistent DS. To provide a clear mechanism to ensure deterministic handling of group state updates and avoid race conditions arising from concurrent update proposals, we propose introducing a designated group administrator responsible for all membership changes which may change in a fixed order (e.g. based on the sequence in which members joined the group) from epoch to epoch. This is consistent with the notion of epoch leaders in previous work [42] except that only the administrator may initiate add or remove proposals; any such proposals from other group members will be ignored. Additionally, to ensure all members can synchronize group state, a "commit transcript" of a tunable length is appended to all messages sent. In the worst case of an eventually consistent DS, this may contain all previous commits since the start of the session. The length can be parameterised to the reliability of the network; with a strongly consistent DS, the length is zero.

4.2 Construction Overview

Our QUIC-MLS construction, detailed in Fig. 2, is composed of KGen, Init, Enc, and Dec. KGen is used to generate public keys, simply by calling CGKA.KGen. In Init, a group admin instantiates the group session (using the intended partner's public keys) using the CGKA algorithms Create, Add and Commit. All welcome messages generated by Init are sent to recipients via QUIC-RL who call Init as a participant ($\rho = \mathsf{p}$) upon receipt to join the group (via CGKA.Join).

Enc enables payload encryption via QUIC 0RTT, and generation of group control proposals (e.g. Add, Rem, Upd). Similarly, Dec decrypts payload messages and processes proposals and commits. To ensure reliability, ciphertexts contain "a commit transcript" ast with a tunable length tl to reconcile group state synchronization. In an asynchronous scenario with a two-party group and strongly consistent DS the tl can be set to 1 when assuming parties are never more than 1 epoch apart. If Dec updates the session's group state, they derive a new key (via CGKA.Key) for payload encryption via QUIC 0RTT.

4.3 Limitations

While our approach is intended as a clean substitution of TLS in QUIC, it introduces a limitation on non-repudiation due to the nature of group communications versus two-party communications. QUIC does not sign messages because non-repudiation is implicit in the channel among two parties who have completed authenticated key exchange. In a group channel, however, insiders can impersonate one-another if messages are not signed with the sender's private key. To avoid this, group channel messages for QUIC-MLS can also be signed using public and private keys of clients used for MLS. However, this composition requires further analysis as we must then also consider allowing adversary access to a signing and verification oracle within the context of the CGKA security model. We leave this for future work and assign handling non-repudiation of insiders to the application layer.

4.4 Changes to Respective Protocol Standards

We make no changes to the underlying cryptographic components of MLS or QUIC-RL as standardized. However, we change the semantics of some QUIC

KGen()
```
(pk, sk) ← CGKA.KGen()
return (pk, sk)
```

Init(ρ, sk, $\overrightarrow{PK}$, welc) → st
```
st ← ϵ
if ρ = a then
    γ ← CGKA.Create()
    for j ∈ [PK⃗] do
        CGKA.Add(γ, id_j, pk_j) → (γ, p_j)
        CGKA.Commit(γ, p_j) → (γ, commit_j, welc_j)
        st.ast ← (p_j, commit_j, welc_j)
        st.eid ← γ.eid
        st.mid_st.eid ← 0
        st.γ ← γ
return st
if ρ = p then
    CGKA.Join(sk, welc) → (γ, G⃗, id)
    st.γ ← γ
return st
```

Enc(st, ctrl, m) → (st, ctxt, eid, mid)
```
req st.γ ≠ ⊥
(m′, id, pk) ← m
if ctrl ≠ ⊥ then
    if ctrl = add then
        CGKA.Add(st.γ, id, pk) → (st.γ, p)
    if ctrl = rem then
        CGKA.Rem(st.γ, id) → (st.γ, p)
    if ctrl = upd then
        CGKA.Upd(st.γ) → (st.γ, p)
    eid′ ← st.eid + 1
    st.ast_eid′.p⃗ ←∪ p
    st.mid_eid′ ←+ 1
    ctxt ← (st.gid, st.id, st.ast_eid′, st.mid_eid′)
    return (st, ctxt, eid′, st.mid_eid′)
let i = min(st.eid_sid) ∀ sid ∈ st.G⃗_st.eid
// tl adjustable based on
// network reliability
let j = max(i, st.eid − tl)
ast′ ← st.ast[j : st.eid]
mid ← st.mid_st.eid++
AD ← st.id||st.gid||st.eid||mid||ast′
l ← |AD|
c ← AuthEnc.Enc(st.kst_eid, m′||AD||l)
ctxt ← (c, st.id, st.gid, st.eid, mid, l, ast′)
return (st, ctxt)
```

Dec(st, ctxt) → (st, sid, ctrl, m, eid, mid)
```
(c, sid, gid, eid, mid, l, ast) ← ctxt
let k = |st.ast| , k′ = |ast|,ctrl ← ⊥
// Update sender's epoch from our POV
if eid > st.eid_sid then
    st.eid_sid ← eid
// Catch up to the sender's epoch
if eid > st.eid then
    let i = max(j)  s.t. ast_j = st.ast_k
    for j ∈ [i, k′ − 1] do
        [commit_j, p⃗_j, welc_j] ← ast_j
        CGKA.Process(st.γ, commit_j, p⃗_j) → (st.γ, info)
        CGKA.Key(st.γ) → (st.γ, st.kst_{k+j−i+1})
        ctrl ← info.propSem
m ← AuthEnc.Dec(st.kst_eid, c||sid||gid||eid||mid||l||ast)
// Check for uncommitted proposals to commit.
// In ast_n,commit/⊥ is stored at index
// 0 and p⃗ at 1
if st.ρ = admin ∧ (ast_k′[0] = ⊥) ∧ Policy(ast_k′[1]) then
    st.eid++
    CGKA.Commit(st.γ, ast_k′.p⃗) → (st.γ, commit, welc)
    st.ast_st.eid ← [commit, ast_k′.p⃗, welc]
    ctrl ← (commit, ast.p⃗)
return (st, sid, ctrl, m)
```

Fig. 2. QUIC-MLS algorithms. All algorithms abort if any CGKA sub-algorithms return ⊥.

terminology in order to adapt MLS. The association of QUIC security levels to certain message types throughout the QUIC handshake is obviated by the single stage MLS key agreement mechanism. As observed in Fig. 3, clients continue to use 0-RTT messages for sending data after the initial volley of messages. This choice conveys the efficiency of QUIC-MLS and that MLS security is obtained from the session start.

To address the requirements for QUIC-HS to offer authenticated transport parameter and application protocol negotiation, we utilize the MLS Safe Extension [32] to add further context to the group. Specifically, for application-layer protocol agreement, a list of protocols would be included in the `data` vector of the `ComponentData` struct within the `app_data_dictionary` in the `GroupContext`. For transport layer parameters advertisement, this can simply be a list added to the `aad_item_data` with an appropriate `component_id` in the `SafeAAD` struct to be more transparent. These changes have been proposed to the MLS working group (see pull requests for [32]).

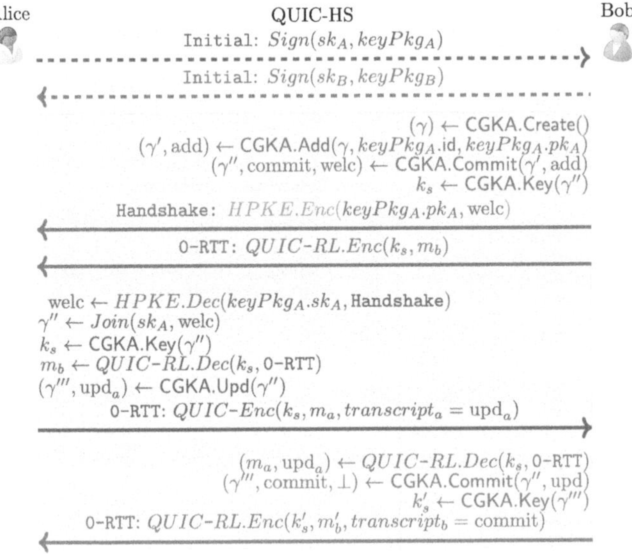

Fig. 3. QUIC-MLS execution with two parties. The use of Initial QUIC packets to send MLS Key Packages is optional if key packages are installed out-of-band/prior.

5 Benchmarking QUIC-MLS

In this section, we present benchmarking results for our proposed QUIC-MLS construction. As part of our benchmarking efforts, we developed a reference implementation[1] prototyping QUIC-MLS functionality in Go, leveraging the

[1] https://osf.io/qun62/?view_only=e814346aa4334fe1be43a81a89f01c8d.

existing libraries (quic-go), (go-mls), and (crypto/aes) (crypto/tls), [33–35]. We note, at the time of writing, our reference implementation is not a complete integration of MLS into QUIC. Instead, it serves as a prototype for assessing the computational and bandwidth costs associated with our proposed QUIC-MLS construction. This is due in part to the tight coupling of the (quic-go) [33] library with Go"s native TLS stack, making it non-trivial to fully replace TLS with MLS without extensive refactoring. However, we simulate the core functionality of the QUIC record layer by encrypting application data using AEAD schemes with session secrets derived from MLS, enabling a functionally comparable evaluation of performance and overhead.

We instantiated QUIC-MLS with the cipher suite P256_AES128GCM_SHA256_P256 and benchmarked its average performance across group sizes of 2, 5, 10, 20, 50, and 100 members, using 100 iterations per group size. For each epoch, the derived ExporterSecret was utilized for 0-RTT encryption of application-layer data.

In Table 1, we compare the average performance of the cryptographic procedures involved in the key package and group creation stages of QUIC-MLS. During key package creation, QUIC-MLS issues each member a set of credentials that can be leveraged in subsequent group operations. We observe that average creation times increase steadily with group size, scaling gradually as more members are added. Within the group creation stage, QUIC-MLS facilitates the formation and management of dynamic groups, where a designated group *admin* handles Add and Remove proposals by processing Join requests and issuing corresponding Welcome messages. Reflecting the increased overhead of managing group state and the complexity of underlying cryptographic operations, average group creation time exhibits a more dramatic rise, particularly as the group becomes large.

Table 1. Average runtime (in milliseconds over 100 iterations) of cryptographic operations during key package and group creation in QUIC-MLS, evaluated on an **Intel(R) Core(TM) i7-11370H CPU @ 3.30 GHz**.

Group Size	KeyPackage Creation	Group Creation
2	$\approx 0.373 \pm 0.235$	$\approx 0.946 \pm 0.723$
5	$\approx 1.42 \pm 0.564$	$\approx 6.72 \pm 1.781$
10	$\approx 2.12 \pm 0.508$	$\approx 15.79 \pm 2.261$
20	$\approx 3.11 \pm 0.9$	$\approx 45.97 \pm 7.129$
50	$\approx 10.09 \pm 2.613$	$\approx 191.49 \pm 27.395$
100	$\approx 17.566 \pm 6.253$	$\approx 712.57 \pm 267.381$

In Table 2, we compare the cost of QUIC-MLS Update operations in terms of both performance and bandwidth overhead. In particular, we model a use case involving a two-member group, where one member processes committed Update messages from the other after 5, 10, 20, 50, and 100 Commit operations. This setup is intended to simulate a scenario in which a QUIC-MLS group member remains part of the group but is inactive for an extended period. When the inactive member resumes communication, they must update their local group state to the latest epoch before re-engaging with the group. Figure 4 illustrates the expected format of a QUIC-MLS Update packet within our construction. Crucially, to resume sending encrypted messages over the QUIC record layer, the inactive member must first derive the most recent ExporterSecret from the updated group state. In a catch-up scenario, the inactive member processes previously committed Commit messages to update its local state. The path field provides the encrypted key material necessary to advance to the latest epoch.

Our evaluation shows that epoch synchronization time grows predictably with the number of missed updates, reflecting the accumulation of cryptographic state. Sync message size follows a similar trend, increasing with the volume of group information that must be communicated.

```
QUICMLSUpdate group_id, epoch, sender, authenticated_data, content: Commit proposals
: [empty], path: DirectPath nodes: [...] , signature, confirmation_tag
```

Fig. 4. QUIC-MLS packet structure for maintaining admin state (See Fig. 2 ast)

Table 2. Average runtime and bandwidth evaluation (in milliseconds for sync time and bytes for message size over 100 iterations) during epoch Update for inactive member in QUIC-MLS evaluated on **Intel(R) Core(TM) i7-11370H CPU @ 3.30 GHz**.

Missed Commit Count	State Sync Time	Message Size
5	$\approx 5.41 \pm 0.501$	$\approx 6,119$
10	$\approx 10.02 \pm 2.873$	$\approx 11,204$
20	$\approx 20.01 \pm 3.325$	$\approx 21,369$
50	$\approx 51.55 \pm 8.062$	$\approx 51,903$
100	$\approx 101.43 \pm 22.756$	$\approx 102,740$

6 Security Analyis of QUIC-MLS

Both TLS and QUIC have been extensively analyzed under various provable security approaches that either separate the key exchange and secure channel phases or consider them together as an intertwined protocol. Security goals commonly analyzed across the various approaches include key indistinguishability, authenticated and confidential channel establishment, protection against replay attacks, defense against state reveals, and forward secrecy. Jager et al. [36] formalized the monolithic approach as *authenticated and confidential channel establishment* (ACCE) protocols, which are separated into pre-accept and post-accept phases (similar to the TLS Handshake and Record Layer phases [37]). Follow-on work from Lychev et al. in [38] take a more holistic approach in analyzing QUIC and define the Q-ACCE model based on how QUIC uses TLS with multiple keys for key agreement and data messages in a two stage approach. Fischlin and Günther in [39] analyze QUIC in their multi-stage key exchange (MSKE) model in the Bellare and Rogaway style of [40], highlighting their model's composability with any symmetric-key application protocol. Tangential to this composability emphasized approach, Dowling et al. in [41] propose the Flexible ACCE (fACCE) model which eliminates the boundary between the handshake and channel yet is able to measure fine-grained security guarantees at each phase.

6.1 gACCE for QUIC-MLS

We use a modified fACCE model we call gACCE in our analysis of QUIC. To this end, we make some changes to the fACCE primitive to accommodate group channel security in what we dub gACCE (Definition 2).

Definition 2 (Flexible ACCE for Groups ([41])**.** *A flexible group ACCE protocol* gACCE *is a tuple of algorithms* $\mathsf{gACCE} = (\mathsf{KGen}, \mathsf{Init}, \mathsf{Enc}, \mathsf{Dec})$ *defined over a secret key space* $\mathcal{SK}$*, a public key space* $\mathcal{PK}$ *and a state space* $\mathcal{ST}$*. The syntax of a* gACCE *protocol is as follows:*

- $\mathsf{KGen} \rightarrow_{\$} (\mathrm{sk}, \mathrm{pk})$ *generates a long-term key pair where* $\mathrm{sk} \in \mathcal{SK}, \mathrm{pk} \in \mathcal{PK}$.
- $\mathsf{Init}(\rho, sk_i, \overrightarrow{\mathsf{PK}}_{\overrightarrow{\mathsf{G}}}, \mathrm{welc}, ad) \rightarrow_{\$} st$ *initializes a session to begin communication, where* sk_i *(optionally) is the caller* i*'s long-term secret key,* $\overrightarrow{\mathsf{PK}}_{\overrightarrow{\mathsf{G}}}$ *(optionally) are the long-term public keys of the intended group session partners* $\overrightarrow{\mathsf{G}}$ *such that* $i \notin \overrightarrow{\mathsf{G}}$*,* $\rho \in \{\mathsf{a}, \mathsf{p}\}$ *the session's role (i.e. admin or partner),* ad *is the data associated with this session, and* $sk \in \mathcal{SK} \cup \{\perp\}, \mathrm{pk} \in \mathcal{PK}\ \forall\ \mathrm{pk} \in \overrightarrow{\mathsf{PK}}_{\overrightarrow{\mathsf{G}}}, ad \in \{0,1\}^*, st \in \mathcal{ST}$.
- $\mathsf{Enc}(\mathsf{st}, \mathsf{ctrl}, m) \rightarrow_{\$} (\mathsf{st}', ctxt, \mathsf{eid}, \mathsf{mid})$ *enables a group member to encrypt a message, or to propose to* evolve *the group by adding, removing or updating members of the group. It takes as input a state* st*, an optional control message* ctrl *and a message* m*, and outputs new state* st'*, and a ciphertext* $ctxt$ *(where* $\mathsf{st}, \mathsf{st}' \in \mathcal{ST}, \mathsf{ctrl} \in \{\perp, \mathsf{Add}, \mathsf{Upd}, \mathsf{Rem}\}, m \in \{0,1\}^*$ *when* $\mathsf{ctrl} = \perp$ *otherwise* $m \leftarrow (\mathsf{st.id}, \mathrm{pk}_{\mathsf{st.id}}), ctxt \in \{0,1\}^* \cup \{\mathrm{propSem}\}, \mathsf{eid} \in \mathbb{N}$ and $\mathsf{mid} \in \mathbb{N}$).
- $\mathsf{Dec}(\mathsf{st}, ctxt) \rightarrow_{\$} (\mathsf{st}', \mathsf{id}, \mathsf{ctrl}, m, \mathsf{eid}, \mathsf{mid})$ *processes any updates to the group or decrypts messages by other group members. It takes as input a state* st *and* $ctxt$ *and outputs new state* st'*, sending partner's identifier* id*, message* m*, control message* $\mathsf{ctrl} \in \{\perp, \mathsf{Upd}, \mathsf{Add}, \mathsf{Rem}, \mathsf{Commit}\}$*, and epoch and message counters* eid *and* mid*, where* $\mathsf{st} \in \mathcal{ST}, st' \in \mathcal{ST} \cup \{\perp\}, m \in \{\{0,1\}^* \cup \perp\}$, $ctxt \in \{0,1\}^*, \mathsf{mid} \in \mathbb{N}$ and $\mathsf{eid} \in \mathbb{N}$. *If* $m = \perp$*, then this denotes a failure to process the message.*

To capture security in a group setting, we need to modify the fACCE's matching conversations and correctness definitions. Two group members share a *matching conversation* when they agree on the *control messages* used to evolve the group, and that any received payload messages are the same as the original sent message. The control messages are held in CT and the payload application messages are held in AT. Due to the propose-and-commit nature of MLS, we introduce the concepts of a *confirmed transcript* and *opportunistic transcript* for CT as an expansion of the message-stage-ciphertext transcripts in [41]: group members can propose changes that are (validly) discarded by the admin.

The confirmed transcript maintained by a group member party is a pair of structures ordered by the currently member $\mathsf{id} \in \overrightarrow{\mathsf{G}}$ and indexed by epoch eid. $(\mathrm{CT}^{\mathrm{c,e}}_{\mathsf{id},\mathsf{eid}}, \mathrm{CT}^{\mathrm{c,d}}_{\mathsf{id},\mathsf{eid}})$: where $\mathrm{CT}^{\mathrm{c,e}}_{\mathsf{id},\mathsf{eid}}$ records all messages that have been encrypted (sent) and $\mathrm{CT}^{\mathrm{c,d}}_{\mathsf{id},\mathsf{eid}}$ that holds decrypted messages (received) from a party $n \in \overrightarrow{\mathsf{G}}$ in epoch eid. The opportunistic transcript is similarly composed of a $\mathrm{CT}^{\mathrm{o,e}}_{n.\mathsf{eid}}$ and $\mathrm{CT}^{\mathrm{o,d}}_{n.\mathsf{eid}}$ except these only hold *proposed* group *control messages*, respectively. The opportunistic transcript control messages have not been committed: when they do, they are moved to the *confirmed* transcript. Together, these allow gACCE to both match application messages and match epoch evolutions through staging pending proposals until a successful decryption of a commit message triggers a new epoch. We now define correct execution of an gACCE protocol. Finally, the application transcript $\mathrm{AT}^{x}_{\mathsf{id},\mathsf{eid}}$ (where $x \in \{e, d\}$) contain all application messages (i.e. payload) encrypted and decrypted by id in epoch eid. Note that the decrypted $\mathrm{CT}^{\mathrm{d}}_{\mathsf{id},\mathsf{eid}}[\mathsf{id}']$ is indexed by the claimed sender partner identifier id'.

Definition 3 (Correctness of gACCE (adopted from [41])). *A* gACCE *protocol is* correct *if, for any pair of keys* $(\mathrm{sk}_i, \mathrm{pk}_i)$ *and* $(\mathrm{sk}_j, \mathrm{pk}_j)$ *output by* KGen *such that* $(i, j) \in \overrightarrow{\mathsf{G}}$, *with* $i \neq j$, *the following holds. Let* $ad \in \{0,1\}^*$. *The session states are initialized as* $\mathsf{st}^{\mathsf{a}}_i \xleftarrow{\$} \mathsf{Init}(\mathsf{a}, \mathrm{sk}_i, \{\mathrm{pk}_{\overrightarrow{\mathsf{G}}}\}, ad)$ *and* $\mathsf{st}^{\mathsf{p}}_j \xleftarrow{\$} \mathsf{Init}(\mathsf{p}, \mathrm{sk}_j, \{\mathrm{pk}_{\overrightarrow{\mathsf{G}}}\}, ad)$. *Application transcripts are initialized as* $\mathrm{AT}^*_* \leftarrow \epsilon$, *and control transcripts as* $(\mathrm{CT}^{*,*}_{i,*}, \mathrm{CT}^{*,*}_{j,*}) \leftarrow \epsilon$ *(indexed by* $\mathsf{id} \in \overrightarrow{\mathsf{G}}$, eid*). Then, for all sequences of operations* $((op^0, \mathsf{id}^0, \mathsf{ctrl}^0, \rho^0, m^0), \ldots, (op^n, \mathsf{id}^n, \mathsf{ctrl}^n, \rho^n, m^n))$, *with* $0 \leq l \leq n$, *the following holds:* $op^l \in \{e, d\}$, $\mathsf{id}^l \in \{i, j\}$, *control actions* $\mathsf{ctrl}^l \in \{\bot, \mathsf{Add}, \mathsf{Rem}, \mathsf{Upd}, \mathsf{Commit}\}$, *role* $\rho^l \in \{\mathsf{a}, \mathsf{p}\}$, *and message* $m^l \in \{0,1\}^*$. *This* gACCE *correctness definition holds provided the protocol is executed precisely as follows.*

- *if* $op^l = e$, *invoke:* $\mathsf{Enc}(\mathsf{st}^{\rho^l}_{\mathsf{id}^l}, \mathsf{ctrl}^l, m^l) \xrightarrow{\$} (\mathsf{st}^{\rho^l}_{\mathsf{id}^l}, ctxt^l, \mathsf{eid}, \mathsf{mid})$ *and,*
  - *if* $\mathsf{ctrl}^l = \bot$, *update:* $\mathrm{AT}^{\mathrm{e}}_{\mathsf{id}^l,\mathsf{eid}} \leftarrow \mathrm{AT}^{\mathrm{e}}_{\mathsf{id}^l,\mathsf{eid}^l} \,\|\, (\mathsf{id}^l, \mathsf{mid}, m^l, ctxt^l)$
  - *else if* $\mathsf{ctrl}^l \in \{\mathsf{Add}, \mathsf{Rem}, \mathsf{Upd}\}$*:*
    - * *if* $\rho_{\mathsf{id}^l} = \mathsf{a}$, *update:* $\mathrm{CT}^{\mathrm{c,e}}_{\mathsf{id}^l,\mathsf{eid}^l} \leftarrow \mathrm{CT}^{\mathrm{c,e}}_{\mathsf{id}^l,\mathsf{eid}^l} \,\|\, (\mathsf{eid}^l, \mathsf{ctrl}^l, m^l, ctxt^l)$
    - * *if* $\rho_{\mathsf{id}^l} = \mathsf{p}$, *update:* $\mathrm{CT}^{\mathrm{o,e}}_{\mathsf{id}^l,\mathsf{eid}^l} \leftarrow \mathrm{CT}^{\mathrm{o,e}}_{\mathsf{id}^l,\mathsf{eid}^l} \,\|\, (\mathsf{eid}^l, \mathsf{ctrl}^l, m^l, ctxt^l)$
- ***OR***, *if* $op^l = d$, *invoke:* $\mathsf{Dec}(\mathsf{st}^{\rho^l}_{\mathsf{id}^l}, ctxt^l) \xrightarrow{\$} (\mathsf{st}^{\rho^l}_{\mathsf{id}^l}, \mathsf{id}_*, \mathsf{ctrl}^l_*, m^l_*, \mathsf{eid}^l_*, \mathsf{mid}^l_*)$

- *if* $\mathsf{ctrl}^l_* = \bot$*, update:*

$$\mathrm{AT}^{\mathrm{d}}_{\mathsf{id}_*,\mathsf{eid}^l_*}[\mathsf{id}_*] \leftarrow \mathrm{AT}^{\mathrm{d}}_{\mathsf{id}_*,\mathsf{eid}^l_*}[\mathsf{id}_*] \,\|\, (\mathsf{id}_*, \mathsf{mid}^l_*, m^l_*, ctxt^l)$$

- *else if* $\mathsf{ctrl}^l_* \neq \bot$*, update:*

$$\mathrm{CT}^{\mathrm{c,d}}_{\mathsf{id}^l,\mathsf{eid}^l_*}[\mathsf{id}_*] \leftarrow \mathrm{CT}^{\mathrm{c,d}}_{\mathsf{id}^l,\mathsf{eid}^l_*}[\mathsf{id}_*] \,\|\, (\mathsf{eid}^l_*, \mathsf{ctrl}^l_*, m^l_*, ctxt^l)$$

If $m^l_* \neq \bot$*, then encrypted and decrypted messages, control messages, and epoch and message counters outputs equal* $m^l_* = m^l_o, \mathsf{ctrl}^l_* = \mathsf{ctrl}^l_o, \mathsf{eid}^l_* = \mathsf{eid}^l_o, \mathsf{mid}^l_* = \mathsf{mid}^l_o$*, that epoch counter outputs increase monotonically* ($\forall l^* < l$ *with* $op^l = op^{l^*} = e$ *and* $\rho^{l^*} = \rho^l$ *it holds that* $\mathsf{eid}^{l^*} \leq \mathsf{eid}^l_o$)*, and the following transcript invariants hold:*

1. $\mathrm{CT}^{\mathrm{c,d}}_{\mathsf{id},\mathsf{eid}}[\mathsf{id}'][1:] \subseteq \{\mathrm{CT}^{\mathrm{c,e}}_{\mathsf{id}',\mathsf{eid},\mathsf{mid}} \cup \mathrm{CT}^{\mathrm{o,e}}_{\mathsf{id}',\mathsf{eid}}\} \wedge$
2. $\mathrm{AT}^{\mathrm{d}}_{\mathsf{id},\mathsf{eid}}[\mathsf{id}'] \subseteq \mathrm{AT}^{\mathrm{e}}_{\mathsf{id}',\mathsf{eid}}$

The gACCE model analyzes QUIC's security properties in various epochs. fACCE captures certain security properties which are given values corresponding to a stage of the protocol that they are guaranteed thereafter: Authentication and integrity, key compromise impersonation (KCI) resistance, forward secrecy, resistance against replay attacks, and reveals against executions' random coins. MLS already provides guarantees for FS and replay attacks which we do not model for brevity. For gACCE, we add PCS as an additional security property denoted by the counter pcs to the ten presented in [41]. Similar to the fs counter, pcs defines the epoch from which post-compromise security (with respect to the group session) is reached. It should be hard, for an epoch $\mathsf{eid} \geq \mathtt{pcs}$, to break the confidentiality of ciphertexts, even if all group members were corrupted previously (*unless* one of the members' random coins were revealed to the adversary). We modify the freshness notion to incorporate PCS security in Fig. 5.

$\mathrm{Fresh}_{\mathtt{fs-pcs}}$

1: **for** $(i, j) \in [n_p]$ **do**
2:   **for** $(s, t) \in [n_s]$: **do**
3:     $\mathtt{ctr} \leftarrow \min(\mathsf{eid}^* : \pi^s_i.fr_{\mathsf{eid}^*} = 1)$
4:     **if** $corr_i = 1$ **then**
5:       $\mathtt{ctr} \leftarrow \max(\mathtt{ctr}, \mathtt{fs})$
6:       $\tau \leftarrow \pi^s_i.\mathsf{eid}$
7:       $\pi^s_i.fr_{\mathsf{eid}^*} \leftarrow 0$ for all $\mathsf{eid}^* < \mathtt{ctr}$
8:       **if** $(\mathsf{Upd} \in \{\pi^s_i.\mathrm{CT}^{\mathrm{c,e}}_{i,\tau'} \cup \pi^s_i.\mathrm{CT}^{\mathrm{o,e}}_{i,\tau'}\}) \wedge ((\pi^t_j.\mathrm{CT}^{\mathrm{c,d}}_{j,\tau'}[i] = \pi^s_i.\mathrm{CT}^{\mathrm{c,e}}_{i,\tau'}) \vee (\pi^t_j.\mathrm{CT}^{\mathrm{c,d}}_{j,\tau'}[i] = \pi^s_i.\mathrm{CT}^{\mathrm{o,e}}_{i,\tau'})) \;\forall \tau' > \tau$ **then**
9:         $\pi^s_i.fr_{\mathsf{eid}^*}, \pi^t_j.fr_{\mathsf{eid}^*} \leftarrow 1$ for all $\mathsf{eid}^* \geq \tau'$
10:         $\mathtt{pcs} \leftarrow \max(\mathtt{pcs}, \tau')$

Fig. 5. Freshness notion for fACCE with PCS modifications in blue. Freshness (fr) is regained after corruption through all parties reaching a new shared group state resulting from processing an update. We abuse notation on line 8 in the second clause to convey that the *commit* to π^s_i's update must appear in π^t_j's transcript (i.e. $(\mathsf{Commit}, \mathsf{Upd}) \in \mathrm{CT}^{\mathrm{c,d}}_{j,\tau+1}[i]$). (Color figure online)

The execution environment of fACCE is also suitable to analyze QUIC. Particularly, it's worth noting that the Honest Partner definition can extend to the group channel formed by QUIC-MLS.

Definition 4 (Honest Group Partner (adapted from [41])). *π_j^t is an honest group partner of π_i^s if $(i, j) \in \overrightarrow{\mathsf{G}}$ where $j \neq i$ and $\overrightarrow{\mathsf{G}} = \{i, \ldots, n\}$ are group partners and all initial variables match (i.e. $\pi_i^s.\overrightarrow{\mathsf{G}}_{\mathsf{eid}} = \pi_j^t.\overrightarrow{\mathsf{G}}_{\mathsf{eid}}$, $\pi_i^s.\mathsf{st}.\gamma = \pi_j^t.\mathsf{st}.\gamma \neq \perp$, $\pi_i^s.\mathsf{eid} = \pi_j^t.\mathsf{eid}$ where $\rho_\iota = \mathsf{a}$ for some $\iota \in \overrightarrow{\mathsf{G}}$), and the received control transcript is a prefix of the partner's sent control transcript for their common epochs, respectively, where at least one of them is not empty (i.e. , for any epoch n s.t. $0 \leq n \leq m$ where m is the $\min(\pi_i^s.\mathsf{eid}, \pi_j^t.\mathsf{eid})$, where $a = |\pi_j^t.\mathrm{CT}_{i,n}^{\mathrm{c,d}}[j]|, b = |\pi_i^s.\mathrm{CT}_{j,n}^{\mathrm{c,d}}[i]|$ such that if $a > 0$ and $b > 0$ then $\forall\, 0 \leq \alpha < a : (\pi_i^s.\mathrm{CT}_{i,n}^{\mathrm{c,e}}[\alpha] = \pi_j^t.\mathrm{CT}_{j,n}^{\mathrm{c,d}}[i][\alpha])$ and $\forall 0 \leq \beta < b : (\pi_i^s.\mathrm{CT}_{i,\mathsf{eid}}^{\mathrm{c,d}}[j][\beta] = \pi_j^t.\mathrm{CT}_{j,n}^{\mathrm{o,e}}[\beta])$). If π_i^s already received ciphertexts from any π_j^t, then π_j^t is an honest group partner of π_i^s only if no other honest partner π^* exists outside the set $\pi_{s.G}^i$.*

Our honest group partner notion changes the honest partnering from fACCE in two major ways. First, gACCE allows for partnering to be a 1-to-many relationship such that there can be up to $n - 1$ honest partners for a particular initiator after decrypting a ciphertext. This reflects the fact that any member of an MLS group can encrypt and decrypt application messages and group control messages. Second, as opposed to matching conversations across all message types, we only require matching control message sequences within CT between honest group partners to enforce group state agreement.

6.2 Adversarial Model

We adopt the adversarial model of fACCE in [41] for our security experiment with modifications for the group setting. Like fACCE, an adversary $\mathcal{A}$ plays a security game with a challenger in which they attempt break the confidentiality (i.e. via guessing a sampled bit b) or integrity (i.e. via forgery) of messages in the gACCE protocol. At the beginning of the experiment, the challenger runs KGen to generate keys for all participants of the protocol and gives $\mathcal{A}$ the list of their public keys. $\mathcal{A}$ is given oracle access to OInit, OEnc, ODec, OReveal, and OCorrupt and can control communications between participants. One way the $\mathcal{A}$ can win the security game by is by triggering a $\mathtt{win} \leftarrow 1$ (indicating breaking the authenticity or integrity of ciphertexts). Otherwise, at the end of the experiment $\mathcal{A}$ terminates and outputs a bit b' against the challenge bit $\pi_i^s.b_{\mathsf{eid}}$. The challenger checks the freshness conditions and if $\mathcal{A}$ has not violated any of the freshness conditions outputs $(b' = \pi_i^s.b_{\mathsf{eid}}) \vee \mathtt{win}$. We detail the modifications to the relevant oracles below:

- $\mathsf{OInit}(i, s, \overrightarrow{\mathsf{G}}, \rho)$ initializes a session π_i^s (if not yet initialized) of party i to be in a group with parties in the list $\overrightarrow{\mathsf{G}} = (i, \ldots, n)$, invoking $\mathsf{gACCE.KGen}() \xrightarrow{\$} (\mathrm{sk}_n, \mathrm{pk}_n)$ for each party in $\overrightarrow{\mathsf{G}}$ (if not yet generated) and then $\mathsf{gACCE.Init}(sk_i, \overrightarrow{\mathsf{PK}}_{\overrightarrow{\mathsf{G}}}, \rho, ad) \xrightarrow{\$} \pi_i^s.st$ under $\$ \leftarrow \pi_i^s.rand$. It also sets $\pi_i^s.\rho \leftarrow \rho$ and $\pi_i^s.\overrightarrow{\mathsf{G}} \leftarrow \overrightarrow{\mathsf{G}}$. This oracle provides no return value. All subsequent invocations of Enc, Dec of this session participant use $\pi_i^s.rand$ for obtaining randomness. Finally freshness flags are updated by invoking $\mathrm{Fresh}_{\mathtt{fs-pcs}}$ (see Fig. 5).
- $\mathsf{OEnc}(i, s, \mathsf{ctrl}, m_0, m_1; \pi_i^s.rand)$ Upon satisfaction of freshness conditions, this triggers either the encryption of a message or a group action proposal according to the given ctrl instruction for the encryption of message m_b for $b = \pi_i^s.b_{\mathsf{eid}}$ by invoking $\mathsf{gACCE.Enc}(\pi_i^s.st, \mathsf{ctrl}, m_b) \rightarrow (st', c, \mathsf{eid}, \mathsf{mid})$ for an initialized π_i^o. It returns $(c, \mathsf{eid}, \mathsf{mid})$ to the adversary. If $m_0 \neq m_1$, the challenger checks the freshness conditions (given by Fig. 5) and outputs $\perp$ if the $\mathcal{A}$ issued this query and $\pi_i^s.fr_{\mathsf{eid}} = 0$. Otherwise, if encryption succeeds (i.e. $c \neq \perp$), this oracle updates the session specific variables $\pi_i^s.st \leftarrow st'$, and appends the private results to the challenger held encryption CT and AT in π_i^s according to Definition 3.
- $\mathsf{ODec}(i, s, c; \pi_i^s.rand)$ triggers invocation of $\mathsf{gACCE.Dec}(\pi_i^s.st, c) \rightarrow (st', m, \mathsf{ctrl}, \mathsf{id}, \mathsf{eid}, \mathsf{mid})$ for initialized π_i^s and returns $(m, \mathsf{eid}, \mathsf{mid})$ to the adversary. If c was not generated by an honest partner and the epoch was fresh according to Definition 4 and Fig. 5, respectively, then $\mathtt{win} = 1$ and the challenger ends the game. Otherwise, if decryption was successful (i.e. $m \neq \perp$), then it appends the results to the decryption CT and AT in π_i^s according to Definition 3.

We define the (insecurity) of gACCE below:

Definition 5 (Breaking gACCE Security). *Let Π be a flexible group ACCE protocol $\Pi = \{\mathsf{KGen}, \mathsf{Init}, \mathsf{Enc}, \mathsf{Dec}\}$. Let $\mathsf{Exp}_{\Pi,\mathcal{A}}^{\mathsf{gACCE}}(n)$ be the gACCE security experiment described in Sect. 6.2 in which an adversary $\mathcal{A}$ breaks the security of gACCE security when $\mathcal{A}$ terminates and outputs (i, s, eid, b'), if there either exists a session π_i^s such that $\pi_i^s.b_{\mathsf{eid}} = b'$ and $\pi_i^s.fr_{\mathsf{eid}} = 1$, or $\mathtt{win} = 1$. We define the advantage of n adversary $\mathcal{A}$that breaks a group flexible ACCE protocol gACCE as: $\mathsf{Adv}_{\Pi,\mathcal{A}}^{\mathsf{gACCE}}(n) = |2 * \mathsf{Pr}(\mathsf{Exp}_{\Pi,\mathcal{A}}^{\mathsf{gACCE}}(n) = 1) - 1| + \mathsf{Pr}[\mathtt{win} = 1]$.*

6.3 Security Proof Outline

Broadly speaking, our construction is simply a composition of a CGKA protocol, Authenticated Encryption (AuthEnc) protocol, and some book-keeping functionalities. There is no change to either protocols nor their primitives. Thus, the game-hopping based proof is split into two cases which are structurally similar:

Case 1 The adversary $\mathcal{A}$ attempts to forge a message. That is, $\mathcal{A}$ succeeds in getting a party to decrypt a ciphertext c for which no honest partner produced.

Case 2 The adversary $\mathcal{A}$ guesses the correct bit b with non-negligible probability.

a) Case 1: We proceed in a series of game-hops as follows:

Game 0 (G0) This is the gACCE experiment as described in Sect. 6.2 with no modifications.

Game 1 (G1) This version is the same as G0 except that we replace all of the keys used for encryption or decryption during an epoch marked fresh by in the gACCE experiment (i.e. $\mathcal{A}$has not triggered a trivial attack) with uniformly random values from a CGKA challenger $\mathcal{C}_{\mathsf{CGKA}}$. This is sound under the standard hybrid argument since CGKA provides uniformly random keys for fresh epochs. Different CGKA challengers are extended, without loss of generality (WLOG), to any of group sessions allowed under the gACCE experiment. For each group session, a CGKA reduction is made as follows. Freshness in the gACCE game then corresponds to freshness in the CGKA game. When $\mathcal{A}$ issues a OReveal query, the challenger first checks the freshness flag of the epoch and if $fr = 1$, it returns a uniformly random value from $\mathcal{C}_{\mathsf{CGKA}}$, otherwise it returns the real key. When $\mathcal{A}$ issues a OCorrupt query against a party for a given epoch, if the epoch in question is not fresh then the real long-term keys of party are exposed, otherwise the query is not allowed. Future corruptions in new epochs against that party are allowed until pcs flips fr back to 1.

Game 2 (G2) This game is the same as G1 except that we replace all instances of encryption and decryption in OEnc and ODec with ones provided by an AuthEnc challenger $\mathcal{B}_{\mathsf{AuthEnc}}$. WLOG, this requires one fresh AuthEnc reduction per epoch per group session (each group has distinct epochs and each epoch has new keys). In each instance, the adversary's advantage in forgery reduces to the AuthEnc.auth security of the AuthEnc scheme.

b) Case 2: This proof follows the series of game hops exactly as in Case 1 except that in G2, the adversary's advantage in guessing bit b reduces the advantage of an adversary guess bit b in the AuthEnc.conf game.

Theorem 1 (gACCE Security for QUIC-MLS). *Let n_s, n_G, and n_e be the number of sessions, number of groups, and number of epochs given by some security parameter n used in the experiment. The QUIC-MLS protocol presented in Fig. 2 is* gACCE*-secure. That is, for any PPT algorithm $\mathcal{A}$ against the* gACCE *security experiment (described in Sect. 6.2), the $\mathsf{Adv}^{\mathsf{gACCE}}_{\Pi,\mathcal{A}}(n)$ is negligible under the* cgka *security of* CGKA *and the* auth *and* conf *security of the* AuthEnc *primitives.*

7 Conclusion

This work introduces the first formalization and analysis of QUIC-MLS, an idea initially proposed for space networking security. We demonstrate feasibility of the concept and provide a cryptographic security proof. With growing needs for low-latency and efficiency, as well as security, this points a way forward for using novel key exchange as a replacement for legacy handshake approaches within networking protocols.

Acknowledgements. The research of B. Dowling was supported by EPSRC grant EP/X016226/2. The research of B. Dowling and B. Wimalasiri was supported by UKRI grant UKRI156.

A QUIC-MLS Protocol Construction

From a high level overview, QUIC-MLS establishes a secure group channel among two or more parties which uses the output of the MLS continuous key agreement component as the input to the QUIC record layer used to send encrypted application layer messages. We detail our assumptions and intuition on different components of the protocol below:

- *Operational Settings* We assume that there is no centralized strongly consistent DS (e.g. server style DS). Rather, we rely on QUIC transport mechanisms to provide reliable in-order delivery of all messages. Furthermore, we assume that QUIC-MLS participants already have the certificate information (i.e. public keys and associated identities) of all other participants as provided by some AS implementation (e.g. PKI from CAs, out-of-band, preinstalled, etc.).
- *Initialization* The initiator of a session may choose one or more participants to form a group. The initiator uses the public keys of the group member(s) to start an MLS session by unilaterally committing their own add proposal and sends individualized Welcome messages out (via their public keys).
- *Group Control* Because we assume there is no DS to arbitrate valid proposals simultaneously sent by multiple group members, we assign a leader to each epoch that is allowed to commit to group control proposals to ensure no conflicts can arise. Leader assignment can be time based, schedule based, or arbitrarily selected to fit a use-case. For example, epoch leaders can be chosen based on a pre-assigned schedule upon group initialization which is exported (i.e. in the `Group Context`) and updated with any group control action. Or, perhaps more elegantly, epoch leaders can be assigned based on their position in the ratchet tree (leftmost to right).
- *Encryption and Decryption* We make no changes to the QUIC AEAD Encryption or Decryption as previously discussed in Sect. 4.3. However, if non-repudiation between group members is desired for application messages, then the use of a sign-then-encrypt procedure can be adapted to messages input to QUIC's AEAD (Table 3).

Table 3. Summary of variable terminology

Term	Description
$\mathrm{AT}^{\mathsf{x}}_{\mathsf{id},\mathsf{eid}}[\mathsf{id}']$	The application message transcript used in the gACCE security model where $x \in (e, d)$. Note, $\mathrm{AT}^{\mathsf{e}}_{\mathsf{id},\mathsf{eid}}$ does not maintain separate vectors for partners (i.e. $\mathrm{AT}^{\mathsf{e}}_{\mathsf{id},\mathsf{eid}} = \mathrm{AT}^{\mathsf{e}}_{\mathsf{id},\mathsf{eid}}[\mathsf{id}]$).
$\mathrm{CT}^{\mathsf{a},\mathsf{b}}_{\mathsf{id},\mathsf{eid}}[\mathsf{id}']$	The group control message transcript used in the gACCE security model where $a \in \{c, o\}$ signifies confirmed or opportunistic, $b \in \{e, d\}$ refers to encrypted or decrypted, id refers to the transcript owner and id′ refers to a partner id, and eid refers to the epoch number. Similarly, id does not maintain encryption transcripts of partners (i.e. $\mathrm{CT}^{\cdot,\mathsf{e}}_{\mathsf{id},\mathsf{eid}} = \mathrm{CT}^{\cdot,\mathsf{e}}_{\mathsf{id},\mathsf{eid}}[\mathsf{id}]$).
st	The gACCE state stored in memory of each group member which includes the following vectors: γ - The CGKA group state as defined in 1 ρ - The role of the st owner which can take the values of $\{\mathrm{a}, \mathrm{p}\}$ for admin or participant. Only admin can commit to proposals sent by other group members. ast - The administrative state which holds a transcript of commits and proposals, and (optional) welcome messages leading to the current epoch formatted as: $[\mathrm{commit}, \vec{\mathrm{p}}, \mathrm{welc}]$ or a proposed epoch (where $\mathrm{commit} = \bot$). eid - The epoch number associated with a particular id: st.eid is shorthand for $\mathsf{st.eid}_{\mathsf{st.id}}$. **0** - The group identifier of the current session id - The ID of the st owner kst - The set of keys stored by the st owner indexed by eid. $\mathsf{mid}_{\mathsf{eid}}$ - The message transcript indexed by eid $\vec{\mathsf{G}}_{\mathsf{eid}}$ - The IDs of group members in a particular epoch

References

1. U. N. O. for Outer Space Affairs (UNOOSA): Online Index of Objects Launched into Outer Space (2025). https://www.unoosa.org/oosa/osoindex/search-ng.jspx
2. Vyncke, E.: Taking IP To Other Planets Charter (2025). https://datatracker.ietf.org/doc/charter-ietf-tiptop/
3. Iyengar, J., Thomson, M.: QUIC: A UDP-Based Multiplexed and Secure Transport. RFC 9000 (2021)
4. Blanchet, M., Eddy, W., Li, T.: An Architecture for IP in Deep Space. Internet-Draft draft-many-deepspace-ip-architecture-01, Internet Engineering Task Force (2024, Work in Progress)
5. Smailes, J., David, R., Kohler, S., Birnbach, S., Martinovic, I.: Poster: spacequic: securing communication in computationally constrained spacecraft (2023)
6. Dowling, B., Hale, B., Tian, X., Wimalasiri, B.: Key establishment in the space environment (2025)
7. Sommer, M., Sterz, A., Vogelbacher, M., Bellafkir, H., Freisleben, B.: QUICL: a QUIC convergence layer for disruption-tolerant networks. In: Proceedings of the Int'l ACM Conference on Modeling Analysis and Simulation of Wireless and Mobile Systems, MSWiM 2023, pp. 37–46. Association for Computing Machinery (2023)

8. Amponis, G., Lagkas, T., Argyriou, V., Radoglou-Grammatikis, P., Kyranou, K., Makris, I., Sarigiannidis, P.: Channel-aware QUIC control for enhanced CAM communications in C-V2X deployments over aerial base stations. IEEE Trans. Veh. Technol. **73**(7), 9320–9333 (2024)
9. Sandvine: The Global Internet Phenomena Report (2023)
10. Aviram, N., Gellert, K., Jager, T.: Session resumption protocols and efficient forward security for TLS 1.3 0-RTT. J. Cryptol. **34** (2021)
11. Günther, F., Hale, B., Jager, T., Lauer, S.: 0-RTT key exchange with full forward secrecy. In: Advances in Cryptology – EUROCRYPT 2017, pp. 519–548. Springer (2017)
12. Cohn-Gordon, K., Cremers, C., Dowling, B., Garratt, L., Stebila, D.: A formal security analysis of the signal messaging protocol. J. Cryptol. **33**, 1914–1983 (2020)
13. Cohn-Gordon, K., Cremers, C., Garratt, L.: On post-compromise security. In: 2016 IEEE 29th Computer Security Foundations Symposium (CSF), pp. 164–178. IEEE (2016)
14. Barnes, R., Beurdouche, B., Robert, R., Millican, J., Omara, E., Cohn-Gordon, K.: The Messaging Layer Security (MLS) Protocol. RFC 9420 (2023)
15. Anastos, M., et al.: The cost of maintaining keys in dynamic groups with applications to multicast encryption and group messaging. In: Theory of Cryptography: 22nd International Conference, TCC 2024, pp. 413–443. Springer (2024)
16. Alwen, J., Coretti, S., Jost, D., Mularczyk, M.: Continuous group key agreement with active security. In: Theory of Cryptography: 18th International Conference. TCC 2020, pp. 261–290. Springer, Heidelberg (2020)
17. Rescorla, E.: The Transport Layer Security (TLS) Protocol Version 1.3. RFC 8446 (2018)
18. Thomson, M., Turner, S.: Using TLS to secure QUIC. RFC 9001 (2021)
19. Brzuska, C., Cornelissen, E., Kohbrok, K.: Security analysis of the MLS key derivation, pp. 2535–2553
20. Cremers, C., Hale, B., Kohbrok, K.: The Complexities of Healing in Secure Group Messaging: Why Cross-Group Effects Matter, pp. 1847–1864 (2021)
21. Wallez, T., Protzenko, J., Bhargavan, K.: TreeKEM: A Modular Machine-Checked Symbolic Security Analysis of Group Key Agreement in Messaging Layer Security (2025). Publication info: Preprint
22. Cohn-Gordon, K., Cremers, C., Dowling, B., Garratt, L., Stebila, D.: A formal security analysis of the signal messaging protocol. In: 2017 IEEE European Symposium on Security and Privacy (EuroS&P), pp. 451–466 (2017)
23. Dowling, B., Hale, B.: Secure messaging authentication against active man-in-the-middle attacks. In: 2021 IEEE European Symposium on Security and Privacy (EuroS&P), pp. 54–70 (2021)
24. Fiedler, R., Günther, F.: Security analysis of signal's PQXDH handshake. In: Public-Key Cryptography – PKC 2025, pp. 137–169. Springer (2025)
25. Bienstock, A., Fairoze, J., Garg, S., Mukherjee, P., Raghuraman, S.: A more complete analysis of the signal double ratchet algorithm. In: Advances in Cryptology – CRYPTO 2022, pp. 784–813. Springer (2022)
26. Dowling, B., Hale, B.: Authenticated continuous key agreement: active MitM detection and prevention. Cryptology ePrint Archive, Paper 2023/228 (2023)
27. Fischlin, M., Günther, F., Janson, C.: Robust channels: handling unreliable networks in the record layers of QUIC and DTLS 1.3. J. Cryptol. **37** (2024)
28. Delignat-Lavaud, A., et al.: A security model and fully verified implementation for the IETF QUIC record layer. In: 2021 IEEE Symposium on Security and Privacy (SP), pp. 1162–1178 (2021)

29. Chen, S., Jero, S., Jagielski, M., Boldyreva, A., Nita-Rotaru, C.: Secure communication channel establishment: TLS 1.3 (over TCP Fast Open) versus QUIC. J. Cryptol. **34** (2021)
30. Lychev, R., Jero, S., Boldyreva, A., Nita-Rotaru, C.: How secure and quick is QUIC? Provable security and performance analyses. In: 2015 IEEE Symposium on Security and Privacy, pp. 214–231 (2015)
31. Beurdouche, B., Rescorla, E., Omara, E., Inguva, S., Duric, A.: The Messaging Layer Security (MLS) Architecture. RFC 9750 (2025)
32. Robert, R.: The Messaging Layer Security (MLS) Extensions. Internet-Draft draft-ietf-mls-extensions-07, Internet Engineering Task Force (2025, Work in Progress)
33. Seemann, M.: quic-go (2025). https://pkg.go.dev/github.com/quic-go/quic-go
34. Cisco Systems: go-mls (2021). https://pkg.go.dev/github.com/cisco/go-mls
35. Google: crypto/tls (2025). https://pkg.go.dev/crypto/tls
36. Jager, T., Kohlar, F., Schäge, S., Schwenk, J.: On the security of TLS-DHE in the standard model. In: Annual Cryptology Conference, pp. 273–293. Springer (2012)
37. Jager, T., Kohlar, F., Schäge, S., Schwenk, J.: On the security of TLS-DHE in the standard model, pp. 273–293
38. Lychev, R., Jero, S., Boldyreva, A., Nita-Rotaru, C.: How secure and quick is quic? provable security and performance analyses. In: Proceedings of the 16th Annual Information Security Symposium, CERIAS 2015, (West Lafayette, IN), CERIAS - Purdue University (2015)
39. Fischlin, M., Günther, F.: Multi-stage key exchange and the case of Google's QUIC protocol, pp. 1193–1204
40. Bellare, M., Rogaway, P.: Entity authentication and key distribution, pp. 232–249
41. Dowling, B., Rösler, P., Schwenk, J.: Flexible authenticated and confidential channel establishment (fACCE): analyzing the noise protocol framework. In: Public-Key Cryptography – PKC 2020, pp. 341–373. Springer (2020)
42. Alwen, J., Coretti, S., Dodis, Y., Tselekounis, Y.: Security Analysis and Improvements for the IETF MLS Standard for Group Messaging. In: Micciancio, D., Ristenpart, T. (eds.) CRYPTO 2020. LNCS, vol. 12170, pp. 248–277. Springer, Cham (2020). https://doi.org/10.1007/978-3-030-56784-2_9

Cryptographic Binding Should Not Be Optional: A Formal-Methods Analysis of FIDO UAF Channel Binding

Enis Golaszewski[1], Alan T. Sherman[1(✉)], Edward Zieglar[2], Jonathan D. Fuchs[1], and Sophia Hamer[1]

[1] Cyber Defense Lab, University of Maryland Baltimore County (UMBC), 1000 Hilltop Circle, Baltimore, MD 21228, USA
{golaszewski,sherman,jfuchs2,chamer1}@umbc.edu

[2] National Security Agency, 9800 Savage Road, 20755 Fort George G. Meade, USA
evziegl@uwe.nsa.gov

Abstract. As a case study in cryptographic binding, we present a formal-methods analysis of the cryptographic channel binding mechanisms in the *Fast IDentity Online (FIDO) Universal Authentication Framework (UAF)* authentication protocol, which seeks to reduce the use of traditional passwords in favor of authentication devices. First, we show that UAF's channel bindings fail to mitigate protocol interaction by a *Dolev-Yao* adversary, enabling the adversary to transfer the server's authentication challenge to alternate sessions of the protocol. As a result, in some contexts, the adversary can masquerade as a client and establish an authenticated session with a server (e.g., possibly a bank server). Second, we implement a proof-of-concept man-in-the-middle attack against eBay's open source FIDO UAF implementation. Third, we propose and formally verify improvements to UAF. The weakness we analyze is similar to the vulnerability discovered in the Needham-Schroeder protocol over 25 years ago. That this vulnerability appears in the FIDO UAF standard highlights the strong need for protocol designers to bind messages properly and to analyze their designs with formal-methods tools. To our knowledge, we are first to carry out a formal-methods analysis of channel binding in UAF and first to exhibit details of an attack on UAF that exploits the weaknesses of UAF's channel binding. Our case study illustrates the importance of cryptographically binding context to protocol messages to prevent an adversary from misusing messages out of context.

Keywords: Authentication · channel binding · cryptographic binding · cryptographic protocols · Cryptographic Protocol Shapes Analyzer (CPSA) · cryptography · cybersecurity · Fast Identity Online (FIDO) · formal-methods analysis of protocols · Universal Authentication Framework (UAF)

H. C. Pöhls and C. J. Mitchell (Eds.): SSR 2025, LNCS 16466, pp. 133–161, 2026.
https://doi.org/10.1007/978-3-032-19567-8_7

1 Introduction

42 years apart, the 1978 *Needham-Schroeder (NS)* public-key protocol [30] and the 2020 *Fast IDentity Online (FIDO) Universal Authentication Framework (UAF)* 1.2 specification [4] share a common flaw: they both fail to cryptographically bind a sensitive value to its source. To protect against a malicious adversary, including a *Dolev-Yao (DY)* network intruder [13], cryptographic binding is necessary. Without correct cryptographic binding, an adversary may violate a protocol's security goals by copying sensitive cryptographic values between protocol sessions to execute *man-in-the-middle (MitM)* attacks. Mitigating such attacks requires emerging protocol standards to apply cryptographic bindings correctly and to perform formal-methods analyses to verify the correctness of these bindings. Using formal methods, we analyze a channel-binding flaw of FIDO UAF, demonstrate a resulting MitM attack against eBay's open-source UAF server, and suggest and formally verify mitigations.

Our analysis reveals MitM attacks on the UAF attestations that enable an adversary to masquerade as a client, for example, when establishing a session with a bank server. A version of this attack follows from any one of the following weaknesses in UAF: (1) Even when performing channel binding, the server might not bind the challenge in a manner that enables the client to authenticate the challenge. (2) The server can selectively accept incorrect channel bindings, potentially accepting attestations from malicious protocol sessions. (3) The standard makes channel bindings optional, creating circumstances in which there is no cryptographic binding between the client's attestation and the server's protocol session. Exploiting these weaknesses, an adversary can trick a legitimate client into acting as a confused deputy [20], producing attestations for a legitimate server's challenge, which the legitimate server accepts.

Cryptographic *channel binding* is an important type of cryptographic binding which binds sensitive values to an underlying authenticated communication channel. A common type of channel binding is *Transport Layer Security (TLS)* channel binding [34], which, through various methods, binds sensitive values to properties of an end-to-end encrypted TLS channel. The UAF specification recommends TLS channel binding to mitigate MitM attacks, in which an adversary might fraudulently authenticate as a legitimate user to steal the user's private information, engage in transactions on the user's behalf, or usurp the user's identity. For emerging protocol standards, channel binding is a critical tool for resisting MitM attacks and other undesirable structural flaws.

Formal-methods protocol analysis is a powerful technique for proving the correctness of a protocol's security properties or, by discovering counterexamples, identifying security flaws. This technique lends itself well to automatic tools (e.g., theorem provers or model checkers), which verify the security properties of a cryptographic protocol specified in a formal language. Generally, these tools assume *symbolic* models with perfect cryptography, and evaluate protocols against a DY adversary to reveal security flaws. Security flaws are subtle, particularly when an adversary manipulates messages between an unbounded number of protocol instances, and can be difficult to identify manually.

We present a formal-methods analysis of channel bindings in the 2020 FIDO UAF 1.2 protocol, which seeks to reduce the use of traditional passwords in favor of authentication devices. Using the *Cryptographic Protocol Shapes Analyzer (CPSA)* [26]—which is one of several tools specialized for formal-methods analysis of protocols—we model several variations of FIDO UAF in the mathematical abstraction of *strand space* and apply CPSA to explore all essentially different possible executions of each model. We do so separately from the perspectives of the client and the server, for specified assumptions about how certain important cryptographic values (e.g., keys, nonces) were generated and who knows them. This exploration includes possible interactions with a DY adversary. CPSA either exhaustively proves that no adverse interaction is possible, or CPSA finds an attack against the model. We summarize our results by stating and proving, or disproving, UAF security properties, focusing on UAF's declared security goals.

While powerful, formal-methods analysis does not address all aspects of protocol security. For example, this type of analysis will not uncover errors in implementation, flaws resulting from using weak cryptographic primitives, or applications of protocols to inappropriate settings. For these reasons, in our review of eBay's implementation of FIDO UAF, we also carefully studied their source code. Despite the limitations of formal-methods analysis, protocols—including UAF—would usually benefit from such analyses.

FIDO UAF. UAF is an attractive emerging standard and the subject of a growing number of studies, including formal-methods studies (see Sect. 3). The FIDO Alliance counts among its members many recognizable technology giants, financial institutions, retailers, government institutes, and standards bodies from nations throughout the world [1]. These members include Google, Apple, Microsoft, and Amazon. UAF is a complicated standard, specified across over a dozen documents, that attempts to support a large number of technologies and use cases. To our knowledge, FIDO developed the standard without any formal verification, resulting in several studies (including this one) identifying flaws. With UAF replacing many traditional password-based systems, it is vital that we analyze and improve the standard's cryptographic bindings.

A core component of UAF is the *authenticator*—a networked device implementing a local authentication mechanism, such as facial recognition, voice detection, or PIN entry. UAF specifies four protocols: registration, authentication, transaction confirmation, and de-registration. In registration, a *client* pairs an authenticator with a server (the "*relying party*") for subsequent use in the other protocols. In authentication, transaction confirmation, and de-registration, the client authenticates to a relying party by presenting *attestations* (assertions) of a user's identity from a subset of paired authenticators (see Fig. 1). To associate an authenticator's assertion with a client's specific request, the relying party issues a cryptographic challenge, which the authenticator signs.

In FIDO UAF, the relying party's challenge, and thus the resulting assertion, may optionally bind to the session's underlying TLS channel using one of several TLS channel bindings. By shedding light on how to channel bind correctly, including the choice of binding method and to which data to bind, our study of UAF's channel binding benefits UAF and future protocol standards. We introduce UAF's available channel bindings in Sect. 2.2.

Our Work. To our knowledge, we are first, including using formal methods, to analyze whether the available TLS channel bindings adequately address the UAF security goals. In particular, prior work by Feng et al. [15] does not perform such analysis.

To analyze channel binding in UAF, we model and analyze variations of the registration and authentication protocols using CPSA. For each protocol, we model five available channel bindings (including no channel binding) using three different versions of TLS: TLS 1.2 with RSA key exchange (TLS1.2-RSA), TLS 1.2 with DH key exchange (TLS1.2-DH), and TLS 1.3. Additionally, we model each protocol using the TLS 1.3 "*TLS-exporter*" channel binding' [37], which UAF does not officially support. Table 1 lists our CPSA models of the UAF protocols. To reflect the interactions between the lower-level TLS connections and the higher-level UAF messages, each CPSA model incorporates existing strand-space models of TLS 1.2 and TLS 1.3. We model and analyze these different binding scenarios to illustrate the binding properties necessary to achieve UAF security goals under a variety of cryptographic assumptions.

As a proof of concept, we implement our MitM attack against eBay's FIDO-certified, open-source UAF server [14], which does not implement channel binding (see Sect. 9). On August 13, 2023, we notified eBay's GitHub maintainers of this vulnerability, but they never responded, and eBay appears to have abandoned their UAF implementation. To carry out this attack, an adversary exploits inadequate binding of the server's challenge to specific sessions of UAF authentication and registration protocols, producing a protocol interaction in which the honest client-authenticator pair generates attestations for the adversary's malicious sessions. This attack demonstrates an example of a harmful protocol interaction resulting from inadequate cryptographic binding and verification.

Our contributions include: (1) A formal-methods analysis of UAF 1.2's optional channel bindings, including bindings for TLS-1.2 (with RSA or DH key exchange) and TLS-1.3. Table 3 summarizes the results of our analysis. (2) A structural weakness and resulting "challenge-reissuing" attack against several FIDO UAF channel bindings, exploiting inadequate binding of the server's challenge to a particular session (Sect. 8). (3) Details of a MitM attack in which an adversary reissues challenges to trick a client and authenticator pair to act as confused deputies to authenticate the adversary (Sect. 8.2). (4) A demonstration of the MitM attack against eBay's open-source UAF server (Sect. 9). (5) Recommendations to improve channel binding in UAF (Sect. 10). We include artifacts of our work, including all of our CPSA and attack source code, and make these artifacts available on GitHub [23].

In the rest of this paper, we (1) introduce the UAF protocols and their channel binding mechanisms, (2) discuss previous work, (3) present our adversarial model, CPSA models, security goals, and security analysis, (4) identify resulting vulnerabilities, attacks, and risks, (5) describe and implement an attack against eBay's UAF implementation, and (6) recommend improvements to the UAF standard. Three appendices include additional technical details: ladder diagrams of the UAF protocols, security goals, and formal-methods analyses. For more background, details, and discussion, see our full paper [17].

2 FIDO

We introduce FIDO UAF and discuss the framework's cryptographic channel binding, authentication protocol, and registration protocol.

2.1 FIDO UAF

In 2013, the FIDO Alliance proposed UAF [4], an open standard supplanting passwords in favor of *authenticator devices*, such as mobile phones, which implement local authentication mechanisms (e.g., biometric, PIN). Major design goals of UAF include enabling *relying parties* (services seeking to authenticate users), to specify to users which types of authenticators they will accept. As of September 2025, the FIDO website lists 508 certified implementations of UAF [2], including the eBay implementation that we attack in Sect. 9.

UAF's design seeks to reduce the use of traditional passwords, which FIDO indicates as problematic due to weak password choices, password reuse, management of many passwords, and phishing attacks. FIDO identifies passwords as responsible for over 80% of all data breaches, and promotes UAF as a potential mitigation. Additionally, relying parties that authenticate users using UAF do not store passwords or password hashes, mitigating common attacks in which the adversary steals password databases.

The FIDO Security Reference [5] specifies informal security goals for UAF network protocols, including strong user authentication (SG-1), forgery resistance (SG-11), parallel session resistance (SG-12), and forwarding resistance (SG-13), for which the reference lists channel binding as a security measure. Despite listing channel binding as a security measure, to encourage adoption of the framework and to maximize compatibility with existing systems, *FIDO made channel binding optional* in the UAF standard. In Sect. B, we formalize these security goals as an "injective agreement" [29] on session context.

UAF protocols build on the principle of *attestation*: clients prove their identities to relying parties by presenting one or more assertions of their identity signed by pre-registered authenticators. Authenticators sign these assertions with asymmetric authentication keys that they generate when registering with a relying party. Additionally, the authenticators sign *endorsement keys* using *attestation signing keys*, which the authenticators back by presenting *attestation certificates* originating from device manufacturers. By relying on authenticator attestations, UAF shifts authentication from traditional passwords ("something you know") to a client's possession of their registered authenticators ("something you have"). Figure 1 illustrates a high-level overview of the assertion process during UAF authentication.

UAF presents challenges to developers and researchers because it is complex—the standard comprises several protocols and variations spanning at

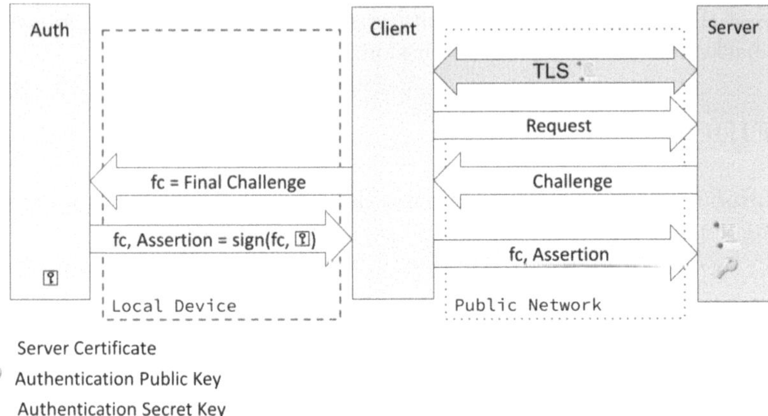

Fig. 1. Architecture of UAF authentication using a pre-registered, embedded authenticator. The server issues a challenge to the client, who incorporates that challenge into a final challenge and transmits it to the authenticator (Auth). Using the authentication secret key, the authenticator signs an assertion, which the client transmits to the server to complete authentication. The server verifies the assertion using the authentication public key that it obtains when the client registers the authenticator. The attestation process in UAF registration reflects a similar structure. In our analysis, we assume that the adversary cannot manipulate local device communication between the client and their authenticator.

least 12 lengthy documents—and specifies security goals only informally. This complexity arises from the framework's effort to be universal: the framework attempts to support many types and models of authenticators, incorporate backwards compatibility with legacy authentication methods, and enable relying parties to specify custom levels of security and authenticator support. To manage UAF's complexity, implementations may forgo optional features such as cryptographic channel binding, and formal-methods analyses may abstract away certain operations. These measures may result in unexpected vulnerabilities.

2.2 Channel Binding

To mitigate potential MitM attacks, UAF specifies an optional channel binding that binds a UAF session's challenge parameters to the underlying TLS channel between the client and the server. UAF implementations may select from several TLS channel binding standards: *token binding* [33], *channel ID binding* [6], *server endpoint binding* [3], and *server certificate binding* (could be done in a manner similar to client certificate binding in OAuth [27]). In token binding and channel ID binding, the client generates an asymmetric key pair, shares the public key with the server using extensions in the TLS handshake, and binds subsequent UAF challenge parameters to this public key. When binding to the server endpoint, the client binds the challenge to a hash of the server's certificate. When binding to the server certificate, the client binds the challenge to the server's certificate.

While the phrase "channel binding" suggests binding to a specific TLS *session*, each of the UAF's channel bindings binds only to one of two *endpoints*: the client or the server. The channel bindings are valid for multiple TLS sessions between endpoints, such as renegotiated sessions, but potentially enable bound UAF session challenge parameters to migrate between different UAF sessions sharing the same endpoints (see Sect. C). We analyze UAF with the framework's supported bindings and a newer channel binding TLS-exporter [37], which binds to a specific TLS session but is unsupported by the current UAF standard. To our knowledge, TLS 1.3 officially supports only TLS-exporter as a valid binding.

UAF allows a server to continue the protocol even when it is unable to verify bindings. For example, the server might accept a binding from a client that binds to a TLS connection between the client and a TLS proxy, rather than between the client and the server.

2.3 Registration

The UAF registration protocol comprises messages between three network entities: a FIDO UAF *client*, a FIDO *server*, and a FIDO *authenticator*. Registration pairs the client's authenticator with a server for future operations requiring authentication. As is default in the UAF specification, we assume a first-factor authenticator integrated with the device running the client. The client and the server communicate over a TLS channel. The authenticator and the client reside together on a single device and communicate using a custom *Application Programming Interface (API)* [5]. Prior to executing the registration protocol, the client first authenticates to the server using a traditional authentication mechanism, such as providing a username and a password.

The relying party initiates the registration protocol by sending to the client four values: (1) $username$, the username under which the client will register, (2) *policy*, a list of allowed and disallowed authenticator types, (3) $appId$, an identifier for the relying party, and (4) *challenge*, a freshly generated cryptographic nonce. The client verifies that $appId$ matches the server's relying party, then proceeds to the next step of the protocol by preparing a registration request.

To prepare the registration request, the client prepares several additional values: (5) $facetId$, a set of identifiers for which the registration is valid, included for the purpose of preventing excess registrations for a relying party with multiple valid identities, (6) $tlsData$, an optional entry of data for channel binding, and (7) fc, a final challenge comprising a hash of $appId$, *challenge*, $facetId$, and $tlsData$. The client transmits $username$, $appId$, and fc to the authenticator via the local API.

The authenticator now generates a registration assertion by generating (8) an asymmetric authentication key pair (K_{pub}, K_{priv}) and (9) a key handle $h = \text{hash}(K_{priv}, username)$. In addition, the authenticator introduces the following values: (10) $aaid$, an identifier for the authenticator's model, (11) $cert_{attest}$, a certificate for a pre-loaded attestation key backed by a manufacturer's root attestation certificate, (12) *reg-cntr* and *cntr*, a pair of operation counters that assist the relying party in detecting duplicate assertion operations, and (13) s, an assertion signed by the authenticator's attestation key and containing *aaid*, fc, *reg-cntr*, *cntr*, and K_{pub}. To the client, the authenticator transmits *aaid*, K_{pub}, fc, h, $cert_{attest}$, *reg-cntr*, *cntr*, and s, which the client forwards to the server over the existing TLS channel. Figure 3 visualizes the cryptographic flow of the UAF registration network protocol.

2.4 Authentication

The UAF authentication protocol is similar to registration, but omits some of the values present in registration messages, and the authenticator signs the assertion using K_{priv} (previously generated during registration) rather than with the device's attestation key. Authentication and registration rely on a TLS channel between the client and the server and apply channel binding in the same manner. Figure 4 illustrates the message flow of UAF authentication.

When initiating the authentication protocol, the server omits *username* and transmits only *policy*, *appId*, and *challenge*. The client now transmits only *appId* (or a similar key identifier for the corresponding relying party) and fc to the authenticator. The authenticator responds with fc, a random nonce n, *cntr*, and an assertion s consisting of a signature of fc, n, and *cntr* signed by K_{priv}, the asymmetric authentication key that the authenticator generated during the registration protocol.

3 Previous Work

In contrast with our work, existing formal-methods studies of FIDO UAF abstract away the TLS channel and neither explicitly model nor analyze the channel bindings. By neglecting to analyze channel binding, previous work fails to examine whether UAF protects against undesirable protocol interactions caused by the various ways UAF binds channels or chooses not to bind channels.

In 2021, Feng et al. [15] presented a formal-methods analysis of the UAF registration and authentication protocols using ProVerif. In their analysis, they formalized and verified UAF authentication goals based on Lowe's authentication hierarchy [29]. They discovered and corrected several attacks on the UAF standard, including attacks against enterprise UAF implementations in finance. Their ProVerif model abstracts away details of the TLS channel, representing it as a communication channel under an identifier. To bind UAF messages to the channel, the model specifies a function that maps a TLS channel identifier to a unique bitstring representing the channel: a perfect channel binding. In contrast, the approved UAF bindings bind only to one of the channel's endpoints, may be valid for multiple TLS channels between the same endpoints, and, when using TLS 1.2, depend on the client generating a fresh premaster secret. Consequently, analysis of their model overlooks potential vulnerabilities resulting from the limitations of UAF's channel bindings.

Using ProVerif, Pereira et al. [32] also present a formal-methods analysis of FIDO's U2F protocol, a similar protocol to those in UAF. They conclude that, if the client verifies the *appId* it receives from the server, the protocol achieves the standard's authentication goals. Notably, their analysis completely omits channel binding, focusing exclusively on the *appId*'s role in helping the client authenticate the server's challenge: they do not present any analysis of U2F with channel binding. We consider the *appId* a poor value to bind because it is a public, not a cryptographic value, and, by FIDO's own admission [4], may be possible for an adversary to spoof (e.g., by compromising a subdomain owned by a legitimate organization).

Hu and Zhang [22] present an informal analysis of UAF, identifying three attacks: (1) a misbinding attack, (2) a parallel-session attack, and (3) a multi-user attack. These attacks do not consider the effect of channel binding and require a stronger adversary than a DY intruder: the adversary corrupts the client, corrupts the authenticator, or exploits multiple users sharing an authenticator.

Panos et al. [31] perform an informal analysis of UAF, presenting several high-level attack vectors. Büttner and Gruschka [9] present MitM attacks on FIDO extensions, design a protocol to protect the extensions, and analyze the protocol using ProVerif. Neither of these works considers channel binding.

Additional studies of FIDO UAF assess social-engineering attacks [36], biometric authenticators [11], informal trust requirements [28], and feasibility [10]. Other studies analyze related standards such as FIDO2 [7,19], for which attacks on UAF are relevant, though these two studies do not consider channel binding.

Protocols which have been analyzed using CPSA include the CAVES multi-party attestation protocol [12], Zooko's forced-latency protocol [24], SRP-3 [35], TLS-1.3 [8], and the Session Binding Proxy [18].

Building on our 2021 initial analysis of UAF authentication, in 2022, Fuchs, Hammer, and Liu [16] analyzed UAF registration. Our analysis of UAF incorporates and evolves their analysis.

4 Adversarial Model

We evaluate UAF against a DY-style adversary that seeks to fool legitimate clients into generating assertions on the adversary's behalf, to enable the adversary to register or authenticate in place of an honest user. To achieve this goal, the adversary transfers challenges from one UAF session to another by exploiting weak or missing cryptographic bindings, including TLS channel bindings.

Our adversary controls all traffic between UAF clients and servers, and is thus capable of adding, dropping, modifying, and replaying arbitrary messages between these entities. The adversary does not have access to communication between the client and the authenticator, which takes place over a local API rather than over a network channel. The adversary cannot break standard cryptographic primitives such as encryption, digital signatures, or hashing, and to compute these primitives requires knowledge of correct keys or hash function inputs. The adversary controls at least one legitimate UAF server on the network, for which they hold appropriate cryptographic keys and certificates. In practice, this assumption may be an obscure UAF server operating under some dubious or compromised certificate, and may require the adversary to trick an honest user into communicating with it.

We assume that all legitimate network participants communicate with a legitimate certificate authority and deploy the same version of TLS and any channel bindings in use. Upon request, the certificate authority produces authenticated certificates for any network entity, including the adversary. Additionally, we assume that any attestation certificate originating from an authenticator is legitimate—in real implementations, the server must check such certificates during UAF registration. The adversary cannot compromise legitimate authenticators to steal key material.

The adversary is capable of spoofing *application identifiers (appIds)*—FIDO acknowledges this possible attack in the UAF network protocol specification [4]. In authentication and registration, servers bind their challenges to the *appId*. Because this value is known to all network participants and is possible to spoof or verify incorrectly, we consider it unsuitable for a cryptographic binding.

Our adversary wishes to access an honest user's accounts to steal information, engage in transactions on the user's behalf, or to usurp the user's identity when interacting with other users. These activities enable an adversary to sell a user's private data to criminals, blackmail the user with details of their private life, steal the user's assets by transferring them to the adversary, and target the user's social network for further attacks. Possible targets include a user's online banking, E-commerce, social media, or business accounts.

5 CPSA Models (Summary)

For our formal-methods analysis, we created eight CPSA models of FIDO UAF (see Table 1), including a baseline using passwords over TLS 1.2 without UAF, six different ways to bind the challenge, and our suggested improvement that binds the challenge to TLS 1.3 channel key material derived using TLS-exporter. For details and sample snippets of our CPSA source code, see our full paper [17] and GitHub [23].

6 Security Goals (Summary)

FIDO informally states several security goals that it aims to achieve via UAF channel binding [5], which we summarize in Table 2 as SG-1, SG-11, SG-12, and SG-13. In the strand space model, we formalize what we call Goal 1, which implies each of the four informally-stated goals. Specifically, we state Goal 1 as an *injective agreement* [29] on a session context between two complementary strands in a UAF strand space (see Sect. B).

7 CPSA Analysis (Summary)

Using CPSA, we analyze for each of our eight models of UAF (see Sect. 5) whether they achieve Goal 1 (see Sect. B). We do so by (1) modeling UAF authentication and registration protocols in the strand space model, (2) for each protocol, defining session contexts (see Sect. B.2), (3) specifying origination assumptions for each of the protocol roles (see Sect. B.2), (4) using CPSA, search the strand space models to produce "shapes" (see [17]), (5) using the shapes, prove Goal 1 (and its constituent sub-goals) true or false.

Table 1. Summary of our CPSA models. Each UAF model includes the registration and authentication protocols. We include two variations of each TLS 1.2 model: (1) with RSA key exchange, (2) with DH key exchange.

Name	Summary
Baseline-NoUAF	Plain passwords over TLS 1.2 without UAF
UAF-NoBinding-TLS1.2	Unbound challenge over TLS 1.2
UAF-TokenBinding-TLS1.2	Client applies TLS 1.2 token binding to challenge
UAF-ChannelId-TLS1.2	Client applies TLS 1.2 channel ID binding to challenge
UAF-Endpoint-TLS1.2	Client binds challenge to hash of server certificate over TLS 1.2
UAF-ServerCert-TLS1.2	Client binds challenge to server's certificate over TLS 1.2
UAF-NoBinding-TLS1.3	Unbound challenge over TLS 1.3
UAF-Exporter-TLS1.3 *	Client binds challenge to TLS 1.3 channel key material

(* Our suggested improvement.)

Table 2. Selected UAF security goals as informally stated by the FIDO Alliance [5], for which FIDO specifies channel binding as a security measure. The goals are vague when referring to notions such as "high cryptographic strength" or resilience, and the goals do not refer to specific variables or messages in the protocol. We formalize these goals and focus on them in our analysis.

Goal ID	Description
SG-1	**Strong User Authentication:** Authenticate (i.e. recognize) a user and/or a device to a relying party with high (cryptographic) strength
SG-11	**Forgery Resistance:** Be resilient to Forgery Attacks (Impersonation Attacks). I.e. prevent attackers from attempting to modify intercepted communications in order to masquerade as the legitimate user and login to the system
SG-12	**Parallel Session Resistance:** Be resilient to Parallel Session Attacks. Without knowing a user's authentication credential, an attacker can masquerade as the legitimate user by creating a valid authentication message out of some eavesdropped communication between the user and the server
SG-13	**Forwarding Resistance:** Be resilient to Forwarding and Replay Attacks. Having intercepted previous communications, an attacker can impersonate the legal user to authenticate to the system. The attacker can replay or forward the intercepted messages

Each search assumes the perspective of a protocol role and its corresponding origination assumptions (which might differ for different roles). CPSA searches exhaustively for unique shapes (possible protocol executions) within a strand space, either proving session-context agreement or finding a counterexample (a possible attack). These searches include intruder strands in strand spaces, where intruders may use an unbounded number of sessions, thereby considering all essentially different possible protocol interaction attacks. For each search, CPSA terminated, thereby achieving provable definite results [25]. Table 3 summarizes our findings.

Table 3. Summary of our security analysis of our UAF models. For each model, a check (✓) indicates that all strands of the corresponding role (indicated by the column header) satisfy context-agreement theorems with a complementary strand under the role's security assumptions. A crossmark (×) indicates that CPSA finds a counterexample to the security goal by disproving context agreement. Only a subset of models using TLS1.2-DH and TLS1.3 achieve context agreement from all perspectives: TLS1.2-DH with server side bindings (endpoint, server certificate), and TLS 1.3 (exporter). These models succeed because they bind to the authenticated server and incorporate mutual freshness in the TLS session via a DH key exchange.

Model	client-reg	server-reg	client-auth	server-auth
Baseline-NoUAF	✓	×	✓	×
UAF-NoBinding-TLS1.2-RSA	✓	×	✓	×
UAF-TokenBinding-TLS1.2-RSA	✓	×	✓	×
UAF-ChannelId-TLS1.2-RSA	✓	×	✓	×
UAF-Endpoint-TLS1.2-RSA	✓	×	✓	×
UAF-ServerCert-TLS1.2-RSA	✓	×	✓	×
UAF-NoBinding-TLS1.2-DH	✓	×	✓	×
UAF-TokenBinding-TLS1.2-DH	✓	×	✓	×
UAF-ChannelId-TLS1.2-DH	✓	×	✓	×
UAF-Endpoint-TLS1.2-DH	✓	✓	✓	✓
UAF-ServerCert-TLS1.2-DH	✓	✓	✓	✓
UAF-NoBinding-TLS1.3	✓	×	✓	×
UAF-Exporter-TLS1.3 *	✓	✓	✓	✓

(* Our suggested improvement.)

8 Vulnerabilities, Attacks, and Risks

We discuss vulnerabilities, attacks, and risks that arise from our analysis of UAF.

8.1 Vulnerabilities

We highlight three vulnerabilities resulting from how UAF binds (or fails to bind) the server's challenge.

Binding to a TLS1.2-RSA Channel Is Insufficient. Because the client is solely responsible for generating the premaster secret in TLS1.2-RSA, the server has no assurances that channel bindings are legitimate. An adversary that learns or guesses the client's premaster secret can forge such a channel binding to fool the server. Possible causes include the adversary compromising the client's machine, the client reusing premaster secrets, or an implementation error exposing the premaster secret to the adversary.

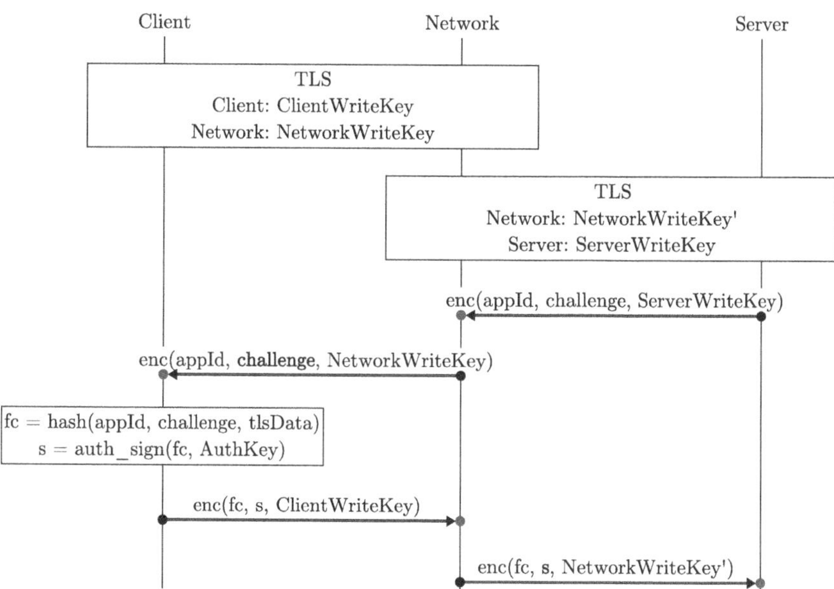

Fig. 2. Challenge-reissuing attack during UAF authentication: CPSA shape for UAF authentication under the server's cryptographic assumptions. When the client omits channel binding, or includes one of the standard UAF bindings in *tlsData*, the client acts as a confused deputy and produces an attestation for the adversary. This shape reveals the following structural weakness: in two scenarios, the adversary can masquerade as the client to the server, or transplant messages from one session to another between the same endpoints. In particular, the adversary can masquerade as the client when the client omits channel binding in the *tlsData*, or when the server fails to verify this binding. The adversary can transplant messages between such sessions because the client binds only to the endpoints of the channel and not to the session.

The Server Cannot Verify All Channel Bindings. Depending on which channel bindings a client applies to the final challenge parameters, the server may be unable to verify the bindings when processing an assertion. For channel bindings relying on client-generated secrets, the server has no assurance that such secrets are not known to the adversary or are unique to the server's TLS session with the client. When channel binding to the server's identity using TLS1.2-RSA, the server may be unable determine to which TLS channel a client's binding applies. Additionally, if the client binds to a TLS channel between itself and a perimeter proxy, the server cannot verify the binding. Under some circumstances, UAF allows a server to continue the protocol even when such bindings fail to verify. We discuss the issue of such proxies in [17].

Channel Binding Is Optional. There is no requirement for certified UAF implementations to implement channel binding. When the client omits a channel binding in the final challenge parameters, the server has no assurance that an adversary does not reissue its challenge in another session. This scenario is equivalent to when a server fails to verify the channel bindings.

8.2 Attacks

Resulting from the weaknesses in UAF's channel binding, an adversary that extracts a challenge from a session of UAF between itself and a legitimate server may reissue this challenge in another session between itself and a legitimate client. In this *challenge-reissuing attack*, an adversary (acting as a MitM) fools honest clients into signing fraudulent assertions with their authenticators. UAF registration and authentication feature a similar format for the challenge, assertion, and response, resulting in this attack applying to both protocols. Figure 2 illustrates a challenge-reissuing attack during UAF authentication.

Challenge reissuing results from a client's inability to identify for which session the server generates a challenge (see Sect. 8.1). Because the server does not cryptographically bind the challenge to any session of UAF, the adversary may forward the challenge to a client who unwittingly uses it to craft an assertion, which the client's authenticator then signs. UAF's mitigation against such an attack is channel binding, which is optional and may still enable an adversary to move challenges between different sessions involving the same TLS endpoints. We implement this attack against eBay's implementation of UAF, which chooses not to use channel binding, as allowed by the UAF standard (see Sect. 9).

An adversary that tricks clients into signing fraudulent assertions can represent themselves as the client to a legitimate UAF server. In registration, the adversary can register a client's authenticators with a relying party without the client's knowledge. In authentication, the adversary authenticates as the legitimate client by sending to the server an assertion that the client's authenticator signs. Without channel binding, the server cannot detect such an assertion.

8.3 Risks

We consider the risks posed by challenge reissuing to UAF's primary goal and consider the resulting harmful effects that threaten users and systems authenticating with UAF.

UAF's primary goal, authenticating users and devices to relying parties with a "high degree of cryptographic strength," does not hold when missing or insufficient channel binding enables challenge reissuing. An adversary can misrepresent themselves as a client and present fraudulent assertions signed by clients unaware that the challenge migrated between UAF sessions. Even when binding is present, a server may disregard or fail to verify the binding correctly, amplifying the risk of this attack.

Because the adversary can fool a client into producing assertions for arbitrary challenges, the adversary can misrepresent themselves as a legitimate user and engage in transactions with the user's authorization. UAF's design is general purpose, broadly applicable to many systems, and well adopted, enabling an adversary to engage in malicious transactions across a wide range of services (e.g., source control systems, E-commerce websites, online banking, health care, social media) that fail to mitigate challenge reissuing. Such transactions can have devastating effects on individual users and organizations, which may be victims of identity theft, fraud, blackmail, and other criminal activities.

9 Attack Implementation

To illustrate the importance of UAF's channel binding, we exploit missing channel binding to carry out a MitM attack against eBay's well-known open-source UAF server [14], which is certified by FIDO and implements a subset of UAF 1.0. Our attack enables us to authenticate as an honest user without access to the user's authenticators.

To carry out the protocol, we implement a basic client in the Python programming language. Our client registers dummy authenticators with the server and responds to authentication requests with valid assertions from these authenticators. We implement a malicious server as a process that passes messages between the client and the UAF server. Our attack source code is available on GitHub [23].

We assume: (1) an honest user wishes to communicate with a DY adversary acting as a server; (2) there is a legitimate server on the network; (3) the adversary controls a subdomain under the server's URL (e.g., the adversary compromises one of the server's trusted facets [21]); and (4) the client does not implement channel binding. The adversary wishes to masquerade as the honest client to a legitimate server.

In addition to not supporting channel binding, the eBay FIDO UAF implementation fails to inspect the contents of an assertion's final challenge parameters, verifying only an authenticator's signature. This egregious omission likely results in additional potential vulnerabilities beyond our work: an adversary can freely substitute challenge parameters without the server's knowledge. For our attack, we assume only that the server does not enforce any channel binding.

The attack proceeds in two steps—registration and authentication—which exploit lack of binding of the UAF challenge.

9.1 Step 1: Registration

In our attack's first phase, the adversary exploits missing binding to register the honest user's authenticator with the legitimate server, claiming to own this authenticator.

An honest user intentionally attempts to register this authenticator with the adversary, who masquerades as an honest server on the network. The adversary then engages in two concurrent UAF registration protocols: one between itself and the user, and one between itself and an honest server, presenting the user with the honest server's challenge. Subsequently, the user issues the challenge to their authenticator, which generates a *key registration data (KRD)* object, including an *authenticator attestation ID (aaid)*, a new public-private key pair, an attestation certificate, a pair of counters (registration and signature), and a hash of these parameters including the malicious challenge. Using the private key, the authenticator signs the KRD and returns an assertion to the user, who forwards it to the adversary. The adversary now claims the assertion to the legitimate server, thereby registering the user's authenticator without their knowledge.

9.2 Step 2: Authentication

The adversary engages in parallel UAF authentication protocols, transplanting the legitimate server's challenge and policy, which includes the user's authenticator maliciously registered by the adversary, into the session between the adversary and the user. The user issues the challenge to the authenticator, which builds an authentication assertion, which the adversary presents to the legitimate server as their own to complete the protocol and authenticate. Claiming the user's identity, the adversary is now free to engage in malicious behaviors under the user's name.

10 Recommendations

We recommend: (1) For applications where it is critical to mitigate protocol interactions, the UAF standard require the client (and potentially the server) to apply a channel binding to the challenge parameters. (2) The server should not accept attestations that bind to channels it cannot verify. (3) Applications should consider using TLS1.3 and implementing the TLS-exporter binding, which avoids the limitations of TLS channel bindings in UAF by binding to a specific TLS session rather than to one of the communication endpoints. Applications should not bind to TLS1.2-RSA channels because these may be vulnerable.

11 Conclusion

Using CPSA, we performed a formal-methods analysis of channel binding in the FIDO UAF standard. From this analysis, we: (1) showed that several of FIDO UAF's channel bindings fail to mitigate protocol interaction, resulting in MitM attacks on the server's challenge. (2) implemented an attack against eBay's open-source FIDO UAF server, allowing an adversary to masquerade as a legitimate client. (3) recommended and formally verified improvements to TLS channel binding in the UAF standard.

Our attack exploits three limitations of channel binding in FIDO UAF: (1) channel binding is optional; (2) the server may accept attestations that bind to incorrect channels; and (3) UAF binds only to the protocol's *endpoints*, not to the underlying TLS *session*.

Although the UAF specification suggests that omitting channel binding may create a vulnerability (see Sect. 2), to our knowledge, we are first to carry out a formal-methods analysis of channel binding in UAF and first to exhibit details of an attack on UAF that exploits the weaknesses of UAF's channel binding. Previous studies of UAF did not analyze the standard's cryptographic channel binding. Policy makers should be aware that omitting channel binding, or accepting attestations that bind to an incorrect channel, creates a serious vulnerability in which the adversary can trick the client and authenticator to act as confused deputies to sign an authentication challenge for the adversary.

Despite decades of progress in protocol design, UAF fails to apply cryptographic binding consistently and correctly, enabling potential attacks by a DY adversary. Our study of UAF channel binding illustrates the necessity of adopting formal-methods tools in protocol analysis—including analysis in the design process—and the need to develop and apply rigorous techniques to ensure that critical protocol values are always properly cryptographically bound to their session context.

Acknowledgments. We thank Joshua Guttman for helpful comments and valuable guidance on proving security goals using CPSA. Our work evolves CPSA models of UAF registration created by Danning Liu [16]. Thanks also to Ted Selker for suggesting ways to clarify the presentation. Alan Sherman and Enis Golaszewski were supported in 2023 in part by the National Security Agency under an INSuRE+C grant via Northeastern University, and by the UMBC cybersecurity exploratory grant program. Alan Sherman was also supported in part by the National Science Foundation under DGE grants 1753681 and 2438185 (SFS), 1819521 (SFS Capacity), and 2138921 (SaTC).

A Ladder Diagrams

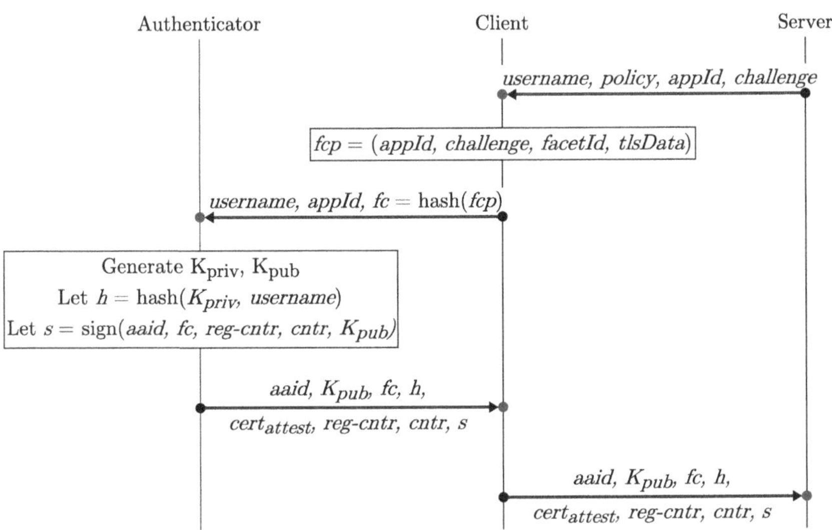

Fig. 3. Idealized message sequence diagram of UAF registration over a network. Vertical lines correspond to protocol roles; horizontal arrows indicate message flows from one role to another; and arrow labels indicate message contents. Information in boxes specify local processing for each role. The client and server communicate over a pre-negotiated TLS channel. The client communicates with the authenticator via the *Authenticator-Specific Module (ASM)* API. The authenticator signs s using the attestation key corresponding to the attestation certificate that the manufacturer loads on the device.

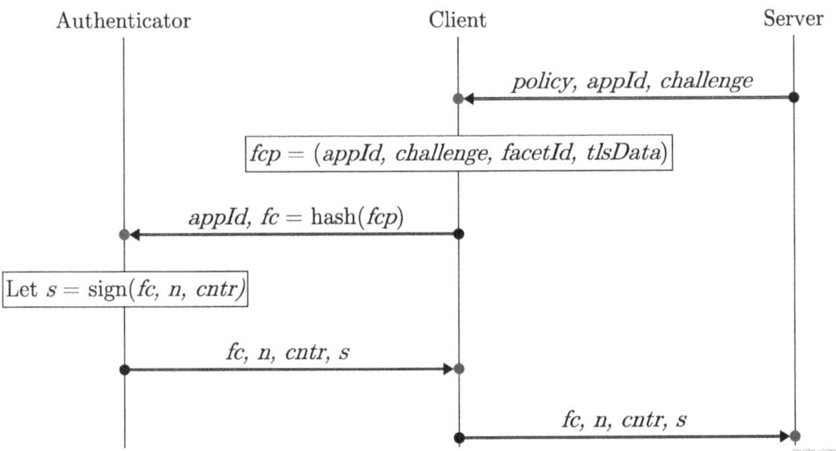

Fig. 4. Idealized message sequence diagram of UAF authentication over a network. As in registration, the client and server communicate over a pre-negotiated TLS channel, and the client communicates with the authenticator using a local API. The authenticator signs s using K_{priv}, which it recalls from a successful run of the registration protocol.

B Security Goals

In the strand space model, we formalize several UAF security goals as an *injective agreement* [29] on a session context between two complementary strands in a UAF strand space. First, we introduce UAF security goals relevant to our study. Second, we define *session context agreement* as an injective agreement on the values and relationships of a protocol's session context variables. Injective agreement means, in part, that the two roles agree on the values of the specified variables. In addition, informally, it means that this agreement was achieved through a unique proper execution of the protocol, and not through an adverse interaction with a DY adversary. Third, we define session contexts and cryptographic assumptions for our UAF models.

B.1 UAF Security Goals

FIDO states several security goals for which TLS channel binding serves as an explicit security measure [5]: SG-1 (user authentication), SG-11 (forgery resistance), SG-12 (parallel session resistance), and SG-13 (forwarding resistance). Table 2 lists these goals. FIDO describes these security goals informally, without explicitly referencing authenticity goals for specific session variables. As such, FIDO's statement of these goals is insufficient for any rigorous evaluation of UAF's authenticity properties.

In Sect. C, we rigorously formalize UAF's SG-1, SG-11, SG-12, and SG-13 security goals collectively as agreements between the server and the client on several session variables: username, server identifier, application ID, challenge, or authenticator public key. Specifically, we collectively formalize these goals as an injective agreement on the variables of a session context between a pair of complementary strands in a UAF strand space. Because UAF protocols run over a TLS connection, there are additional implicit variables on which honest, complementary communicants must agree: server random nonce, client random nonce, premaster secret (RSA key exchange), or DH exponents. As explained in Sect. B.2, this injective agreement on session context between complementary client and server strands implies that UAF achieves its informally stated security goals.

B.2 Session Context Agreement

First, we define (1) session contexts, (2) origination assumptions, and (3) unique and successful completion. Second, we combine these ideas to generalize a session context-agreement security goal.

Session Context. Session contexts comprise variables that express a single, unique session of a protocol, such as the identifiers of the communicating parties, cryptographic nonces that provide the session's freshness, and other values, such as challenges, on which participants completing a protocol session must agree.

A well-constructed session context specifies the required relationships between two complementary protocol roles for a correct execution, and can be challenging to define when a protocol features many terms with potentially complex relationships.

For any arbitrary two-party protocol π with a corresponding strand space Σ_π, a session context $Ctx[\pi]$ is a list of facts on which a pair of complementary strands $s \in \Sigma_\pi$ and $s' \in \Sigma_\pi$ must agree. Facts reflect equivalences between values (e.g., s and s' must map a nonce n to the same value) or relationships (e.g., s generates a nonce n for which s' holds hash(n)). If all facts in $Ctx[\pi]$ hold for a pair of strands s and s', then s and s' satisfy $Ctx[\pi]$. Within a strand space, it is possible for s and s' to take on the value of any strands, including the case where $s = s'$, or the case where one of s and s' is an intruder strand.

Origination Assumptions. Origination assumptions are secrecy and freshness assumptions of a protocol's variables, such as keys, nonces, or passwords. In the strand space model, these assumptions place constraints on the values penetrator strands may know or learn. *Non-originating* variables (typically used for private keys) cannot appear (i.e., be carried) as terms in any message, and are unavailable to the penetrator to know or learn, but are available to honest strands for encrypting information. Several origination assumptions are available to constrain the origination of sensitive values. *Uniquely originating* variables (typically used for nonces) generate on a single honest strand at the node where they are first carried in a message. *Uniquely generated* variables (typically used for DH exponents) generate on a single honest strand at the node where they first appear, but are not necessarily carried in a message. As such, they begin unknown to the adversary and the adversary cannot know the values of uniquely originating or generated variables until after the node where they first generate. *Penetrator non-originating* variables (typically used for passwords) are unknown to the adversary, but unlike non-originating terms, can be carried in a message and can be learned by the adversary.

Often, different protocol roles are unable to share the same assumptions—for example, a client may know that they generate a fresh nonce, but from a server's perspective, the client may reuse a previous nonce. As a result, a protocol might achieve injective agreement on a term from one perspective, but not from another perspective.

Successful and Unique Completion. We define two necessary predicates for injective agreement on the facts of a session context: *successful completion* and *unique completion*. Together, these properties define an injective agreement: if both properties hold, two complementary strands complete a unique run of the protocol with each other and agree on the resulting session context.

Honest strands derive their terms from protocol *roles*. For an ideal execution, a strand that belongs to a role $\mathcal{R}_a \in \Sigma_\pi$ completes the protocol π with a complementary strand that belongs to a role $\mathcal{R}_b \in \Sigma_\pi$.

For successful completion, two strands s and s' must execute the protocol with each other and agree on the resulting session context $Ctx[\pi]$ under a set of origination assumptions for the role of s, which we define as $Orig[\mathcal{R}_a]$, where $\mathcal{R}_a$ is the role of s. Without an additional property specifying the protocol execution as unique, successful completion alone yields a non-injective agreement on the session context $Ctx[\pi]$.

In cases where s transmits the final message, s completes without assurance that s' fully executes. As a result, a bundle $\mathcal{B}$ may incorporate a strand s' with the final node missing, which is a common occurrence when modeling protocols. To describe this scenario, let $\mathcal{B}$-height be the node-height (number of terms transmitted and received) of a strand that appears in $\mathcal{B}$. For any natural number i, a strand of integer height i has sent or received at least i of its terms.

Definition 1 (Successful Completion)
Let π be any two-party protocol; let $\mathcal{B}$ be any bundle in any strand space Σ_π; let $\mathcal{R}_a$ and $\mathcal{R}_b$ be roles in Σ_π; let s and s' be any pair of complementary strands in Σ_π; let $Ctx[\pi]$ be any session context for π; and let $Orig[\mathcal{R}_a]$ be any set of origination assumptions for s. Let i and j be any natural numbers.

$Succ(\mathcal{R}_a, \mathcal{R}_b, Ctx[\pi], Orig[\mathcal{R}_a], i, j)$ if and only if (iff) for all bundles $\mathcal{B}$ that yield from Σ_π and strands $s \in \mathcal{R}_a \cap \mathcal{B}$, there exists a strand $s' \in \mathcal{R}_b \cap \mathcal{B}$ such that under $Orig[\mathcal{R}_a]$, s with $\mathcal{B}$-height i and s' with $\mathcal{B}$-height j satisfy $Ctx[\pi]$.

Unique completion asserts that, if $\mathcal{B}$ contains executions of the strands s, s', and s'' such that all strands agree on $Ctx[\pi]$, strands s' and s'' must share role $\mathcal{R}_b$. Because they share a role and agree on the same context, for the analysis we can assume $s' = s''$ and s' is not an intruder strand. Based on this observation, we can assert that only s and s' agree on $Ctx[\pi]$—in other words, s and s' are a unique completion of the protocol.

Definition 2 (Unique Completion)
Let $\mathcal{R}_a$ be any role in Σ_π; let $Ctx[\pi]$ be any session context for π; and let $Orig[\mathcal{R}_a]$ be any set of origination assumptions for s. Let i and j be any natural numbers.

$Uniq(\mathcal{R}_a, Ctx[\pi], Orig[\mathcal{R}_a], i, j)$ iff for all roles $\mathcal{R}_b, \mathcal{R}_c$ in Σ_π, $Succ(\mathcal{R}_a, \mathcal{R}_b, Ctx[\pi], Orig[\mathcal{R}_a], i, j) \wedge Succ(\mathcal{R}_a, \mathcal{R}_c, Ctx[\pi], Orig[\mathcal{R}_a], i, j) \implies \mathcal{R}_b = \mathcal{R}_c$.

Session Context Agreement. We now define *session context-agreement* (Goal 1) as a conjunction of unique and successful completion. Using Goal 1, which we model explicitly in CPSA, we prove or disprove injective agreement of $Ctx[\pi]$ between the roles $\mathcal{R}_a$ and $\mathcal{R}_b$ under origination assumptions $Orig[\mathcal{R}_a]$ within a strand space Σ_π. For any strand space Σ_π, if CPSA terminates and produces a counterexample to Goal 1, the counterexample describes an attack on the protocol. In Sect. C, we analyze our baseline and UAF models for session context agreement.

As a comprehensive authentication goal, Goal 1 implies all of the weaker, informal UAF security goals (see Table 2) in accordance with the Lowe authentication hierarchy [29]. Models that satisfy Goal 1 express a one-to-one correspondence between the client and the server's UAF session context variables, implying SG-1. Additionally, the SG-11, SG-12, and SG-13 UAF goals specify resistance against an adversary that impersonates a legitimate user via executing parallel sessions, forging messages, or forwarding existing messages. Because Goal 1 assumes an unbounded number of sessions, Goal 1 implies SG-11. Because the UAF strand space includes penetrator strands that forge and forward messages, Goal 1 also implies SG-12 and SG-13.

Goal 1 (Session Context Agreement)
Let Σ_π be any strand space; let $\mathcal{R}_a$ and $\mathcal{R}_b$ be any complementary roles in Σ_π; let $Orig[\mathcal{R}_a]$ be any set of origination assumptions for role $\mathcal{R}_a$; and let $Ctx[\pi]$ be any session context for π. For any role ρ, let $height(\rho)$ be the height of any fully executing strand in role ρ. Let i and j be natural numbers such that $i = height(\mathcal{R}_a)$ and $j \leq height(\mathcal{R}_b)$.

Session context agreement means $\exists j$ such that
$Succ(\mathcal{R}_a, \mathcal{R}_b, Ctx[\pi], Orig[\mathcal{R}_a], i, j) \wedge Uniq(\mathcal{R}_a, Ctx[\pi], Orig[\mathcal{R}_a], i, j)$.

B.3 UAF Session Contexts

To define UAF session contexts, we identified key terms on which honest communicants must agree to achieve the UAF security goals, including terms crucial for a correct TLS session. For comparison, we include a session context for the baseline model. Because UAF session contexts depend on TLS session contexts, we begin by defining TLS session contexts.

TLS Session Contexts. We first specify a session context for TLS-1.2-RSA, followed by a session context for TLS using ephemeral DH key exchange (TLS-1.2-DH, TLS-1.3). The TLS contexts are interchangeable parameters for the baseline context and the UAF contexts that follow. Both TLS contexts specify agreement for the client and server random nonces. The TLS-1.2-RSA context specifies an additional condition on which communicants must agree involving the premaster secret. To reflect a successful DH key exchange, the TLS-DH context specifies that communicants must agree on each communicant's private DH exponent. It is possible for strands to agree on values that they do not know, such as the private exponent corresponding to a communicant's public DH value.

Session Context 1 (TLS1.2-RSA)
Let s and s' be complementary strands that carry out a TLS 1.2 handshake with a RSA key exchange. For any pair (s, s'), the following facts hold: strands s and s' agree on the identifiers for the session's server (server) and the certificate authority (ca) that signed the server's certificate. Strands s and s' agree on the client's random nonce (cr), the server's random nonce (sr), and the client-generated premaster secret (pms).

Session Context 2 (TLS-DH)
Let s and s' be complementary strands that carry out a TLS 1.2 or TLS 1.3 handshake with an ephemeral DH key exchange. For any pair (s, s'), the following facts hold: strands s and s' agree on the identifiers for the session's server (server) and the certificate authority (ca) that signed the server's certificate. Strands s and s' agree on the client's random nonce (cr), the server's random nonce (sr), the client's DH exponent (x), and the server's DH exponent (y).

Baseline Session Context. Incorporating our TLS contexts, we now specify the baseline session context (see Session Context 3) for traditional, password-based authentication across a TLS channel. In 2024, the baseline reflects a still prevalent manner by which clients authenticate to websites and other web-based services. Successful authentication between a client and a server in this baseline implies that a client strand and a server strand agree on the user's identifier, the server's identifier (e.g., URL), the user's password, and the cryptographic details of the underlying TLS session.

Session Context 3 (No-UAF)
Let s and s' be any strands in the Baseline-NoUAF strand space. For any pair (s, s'), the following facts hold: strands s and s' agree on a TLS session context [TLS-1.2-RSA or TLS-DH]. s and s' agree on the terms username, server, and pw, where pw is the password.

UAF Registration Session Context. We now define the UAF registration session context. Similar to the baseline session context, this context require strands to agree on an appropriate TLS session context—the TLS context varies depending on which version of TLS our models assume. Successful registration requires client and server strands participating in the same session to agree on the user's identifier, the server's cryptographic challenge, the server's identifier, and the *appId*.

Session Context 4 (UAF Registration)
Let s and s' be any strands in any UAF strand space. For any pair (s, s'), the following facts hold: strands s and s' agree on a TLS session context. s and s' agree on the terms challenge, username, server, and appId.

UAF Authentication Session Context. Because the authentication protocol is simpler, we define UAF authentication session context as a subset of the registration context's facts. Specifically, a client and a server strand for authentication must agree only on the server identifier, challenge, and *appId*.

Session Context 5 (UAF Authentication)
Let s and s' be any strands in any UAF strand space. For any pair (s, s'), the following facts hold: s and s' agree on a TLS session context. s and s' agree on the terms challenge, server, and appId.

B.4 UAF Origination Assumptions

We specify *origination assumptions* (see Sect. B.2) from the perspectives of the client and server roles for the baseline, UAF registration, and UAF authentication protocols. In Sect. C, we use these assumptions to analyze the baseline, UAF authentication, and UAF registration protocols. Several assumptions apply only to a subset of the models we analyze, and carry labels to indicate such.

Assumption 1 (Client Assumptions)
For any initial client strand $\mathcal{C}$ in any bundle, we make the following assumptions:

(1) Private keys of legitimate parties are unknown (non-originating) to the adversary and are never transmitted on the network.
(2) $\mathcal{C}$ generates (uniquely originates) a fresh client-random nonce for TLS, and [for TLS-1.2-RSA] a fresh premaster secret or [for TLS-1.2-DH or TLS-1.3] a fresh DH value.
(3) [Baseline model only] The adversary does not know the client's password pw (penetrator non-originating).

Assumption 2 (Server Assumptions)
For any initial server strand $\mathcal{S}$ in any bundle, we make the following assumptions:

(1) Private keys of legitimate parties are unknown to the adversary and are never transmitted on the network.
(2) $\mathcal{S}$ generates a fresh server-random nonce for TLS, and [for TLS-1.2-DH or TLS-1.3] a fresh DH value.
(3) [Baseline model only] The adversary does not know the client's password pw (penetrator non-originating).
(4) [UAF models only] The server uniquely originates the challenge for each session.
(5) [UAF registration only] The server uniquely originates the client's username.

C CPSA Analysis

We overview our analysis method and then state and prove session context-agreement theorems for our UAF registration and authentication models.

C.1 Method

We analyze UAF by (1) modeling UAF authentication and registration protocols in the strand space model, (2) for each protocol, defining session contexts, (3) specifying origination assumptions for each of the protocol roles, (4) using CPSA, search the strand space models to produce "shapes", (5) using the shapes, prove these goals true or false. Our analysis builds from the models in [17], session contexts from Sect. B.2, origination assumptions for the client and server role perspectives from Sect. B.2, and successful session context-agreement (Goal 1).

In this section, we prove or disprove session context agreement by using CPSA to search exhaustively for unique shapes within a strand space. Each search assumes the perspective of a role and its corresponding origination assumptions. Each search outputs shapes that support or serve as a counterexample to a session context agreement security goal. When searching, CPSA includes intruder strands in strand spaces.

For comparison, our analysis includes baseline authentication without UAF.

C.2 Analysis of Registration

We specify and prove theorems for UAF registration. Table 3 summarizes our results.

Theorems 2 and 3 address UAF registration from the perspective of a server. Theorem 2 asserts that the session context-agreement Goal 1 is false. Theorem 3 applies to *UAF-Endpoint-TLS1.2-DH*, *UAF-ServerCert-TLS1.2-DH*, and *UAF-Exporter-TLS1.3*, for which Goal 1 holds under the server's perspective and origination assumptions. We refer to multiple models that model the same channel binding (e.g., *UAF-NoBiding-TLS1.2-RSA* and *UAF-NoBinding-TLS1.3*) by substituting a wildcard (*) for the TLS version (e.g., *UAF-NoBiding-**).

Theorem 1. *For any initial client-reg role holding the client origination assumptions, and for any complementary server-reg role in the [UAF-NoBinding-*, UAF-TokenBinding-*, UAF-ChannelId-*, UAF-Endpoint-*, UAF-ServerCert-*, UAF-Exporter-TLS1.3] strand spaces, Goal 1 is true.*

*Proof (***Proof** *(By enumeration)).* For each UAF model, CPSA terminates and discovers a single shape that reflects an ideal execution between a client and a server, satisfying Goal 1. Because CPSA terminated and discovered all essentially different shapes for these models, no counterexample exists.

Theorem 2. *For any initial server-reg role holding the server origination assumptions, and for any complementary client-reg role in the [UAF-NoBinding-*, UAF-TokenBinding-*, UAF-ChannelId-*, UAF-Endpoint-TLS1.2-RSA, UAF-ServerCert-TLS1.2-RSA] strand spaces, Goal 1 is false.*

*Proof (***Proof** *(By counterexample)).* For each model, finds a shape that contradicts Goal 1. Moreover, CPSA fails to find any shape that satisfies Goal 1.

Under the server assumptions, each UAF-NoBinding-* model produces a shape that illustrates a similar issue: because the server fails to bind its challenge to a session, the adversary may reissue the server's challenge to a client responding in a different session. The server binds the challenge to the relying party's *appId*, which is not a unique value. As we discuss in Sect. 4, is possible for an adversary to spoof the *appId* to a client. An additional shape when using TLS with RSA indicates that the server additionally has no assurance that the client generates a unique premaster secret, enabling the adversary to compromise the channel.

Similarly, the UAF-TokenBinding-* and UAF-ChannelId-* models produce shapes that fail to satisfy the goal. Because the server does not assume that the client's binding key is unique to the TLS session with the server, the server has no assurance that the adversary did not reissue the challenge in a separate UAF session. The server cannot know if a client reused a binding key or if the adversary compromised the key.

The *UAF-Endpoint-TLS1.2-RSA* and *UAF-ServerCert-TLS1.2-RSA* models, in which the client binds the challenge parameters to the server's certificate, present several shapes that illustrate a more subtle issue: the binding does not bind to a specific session of UAF registration. While there is some guarantee that the client intends to communicate with the server, it is possible for the client to confuse the session for which the server issues a challenge. As in the other models, this issue arises from the server failing to bind the challenge to the underlying TLS session.

Theorem 3. *For any initial server-reg role holding the server assumptions, and for any complementary client-reg role in the [UAF-Endpoint-TLS1.2-DH, UAF-ServerCert-TLS1.2-DH, UAF-Exporter-TLS1.3] strand spaces, Goal 1 is true.*

*Proof. (***Proof** *(By enumeration)).* Each model produces a single shape that satisfies Goal 1.

Each of the he *UAF-Endpoint-TLS1.2-DH*, *UAF-ServerCert-TLS1.2-DH*, and *UAF-Exporter-TLS1.3* models overcomes the limitations of the other models. Because these models use TLS with DH key exchange (TLS1.2-DH and TLS1.3), they ensure that both the client and the server contribute confidential freshness to the TLS channel. The endpoint, server certificate, and exporter bindings ensure that the challenge binds to an authenticated entity—either to the server's identity, or the cryptographic context of the TLS channel itself.

C.3 Analysis of Authentication

Our analysis of UAF authentication is similar to that of registration because in both protocols, the server issues a challenge and receives a similar response. Because the server issues the challenge in the same manner, it shares the main issue with the registration protocol: the challenge does not bind to a unique session in a manner that the client can verify. Table 3 includes columns summarizing our security goal theorems for our authentication roles.

Theorem 4. *For any initial client role holding the client assumptions, and for any complementary server role in the [UAF-NoBinding-*, UAF-TokenBinding-*, UAF-ChannelId-*, UAF-Endpoint-*, UAF-ServerCert-*, UAF-Exporter-TLS1.3] strand spaces, Goal 1 is true.*

*Proof (***Proof** *(By enumeration).).* As for the client perspective in UAF registration, CPSA terminates and discovers only a single shape for each model, which shape illustrates correct execution, satisfying Goal 1.

Theorem 5. *For any initial server-auth role holding the server assumptions, and for any complementary client-auth role in the [UAF-NoBinding-*, UAF-TokenBinding-*, UAF-ChannelId-*, UAF-Endpoint-TLS1.2-RSA, UAF-ServerCert-TLS1.2-RSA] strand spaces, Goal 1 is false.*

*Proof (***Proof** *(By counterexample)).* For each model, CPSA finds at least one counterexample. As in the analysis of UAF registration, in the counterexamples, the server has no guarantee that its challenge remains within the server's session with the client. In the unbound models, this issue results from a lack of binding between the challenge and the session outside of the *appId*, which is an inadequate binding. For the client-oriented channel bindings (token binding, channel ID), the server has no assurance that the client's key material for the binding is unique to the session. For the server-oriented channel bindings (endpoint, server certificate), the server cannot determine to which TLS session between the server and the client the challenge binds. In RSA-based models, the server has no assurance that the client contributes confidential freshness to the session.

Theorem 6. *For any initial server-auth role holding the server assumptions, and for any complementary client-auth role in the [UAF-Endpoint-TLS1.2-DH, UAF-ServerCert-TLS1.2-DH, UAF-Exporter-TLS1.3]strand spaces, Goal 1 is true.*

*Proof (***Proof** *(By enumeration).).* As in Theorem 3, implementing exporter channel binding or binding to the server's authenticated identity when using TLS1.2-DH satisfies Goal 1 for the UAF authentication server role.

References

1. Alliance, F.: FIDO alliance member companies and organizations, January 2023. https://fidoalliance.org/members/
2. Alliance, F.: FIDO certified products, January 2023. https://fidoalliance.org/certification/fido-certified-products/
3. Altman, J.E., Zhu, L., Williams, N.: Channel bindings for TLS. RFC 5929, July 2010. https://doi.org/10.17487/RFC5929. https://rfc-editor.org/rfc/rfc5929.txt
4. Baghdasaryan, D., Balfanz, D., Hill, B., Hodges, J., Yang, K.: FIDO UAF protocol specification v1.2. Technical report, FIDO Alliance (2020)
5. Baghdasaryan, D., Hill, B., Sasson, R., Hodges, J., Yang, K.: FIDO UAF authenticator-specific module API (2022)
6. Balfanz, D., Hamilton, R.: Transport Layer Security (TLS) Channel IDs, June 2013. https://datatracker.ietf.org/doc/draft-balfanz-tls-channelid/01/. Work in Progress
7. Barbosa, M., Boldyreva, A., Chen, S., Warinschi, B.: Provable security analysis of FIDO2. In: Annual International Cryptology Conference, pp. 125–156. Springer (2021)

8. Bhandary, P., Zieglar, E., Nicholas, C.: Searching for selfie in TLS 1.3 with the cryptographic protocol shapes analyzer. In: Dougherty, D., Meseguer, J., Mödersheim, S.A., Rowe, P.D. (eds.) Protocols, Strands, and Logic - Essays Dedicated to Joshua Guttman on the Occasion of his 66th Birthday. LNCS, vol. 13066, pp. 50–76. Springer (2021). https://doi.org/10.1007/978-3-030-91631-2_3
9. Büttner, A., Gruschka, N.: Protecting FIDO extensions against man-in-the-middle attacks. In: Emerging Technologies for Authorization and Authentication: 5th International Workshop, ETAA 2022, Copenhagen, Denmark, 30 September 2022, Revised Selected Papers, pp. 70–87. Springer, Berlin, Germany (2023)
10. Chadwick, D.W., Laborde, R., Oglaza, A., Venant, R., Wazan, S., Nijjar, M.: Improved identity management with verifiable credentials and FIDO. IEEE Commun. Stand. Mag. **3**(4), 14–20 (2019)
11. Chae, C.J., Cho, H.J., Jung, H.M.: Authentication method using multiple biometric information in FIDO environment. J. Digit. Convergence **16**(1), 159–164 (2018)
12. Coker, G., et al.: Principles of remote attestation. Int. J. Inf. Sec. **10**(2), 63–81 (2011). https://doi.org/10.1007/S10207-011-0124-7
13. Dolev, D., Yao, A.: On the security of public key protocols. IEEE Trans. Inf. Theory **29**(2), 198–208 (1983). https://doi.org/10.1109/TIT.1983.1056650
14. eBay: eBay FIDO UAF Implementation (2022). https://github.com/eBay/UAF. Accessed 31 Mar 2023
15. Feng, H., Li, H., Pan, X., Zhao, Z., Cactilab, T.: A formal analysis of the FIDO UAF protocol. In: Proceedings of 28th Network And Distributed System Security Symposium (NDSS) (2021)
16. Fuchs, J., Hamer, S., Liu, D.: A man-in-the-middle attack on the FIDO UAF registration protocol. In: CMSC-691 Special Topics: Cybersecurity Research (INSuRE) Course Project, CSEE Department, UMBC (2022, unpublished manuscript)
17. Golaszewski, E., Sherman, A.T., Zieglar, E., Fuchs, J.D., Hamer, S.: Cryptographic binding should not be optional: a formal-methods analysis of FIDO UAF channel binding. arXiv preprint http://arxiv.org/abs/2511.06028 (2025)
18. Golaszewski, E., Zieglar, E., Sherman, A.T., Elsaad, K.A., Fuchs, J.: Limitations of wrapping protocols and TLS channel bindings: formal-methods analysis of the Session Binding Proxy protocol. CSEE Department, UMBC, March 2024. Unpublished manuscript
19. Guan, J., Li, H., Ye, H., Zhao, Z.: A formal analysis of the FIDO2 protocols. In: European Symposium on Research in Computer Security, pp. 3–21. Springer (2022)
20. Hardy, N.: The confused deputy: (or why capabilities might have been invented). ACM SIGOPS Oper. Syst. Rev. **22**(4), 36–38 (1988)
21. Hill, B., Balfanz, D., Baghdasaryan, D.: FIDO AppID and facet specification. Technical report, FIDO Alliance (2018)
22. Hu, K., Zhang, Z.: Security analysis of an attractive online authentication standard: FIDO UAF protocol. China Commun. **13**(12), 189–198 (2016)
23. UPA Lab: PAL GitHub repository, April 2023. https://tinyurl.com/3d2wnhuf
24. Lanus, E., Zieglar, E.: Analysis of a forced-latency defense against man-in-the-middle attacks. J. Inf. Warfare **16**(2), 66–78 (2017)
25. Liskov, M., Rowe, P., Thayer, J.: Completeness of CPSA. Technical report, MITRE (2011). https://www.mitre.org/sites/default/files/pdf/12_0038.pdf
26. Liskov, M.D., Ramsdell, J.D., Guttman, J.D., Rowe, P.D.: The cryptographic protocol shapes analyzer: a manual. The MITRE Corporation (2016)
27. Lodderstedt, T., Bradley, J., Labunets, A., Fett, D.: RFC 9700: Best current practice for OAuth 2.0 security (2025)

28. Loutfi, I., Jøsang, A.: FIDO trust requirements. In: Nordic Conference on Secure IT Systems, pp. 139–155. Springer, Berlin, Germany (2015)
29. Lowe, G.: A hierarchy of authentication specifications. In: Proceedings 10th Computer Security Foundations Workshop, pp. 31–43. IEEE (1997)
30. Needham, R.M., Schroeder, M.D.: Using encryption for authentication in large networks of computers. Commun. ACM **21**(12), 993–999 (1978). https://doi.org/10.1145/359657.359659
31. Panos, C., Malliaros, S., Ntantogian, C., Panou, A., Xenakis, C.: A security evaluation of FIDO's UAF protocol in mobile and embedded devices. In: International Tyrrhenian Workshop on Digital Communication, pp. 127–142. Springer, Berlin, Germany (2017)
32. Pereira, O., Rochet, F., Wiedling, C.: Formal analysis of the FIDO 1.x protocol. In: Foundations and Practice of Security: 10th International Symposium, FPS 2017, Nancy, France, 23–25 October 2017, Revised Selected Papers 10, pp. 68–82. Springer, Berlin, Germany (2018)
33. Popov, A., Nystrom, M., Balfanz, D., Langley, A., Hodges, J.: The Token Binding Protocol Version 1.0. RFC 8471, October 2018. https://doi.org/10.17487/RFC8471. https://rfc-editor.org/rfc/rfc8471.txt
34. Rescorla, E.: SSL and TLS: Designing and Building Secure Systems. Addison-Wesley (2001)
35. Sherman, A.T., et al.: Formal methods analysis of the secure remote password protocol. In: Logic, Language, and Security, pp. 103–126. Springer (2020)
36. Ulqinaku, E., Assal, H., Abdou, A., Chiasson, S., Capkun, S.: Is real-time phishing eliminated with FIDO? Social engineering downgrade attacks against FIDO protocols. In: 30th USENIX Security Symposium (USENIX Security 21), pp. 3811–3828. USENIX Association, Berkley, CA, August 2021. https://www.usenix.org/conference/usenixsecurity21/presentation/ulqinaku
37. Whited, S.: Channel Bindings for TLS 1.3. RFC 9266, July 2022. https://doi.org/10.17487/RFC9266. https://www.rfc-editor.org/info/rfc9266

CRA and Cryptography: The Story Thus Far

Markku-Juhani O. Saarinen(✉)

Information Security Laboratory, Tampere University, Tampere, Finland
markku-juhani.saarinen@tuni.fi

Abstract. We report on our experiences with the ongoing European standardisation efforts related to the EU Cyber Resilience Act (CRA) and provide interim (November 2025) estimates on the direction that European cryptography regulation may take, particularly concerning the algorithm "allow list" and PQC transition requirements in products.

The CRA has a wide-ranging set of security requirements, including security patching and the use of cryptography (data integrity, confidentiality for data at rest and data in transit). However, the Cyber Resilience Act itself is a legal text devoid of technical detail – it does not specify the type of cryptography deemed appropriate to satisfy its requirements.

The technical implications of CRA are being detailed in approximately 40 new standards from the three European standardisation organisations, CEN, CENELEC, and ETSI. While the resulting ETSI standards can be expected to be available for free even in the drafting stage, the CEN and CENELEC standards will probably require a per-reader license fee. This, despite recent legal rulings asserting that product security and safety standards are part of EU law due to their legal effects. We outline some of the risks associated with the partially closed standardisation process, including active impact minimisation by vendors concerned with engineering costs, a lack of public review leading to lower technical quality, and an increased potential for backdoors.

Taking a recent (2024) example of cryptographic requirements in such standards, we observe that the definitions and language in the Radio Equipment Directive (RED DA) harmonised standard (EN 18031 series) may allow vendors to take an approach where weak cryptography is considered "best practice" right until exploitation is feasible.

Recognising recent developments such as the EU Post-Quantum Cryptography transition roadmap, many CRA standardisation working groups are moving towards a "State-of-the-Art Cryptography" (SOTA Cryptography) model where approved mechanism listings are published by the European Cybersecurity Certification Group (ECCG). CRA-compliant products may still support other cryptographic mechanisms, but only SOTA is permitted as a safe default for Internet-connected products.

Keywords: CRA – Cyber Resilience Act · RED-DA · Agreed Cryptographic Mechanisms · Cryptographic Agility · PQC Transition

H. C. Pöhls and C. J. Mitchell (Eds.): SSR 2025, LNCS 16466, pp. 162–180, 2026.
https://doi.org/10.1007/978-3-032-19567-8_8

1 Introduction

Our research interest in Cyber Resilience Act (CRA) standardisation was initially motivated by a simple desire to "find out" about its potentially huge implications on cryptography and product security testing in Europe. However, it soon became apparent that there were no public working documents, discussion forums, and very few open sources with detailed technical information.

Even after the standardisation process is finished, CEN and CENELEC standards in particular are not freely available, and their contents are protected by copyright. In our experience, a rather common attitude in cybersecurity engineering is to ignore such technical standards. Paywalled, per-seat licensed documents are challenging for actual cybersecurity engineering and testing teams to use. However, due to the wide-ranging and legally binding obligations of the CRA regulation, these particular standards can't be easily dismissed.

Due to lack of transparency, studuing the CRA security standards requires "participatory fieldwork". A security researcher must invest time and effort to gain access to the institutions and participate in the processes to gain technical information. This work is primarily based on subjective observations as a national expert and as an interim rapporteur of one of the vertical standards.

At the time of writing, the standards are not yet finished, so the reader must understand that all information contained herein is preliminary. Furthermore, it is essential to note that the author is not a legal expert. This work should not be interpreted as a legally accurate description of the rules and regulations governing the creation of standards, but as a subjective description.

Structure and Contributions. Section 2 contains a brief introduction to the European product legislation system and harmonised standards, and also offers a critique of the practical and security implications of the relatively closed standardisation process. Section 3 discusses the contents of the Cyber Resilience Act in the context of cryptography and the upcoming cybersecurity standards. Section 4 discusses cryptographic requirements in the related Radio Equipment Directive Delegated Act (RED-DA) standards (EN 18031) from 2024; we focus on an apparent "best practice loophole" in its wording, which can allow weak cryptography. This is followed by a discussion of cryptography in CRA (Sect. 5) and the proposed "State-of-the-Art Cryptography" concept and its "allow list" approach, which mainly determines the methods allowed in "secure default" settings of self-assessed products. We conclude in Sect. 6.

2 CRA and EU Product Regulation: A Crash Course

On 10 December 2024, the EU Cyber Resilience Act (CRA) [13] entered into force. The main obligations introduced by the Act will take effect on 11 December 2027. Compliance with this law would be required to sell "products with digital elements" (most types of software and consumer electronics) in the European common market of 450 million people. Compliance with CRA is needed to obtain the "CE-mark" (See Fig. 1) that is required in electrical gadgets, raincoats, toys, industrial machinery, and many other classes of products to be sold in Europe.

The CE-mark (from "Conformité Européenne") means that the product conforms to relevant European regulations – whatever they may be for that particular product. It is not a "Made in Europe" mark, nor does it necessarily indicate that the product is of particularly high quality. CRA is just the latest addition to a long list of regulations that consumer electronics and many other types of products must meet to have the CE mark; they must be safe for the voltages that they use, should not cause electromagnetic/radio interference, etc. The general product rules are laid out in the "Blue Guide" [10], which has traditionally been one of the most essential references for compliance engineers. The Blue Guide is crucial when interpreting the implications of the CRA, as it also describes many relevant concepts and legal mechanisms such as *"market surveillance"* – the actual monitoring and enforcement of these European product regulations.

Fig. 1. The CE mark is required to sell many kinds of consumer products, including almost any kind of electrical device, on the European single market. CRA compliance will be a requirement for the CE mark from 2027.

2.1 European Standards and Harmonised Standards

European standards carry an EN number and have the format EN [number]:[year]. There are three European standardisation organisations[1]:

- European Committee for Standardisation (CEN)
- European Committee for Electrotechnical Standardisation (CENELEC)
- European Telecommunications Standards Institute (ETSI)

The areas of work of CEN, CENELEC, and ETSI generally mirror the international organisations (largely unrelated to CRA – here just for completeness):

- International Organization for Standardization (ISO)
- International Electrotechnical Commission (IEC)
- International Telecommunication Union (ITU)

Broadly speaking, electrotechnical matters are in the scope of IEC/CENELEC, ITU/ ETSI handles telecommunication matters, while ISO/CEN addresses the remainder. Most European countries also have a matching national layer that can specify national standards (Fig. 2), which also forms the representation on upper layers (European and International). There are significant areas of overlap, resulting in joint ISO/IEC (CEN/CENELEC) standards in particular.

[1] The roles of CEN, CENELEC, and ETSI are laid out in Regulation (EU) No 1025/2012 of 25 October 2012 on European standardisation. https://eur-lex.europa.eu/eli/reg/2012/1025/oj/eng.

	General	Electrotechnical	Telecomms.
International	ISO	IEC	ITU
European	cen	CENELEC	ETSI
National *(Example: Finland)*	SFS Suomen Standardit	SESKO	TRAFICOM Liikenne- ja viestintävirasto

Fig. 2. The division of duties between the three main international standardisation organisations ISO (General), IEC (Electrotechnical), and ITU (Telecommunications) is reflected on the European level (CEN-CENELEC-ETSI), and often even on the national level. The three national standardisation organisations of Finland are given as an example, but each of the 27 EU member states has its own national organisations.

A *harmonised standard* is a standard from CEN, CENELEC, or ETSI that is a result of a standardisation request from the European Commission[2]. The publication of a reference to a harmonised standard in the Official Journal of the European Union (OJEU) gives it a specific legal status, *presumption of conformity*. This means that if a product fully complies with the technical requirements of a harmonised standard, it is also presumed to be compliant with the related product regulation (e.g., safety or security laws).

2.2 Participation in CEN and CENELEC

In theory, the standardisation bodies operate within a system where national standardisation bodies (in each of the 27 European Union member states) select representatives to work on the European and international levels. However, the opportunities for participation vary significantly from one country to another. Based on our observations, a majority of the 27 EU countries do not have even a single active participant in the CRA standards-writing process, even though the standards form a part of the ruleset that affects everyone in Europe.

While ETSI has adopted an open policy regarding CRA standard drafts and other working documents, the distribution of CEN and CENELEC documents tends to be strictly limited to members of the relevant working groups.

[2] A list of harmonised standards: https://single-market-economy.ec.europa.eu/single-market/goods/european-standards/harmonised-standards_en.

In practical terms, one often has to first pay a fee to participate in the national standardisation group (in the author's case, 600 € for SESKO membership to monitor the CENELEC TC 47X group, responsible for semiconductor security), and then ask the national standards body or industry association to appoint oneself as a representative on the European level. Large companies do this routinely to protect their interest in the standardisation front. In the particular case of the author, the Finnish associations were supportive of academic representation, but most European experts will face significant difficulty accessing CEN and CENELEC drafts.

2.3 Accessing the Final Standards

While the ETSI CRA standards (the majority of the software-oriented CRA vertical standards) are expected to be publicly available (and some already are, in draft format: https://www.stan4cra.eu/etsi-tc-cyber), the cybersecurity standards being developed by CEN and CENELEC are not expected to be available for free. As can be seen in Table 1, this would primarily impact the horizontal standards (that are somehow intended to assist all European product vendors), and also chip standards from CENELEC.

The standards continue to be non-free despite harmonised standards forming an integral part of the regulatory framework for the European internal market[3] This has been recognized in a recent judgment by the Court of Justice of the European Union on the free availability of CEN standards related to the safety of toys.[4] It appears that fundamental changes in the standardisation system are required to overcome this restriction.

While the price point of standards is not overwhelming, it remains prohibitive for casual review or everyday use. Almost all European standardisation bodies sell the same English-language standards, but with wildly varying prices. Let us take the RED-DA standard EN 18031-1 as an anecdotal example: Checking for the cost of a 1-seat licence in October 2025, the price ranged from 43.72 € in Lithuania (LVS), to 161,00 € in Finland (SFS), and 327,70 € in Germany (DIN).

Even if a copy of the standard is purchased, its license prohibits the passing of the standard text to colleagues; hence, ISO, IEC, CEN, and CENELEC cybersecurity standards are difficult to reference in engineering specifications. In fact, it has been argued that it is best practice not to use closed (non-free) standards in security engineering as it prohibits open review (related to Kerckhoffs' principle [4] in cryptography.)

[3] This system originates with the so-called "New Approach" Council Resolution of 7 May 1985, https://eur-lex.europa.eu/legal-content/EN/TXT/?uri=celex:31985Y0604(01).

[4] Court of Justice of the European Union press release on 5 March 2024: "Judgment of the Court in Case C-588/21: The European harmonised technical standards on the safety of toys should be accessible to EU citizens." https://curia.europa.eu/jcms/upload/docs/application/pdf/2024-03/cp240041en.pdf.

By comparison, NIST has worked through open competitions to create the well-received cryptographic standards [23] that Europe has also included in its ACM listing [7]. From a European perspective, it is relatively easy to have faith in these algorithms thanks to the transparency of the NIST process and the historical fact that European academic researchers were strongly involved in the design of many of them. Apart from a few exceptions, their design criteria are well-known. For cryptographic protocols (such as TLS and IPSec), the IETF creates standards via an open consensus method driven by individuals (the IETF doesn't even have formal membership). Both NIST and IETF standards are freely distributed.

2.4 Security Risks in the CEN-CENELEC Process

As discussed, European citizens have very limited opportunities to review and influence CEN and CENELEC harmonised standards before they take legal effect – and afterwards, the standards are only available for a fee. Due to their licensing fee structure, they are not generally available even in academic libraries. There are obvious risks stemming from such a lack of transparency when developing what, in effect, is a legally binding security regulation.

We will list some information security and operational risks we have observed in the current CEN-CENELEC standardisation process (and to a somewhat lesser degree, in the ETSI processes), which would be significantly reduced if the process were made more open and transparent.

Vendors Participate in the Process Solely to Minimise the Impact of Security Standards. Particularly CEN and CENELEC standardisation working groups are generally composed through nominations from national industrial bodies. These are commercial entities – the primary goal for some companies is to simply minimize the impact of CRA on their product lines and the need for costly security engineering. While the technical input from the industry is welcome to help arrive at workable standards, there should be a balance that prevents committee members with apparent conflicts of interest from rendering security standards ineffective.

Limited Public Review Leads to Low Quality. Trust in cryptographic mechanisms is almost entirely derived from the amount and the quality of review they have received. The participation of scientific experts in CEN and CENELEC work, even in the development phase, is challenging, as non-public work is contrary to their performance indicators and the principles of open science. The lack of expert participation and critical review leads to lower-quality standards.

Potential for Security Backdoors. The infamous example of the "Dual EC" cryptographic back door [3] (and possibly others [6]) contained in the ISO/IEC 18031 [14] (not to be confused with EN 18031!) Random Bit Generator standard emphasizes that not only must the final standards be available for public review, but their entire design process, origins, and selection criteria must also be publicly disclosed. This does not happen in the closed process.

3 CRA's Essential Cybersecurity Requirements

One of the main functions of the CRA harmonised standards is to codify an interpretation of *Essential Cybersecurity Requirements* (ECR) contained in Annex I of the CRA law itself [13]. The ECRs are structured into two parts:

Part 1: Cybersecurity Properties of the Products. There are two main technical requirements in this part. The first one is a catch-all: *"Products with digital elements shall be designed, developed, and produced in such a way that they ensure an appropriate level of cybersecurity based on the risks."*

The second requirement (ECR P1-2) is divided into a list of 13 technical points, (a) to (m), all of which are applied "on the basis of the cybersecurity risk assessment". The main cryptographic requirements are:

(e) *protect the confidentiality of stored, transmitted or otherwise processed data, personal or other, such as by encrypting relevant data at rest or in transit by state of the art mechanisms, and by using other technical means*
(f) *protect the integrity of stored, transmitted or otherwise processed data, personal or other, commands, programs and configuration against any manipulation or modification not authorised by the user, and report on corruptions*

There are further requirements that less directly require the use of cryptography, including (c) on automated updates, (d) on authentication, (l) on logging, and (m) on secure erase and backup. The technical interpretation of all of these requirements is left to the harmonised standards.

Part 2: Vulnerability Handling Requirements. The draft horizontal standard on vulnerability handling requirements (known as Work Item JT013090) has normative dependencies on existing standards EN ISO/IEC 30111 ("vulnerability handling processes") and EN ISO/IEC 29147 ("Vulnerability disclosure"), and generally follows the procedures outlined there. This standard is expected to have a presumption of conformity in relation to vulnerability handling.

Technical cryptographic requirements are generally outside the scope of Part 2, although the standard is likely to include secure communication requirements for vulnerability information. The underlying standard (EN ISO/IEC 29147:2020 clause 5.8.2) has references to TLS, S/MIME, and OpenPGP as potential tools for this task.

3.1 Interpreting the ECRs

While the language around "confidentiality" and "integrity" ECRs appears unambiguous, they are dependent on a risk assessment. Some vendors in the standardisation groups have an interpretation that allows the risk assessment to be used to escape relatively costly updates of their product lines. To support such a claim, a vendor would have to demonstrate that the risk arising from the use of weak, proprietary, or legacy cryptographic methods is so low "in practice" that their use is acceptable under the Cyber Resilience Act.

Vendors can always try this tactic in a third-party assessment with *notified bodies* (independent third-party conformance evaluation bodies accredited by

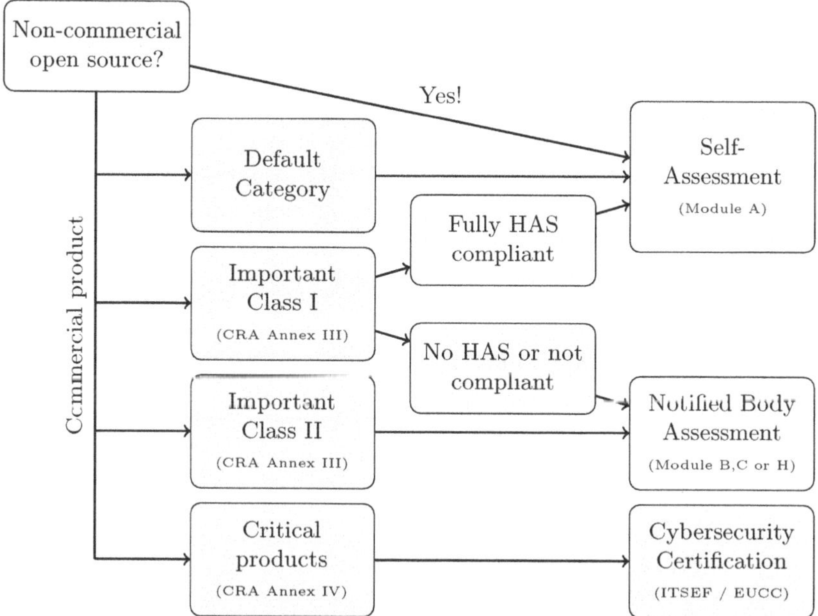

Fig. 3. Typical paths for (presumption of) conformance for various CRA product categories. The vast majority of products are in the "default category" – vendors can place a CE mark on their products after a self-assessment if they meet all relevant requirements. For Important Class I, "HAS" refers to a vertical harmonised standard with a presumption of conformity.

member countries). It remains to be seen under what conditions such claims of "low-risk bad cryptography" will be successful – the notified bodies will utilise relevant harmonised standards, document review, and product tests for the determination.

An important question arises about what kind of risk assessment (and resulting selection of cryptographic mechanisms) will be considered valid in self-assessment (internal control) – after all, the majority of products are expected to receive their CE mark this way. The relevant harmonised standards will also determine this. The monitoring of self-assessments (and the possibly resulting enforcement actions) will be left to market surveillance authorities after the product is already placed on the market. Market surveillance should utilise the same rules and standards as the notified bodies.

3.2 CRA Product Classes

CRA Annexes III and IV have lists of product categories that can be used to establish if a third-party assessment is required, and what type of assessment is sufficient:

- **Default category**: Low risk usage where self-assessment can be used. The expectation is that the vast majority of products are in this category.
- **Important Class I**: Products listed in CRA Annex III, where self-assessment suffices if the European Commission has approved a suitable Harmonised Standard, and the product is fully compliant with its requirements.
- **Important Class II**: Products listed in CRA Annex III, where compliance is assessed by a Notified Body based on evidence from the vendor.
- **Critical products**: The use of a European Cybersecurity Certification Scheme is expected. Currently, the only such scheme is the EUCC [11] Common Criteria-based scheme.

Figure 3 shows some common pathways through the compliance process for various product categories. For an indication of various products in each class, see the listing of vertical standards in Table 1. There are many complications and additional rules to the decision diagram, so this figure should not be considered complete.

3.3 The CRA Standardisation Request

The European Commission issued a standardisation request[5] related to CRA to European standardisation agencies in February 2025. There are two main kinds of standards in the standardisation request:

- **Horizontal standards** which apply to a wide range of products; in the case of CRA, essentially all products are under their scope, but "default category" standards in particular are impacted by horizontal standards.
- **Vertical standards** which are more specific, and generally tied to the product classes in Annexes III and IV in CRA (see Sect. 3.1).

An annex to the standardisation request listed 41 different items for standardisation. CEN, CENELEC, and ETSI then divided this enormous standardisation task among their Technical Committees (TCs) and Working Groups (WGs) – some requested standards were combined while others were further split into separate standards.

The standardisation request resulted in the work programme M/606[6] that is currently being executed by the standardisation bodies. Table 1 contains a preliminary (and still partial) list of standards currently being developed at ETSI, CEN, and CENELEC.

---

[5] The 3 February 2025 European Commission Standardisation Request related to CRA (and its annexes) is available from: https://ec.europa.eu/transparency/documents-register/detail?ref=C(2025)618&lang=en.

[6] CEN, CENELEC and ETSI Work Programme M/606, dated 2 Apr 2025: https://www.cencenelec.eu/media/CEN-CENELEC/News/Newsletters/2025/m_606_work_programme_final.pdf.

Table 1. A list of draft (CEN-CENELEC) horizontal standards and a rough mapping from the product classification in CRA [13] Annexes to related vertical standards under development at ETSI, CEN, and CENELEC, based on information available in November 2025. All of the standards are works in progress.

Horizontal Standards: CEN-CENELEC JTC 13/WG 9

(October 2025 development status of drafts.)

Std Number	Work Item	Status	Title
EN 40000-1-1	JT013095	ENQ	Vocabulary
EN 40000-1-2	JT013089	ENQ	Principles for cyber resilience
EN 40000-1-3	JT013090	ENQ	Vulnerability Handling
EN 40000-1-4	JT013091	On hold	Generic Security Requirements
TR 40000-1-5	JT013097	On hold	Threats and Security Objectives

CRA Annex III, "Important Class I" Verticals

1.	CEN	(Line 16)	Identity and privileged access management products.
2.	ETSI	EN 304 617	Standalone and embedded browsers.
3.	ETSI	EN 304 618	Password managers.
4.	ETSI	EN 304 619	software that searches for, removes, or quarantines malicious software ("anti-virus".)
5.	ETSI	EN 304 620	Virtual Private Networks (VPNs) (parts 1 and 2).
6.	ETSI	EN 304 621	Network Management systems.
7.	ETSI	EN 304 622	Security information and event management (SIEM).
8.	ETSI	EN 304 623	Boot managers.
9.	ETSI	EN 304 624	PKI and digital certificate issuance software.
10.	ETSI	EN 304 625	Physical and virtual network interfaces.
11.	ETSI	EN 304 626	Operating systems.
12.	ETSI	EN 304 627	Routers, internet modems, switches.
13+14.	CLC	EN 50765	CPUs and MCUs (low-risk environment.)
15.	CLC	EN 50767	ASICs and FPGAs with security functionalities.
16.	ETSI	EN 304 631	Smart home general-purpose virtual assistants.
17.	ETSI	EN 304 632	Smart home products with security (locks, cameras, baby monitoring, alarm, ...)
18.	ETSI	EN 304 633	Internet-connected toys (interactive features or tracking).
19.	ETSI	EN 304 634	Personal wearables (health monitoring, tracking)

CRA Annex III, "Important Class I" Verticals

1.	ETSI	EN 304 635	Hypervisors and container runtime systems.
2.	ETSI	EN 304 636	Firewalls, intrusion detection, and/or prevention
3+4.	CLC	EN 50766	CPUs and MCUs (higher-risk: "tamper-resistant.")

CRA Annex IV, "Critical" Verticals

1.	CEN	(Line 39)	Hardware devices with security boxes.
2.	CEN CLC	(Line 40)	Smart meter gateways within smart metering, secure cryptoprocessing.
3.	CLC	EN 50764	Smartcards or similar devices, secure elements.

Note: Six additional standardisation items that apply CRA to industrial automation and control systems and their networks are being developed by CLC/TC 65X WG 3.

4 Cryptography and the Radio Equipment Directive

One of the main models for the development of the CRA standards is the EN 18031-{1,2,3} series [17–19] of harmonised standards related to the Radio Equipment Directive Delegated Act (RED-DA)[7]. Since August 1, 2025, manufacturers placing radio equipment on the European market have been required to comply with the requirements of RED-DA.

Somewhat similar to the CRA (but with a smaller scope), RED is part of European product regulation and includes cybersecurity requirements. The scope of the earlier RED regulation is essentially a subset of products covered by CRA. The EN 18031 harmonised standards [17–19] can be used for conformity self-assessment with some caveats[8].

Many of the RED cybersecurity requirements imply the use of cryptographic mechanisms, so-called "[CRY-1] best practice cryptography." The EN 18031 standards offer guidance for this, including references to relevant NIST, BSI, and SOG-IS documents. However, each EN 18031 standard also contains the following characterisation:

> *"A commonly used cryptographic method for a certain use case, with the lack of evidence for a feasible attack with current readily available techniques, can be considered as best practice."* – EN 18031-{1,2,3} [17–19]

A vendor performing self-assessment can interpret this statement (or definition) to mean that a cryptographic mechanism with known weaknesses or potential vulnerabilities can be considered "best practice cryptography", as long as others also use it and the exploits are "difficult" or not readily available.

This definition is close to the one used in ETSI IoT Cybersecurity standard EN 303 645 [8]. Although its assessment specification, ETSI TS 103 701 [9], encourages the use of SOG-IS reference catalogues (a predecessor to current ECCG catalogues [7]), it also allows arbitrary algorithms based on "competent cryptanalytic reports" from vendors. ETSI TS 103 701 is primarily designed for independent Testing Laboratories (TL) and notes that *"The competence of the TL has a strong influence on the validity of the assessment results."* [9]. Its use in CRA self-assessment seems especially hazardous, with vendors potentially self-approving arbitrary (or even proprietary) cryptographic mechanisms.

Typically, cryptographic methods are known to be vulnerable long before exploitation with "current readily available techniques" starts. A prominent example is the SHA-1 hash function, which was considered cryptanalytically broken by 2005 [24] but remained in use even after practical attacks were demonstrated in 2017 [22].

To most cryptographers, the no-foresight "currently feasible attack" approach allowed by EN 18031 represents the opposite of what would be considered best

[7] RED-DA: Commission Delegated Regulation (EU) 2022/30 of 29 October 2021. http://data.europa.eu/eli/reg_del/2022/30/2023-10-27.

[8] In OJEU, the European Commission imposed limitations to presumption of conformance when using EN 18031 standards, but those are not related to its "best practice cryptography": http://data.europa.eu/eli/dec_impl/2025/138/oj.

practice. In the case of encryption, the implied approach contradicts policies such as the EU Post-Quantum Cryptography Transition Roadmap [12] (quantum computers are not "readily available") and the well-known "store now, decrypt later" threat model, which is unique to confidentiality protection.

5 CRA Cryptography and Harmonised Standards

We emphasise that no binding decisions have been taken on CRA cryptologic matters at the time of writing; this section simply reflects information and the status of the proposals as it is available to the author at the time of writing.

5.1 Defining "State of the Art"

The standardisation request[9] states that the resulting standards shall reflect the generally acknowledged state of the art, with a further explanation in a footnote:

> *"The state of the art does not necessarily imply the latest scientific research still in an experimental stage or with insufficient technological maturity. The state-of-the-art is not to be intended as minimum requirements to access the market."*

Based on discussions with the European Commission, the RED-DA "Best Practice Cryptography" approach, or at least its wording (Sect. 4), is being recognized to be insufficient to meet the criteria set in the CRA standardisation request. Since it is difficult to change definitions that are already in harmonised standards, and the language in the CRA Annex I confidentiality requirement ECR P1-2-e (Sect. 3), a new concept of practical "State-of-the-Art Cryptography" is being defined for the harmonised standards.

5.2 A Single Source of Truth

Presently, the European Commission supports an *allow list* policy in selecting cryptographic mechanisms that are considered secure in CRA vertical standards. Under this policy, use of a cryptography mechanism that is not explicitly allowed by the harmonised standards requires a third-party assessment (or some explicitly defined mitigation). Furthermore, rather than having all of the vertical standards contain their own lists and recommendations, a central, frequently updated "single source of truth" on allowed cryptography is preferred.

For a number of reasons, it is not feasible to completely prohibit legacy or non-listed cryptography under a broad product legislation such as CRA:

- There is a need to access (decrypt) legacy encrypted information, and to verify its authenticity and integrity using legacy mechanisms.

[9] EC Std. request dated 03.02.2025, C(2025) 618, Annex II, Objectives. https://ec.europa.eu/transparency/documents-register/detail?ref=C(2025)618&lang=en.

- Devices must be able to communicate and interoperate with older devices and with devices in other regulatory frameworks.
- There must be a way to introduce new cryptographic mechanisms into use without the need to insert them into ACM listings first.

A guiding principle for the application of the *allow list* is the "secure defaults" requirement (ECR P1-2-b) – the *allow list* defines what those defaults can be, but a user may reconfigure a product to use other mechanisms. Furthermore, in the case of a protocol negotiation, the product should opt for a mechanism in the *allow list* by default.

We observe that while CRA requires, e.g., automated updates, it also mandates that a user must have a way to postpone or opt out of them (ECR P1-2-c). Consumer devices are always ultimately under the control of their owners.

5.3 ACM and the Need for Public Consultation

Cryptographic algorithms supported in CRA will need to be compatible with other European regulations and policies, as well as the requirements of the individual national cybersecurity certification authorities (NCCAs).

With the 2019 EU Cybersecurity Act updates[10], many elements of the long-running SOG-IS (Senior Officials Group - Information Systems Security) were adopted under ENISA and the European Cybersecurity Certification Group (ECCG)[11], including the widely-cited document "Agreed Cryptographic Mechanisms" (ACM) [7]. This document is already used for EUCC (Critical products).

As stated in ECCG's ACM document itself: *"Its purpose is to specify which cryptographic mechanisms are recognised agreed, i.e., ready to be accepted by all national cybersecurity certification authorities (NCCAs)."* Hence, the ACM listing can be seen as a least-common-denominator set that is acceptable to all NCCAs. As the CRA is an European regulation, and products placed on the market in any single country can be sold in any other European country, the definition of pre-approved cryptographic mechanisms seems to be most logically placed under ECCG.

The ECCG is relatively new, and based on our observations, the process for selecting cryptographic mechanisms for ACM appears to be mostly closed. It seems uncontroversial to suggest that the selection process would benefit from a more direct involvement of the open cryptography research community – the same community of cryptanalysts and cryptography engineering experts who have designed most of the recommended algorithms on the ACM list. Hence, we hope that a broader public consultation will be established for the purpose of maintaining the "allow list" for CRA. This could also make the process more forward-looking and responsive to emerging threats and technology demands.

---

[10] Regulation (EU) 2019/881 of 17 April 2019 (Cybersecurity Act) https://eur-lex.europa.eu/eli/reg/2019/881/oj.

[11] European Cybersecurity Certification Group (ECCG): https://digital-strategy.ec.europa.eu/en/policies/cybersecurity-certification-group.

5.4 What is in the ACM Right Now and What Is Missing?

All cryptographic mechanisms listed in ACM v2.0 [7] are considered suitable for use, but they are divided into two classes:

- **Recommended mechanisms**: Considered practical state-of-the-art and have a security level of at least 125 bits.
- **Legacy mechanisms**: Acceptable, with a security level of at least 100 bits. Legacy mechanisms have a specified depreciation/sunset date after which they will be removed from the list.

The set of algorithms in ACM is presently quite limited, but it is (for the most part) a superset of algorithms approved by the U.S. NIST. The expectation is that the list will need to be expanded to accommodate the broader range of products under CRA.

- **Symmetric**: AES, 3DES (legacy – 2027), SHA2-256+, SHA3, MAC modes (including HMAC-SHA-1 with depreciation date 2030), Key derivation mechanisms, PBKDF2.
- **Asymmetric traditional**: RSA (key sizes under 3000 bits have a depreciation after 2025), DSA, DH, ECDH, ECDSA (many variants).
- **Asymmetric PQC**: ML-KEM, FrodoKEM, ML-DSA, SLH-DSA, XMSS, LMS. Generally, only PQC Category 3 ("192-bit") and above is allowed.

There are some obvious gaps: The ACM list includes TLS 1.2 and 1.3 (with specific ciphersuites), but currently does not mention IPSec or SSH protocols, commonly used for VPN and remote administration.

The ACM also includes brief discussions about person authentication, but this seems to be written for Common Criteria use cases only, such as Hardware Security Modules (HSMs). It is likely that vertical standards (such as those related to "smart home" and wearable devices) will require this to be substantially expanded.

5.5 Impact of Risk Environment: Implementation Testing

In quantitative risk analysis, after a certain threshold (currently the 125-bit minimum strength of ACM-recommended algorithms), cryptographic key lengths and other parameter settings do not significantly affect the risk of cryptanalytic compromise. However, implementation quality always has a non-negligible impact on exploitation risk – for example, via simple logical vulnerabilities from implementation bugs, or through a lack of countermeasures against side-channel attacks and fault injection attacks in more advanced cases.

Current proposal maps CRA product categories (Sect. 3.1) to implementation testing regimes as follows:

- **Default:** Vendors who have not implemented their own cryptographic libraries but use standard ones can refer to their documentation. Products with bespoke cryptography are elevated to the Important class.

- **Important Class I and II:** Functional testing based on test vectors (either self-certification or with a notified body).
- **Critical:** European Cybersecurity Certification Scheme at "high" assurance level (AVA_VAN.3 or higher in case of EUCC [11]).

Note that U.S. FIPS 140-3 [20,21] testing mostly remains limited to functional testing. Plans are underway to establish a test vector service similar to NIST's CAVP (Cryptographic Algorithm Validation Program) under ECCG.

5.6 Cryptographic Agility?

One further factor presently affecting the selection of algorithms is the transition to Post-Quantum Cryptography. While the current 2.0 (April 2025) version of the ACM [7] document includes warnings about quantum threat, it does not (yet) specify concrete sunset dates for traditional algorithms.

Previously, various European nations have offered their own guidance on this matter, but in June 2025, EU member states issued a "A Coordinated Implementation Roadmap for the Transition to Post-Quantum Cryptography" [12]. CRA is discussed in the PQC Roadmap with the expectation of incorporating its transition requirements. Since it is expected that ACM will incorporate the sunset dates of the PQC Roadmap, it can indirectly serve as an enforcement mechanism for the European PQC transition in the context of CRA.

Table 2 summarizes the proposed transition timelines in the initial version of the European PQC roadmap. We note that the transition dates are mostly compatible with those proposed in the United States by NIST [16]. The timelines (as well as the algorithm selection) of CNSA 2.0 [5] seem stricter, but the scope of CNSA 2.0 is limited to U.S. National Security Systems (NSS – Defence and Intelligence Community systems).

When examining PQC transition guidance, it is useful to note that CRA is product legislation. CRA does not concern organisations that merely use products with cryptographic features; the CRA standards directly impose requirements on vendors and manufacturers that make the products. The approach in EU Coordinated Roadmap [12] and its referenced risk-analysis methodology [1] is largely organisation-oriented; there is a suggestion to "include supply chain" and to start the dialogue with product and service suppliers because the transition depends on them (in *first steps*) and to include cryptographic agility in procurement and NIS2 conformity (in *next steps*). The NIST White Paper on Cryptographic Agility [2] is also largely organisation-centric, but includes some technical and product-oriented guidance as well.

As cryptographic transitions are a continuous process, and unlikely to be limited to the current modernization process related to PQC, CRA may adopt more abstract design requirements loosely derived from a cryptographic agility definition given in [15]:

1. products should have the capability to select their security algorithms flexibly, either via configuration or (for communication protocols) in real time, based on the combined security functions of communicating parties

Table 2. The Initial European PQC Transition timetable, reproduced from Sect. 4.1 of [12], dated June 2025. We refer the reader to that document for more detailed information about First Steps and Next Steps, and the risk levels used.

1. **By 31.12.2026:**
   - At least the *First Steps* have been implemented by all Member States.
   - Initial national PQC transition roadmaps have been established by all Member States.
   - PQC transition planning and pilots for high- and medium-risk use cases have been initiated.

2. **By 31.12.2030:**
   - The *Next Steps* have been implemented by all Member States.
   - The PQC transition for high-risk use cases has been completed.
   - PQC transition planning and pilots for medium-risk use cases have been completed.
   - Quantum-safe software and firmware upgrades are enabled by default.

3. **By 31.12.2035:**
   - The PQC transition for medium-risk use cases has been completed.
   - The PQC transition for low-risk use cases has been completed as much as feasible.

2. products should have the ability to add new cryptographic mechanisms to existing hardware or software, resulting in new, stronger security features
3. products should have the ability to gracefully retire cryptographic mechanisms that have become either vulnerable or obsolete

For testable product requirements related to cryptographic agility, we note that the CRA [13] discusses product support periods in detail, as well as the mechanisms for dealing with artificially short ones. Generally, this is expected to be at least 5 years; especially for hardware products, it can be significantly longer.

One proposal is to require demonstrable cryptographic agility (to some alternative scheme, not necessarily the final replacement scheme used) if the product has a legacy cryptography mechanism (as defined in ACM [7]) as a default, and the announced depreciation of that cryptographic mechanism occurs during the product's support period.

6 Conclusions

This work examines the current state of development of European product standards related to the EU Cyber Resilience Act (CRA), with a focus on their impact on cryptography. CRA may have a positive effect, particularly by facilitating the transition to more robust algorithms and accelerating the Post-Quantum transition in internet-connected consumer electronics.

The cryptographic definitions in the closely related Radio Equipment Act (RED) standard series EN 18031 can be considered unsatisfactory (Sect. 4), and we hope that CRA will bring improvement to this by requiring strong cryptography as a default setting in products (users must still be able to use arbitrary cryptographic mechanisms). This work discusses the possible organisation of the cryptography approvals with ECCG (European Cybersecurity Certification Group) as the "single source of truth", and the impact of the Post-Quantum Cryptography transition on product requirements expressed in the standards.

Based on our experience with CEN and CENELEC, we offer criticism of their closed standardisation processes. To work on these standards (or even to find out about their direction), the author had to be appointed to CEN and CENELEC by two national-level Finnish standardisation committees (which mostly work as industrial associations). This path is not even feasible for citizens of some other EU countries. Furthermore, a member of a specific committee is generally not allowed to share working documents, even with members of other CRA standardisation committees, let alone with outsiders such as independent security researchers.

In addition to the fundamental problems of inaccessibility of technical information leading to low-impact standards, a closed standardisation approach is especially dangerous when applied to regulation related to cryptography and information security, where deliberate backdoors are a distinct risk in addition to simpler security issues stemming from a lack of an open, critical review by outside experts.

References

1. Amadori, A., et al.: AIVD Cryptologists: The PQC Migration Handbook, revised and extended 2nd edn, December 2025, https://publications.tno.nl/publication/34643386/fXcPVHsX/TNO-2024-pqc-en.pdf
2. Barker, E., et al.: Considerations for achieving crypto agility – strategies and practices, second public draft. NIST Cybersecurity White Paper NIST CSWP 39 2pd, National Institute of Standards and Technology, July 2025. https://doi.org/10.6028/NIST.CSWP.39.2pd
3. Bernstein, D.J., Lange, T., Niederhagen, R.: Dual EC: a standardized back door. In: Ryan, P.Y.A., Naccache, D., Quisquater, J. (eds.) The New Codebreakers - Essays Dedicated to David Kahn on the Occasion of His 85th Birthday. Lecture Notes in Computer Science, vol. 9100, pp. 256–281. Springer (2016). https://doi.org/10.1007/978-3-662-49301-4_17, https://eprint.iacr.org/2015/767
4. Caraco, J., Géraud-Stewart, R., Naccache, D.: Kerckhoffs' legacy (2020), https://eprint.iacr.org/2020/556
5. CNSS: use of public standards for secure information sharing. CNSSP 15 – Committee on National Security Systems (CNSS) Policy No. 15, December 2024, https://www.cnss.gov/CNSS/issuances/Policies.cfm

6. Davis, H., Green, M.D., Heninger, N., Ryan, K., Suhl, A.: On the possibility of a backdoor in the Micali-Schnorr generator. In: Tang, Q., Teague, V. (eds.) Public-Key Cryptography - PKC 2024 - 27th IACR International Conference on Practice and Theory of Public-Key Cryptography, Sydney, NSW, Australia, 15–17 April 2024, Proceedings, Part I, LNCS, vol. 14601, pp. 352–386. Springer (2024). https://doi.org/10.1007/978-3-031-57718-5_12, https://eprint.iacr.org/2023/440
7. ECCG: Agreed cryptographic mechanisms. European cybersecurity certification group sub-group on cryptography, Version 2.0, April 2025, https://certification.enisa.europa.eu/publications/eucc-guidelines-cryptography_en
8. ETSI: CYBER; cyber security for consumer internet of things: baseline requirements. European standard ETSI/EN 303 645 V3.1.3, European telecommunications standards institute, September 2024, https://www.etsi.org/deliver/etsi_en/303600_303699/303645/03.01.03_60/en_303645v030103p.pdf
9. ETSI: Cyber security (CYBER); cyber security for consumer internet of things: Conformance assessment of baseline requirements. Technical Specification ETSI TS 103 701 V2.1.1, European Telecommunications Standards Institute, May 2025, https://www.etsi.org/deliver/etsi_ts/103700_103799/103701/02.01.01_60/ts_103701v020101p.pdf
10. European commission: the 'blue guide' on the implementation of EU product rules 2022. Official Journal of the European Union (2022/C 247/01), June 2022, https://eur-lex.europa.eu/legal-content/EN/TXT/?uri=OJ:C:2022:247:TOC
11. European Commission: EUCC. Official Journal of the European Union (2024/482), February 2024, https://eur-lex.europa.eu/eli/reg_impl/2024/482/oj
12. European commission: a coordinated implementation roadmap for the transition to post-quantum cryptography. Part 1, Version: 1.1, EU PQC Workstream, June 2025, https://digital-strategy.ec.europa.eu/en/library/coordinated-implementation-roadmap-transition-post-quantum-cryptography
13. European parliament: cyber resilience act. Official Journal of the European Union (2024/2847), November 2024, https://eur-lex.europa.eu/eli/reg/2024/2847/oj
14. ISO: information technology– security techniques – random bit generation. Standard ISO/IEC 18031:2011, International organization for standardization (2011), https://www.iso.org/standard/54945.html
15. McKay, K.: How the national institute of standards and technology thinks about cryptography. In: Johnson, A.F., Millett, L.I. (eds.) Cryptographic Agility and Interoperablity – Proceedings of a Workshop, pp. 19–23. The National Academies Press (2017). https://doi.org/10.17226/24636, https://nap.nationalacademies.org/24636
16. Moody, D., Perlner, R., Regenscheid, A., Robinson, A., Cooper, D.: Transition to post-quantum cryptography standards. Internal Report NISTIR 8547 ipd, National Institute of Standards and Technology, November 2024. https://doi.org/10.6028/NIST.IR.8547.ipd
17. NEN: Common security requirements for radio equipment - part 1: Internet connected radio equipment. Standard NEN-EN 18031-1:2024, Nederlands Normalisatie Instituut (2024), https://connect.nen.nl/Standard/Detail?name=NEN-EN+18031-1%3A2024+en
18. NEN: Common security requirements for radio equipment - part 2: radio equipment processing data, namely internet connected radio equipment, childcare radio equipment, toys radio equipment and wearable radio equipment. Standard NEN-EN 18031-2:2024, Nederlands Normalisatie Instituut (2024), https://connect.nen.nl/Standard/Detail?name=NEN-EN+18031-2%3A2024+en

19. NEN: Common security requirements for radio equipment - part 3: Internet connected radio equipment processing virtual money or monetary value. Standard NEN-EN 18031-3:2024, Nederlands Normalisatie Instituut (2024), https://connect.nen.nl/Standard/Detail?name=NEN-EN+18031-3%3A2024+en
20. NIST: security requirements for cryptographic modules. Federal information processing standards Publication FIPS 140-3, March 2019. https://doi.org/10.6028/NIST.FIPS.140-3
21. NIST, CCCS: implementation guidance for FIPS 140-3 and the cryptographic module validation program. CMVP, September 2025, https://csrc.nist.gov/Projects/cryptographic-module-validation-program/fips-140-3-ig-announcements
22. Stevens, M., Bursztein, E., Karpman, P., Albertini, A., Markov, Y.: The first collision for full SHA-1. In: Katz, J., Shacham, H. (eds.) Advances in Cryptology - CRYPTO 2017 - 37th Annual International Cryptology Conference, Santa Barbara, CA, USA, 20–24 August 2017, Proceedings, Part I, LNCS, vol. 10401, pp. 570–596. Springer (2017). https://doi.org/10.1007/978-3-319-63688-7_19
23. Trummová, I., Schmüser, J., Huaman, N., Fahl, S.: Competing for attention: an interview study with participants of cryptography competitions. In: Proceedings of 32nd ACM Conference on Computer and Communications Security (CCS 2025), p. to appear. ACM (2025)
24. Wang, X., Yin, Y.L., Yu, H.: Finding collisions in the full SHA-1. In: Shoup, V. (ed.) Advances in Cryptology - CRYPTO 2005: 25th Annual International Cryptology Conference, Santa Barbara, California, USA, 14–18 August 2005, Proceedings, LNCS, vol. 3621, pp. 17–36. Springer (2005). https://doi.org/10.1007/11535218_2

Post-quantum Cryptography in eMRTDs Evaluating PAKE and PKI for Travel Documents

Nouri Alnahawi[1,2,3], Melissa Azouaoui[4], Joppe W. Bos[5], Gareth T. Davies[5(✉)], SeoJeong Moon[5], Christine van Vredendaal[6], and Alexander Wiesmaier[1,2,7]

[1] Darmstadt University of Applied Sciences, Darmstadt, Germany
[2] European University of Technology, European Union, Darmstadt, Germany
[3] University of Regensburg, Regensburg, Germany
[4] NXP Semiconductors, Hamburg, Germany
[5] NXP Semiconductors, Leuven, Belgium
[6] NXP Semiconductors, Eindhoven, The Netherlands
[7] National Research Center for Applied Cybersecurity ATHENE, Darmstadt, Germany

Abstract. Passports, identity cards and travel visas are examples of machine readable travel documents (MRTDs) or eMRTDs for their electronic variants. The security of the data exchanged between these documents and a reader is secured with a standardized password authenticated key exchange (PAKE) protocol known as PACE.

A new world-wide protocol migration is expected with the arrival of post-quantum cryptography (PQC) standards. In this paper, we focus on the impact of this migration on constrained embedded devices as used in eMRTDs. We present a feasibility study of a candidate post-quantum secure PAKE scheme as the replacement for PACE on existing widely deployed resource-constrained chips. In a wider context, we study the size, performance and security impact of adding post-quantum cryptography with a focus on chip storage and certificate chains for existing eMRTDs.

We show that if the required post-quantum certificates for the eMRTD fit in memory, the migration of existing eMRTD protocols to their post-quantum secure equivalent is already feasible but a performance penalty has to be paid. When using a resource constrained SmartMX3 P71D600 smart card, designed with classical cryptography in mind, then execution times of a post-quantum secure PAKE algorithm using the recommended post-quantum parameter of the new PQC standard ML-KEM can be done in under a second. This migration will be aided by future inclusion of dedicated hardware accelerators and increased memory to allow storage of larger keys and improve performance.

This research work was supported by the National Research Center for Applied Cybersecurity ATHENE.

H. C. Pöhls and C. J. Mitchell (Eds.): SSR 2025, LNCS 16466, pp. 181–201, 2026.
https://doi.org/10.1007/978-3-032-19567-8_9

Keywords: post-quantum cryptography · electronic travel documents · password-authenticated key exchange · cryptography implementations

1 Introduction

Virtually all security building blocks, components and systems of the world's digital infrastructure rely today on traditional[1] asymmetric or public-key cryptography, based on RSA or elliptic curve cryptography (ECC) whose security relies on the hardness of the integer factorization or variants of the discrete logarithm problem. With a powerful quantum computer these problems can be efficiently solved [62] compromising the security of world-wide security standards. Symmetric cryptography algorithms, such as AES, are not as critically impacted by the development of quantum computers and can be made more resistant to quantum cryptanalysis by increasing their key sizes (where deemed necessary). The main solution to remain secure in a post-quantum era is the use of post-quantum cryptography (PQC), i.e. asymmetric cryptography schemes that have been designed to resist attacks from both classic and quantum computers.

In 2016, the USA's National Institute of Standards and Technology (NIST) launched a standardization process for PQC schemes [48]. After almost eight years the first three PQC standards have been selected and published. These schemes have different trade-offs in terms of data size (e.g. key, certificate, signature or ciphertext) versus execution performance and infrastructure complexity compared to traditional systems based on ECC or RSA. In 2024 the schemes ML-KEM [51], ML-DSA [50] and SLH-DSA [52] were standardized. In addition, the digital signature scheme FALCON [59] and the key encapsulation mechanism HQC [3] will be standardized by NIST at a later date. Many other national bodies are developing their own algorithms through competitions such as in Korea [53] and China [36]. The fragmented situation is further exacerbated by government agencies in Europe recommending schemes such as FrodoKEM [47] and Classic McEliece [4] (see Sect. 2.1), these schemes are now in the process of standardization in bodies such as ISO and the IETF.

The PQC migration of public key infrastructures, software and all affected systems with heterogeneous hardware platforms is a significant effort [54]. It is not as simple as using PQC as another plug-in to existing cryptographic protocols, and it is often crucial for applications to guarantee continuity and backwards compatibility. Governmental agencies have already begun to issue migration guidance for the upcoming transition [46]. An example of such an application where migration is essential but also challenging is electronic Machine Readable Travel Documents (eMRTDs) [5]. The International Civil Aviation Organization (ICAO) supports the international coordination of global civil aviation systems, and publishes standards for machine-readable passports [37]. In particular, parts 11 [34] and 12 [35] of the ICAO Doc 9303 series [37] describe the cryptographic protocols and the public key infrastructure for eMRTDs, respectively (Table 1).

[1] In this document we follow IETF nomenclature for PQC [27].

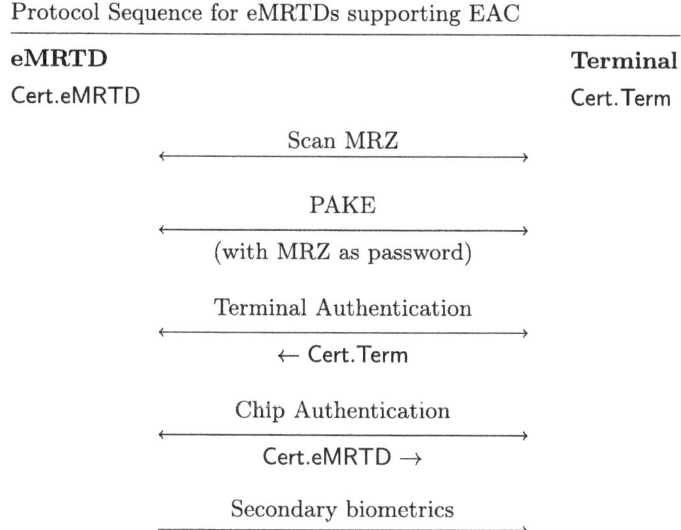

Fig. 1. EAC is the combination of Terminal Authentication and Chip Authentication; passive authentication is a subroutine of Chip Auth. EAC occurs in a channel secured by a PAKE session key, and produces a further session key that is used to encrypt secondary biometrics. PAKE migration is described in Sect. 3; PKI migration is described in Sect. 4.

Electronic MRTDs vary considerably due to the global nature of the ecosystem. Nations have different policies regarding cryptographic recommendations and different generations of chips (that enable cryptography in the documents) and reader terminals, which leads to differences in capabilities. In this high-security setting, the need for interoperability across borders means that chips need to be able to securely communicate with as many terminals as possible, leading to a need for maximal backwards compatibility. The advent of PQC and the new generation of standardized cryptographic algorithms that it brings, will further complicate these constraints: the size of PQC certificates, physi-

Table 1. Security Protocols for eIDs and eMRTDs, where DS denotes digital signatures, SKE denotes symmetric-key encryption and MAC denotes Message Authentication Code.

Protocol	Security Goal	Cryptographic Mechanism
Passive Authentication	Check Authenticity of Chip Data	DS (on chip data)
Active Authentication	Check Chip Genuineness	Challenge-Response (DS)
Basic Access Control	Initial comms. channel, prevent eavesdropping	Challenge-Response (SKE)
PACE	Initial comms. channel, prevent eavesdropping	PAKE (incl. ephemeral DH)
Chip Authentication	Check Chip Genuineness	Ephemeral-Static DH
Terminal Authentication	Check terminal authorized to read secondary biometrics	Challenge-Response (DS)
Payload Comms.	Confidentiality/Data Integrity	SKE, MAC

cal attack protection requirements, hybrid usage of cryptographic algorithms and backward compatibility should all be considered[2]. Figure 1 depicts the flow between an eMRTD chip and the terminal (reader) device.

One of the components of the eMRTD protocol flow is password-authenticated key exchange (PAKE), instantiated using the (quantum-vulnerable) PACE protocol [17,37], with the goal of establishing an initial secure channel between chip and reader based on the visually-readable data in the travel document. Constructing post-quantum secure PAKE is a challenging task (see Sect. 2.4) and at present no clear frontrunners exist for future standardization. This makes it important to evaluate the performance of candidate schemes on the real hardware (chips and readers) that are used in high-security environments, such as protection of sensitive data as provided by eMRTD protocols.

Prior Work. Pradel and Mitchell were the first to investigate the migration of eMRTD applications to PQC [58]. In particular, they proposed a PKI based on post-quantum X.509 certificates and considered qTESLA [19] (a NIST round 2 candidate), both at the country Certificate Authority (CA) and document signer levels. They showed the practicality (efficiency of document verification and signing request generation) of migrating an eMRTD PKI to PQC however the focus on qTESLA makes it difficult to extend their conclusions to other signature schemes: we discuss options for now-standardized schemes in Sect. 4.

In [28] the Extended Access Control (EAC) protocol was investigated in the context of the PQC migration, and suggested two modes for terminal authentication, via signatures and via KEMs. The first approach corresponds to what is done now in EAC: the chip generates a random challenge value which is then signed by the terminal and the resulting signature is then verified by the chip. The KEM-based approach has a few benefits including privacy of the eMRTD certificate and possibly replacing a variable-time operation, such as ML-DSA signing with a constant-time one, namely a KEM decapsulation. They did not discuss the PQC migration of the PACE protocol used for initial channel establishment, which is executed before EAC, nor the impact of signature scheme choice on transferred data in the PKI. We aim to close this gap by analyzing the practical use of a PQ-PAKE in the context of eMRTDs.

A variety of PQ-PAKEs have been proposed and are surveyed in [7]. Of the around 50 investigated PAKEs 26 provide benchmarks on CPU platforms (laptop grade or higher) but none on the constrained chips used in eMRTDs. Of the six PAKEs that provide an implementation two are augmented[3] which does not fit our use case [26,43]. Of the four remaining balanced PAKEs two are non-generic (cannot be instantiated with KEMs) [60,61]. Of the two remaining

[2] Some nations are beginning to step up their preparation through demonstrators, for example Germany's BSI and Bundesdruckerei: https://www.bundesdruckerei.de/en/newsroom/press-releases/deutschland-setzt-massstabe-fur-sichere-ausweisdokumente-im-zeitalter-der-quantencomputer.

[3] While augmented PAKEs use a one-way-transformation of the password on server side, balanced PAKEs assume the possession of the same password on both sides.

generic PAKEs [12] needs KEMs with splittable public keys[4] while [8] works with general KEMs.

Contributions. In this paper, we discuss and show the feasibility of developing a PQC migration strategy for eMRTDs. We build on the work performed in [28] and [8], but add design choices and recommendations that ease implementation on embedded devices involved in eMRTD protocols: the chips and the terminals. Our main contributions are twofold:

1. A demonstration of the feasibility of a candidate post-quantum PAKE scheme as the replacement for the PACE protocol on existing constrained chips. We show that a PAKE scheme using the level 3 parameter set of ML-KEM can be completed in under a second on existing resource-constrained hardware (not designed and optimized for PQC);
2. A study of the size, performance and security impact of adding post-quantum cryptography in the context of chip storage and certificate chains for existing eMRTD protocols. This includes protocol solutions to ease protection against physical attacks, as well as the impact of PQC scheme choices on the system.

These two aspects have received little attention in prior work and therefore we believe that our contribution can serve as a guidance document to government stakeholders for planning PQC migration in the eMRTD context.

2 Preliminaries

2.1 PQC Schemes and Hybrid PQC

Since eMRTDs make use of ECDH and ECDSA, migrating their infrastructures and protocols to PQC requires both a KEM for secure session establishment and a digital signature for proving authenticity and integrity of data. ML-KEM [51] was selected by NIST as the recommended KEM for standardization, and later HQC [3] was selected as a secondary choice. The German Federal Office for Information Security (BSI) has additionally recommended FrodoKEM [47] (a Round 3 candidate in the NIST PQC standardization process that did not progress further) and Classic McEliece [4] (a Round 4 candidate that did not progress further). ML-DSA [50] was selected as the recommended digital signature algorithm by NIST. Additionally, the schemes SLH-DSA [52] and FALCON [59] were also selected by NIST. The stateful hash-based signature schemes XMSS and LMS [49] were also standardized for particular use cases, e.g., software signing, due to their statefulness and the need to carefully maintain the state.

Many national information security bodies such as the German BSI [24] and the French ANSSI [9] recommend the use of hybrid PQC schemes. Hybrid PQC combines a PQC scheme along with a standard public-key cryptography scheme based on RSA or ECC. This thwarts attacks using a quantum computer against

[4] Splittable public keys usually consist of a structured part and an unstructured part which can be transferred separately.

traditional cryptography, but also caters to the possibility that the PQC scheme used is weakened or compromised by a classic attack, while no sufficiently powerful quantum computer has been yet realized.

A major challenge in deploying hybrid PQC relates to interoperability and in particular certificate formats. ICAO and eMRTDs, like numerous other applications, use the X.509 certificate format. There have been a few proposals, mainly in IETF working groups, on how to adopt hybrid X.509 certificates [20,55], and case studies, e.g. [38,57]. The set of proposals includes having two independent certificates, one classic and one PQC. For a certificate authority this proposal would translate into having two independent parallel certificate authorities, one signing with a classic RSA or ECC key and the other with a PQC digital signature scheme. Another proposal includes combining the traditional certificates with a PQ signature, included in the extension field of an X.509 certificate. The benefit of this approach is backwards compatibility, since processing or taking into account the extension field of a X.509 certificate is optional.

2.2 ICAO eMRTD PKI

In the context of eMRTDs, certificates are used to attest to the authenticity of the eMRTD key, eMRTD data and terminal key. A country's CA consists of two CAs: the Country Signing Certificate Authority (CSCA) and the Country Verifying Certificate Authority (CVCA). The CSCA generates root certificates to sign document signers' certificates. In turn, the document signer's key signs the eMRTD data contained in the chip, including its public key. The document signer's certificate is also stored on the eMRTD, along with the eMRTD's own certificate, for verification by a terminal during Chip Authentication. The CVCA also generates root certificates used to sign document verifiers' certificates, which in turn sign certificates to authorize terminals after Terminal Authentication to read MRTD data and verify them. Authorization certificates are also issued separately to authorities of other countries such that other countries and terminals can verify documents. More details are provided in ICAO Doc 9303 part 12 [35].

2.3 ICAO eMRTD Protocols

The protocols described by ICAO Doc 9303 part 11 [34] are carried out between a *chip* (travel document) and a *terminal* (reader). The terminal is sometimes referred to as an *inspection system* in ICAO documents. Figure 1 depicts the flow between an eMRTD chip and the terminal (reader) device and which protocols are used for each step. At the beginning of the communication between the terminal and the chip, the terminal requests the `SecurityInfos` data held by the chip in Data Group 14 to learn which protocols/algorithms the chip supports (refer to ICAO Doc 9303 part 11 [34] for more details). We assume that any chip or terminal upgraded to support PQC will also include these capabilities in its `SecurityInfos` data (in the case of a chip) or will be able to interpret these capabilities (in the case of a terminal).

Primary biometrics and identifiers are visibly available in the machine-readable zone (MRZ) of the eMRTD. These fields are read by a terminal using optical character recognition and not RFID, to thwart eavesdropping. Anyone in possession of the document can see these values by opening it: the MRZ values are used for initial channel establishment via either Basic Access Control (BAC) or Password-Authenticated Channel Establishment (PACE). BAC derives a cryptographic key from a subset of the primary biometrics/identifiers, whereas PACE uses a password extracted from the eMRTD's MRZ in combination with Diffie-Hellman key exchange to derive a shared session key. Since post-quantum PACE for eMRTDs is the main topic explored in this paper, it will be later discussed in more detail in Sects. 2.4 and 3.

After establishing a secure communication channel, authentication is carried out. Passive Authentication is the minimal level of authentication security we consider in this paper: the data groups in the MRZ are signed by the document signer and the chip stores this signature in a Document Security Object ($\text{SecObj}_{\text{Doc}}$), to protect their integrity. Passive Authentication does not protect against cloning of the eMRTD's chip.

Secondary biometrics such as fingerprints and iris scans are only transmitted from the chip to the terminal after successful completion of Terminal Authentication. Terminal Authentication is performed as part of the Extended Access Control (EAC) protocol. EAC is the combination of Chip Authentication, which includes passive authentication, and terminal authentication. For more information on EAC and its migration to PQC we refer the interested readers to [28].

2.4 Password-Authenticated Key Exchange in eMRTDs

The Password Authenticated Connection Establishment (PACE) protocol is a balanced two-party PAKE protocol (with MRZ data as the password), and was defined in BSI TR-03110 [23] as a successor BAC (based on symmetric cryptography). PACE establishes a secure communication channel before the transmission of primary biometrics and certificates, providing privacy by prohibiting eavesdroppers from learning unique document certificates. PACE relies mainly on a password and an asymmetric key agreement to protect against two types of known attacks against PAKE protocols: offline dictionary attacks targeting the password, and man-in-the-middle (MitM) attacks targeting the key agreement. Further, PACE also provides forward secrecy, untraceability, and unlinkability.

While PACE shares many aspects with other PAKEs, its design rationale differs slightly. Conceptually PACE utilizes an additional DH key agreement to protect the password, whereas the use of the password protects the real DH key agreement that leads to a final session key. This is realized by adding a random nonce (generated by the chip) as a required dependency to the DH public parameters (group generator), without actually becoming part of the final key. This is naturally possible thanks to the mathematical properties of (EC)DH, and its underlying algebraic structure (commutativity under addition and scalar multiplication). However, since PACE is built from classical number theoretic hardness assumptions ((EC)DH), it is not quantum-safe and can be considered vulnerable to multiple types of attacks that can be executed with a CRQC. The first type is a Store-Now-Decrypt-Later (SNDL) attack, where an attacker with a CRQC would be able to compute PACE session keys, even a long time after capturing a session transcript, and therefore read any primary biometrics/certificates sent in session traffic and obviate the privacy goals. The second type actively targets the DH key agreement in MitM manner. Although an attacker cannot directly read the password used as input using a CRQC, they would be able to break the first DH and thus determine the exact value of the used nonce and trace it back to the correct password (or its hash). Guessing the password breaks the security for all following sessions, and in the worst case may also lead to active establishment of a compromised communication channel.

Post-quantum PAKE. Although there is a significant amount of work on quantum-safe PAKEs, most of the proposed constructions in the literature are based on direct constructions from PQC primitives (e.g. [1,25,40,42]) and strongly vary in their designs and security properties [7]. In the last two years, a number of KEM-based PQC PAKEs were proposed, which mainly aim at achieving concrete and secure instantiations utilizing CRYSTALS-Kyber (ML-KEM) in a black-box manner [6,8,10–12,16,33,56,63]. Nevertheless, there is still little consensus on how to build post-quantum secure PAKEs [6,7], considering aspects related to formal analysis (e.g., ROM vs QROM and IC vs QIC) and KEM security properties (e.g., key uniformity and ciphertext robustness). There is hence still no standardized construction and no official standardization process for PQC PAKEs. Given the requirement of active CRQC attacks and the relatively small gain—the secondary biometrics would remain secure if PQC algorithms were used in the EAC phase—it appears less urgent to plan PQC migration of the PACE component. However, the long lead time for standardization indicates that work needs to start as soon as possible to assess the viability of PQC PAKE candidates on current and future hardware platforms.

3 Implementation of a Candidate Post-Quantum PAKE

All KEM-based PQC PAKEs (i.e., generic PQC PAKEs) follow the design approach of the classical PAKE Encrypted Key Exchange (EKE) and its variant OEKE. This trend can be clearly seen in the first proposed generic PQC PAKE CAKE [16] and its variant OCAKE shown in Fig. 2. The design idea of CAKE is to encrypt the KEM public key and the ciphertext using a password derived symmetric key using a block cipher modeled as an ideal cipher (IC). Alternatively, the ciphertext is authenticated with a key confirmation tag in OCAKE, which is modeled as a random oracle (RO). Additionally, mutual explicit authentication can be achieved via a key confirmation round at the end of the protocol. This design concept is especially appealing, as it allows relying on well studied idealized models and abstract KEM properties for the overall PAKE security (session key indistinguishability and public key anonymity). On the other hand, it is much more feasible to implement such constructions in practice, as opposed to PAKEs relying on hash to group (H2G) operations in the RO model [7], which are often accompanied with expensive computational costs. In this work, we provide an evaluation of an OCAKE instantiation using an optimized ML-KEM implementation, which also utilizes optimized cryptographic building blocks.

Initiator $\mathcal{I}$ (Client)	**OCAKE**	**Responder $\mathcal{R}$ (Server)**
Password pw		Password pw
	Transmit Encrypted Public Key	
$k_{pw} \leftarrow \mathsf{KDF}(pw)$		$k_{pw} \leftarrow \mathsf{KDF}(pw)$
$(pk, sk) \leftarrow \$\mathsf{KGen}$		
$apk \leftarrow \mathsf{IC}(k_{pw}, pk)$	$\xrightarrow{apk}$	$pk' \leftarrow \mathsf{IC}^{-1}(k_{pw}, apk)$
	Establish Session Pre-Key	
$K' \leftarrow \mathsf{Decap}(sk, c)$	$\xleftarrow{c}$	$(c, K) \leftarrow \$\mathsf{Encap}(pk')$
	$\xleftarrow{tag_1}$	$tag_1 \leftarrow \mathsf{H}(pw, apk, pk', c, K, "r")$
$tag_2 \leftarrow \mathsf{H}(pw, apk, pk, c, K', "i")$	$\xrightarrow{tag_2}$	
	Key Confirmation & Key Derivation	
$tag_1' \leftarrow \mathsf{H}(pw, apk, pk, c, K', "r")$		$tag_2' \leftarrow \mathsf{H}(pw, apk, pk', c, K, "i")$
`if` $tag_1' = tag_1$		`if` $tag_2' = tag_2$
$SK \leftarrow \mathsf{KDF}'(tag_1, K')$		$SK' \leftarrow \mathsf{KDF}'(tag_1, K)$
`output` SK `and accept`		`output` SK' `and accept`
`terminate`		`terminate`

Fig. 2. The OCAKE protocol adapted from [16].

3.1 Implementing OCAKE on Low-Memory Chips

The implementation environment was an NXP SmartMX3 P71D600 microcontroller[5] in a smartcard form factor and an Identive 4700F dual-interface smart card reader[6]. Testing was performed on the ISO/IEC 7816 contact interface. This chip and reader were both chosen to be low-cost and commercially available, reflecting real-world usage of eMRTDs.

In addition to providing benchmarks for ML-KEM-based OCAKE, we also provide performance numbers for PACE using the BrainpoolP256r1 curve. This allows a comparison to pre-quantum alternatives. The chip was loaded with a proprietary, memory-optimized Java Card implementation of ML-KEM (following a similar strategy as described for ML-DSA in [22]): performing various time-memory trade-offs to ensure an implementation which reduces footprint. The library and the reader used a C-implementation on a mid-range Dell laptop

[5] https://www.nxp.com/products/security-and-authentication/security-microcontrollers:MC_71108.

[6] https://www.cardlogix.com/product/identive-utrust-4700f-dual-interface-contactless-smart-card-reader-905320.

(connected via USB). Aligning these two implementations required careful construction of the appropriate APDUs. The chip had approximately 4.5kB of RAM available for our cryptographic operations, and around 3kB of this was used during execution. The on-chip cryptographic library did not expose SHAKE/SHA3 directly, therefore the hash function SHA2 has been used for the OCAKE experiments. AES was used as the symmetric encryption component for PACE and OCAKE, with security levels aligned to the Kyber/PACE parameter set.

The classical cryptography on the SmartMX3 P71D600 includes side-channel and fault attack countermeasures to achieve the highest certification levels and is FIPS 140-3 certified[7]. The ML-KEM implementation does not include such advanced countermeasures.

3.2 Results and Analysis

Using the on-chip cryptographic library, which provided the core (post-quantum) cryptography, we implemented the OCAKE protocol in the provided Securebox environment: this allows developpers to implement, manage, and load assets independently. Performance figures for the different parameter sets are provided in Table 2. Timings are an average of 10 protocol runs, however there was very little variation in runtime (as one would expect).

As expected the runtime of OCAKE is slower than PACE: this is inherent to the change of algorithm and protocol. This slowdown varies between a factor 3.0 and 10.4 depending on the role of the card and the parameter set resulting in a running time of 652 and 2257 ms, respectively. A running time of `OCAKE-ML-KEM-512` and `OCAKE-ML-KEM-768` of less than a second (independent of the role of the card) is already impressive taking into account that this constrained chip that was not designed to support post-quantum cryptography. We note that next-generation chips will have dedicated hardware accelerators for PQC operations. These accelerators in combination with more memory will

Table 2. Performance results for OCAKE and PACE on the NXP SmartMX3 P71D600 microcontroller.

Protocol		Runtime (ms)
PACE-BrainpoolP256r1		217
Card as Responder	`OCAKE-ML-KEM-512`	652
	`OCAKE-ML-KEM-768`	995
	`OCAKE-ML-KEM-1024`	1 406
Card as Initiator	`OCAKE-ML-KEM-512`	917
	`OCAKE-ML-KEM-768`	1 500
	`OCAKE-ML-KEM-1024`	2 257

[7] https://csrc.nist.gov/projects/cryptographic-module-validation-program/certificate/4679.

lead to performance that is significantly better, and even with side-channel countermeasures it can be anticipated that ML-KEM runtimes will be an order of magnitude faster compared to Table 2 on dedicated hardware.

It should also be noted that OCAKE uses an ephemeral KEM plus symmetric cryptography, therefore other KEM-based PAKEs that only additionally use (standardized) symmetric crypto will have comparable performance on similar platforms when implemented with ML-KEM.

Deploying Post-quantum PAKE in Future eMRTDs. The chips in eMRTDs are constrained in memory and processing power but also the gate area allocated to cryptography acceleration. Component/sub-routine re-use is therefore very beneficial: a PAKE scheme built using KEMs is more likely to be adopted in eMRTD hardware than a dedicated non-generic construction, even if the non-generic construction appears to perform faster in software in laptop/server-grade environments. Physical attack protection is inherited from the KEM implementations, yielding faster certification at higher assurance levels.

For KEM-based PAKE schemes ML-KEM is particularly well suited for PAKE on constrained devices due to its balanced profile for performance and its data sizes. This is especially apparent when considering the constrained nature of the communication channel between the eMRTD chip and the terminal, and the APDUs in which data must be transported. An ephemeral public key and an encapsulation ciphertext inherently need to be transmitted, therefore schemes such as HQC [3], Classic McEliece [4] and FrodoKEM [47] are unsuitable even before considering their performance efficiency issues.

If in the future an ephemeral KEM-based PAKE were to be recommended for usage by ICAO, then it would be desirable for the terminal to perform key generation and decapsulation while the chip performs encapsulation, for two reasons. First, the terminal would incur the bulk of the operations, i.e. key generation and decapsulation, instead of the chip, which would only have to perform encapsulation (in our on-chip experiments, decapsulation was slightly slower than encapsulation which was slightly slower than key generation, for all parameter sets). Second, as has been described extensively in the literature [13,64], a PQ KEM decapsulation involves a critical physical attack vector. Avoiding decapsulation on an eMRTD chip also implies reducing the attack surface and overhead, assuming a terminal can better and more efficiently handle the overhead incurred by stronger countermeasures and hardened implementations. Furthermore, in any future recommendation for PQC PAKE, communication bandwidth could be saved by deploying KEMs with smaller keys and ciphertexts by requiring a lower security level parameter set (e.g. ML-KEM-512 at NIST level 1). We also note that this component is unaffected by the CSR issues described in Sect. 4.2, as the KEM keys used here are ephemeral and not static.

Hybrid PAKE. Since hybrid approaches are recommended in the migration phase, it is natural to consider how a traditional PAKE scheme (such as PACE) could be securely combined with a post-quantum-secure PAKE scheme (such as OCAKE). Hybrid KEMs have already been proposed in the literature as generic combiners [29] and dedicated constructions such as X-Wing [14] that rely on non-standard security properties of their underlying components to achieve greater efficiency. Considering hybrid PAKEs, there was no clear path to finding a generic approach [41]. Nonetheless, Hesse and Rosenberg [32], and Lyu and Liu [44] address this issue in two very recent publications: both suggest a generic recipe for the construction of hybrid PQC PAKEs based on parallel and sequential (serial) combiners [7]. Further, Günther et al. recently showed how to realize a secure hybrid PAKE from Obfuscated KEMs [31], working around issues related to the public key uniformity of ML-KEM. A very recent work by Vos et al. [66] builds upon said works and combines the classical CPACE protocol with the PQC NoIC-PAKE. The proposed hybrid PAKEs (symmetric CPaceO-QUAKE and asymmetric CPaceOQUAKE+) are both instantiated using DH and obfuscated ML-KEM. We note that this proposal appeared previously as IETF draft [65], which was submitted by three of the same authors of the research paper.

4 Post-quantum Migration for eMRTD PKIs

In this section we focus on migration prioritization and identify the impacts of scheme choices in different parts of the eMRTD ecosystem. Compromise of the signing key of a country's signing certificate authority is the most critical threat and forms the highest risk to eMRTD security. An adversary would be able to create (valid) document signing authorities and issue documents on their behalf: this would remove the trust even for the minimum level of security provided by Passive Authentication (PA). The data groups in the MRZ on the eMRTD are signed and stored in a Document Security Object ($\mathrm{SecObj}_{\mathrm{Doc}}$) to ensure the integrity and authenticity of the document through PA (see Sect. 2.3). Hence, an attacker able to compromise the signing algorithm and recovering the secret signing key can forge eMRTDs. On the other hand, the compromise of a country's verifying certificate authority, document verifier or terminal secret key is less critical, but nonetheless would imply that all eMRTD data can be read.

4.1 Migration Options and Impact

As mentioned in Sect. 2.1, using hybrid PQC is a pragmatic option to protect against attacks on standard cryptography and attacks on PQC. However, to simplify the analysis and comments, we restrict them to only the PQC schemes and to NIST-standardized schemes. An overview for a hybrid scheme including RSA or ECC can be deduced from the following analysis, based on the selected certificate format and hybrid mechanism. In this work, we are mainly interested in the impact of the PQC migration on eMRTD chips. For many eMRTDs and countries, the embedded chips used are constrained devices. Long-term key/credential storage in non-volatile memory can be considered as a criteria when selecting schemes for the PKI. Note, however, that since PACE/PAKE uses ephemeral keys it does not affect the PKI and vice versa.

Relevant KEMs and Signature Schemes. ML-KEM is the only suitable choice since other KEMs are neither (currently) standardized nor can be efficiently supported by constrained devices [39]. Although efforts have been made to make FrodoKEM more embedded friendly and optimize its implementation [21], it remains significantly more challenging to deploy than ML-KEM.

For signatures, some level of flexibility is available. We consider ML-DSA suitable for most use cases, including certificate generation at the certificate authority level and signature generation on the terminals. In addition, we also consider the stateful HBS scheme LMS, but only at the certificate authorities' level. LMS seems significantly more suitable than their stateless counterpart SPHINCS+ for such an application since they have smaller signatures. Furthermore, it can be assumed that a certificate authority can securely and reliably handle the signing state and does not require a prohibitive number of signatures during the lifetime of its root certificate.

FALCON can be considered at the certificate authorities' and document signers' levels. Its main advantage is its relatively smaller signature size. However, its implementation requires specific hardware for floating-point computation during signing. In eMRTDs signing only happens on the terminal and not on the chip (only signature verification is required on the chip which doesn't require floating-point support), however this still represents a significant implementation challenge for performance and physical security, e.g. protection against side-channel attacks. Hence, in the following we do not consider FALCON.

Scheme Combinations Size Comparison. Tables 3 and 4 provide an overview of the impact of scheme choices on the long term post-quantum cryptographic data that has to be stored on the eMRTD chip. The analysis considers combinations of the previous set of schemes as choices for each level of the certificate chain. The long term cryptographic data includes the following. The *CVCA public key*, which is needed to verify the terminal's certificate during TA. The *document signer's certificate*, which is needed during passive and chip authentication for the terminal to verify the eMRTD's certificate chain. For document signers we only consider ML-DSA due to the large number of signatures that a document signer has to produce making stateful HBS schemes impractical. The *chip's certificate*, containing its public key and a signature from the document signer, which is used for the purpose of chip authentication and to perform key establishment with a terminal. The *chip's secret key* for key establishment, corresponding to the previous certified public key.

Note that the tables do not include the choice of the signature scheme on the terminal. This choice does not impact the *long-term* cryptographic data stored on the eMRTD chip, it however impacts the data stored during the execution of ICAO protocols and the code size on the eMRTD chip.

First, Table 3 displays numbers for key sizes based on the specification or the standard of each scheme for the following cases: when both the certificate authority and document signer use ML-DSA-65, corresponding to NIST security level 3, when the certificate authority uses LMS-h20-192-w8 and the document signer ML-DSA-65 and finally when the certificate authority uses LMS-h20-256-

w8 and the document signer ML-DSA-65. The parameter sets considered for LMS are based on a presentation related to the BSI's PKI [15]. Naturally, the table can be easily adapted to many more parameter sets, however in this work it serves the purpose of giving initial estimates of the impact on the eMRTD chip requirements of different schemes and their combinations along the certificate chain. We assume that both the CSCA and the CVCA use the same scheme and parameter set for signing.

Table 3. eMRTD long term PQ data based on scheme choice at different levels of the PKI. This table uses ML-DSA-65 and ML-KEM-768 (NIST security level 3).

scheme choice	CSCA/CVCA	ML-DSA-65	LMS-h20-192-w8	LMS-h20-256-w8
	DS	ML-DSA-65		
	C	ML-KEM-768		
pk_{CVCA}		1 952	56	64
$Cert_{DS}$	pk_{DS}	1 952	1952	1952
	Signature $_{\text{by CSCA}}$	3 293	1 140	1 772
$Cert_C$	pk_C	1 184	1 184	1 184
	Signature $_{\text{by DS}}$	3 293	3 293	3 293
sk_C		2 400	2 400	2 400
Total (Bytes)		14 074	10 025	10 665

Looking at the last row of Table 3, it highlights that the migration to PQC will have a significant impact on certificate and credential sizes. The usage of a stateful HBS scheme such as LMS, even only at the CSCA/CVCA level, already reduces the total footprint by a few kBytes. The selected LMS parameter $w = 8$ is helpful in this context, since it reduces the signature size by a factor two or four compared to using $w = 4$ and $w = 2$, respectively at the cost of a slower key generation, signature generation and signature verification which is typically not a problem at the CSCA/CVCA level.

Table 4 displays the impact for the same combination of schemes as Table 3 but using ML-DSA-87 and ML-KEM-1024 corresponding to NIST security level 5. In practice, it may not be necessary to match security levels of schemes used at different levels of the eMRTD PKI. For instance, it may be the case that since ML-DSA is used for a more critical target, i.e. the certificate authority and the authenticity of the eMRTD, compared to the ML-KEM key pair which is device specific, one could use a higher security level parameter set for ML-DSA than for ML-KEM. The main benefit would be to reduce the footprint on the eMRTD's embedded chip in terms of stored data and the execution of the ML-KEM functions during chip authentication.

4.2 Certificate Signing Requests

One potential challenge when using a KEM is acquiring certificates for chip public keys from a certificate authority, namely the Document Signer, in an

Table 4. eMRTD long term PQ data based on scheme choice at different levels of the PKI. This table uses ML-DSA-87 and ML-KEM-1024 (NIST security level 5).

scheme choice	CSCA/CVCA	ML-DSA-87	LMS-h20-192-w8	LMS-h20-256-w8
	DS	ML-DSA-87		
	C	ML-KEM-1024		
pk_{CVCA}		2 592	56	64
$Cert_{DS}$	pk_{DS}	2 592	2 592	2 592
	Signature $_{\text{by CSCA}}$	4 595	1 140	1 772
$Cert_C$	pk_C	1 568	1 568	1 568
	Signature $_{\text{by DS}}$	4 595	4 595	4 595
sk_C		3 168	3 168	3 168
Total (Bytes)		19 110	13 119	13 750

efficient and asynchronous manner without further interaction. For digital signatures the Certificate Signing Request (CSR) is straightforward: the requester provides alongside its request a signature on the request itself, thus proving that it is indeed in possession of the secret signing key.

For KEMs it is not straightforward to do this in a non-interactive, 'offline' manner: the owner of the secret decapsulation key needs to prove that it can decapsulate arbitrary ciphertexts that were generated by some other entity. It has been observed that using advanced cryptographic techniques such as multi-party-computation-in-the-head (MPCitH) proof systems, it is possible for the owner of an ML-KEM-512 secret key to prove this fact with proof sizes ranging from 17.8–52.9 kB (with clear speed-size trade-offs) and proofs starting at around 130 kB for ML-KEM-1024 [30]. This approach is not standardized, and invokes considerable overhead in key management and trust provisioning systems.

4.3 Backwards Compatibility

In the (hybrid) post-quantum setting, backwards compatibility mandates that if only one party supports PQC, then the parties should still be able to perform the traditional authentication mechanism that maximizes security (e.g. if the chip supports PQC-Hybrid EAC but the terminal only supports traditional PA then the traditional PA should still occur). If this is a requirement for the next generation protocol, then hybrid PQC must allow fall back in every possible configuration, and this is made easier by the already available eMRTD mechanisms described by ICAO, namely that the terminal can read the capabilities of the chip at the beginning of the communication protocol and proceed accordingly.

4.4 Downgrade Attacks

A downgrade attack is successful when an attacker forces the algorithm/protocol negotiation process (that defines the establishment of the communication channel and/or the authentication mechanism) to agree on something weaker than what would have been agreed in an unattacked session, often by exploiting deprecated cryptography. Notable examples of protocol downgrade attacks are FREAK [18], LogJam [2] and POODLE [45] on TLS.

The existence of CRQCs would deem (almost all widely used) traditional asymmetric cryptography to be considered broken. For eMRTDs the terminal chooses which cryptographic algorithms to use in the subsequent protocol and therefore it is very difficult to protect against a malicious terminal that downgrades communication, however this attack vector is not necessarily important to prevent anyway since this terminal can always read all sensitive information from an eMRTD. In the other direction there no threat, since in the protocol flow there is no secret information passed from the terminal to the chip.

5 Conclusions

In this paper we analyzed different aspects of migrating eMRTD applications and infrastructures to their post-quantum secure versions. Previous work on PQC eMRTDs considered only part of the protocol flow and previous work on PQ-PAKEs did not consider the eMRTD PACE context, whereas we closed this gap by analyzing the complete, practical use of a PQ-PAKE in the context of eMRTDs. We show that post-quantum PAKE is already feasible to implement on current generation constrained HW, although naturally a performance penalty must be paid. As a result, the PAKE scheme using the level 3 parameter set of ML-KEM can be completed in under a second on existing resource-constrained hardware (not designed and optimized for PQC).

Since the eMRTD PKI involves different actors at different levels of the certificate chains, we considered different combinations of PQC schemes and analyzed the impact of scheme choices on the constrained eMRTD chips. We show LMS is a good choice at the certificate authority level, since it allows for relatively smaller certificates. While FALCON's signature size is advantageous compared to other PQC schemes, its practicality in terms of an efficient and secure implementation is unclear. ML-DSA seems to be suitable for many applications, including document signers and terminals.

By considering physical security and its impact on scheme selection for eMRTDs, our work closes the gap with the state-of-the-art by providing a comprehensive overview of PQC considerations in the eMRTD ecosystem.

Acknowledgements. The authors would like to thank Erik Mauß, Bernhard Teuschl and Lutz Jordan for their significant contributions to the OCAKE implementations.

References

1. Abdalla, M., Eisenhofer, T., Kiltz, E., Kunzweiler, S., Riepel, D.: Password-authenticated key exchange from group actions. In: Dodis, Y., Shrimpton, T. (eds.) CRYPTO 2022, Part II. LNCS, vol. 13508, pp. 699–728. Springer, Cham (2022). https://doi.org/10.1007/978-3-031-15979-4_24

2. Adrian, D., et al.: Imperfect forward secrecy: how Diffie-Hellman fails in practice. In: Ray, I., Li, N., Kruegel, C. (eds.) ACM CCS 2015. pp. 5–17. ACM Press (Oct 2015)https://doi.org/10.1145/2810103.2813707
3. Aguilar-Melchor, C., et al.: HQC. Technical report, National Institute of Standards and Technology (2022). https://csrc.nist.gov/Projects/post-quantum-cryptography/round-4-submissions
4. Albrecht, M.R., et al.: Classic McEliece. Technical report, National Institute of Standards and Technology (2022). https://csrc.nist.gov/projects/post-quantum-cryptography/round-4-submissions
5. Alnahawi, N., Schmitt, N., Wiesmaier, A., Zok, C.: Toward next generation quantum-safe eIDs and eMRTDs: a survey. ACM Trans. Embed. Comput. Syst. **23**(2) (2024). https://doi.org/10.1145/3585517
6. Alnahawi, N., Alperin-Sheriff, J., Apon, D., Davies, G.T., Wiesmaier, A.: NICE-PAKE: on the security of KEM-based PAKE constructions without ideal ciphers. Cryptology ePrint Archive, Report 2024/1957 (2024). https://eprint.iacr.org/2024/1957
7. Alnahawi, N., Haas, D., Mauß, E., Wiesmaier, A.: SoK: PQC PAKEs - design, security and performance. Cryptology ePrint Archive, Report 2025/119 (2025). https://eprint.iacr.org/2025/119
8. Alnahawi, N., Hövelmanns, K., Hülsing, A., Ritsch, S.: Towards post-quantum secure PAKE - a tight security proof for OCAKE in the BPR model. In: Kohlweiss, M., Di Pietro, R., Beresford, A.R. (eds.) CANS 2024, Part II. LNCS, vol. 14906, pp. 191–212. Springer, Singapore (2024). https://doi.org/10.1007/978-981-97-8016-7_9
9. Follow up position paper on post-quantum cryptography (2023). ANSSI France. https://cyber.gouv.fr/en/publications/follow-position-paper-post-quantum-cryptography
10. Arriaga, A., Barbosa, M., Jarecki, S.: NoIC: PAKE from KEM without ideal ciphers. Cryptology ePrint Archive, Report 2025/231 (2025). https://eprint.iacr.org/2025/231
11. Arriaga, A., Barbosa, M., Jarecki, S.: Tempo: ML-KEM to PAKE compiler resilient to timing attacks. Cryptology ePrint Archive, Report 2025/1399 (2025). https://eprint.iacr.org/2025/1399
12. Arriaga, A., Barbosa, M., Jarecki, S., Skrobot, M.: C'est Très CHIC: a compact password-authenticated key exchange from lattice-based KEM. In: Chung, K.M., Sasaki, Y. (eds.) ASIACRYPT 2024, Part V. LNCS, vol. 15488, pp. 3–33. Springer, Singapore (2024). https://doi.org/10.1007/978-981-96-0935-2_1
13. Azouaoui, M., Bronchain, O., Hoffmann, C., Kuzovkova, Y., Schneider, T., Standaert, F.X.: Systematic study of decryption and re-encryption leakage: the case of Kyber. In: Balasch, J., O'Flynn, C. (eds.) COSADE 2022. LNCS, vol. 13211, pp. 236–256. Springer, Cham (2022). https://doi.org/10.1007/978-3-030-99766-3_11
14. Barbosa, M., et al.: X-Wing. CiC **1**(1), 21 (2024). https://doi.org/10.62056/a3qj89n4e
15. Bashiri, K.: Quantum-safe PKI for the German administration (2023). https://pkic.org/events/2023/pqc-conference-amsterdam-nl/pkic-pqcc_kaveh-bashiri_bsi_quantum-safe-pki-for-the-german-administration.pdf, Post-Quantum Cryptography Conference, PKI Constortium
16. Beguinet, H., Chevalier, C., Pointcheval, D., Ricosset, T., Rossi, M.: GeT a CAKE: generic transformations from key encaspulation mechanisms to password authenticated key exchanges. In: Tibouchi, M., Wang, X. (eds.) ACNS 2023, Part II. LNCS, vol. 13906, pp. 516–538. Springer, Cham (2023). https://doi.org/10.1007/978-3-031-33491-7_19

17. Bender, J., Fischlin, M., Kügler, D.: Security analysis of the PACE key-agreement protocol. In: Samarati, P., Yung, M., Martinelli, F., Ardagna, C.A. (eds.) ISC 2009. LNCS, vol. 5735, pp. 33–48. Springer, Heidelberg (2009). https://doi.org/10.1007/978-3-642-04474-8_3
18. Beurdouche, B., et al.: A messy state of the union: Taming the composite state machines of TLS. In: 2015 IEEE Symposium on Security and Privacy, pp. 535–552. IEEE Computer Society Press (2015). https://doi.org/10.1109/SP.2015.39
19. Bindel, N., et al.: qTESLA. Technical report, National Institute of Standards and Technology (2019). https://csrc.nist.gov/projects/post-quantum-cryptography/post-quantum-cryptography-standardization/round-2-submissions
20. Bonnell, C., Gray, J., Hook, D., Okubo, T., Ounsworth, M.: A mechanism for encoding differences in paired certificates. Internet-Draft draft-bonnell-lamps-chameleon-certs-07, Internet Engineering Task Force (2025). https://datatracker.ietf.org/doc/draft-bonnell-lamps-chameleon-certs/07/, work in Progress
21. Bos, J.W., Bronchain, O., Custers, F., Renes, J., Verbakel, D., van Vredendaal, C.: Enabling FrodoKEM on embedded devices. IACR TCHES **2023**(3), 74–96 (2023). https://doi.org/10.46586/tches.v2023.i3.74-96
22. Bos, J.W., Renes, J., Sprenkels, A.: Dilithium for memory constrained devices. In: Batina, L., Daemen, J. (eds.) AFRICACRYPT 22. LNCS, vol. 2022, pp. 217–235. Springer, Cham (2022). https://doi.org/10.1007/978-3-031-17433-9_10
23. BSI TR-03110: Technical guideline advanced security mechanisms for machine readable travel documents and eIDAS token (2016). https://www.bsi.bund.de/EN/Themen/Unternehmen-und-Organisationen/Standards-und-Zertifizierung/Technische-Richtlinien/TR-nach-Thema-sortiert/tr03110/tr-03110.html
24. BSI TR-02102-1: Cryptographic mechanisms: Recommendations and key lengths, version: 2024-1 (2024). https://www.bsi.bund.de/EN/Themen/Unternehmen-und-Organisationen/Standards-und-Zertifizierung/Technische-Richtlinien/TR-nach-Thema-sortiert/tr02102/tr02102_node.html
25. Ding, J., Alsayigh, S., Lancrenon, J., RV, S., Snook, M.: Provably secure password authenticated key exchange based on RLWE for the post-quantum world. In: Handschuh, H. (ed.) CT-RSA 2017. LNCS, vol. 10159, pp. 183–204. Springer, Cham (2017). https://doi.org/10.1007/978-3-319-52153-4_11
26. Ding, R., Cheng, C., Qin, Y.: Further analysis and improvements of a lattice-based anonymous PAKE scheme. IEEE Syst. J. **16**(3), 5035–5043 (2022). https://doi.org/10.1109/JSYST.2022.3161264
27. Driscoll, F., Parsons, M., Hale, B.: Terminology for Post-Quantum Traditional Hybrid Schemes. RFC 9794 (2025). https://doi.org/10.17487/RFC9794, https://www.rfc-editor.org/info/rfc9794
28. Fischlin, M., von der Heyden, J., Margraf, M., Morgner, F., Wallner, A., Bock, H.: Post-quantum security for the extended access control protocol. In: Günther, F., Hesse, J. (eds.) SSR 2023. LNCS, vol. 13895, pp. 22–52. Springer, Cham (2023). https://doi.org/10.1007/978-3-031-30731-7_2
29. Giacon, F., Heuer, F., Poettering, B.: KEM combiners. In: Abdalla, M., Dahab, R. (eds.) PKC 2018, Part I. LNCS, vol. 10769, pp. 190–218. Springer, Cham (2018). https://doi.org/10.1007/978-3-319-76578-5_7
30. Güneysu, T., Hodges, P.W., Land, G., Ounsworth, M., Stebila, D., Zaverucha, G.: Proof-of-possession for KEM certificates using verifiable generation. In: Yin, H., Stavrou, A., Cremers, C., Shi, E. (eds.) ACM CCS 2022, pp. 1337–1351. ACM Press (2022). https://doi.org/10.1145/3548606.3560560

31. Günther, F., Rosenberg, M., Stebila, D., Veitch, S.: Hybrid obfuscated key exchange and KEMs. In: Kalai, Y.T., Kamara, S.F. (eds.) CRYPTO 2025, Part III. LNCS, vol. 16002, pp. 575–609. Springer, Cham (2025).https://doi.org/10.1007/978-3-032-01881-6_18
32. Hesse, J., Rosenberg, M.: PAKE combiners and efficient post-quantum instantiations. In: Fehr, S., Fouque, P.A. (eds.) EUROCRYPT 2025, Part II. LNCS, vol. 15602, pp. 395–420. Springer, Cham (2025)https://doi.org/10.1007/978-3-031-91124-8_14
33. Hövelmanns, K., Hülsing, A., Kudinov, M., Ritsch, S.: CAKE requires programming - on the provable post-quantum security of (O)CAKE. Cryptology ePrint Archive, Report 2025/458 (2025). https://eprint.iacr.org/2025/458
34. ICAO machine readable travel documents, 9303-part 11: Security Mechanisms for MRTDs (2021). https://www.icao.int/publications/Documents/9303_p11_cons_en.pdf
35. ICAO machine readable travel documents, 9303-part 12: Public Key Infrastructure for MRTDs (2021). https://www.icao.int/publications/Documents/9303_p12_cons_en.pdf
36. Institute of Commercial Cryptography Standards (ICCS): Next-generation Commercial Cryptographic Algorithms Program (NGCC). https://www.niccs.org.cn/en/
37. International Civil Aviation Organization: Doc 9303. Machine Readable Travel Documents. https://www.icao.int/publications/pages/publication.aspx?docnum=9303
38. Kampanakis, P., Panburana, P., Daw, E., Van Geest, D.: The viability of post-quantum X.509 certificates. Cryptology ePrint Archive, Report 2018/063 (2018). https://eprint.iacr.org/2018/063
39. Kannwischer, M.J., Krausz, M., Petri, R., Yang, S.Y.: pqm4: Benchmarking NIST additional post-quantum signature schemes on microcontrollers. Cryptology ePrint Archive, Report 2024/112 (2024). https://eprint.iacr.org/2024/112
40. Karbasi, A.H., Atani, R.E., Atani, S.E.: A New Ring-Based SPHF and PAKE Protocol on Ideal Lattices. ISeCure (2019)
41. Katz, J., Rosenberg, M.: LATKE: a framework for constructing identity-binding PAKEs. In: Reyzin, L., Stebila, D. (eds.) CRYPTO 2024, Part II. LNCS, vol. 14921, pp. 218–250. Springer, Cham (2024). https://doi.org/10.1007/978-3-031-68379-4_7
42. Katz, J., Vaikuntanathan, V.: Smooth projective hashing and password-based authenticated key exchange from lattices. In: Matsui, M. (ed.) ASIACRYPT 2009. LNCS, vol. 5912, pp. 636–652. Springer, Heidelberg (2009). https://doi.org/10.1007/978-3-642-10366-7_37
43. Liu, C., Zheng, Z., Jia, K., You, Q.: Provably secure three-party password-based authenticated key exchange from RLWE (full version). Cryptology ePrint Archive, Report 2019/1386 (2019). https://eprint.iacr.org/2019/1386
44. Lyu, Y., Liu, S.: Hybrid password authentication key exchange in the UC framework. In: Fehr, S., Fouque, P.A. (eds.) EUROCRYPT 2025, Part II. LNCS, vol. 15602, pp. 421–450. Springer, Cham (2025).https://doi.org/10.1007/978-3-031-91124-8_15
45. Möller, B., Duong, T., Kotowicz, K.: This poodle bites: exploiting the ssl 3.0 fallback. Security Advisory **21**, 34–58 (2014). https://security.googleblog.com/2014/10/this-poodle-bites-exploiting-ssl-30.html

46. Moody, D., Perlner, R., Regenscheid, A., Robinson, A., Cooper, D.: NIST IR 8547 - transition to post-quantum cryptography standards (initial public draft). Technical report, National Institute of Standards and Technology (2024). https://csrc.nist.gov/pubs/ir/8547/ipd
47. Naehrig, M., et al.: FrodoKEM. Technical report, National Institute of Standards and Technology (2020). https://csrc.nist.gov/projects/post-quantum-cryptography/post-quantum-cryptography-standardization/round-3-submissions
48. National Institute of Standards and Technology: Post quantum cryptography standardization. https://csrc.nist.gov/Projects/Post-Quantum-Cryptography/Post-Quantum-Cryptography-Standardization
49. National Institute of Standards and Technology: Recommendation for Stateful Hash-Based Signature Schemes (2020). nIST Special Publication 800-208. https://nvlpubs.nist.gov/nistpubs/SpecialPublications/NIST.SP.800-208.pdf
50. National Institute of Standards and Technology: Module-Lattice-Based Digital Signature Standard (ML-DSA) (2024). federal Information Processing Standards Publication 204, https://doi.org/10.6028/NIST.FIPS.204
51. National Institute of Standards and Technology: Module-Lattice-Based Key-Encapsulation Mechanism Standard (ML-KEM) (2024). federal Information Processing Standards Publication 203, https://doi.org/10.6028/NIST.FIPS.203
52. National Institute of Standards and Technology: Stateless Hash-Based Digital Signature Standard (SLH-DSA) (2024). federal Information Processing Standards Publication 205, https://doi.org/10.6028/NIST.FIPS.205
53. National Security Research Institute (NSR) and National Intelligence Service (NIS): Korean Post-Quantum Cryptography (KpqC) Competition. https://www.kpqc.or.kr/competition.html
54. von Nethen, N., Wiesmaier, A., Alnahawi, N., Henrich, J.: PMMP - PQC migration management process. In: EICC'24. pp. 144–154. ACM (2024). https://doi.org/10.1145/3655693.3655719
55. Ounsworth, M., Gray, J., Pala, M., Klaußner, J., Fluhrer, S.: Composite ML-DSA for use in X.509 public key infrastructure. Internet-Draft draft-ietf-lamps-pq-composite-sigs-13, Internet Engineering Task Force (2025). https://datatracker.ietf.org/doc/draft-ietf-lamps-pq-composite-sigs/13/, work in Progress
56. Pan, J., Zeng, R.: A generic construction of tightly secure password-based authenticated key exchange. In: Guo, J., Steinfeld, R. (eds.) ASIACRYPT 2023, Part VIII. LNCS, vol. 14445, pp. 143–175. Springer, Singapore (2023). https://doi.org/10.1007/978-981-99-8742-9_5
57. Paul, S., Scheible, P., Wiemer, F.: Towards post-quantum security for cyber-physical systems: integrating PQC into industrial M2M communication. J. Comput. Secur. **30**(4), 623–653 (2022). https://doi.org/10.3233/JCS-210037
58. Pradel, G., Mitchell, C.J.: Post-quantum certificates for electronic travel documents. In: Boureanu, I., Dragan, C.C., Manulis, M. (eds.) DETIPS Workshop, ESORICS 2020. LNCS, vol. 12580, pp. 56–73. Springer (2020). https://doi.org/10.1007/978-3-030-66504-3_4
59. Prest, T., et al.: FALCON. Technical report, National Institute of Standards and Technology (2022). https://csrc.nist.gov/Projects/post-quantum-cryptography/selected-algorithms-2022
60. Ren, P., Gu, X., Wang, Z.: Efficient module learning with errors-based post-quantum password-authenticated key exchange. IET Inf. Secur. **17**(1), 3–17 (2023). https://doi.org/10.1049/ISE2.12094

61. Seyhan, K., Akleylek, S.: A new password-authenticated module learning with rounding-based key exchange protocol: saber. PAKE. J. Supercomput. **79**(16), 17859–17896 (2023). https://doi.org/10.1007/S11227-023-05251-X
62. Shor, P.W.: Algorithms for quantum computation: discrete logarithms and factoring. In: 35th FOCS, pp. 124–134. IEEE Computer Society Press (1994). https://doi.org/10.1109/SFCS.1994.365700
63. Tiepelt, M., Eaton, E., Stebila, D.: Making an asymmetric PAKE quantum-annoying by hiding group elements. In: Tsudik, G., Conti, M., Liang, K., Smaragdakis, G. (eds.) ESORICS 2023, Part I. LNCS, vol. 14344, pp. 168–188. Springer, Cham (2023). https://doi.org/10.1007/978-3-031-50594-2_9
64. Ueno, R., Xagawa, K., Tanaka, Y., Ito, A., Takahashi, J., Homma, N.: Curse of re-encryption: a generic power/EM analysis on post-quantum KEMs. IACR TCHES **2022**(1), 296–322 (2022)https://doi.org/10.46586/tches.v2022.i1.296-322
65. Vos, J., Jarecki, S., Wood, C.A.: Hybrid post-quantum password authenticated key exchange. Internet-Draft: draft-vos-cfrg-pqpake-00 (2025). https://datatracker.ietf.org/doc/draft-vos-cfrg-pqpake/
66. Vos, J., Jarecki, S., Wood, C.A., Yun, C., Myers, S., Sierra, Y.: A hybrid asymmetric password-authenticated key exchange in the random oracle model. Cryptology ePrint Archive, Report 2025/1343 (2025). https://eprint.iacr.org/2025/1343

Towards Cryptography Bill of Materials Compliance

Claudio Foroncelli[1], Pietro De Matteis[2], Luis Augusto Dias Knob[3], Luca Piras[3], Alessandro Tomasi[3(✉)], and Silvio Ranise[3,4]

[1] Department of Control and Computer Engineering, Polytechnic University of Turin, Turin, Italy
claudio.foroncelli@studenti.polito.it
[2] Co-Innovation Lab, FBK - Dedagroup SpA, Trento, Italy
pietro.dematteis@dedagroup.it
[3] Center for Cybersecurity, Fondazione Bruno Kessler, Trento, Italy
{l.diasknob,l.piras,altomasi,ranise}@fbk.eu
[4] Department of Mathematics, University of Trento, Via Sommarive 14, Trento, Italy
https://cs.fbk.eu

Abstract. Discovering, managing, and reporting on cryptographic assets is a critical step for the transition to quantum-safe systems and applications. Cryptography Bills of Materials (CBOMs) have been proposed as an aid to cryptographic inventory, agility, and compliance with guidelines to create more secure software and services.

Writing policies and automating compliance checks for cryptography is a valuable but complex task. We present a prototype framework for automated evaluation of cryptographic compliance extending existing CBOM tools with a policy-driven engine that classifies cryptographic assets according to customizable rules and compliance levels. Machine-readable policies enable flexible adaptation to different guidelines while supporting analysts in performing semi-automatic assessments.

The prototype is validated through experiments on both synthetic and real-world software. Results show that the system correctly identifies deprecated and disallowed primitives, producing clear compliance reports. While we highlight some difficulties common to automating compliance checks, our findings demonstrate the potential of CBOM-based approaches to enhance visibility, governance, and readiness for the post-quantum cryptography transition.

Keywords: CBOM · Compliance · Cryptography · Policy Evaluation · Post-Quantum Transition

1 Introduction

With the transition to Post-Quantum Cryptography (PQC) no longer a question of if but when [3,6,23,29], organizations must be able to discover, catalog, and manage their cryptographic assets. This is essential to identify which cryptographic components they are using, and also to assess whether these components

H. C. Pöhls and C. J. Mitchell (Eds.): SSR 2025, LNCS 16466, pp. 202–221, 2026.
https://doi.org/10.1007/978-3-032-19567-8_10

comply with evolving guidelines. Accurate visibility of cryptographic assets can significantly contribute to both security and regulatory compliance processes in the PQC era.

Based on the Software Bill of Materials (SBOM), CycloneDX recently developed a tool to discover, manage, and report on cryptographic assets. This object model was called Cryptography Bill of Materials (CBOM) [31], and it was explicitly designed to enable automated reasoning and compliance checking. As reported in [6], CBOMs can assist in managing and reporting the usage of cryptography when integrated into reporting and software development practices.

Generating a CBOM is a complex task, since several steps are needed to assess the software under maintenance thoroughly. First, the cryptography assets need to be mapped and added to an inventory. To generate this inventory, the application's source code needs to be analyzed and classified, a process that is typically performed through static analysis tools, such as the CBOMKit plugin [32]. To quickly react to changes in the code, these tools are often integrated into continuous integration and deployment (CI/CD) pipelines, providing developers with immediate feedback to approve or remediate potential issues.

Notwithstanding, the simple generation of the CBOM inventory presents a great value to the administrator. It is not immediately apparent how a developer or an automated agent should take action based on these findings. To help in this process, tools like the *CBOMkit* frontend viewer provide a foundational proof-of-concept compliance check, categorizing assets into "quantum-safe" or otherwise. This feature, though useful, relies on a single hardcoded policy within the application logic, which limits its ability to validate the inventory against other standards, such as NIST SP 800-131A Rev. 3 [6].

To address this limitation, we propose a CBOM-based framework for analyzing compliance with cryptographic guidelines. The proposed approach extends the current implementation of *CBOMkit* enabling the definition of custom compliance policies and the validation of inventories against them. The definition of the policy structure ensures that each policy specifies a set of compliance levels and associated rules, which are dynamically loaded and mapped to the cryptographic assets contained in a previously generated CBOM. To demonstrate the correctness of our solution, we define custom policies derived from [6], expressed in TOML and managed independently from the application code.

To evaluate the results of our compliance analysis, we first validate the framework against a synthetic library designed to demonstrate coverage. We then apply it to the same Keycloak library used by *CBOMkit* , a widely adopted open-source identity and access management system. Based on these experiments, we identify several limitations of our approach. These limitations are further analyzed and discussed, highlighting the challenges of defining a generic compliance model across a diverse set of guidelines.

Finally, we can describe our main contributions as: (i) the definition of a policy structure, (ii) the algorithm that matches policies with CBOM, (iii) the definition of concrete rules based on an authoritative source, and (iv) an implementation thereof. Also, our source code can be found at https://github.com/claudioforoncelli/cbomkit.

2 Background

2.1 Compliance and Cryptography

Cybersecurity standards agencies and groups publish recommendations and guidelines on how a service deployment should be configured to avoid insecure configurations—defining which algorithms, key lengths, and modes of operation are approved. Examples of authoritative sources include documents published by NIST [2] for the US, SOG-IS [37] for contributing European states, and individual EU member state agencies, e.g., ANSSI [1] in France or BSI [8] in Germany.

Each guideline may specify a requirement for every configurable element of a service by considering published standards, deprecated features, and known attacks. Requirement levels may be expressed using well-defined common terms [7] or custom wording. The scope of individual recommendations can be broad or specific to individual protocols, like TLS or SSH.

The existence of technical guidelines can help raise awareness and set a minimum security level. However, the lack of a standardized, machine-readable version of these documents can delay the application of recommendations and complicate the comparison between them. To manually comply with a given guideline, a system administrator must examine each requirement, speak the language, and understand the way the requirement is written, and verify that the deployment value matches the required value both by design and at runtime.

Automating compliance checks, however, is a complex endeavour, particularly for protocols that are negotiated between client and server and have gone through several versions, like TLS, but intrinsically due to the discretionary nature of the task: while some rules are mandatory, many rules are permissive and expect developers and administrators to make informed decisions. By way of example, recent work addresses the difficulty of compliance checking in TLS deployments [14]. One of the challenges involved is to map recommendations from authoritative sources into individual rules and standard requirement levels, such as [7], then defining how to combine the evaluation of individual rules on data to reach a final assessment level.

In this work, a CBOM constitutes the data, and we aim to define rules to automate compliance with the authoritative source in NIST SP 800-131A r3 [6].

2.2 The Evolution of Software Bills of Materials (SBOM)

In traditional manufacturing, a **Bill of Materials (BOM)** refers to a comprehensive list of raw materials, components, and assemblies required to construct a product. This concept has been adapted to the software domain to address the growing complexity of software supply chains and the increasing emphasis on cybersecurity.

A **Software Bill of Materials (SBOM)** is an inventory of all components within a software product, with particular attention to third-party and open-source software (OSS) libraries. SBOMs provide visibility into nested dependencies, licensing information, and known vulnerabilities, such as those cataloged by the *Common Weakness Enumeration (CWE)* and *Common Vulnerabilities and Exposures (CVE)* systems.

The importance of SBOMs was boosted by major cybersecurity incidents, notably the *SolarWinds breach (2020)* [24] and the *Log4j vulnerability (2021)* [25]. In response, the U.S. government issued **Executive Order 14028** [40] in 2021, mandating the use of SBOMs for software used by federal agencies. This directive catalyzed global recognition of SBOMs as a foundational element in enhancing software supply chain security. The relevance of SBOMs is further reflected in international regulatory frameworks, such as the European Union's **Cyber Resilience Act (CRA)** [13], or guidances that present a shared vision of the importance of SBOMs in the global community [10].

SBOMs enhance security by enabling rapid identification and mitigation of vulnerabilities in third-party components. They support risk management by providing a comprehensive view of software composition, allowing organizations to assess and control risks associated with untrusted dependencies. SBOMs also facilitate license compliance by clarifying the legal status of included libraries, and contribute to regulatory compliance by supporting adherence to standards, policies, and legal requirements.

The *NTIA Software Transparency Working Group on Standards and Formats* [27] considers two of the major open source Standard formats for SBOMs:

- **Software Package Data Exchange (SPDX)**: Developed by the Linux Foundation, SPDX is a machine-readable format standardized as ISO/IEC 5962:2021 [39].
- **CycloneDX (CDX)**: Originating from the OWASP community, CycloneDX is also a machine-readable format and has been standardized as ECMA-424 [30].

Both SPDX 3.0 and CycloneDX 1.6 are evolving to cover emerging domains and technologies. This evolution has led to the conceptual expansion of SBOMs into specialized variants, such as the AI Bill of Materials (AIBOM), the Cryptography Bill of Materials (CBOM), the Operations Bill of Materials (OBOM), and the Hardware Bill of Materials (HBOM). These extensions aim to provide comprehensive transparency across diverse technological ecosystems, further reinforcing the role of BOMs in securing digital infrastructure.

2.3 Cryptography Bill of Materials (CBOM)

Cryptography Bill of Materials (CBOM) is a structured, machine-readable inventory that enumerates all cryptographic components present in a software system. Created as an extension of the Software Bill of Materials (SBOM), the CBOM focuses specifically on cryptographic assets, including algorithms, keys, certificates, and protocols. By providing an authoritative record of these elements, the

CBOM becomes a valuable resource for security audits, compliance verification, and cryptographic risk assessments.

By representing cryptographic information in a uniform format, CBOMs enable automation, interoperability, and traceability across tools and processes. They also offer visibility into the cryptographic posture of a system, allowing for the detection of deprecated algorithms, weak key lengths, or misconfigured protocols. At the same time, it provides input for compliance checks against guidelines and standards from bodies such as NIST, ENISA, and national cybersecurity agencies.

Although documents from the Office of Management and Budget (OMB) [41], and NIST [26] focused on the preparation for a post-quantum cryptography (PQC) migration, do not explicitly create the definition of a specific Bill of Materials for cryptographic assets. These guidelines highlighted the importance of establishing deprecation and disallowance timelines, as well as prioritizing the inventory of cryptographic systems. Therefore, it was natural that this inventory would eventually be formalized and its structure well-defined for an external organization or company.

NIST SP 1800-38B [28] uses a profile of *CycloneDX* [31], an SBOM specification maintained by the OWASP Foundation, to generate a cryptography inventory. CycloneDX was initially designed for software component inventories. However, its extensibility allows for domain-specific extensions. The CBOM profile originally defined at IBM contains cryptography-specific component types (e.g., `cryptographic-asset`) and properties (e.g., `cryptoProperties`, `protocolProperties`, `tlsCipherSuites`); this aligns cryptographic asset inventories with a widely supported standard while tailoring them to meet the needs of PQC migration.

2.4 CBOM Structure

CycloneDX CBOM is an SBOM profile that defines an object model to describe cryptographic assets and their dependencies. The CBOM object model is a standardized representation of cryptographic assets. Figure 1 shows a graphical definition of the asset types and subtypes available. More specifically, four main asset types are defined:

`Algorithm` assets can specify fields such as `primitive`, `mode` (mode of operation), `padding`, or `cryptoFunctions`.

`Certificate` assets expose fields like `issuerName`, `subjectName`, `notValidAfter`, and `signatureAlgorithmRef`, but do not have attributes such as `mode` or `primitive`.

`Protocol` assets include `type`, `version`, and potentially a list of `cipherSuites`.

`Related crypto material` assets include fundamental and ancillary building blocks of different kinds, such as `key`, `salt`, `token`, `credential`, etc.

The granular nature of the object model lends itself to the definition of fine-grained policies. For instance, a policy for a signature algorithm as in Listing 1.1 can be written as separate rules for the functions `sign` and `verify`.

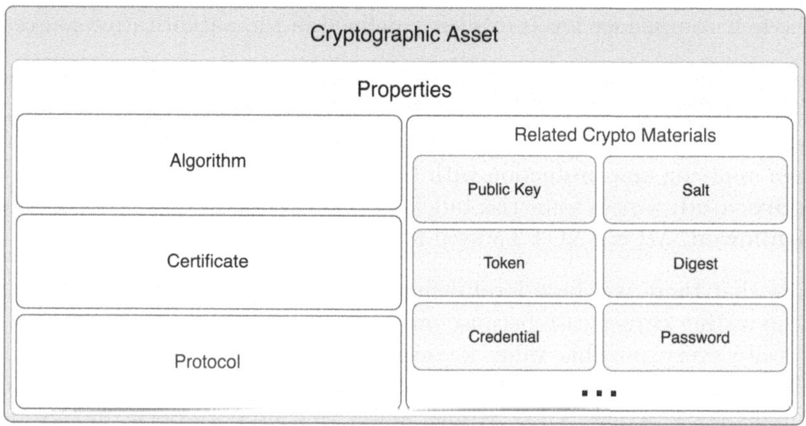

Fig. 1. CBOM Object Model

2.5 CBOM Generation

Several solutions have been published to generate CBOM in the CI/CD pipeline: *CBOMkit* [32] via SonarQube rules [33], *cdxgen* [11], and *cbom-action* [15] via GitHub CodeQL [16]. Other sources have been demonstrated, such as *CryptoMon* for network traffic [35].

cdxgen can generate CBOMs, but its primary focus remains on SBOMs, and its cryptographic modeling is still basic. *cbom-action* is centered on generation alone, without providing a viewer, compliance analysis, or management features.

CBOMkit stands out as the only solution capable of analyzing source code directly, not just compiled binaries. It offers a viewer for interactive exploration and a compliance engine to evaluate CBOMs against policies.

3 A CBOM-Based Framework for Analysing Compliance with Standards and Guidelines

Each rule defines one or more constraints on the properties of cryptographic assets. When an asset matches all of the constraints defined in a rule, that rule's compliance level is assigned. Compliance levels are asset-specific; the compliance tool translates fine-grained, asset-specific policies into an assessment level—a single global result. These elements are shown summarily in Fig. 2 and discussed in the following in more detail.

3.1 Compliance Levels

Compliance levels are derived from the guideline with which compliance is to be checked. For [6], a distinction is made between applying new protection – e.g., encrypting signing – and processing already protected information, e.g., decrypting or verifying. Further details on this are discussed in Sect. 4.3.

The four compliance levels explicitly defined in the authoritative source are:

2: **Acceptable.** The algorithm, key length/strength, parameter set, or scheme MAY be used.
3: **Legacy Use.** MAY be used for processing already protected information when applying new protection with the same algorithm would be disallowed.
4: **Deprecated.** carries some risk but MAY be used following a risk assessment.
5: **Disallowed.** MUST NOT be used to apply new protection.

Note that there is a base level defined by *CBOMkit* as "1: Unknown". This is an interesting corner case because on the one hand, guidelines do not explicitly specify every possible value for every constraint, but on the other, they do sometimes prohibit anything not explicitly specified. For example, in NIST TLS guidelines [22] Sect. 3.3.1, "Cipher suites that do not appear in this [document] **shall not** be used". The full public list of cipher suites is maintained by IANA [17], so a compliance policy may be written as either assigning a higher compliance severity level to unknown findings, or explicitly assigning a Disallowed level to all possible values not explicitly listed in the authoritative source.

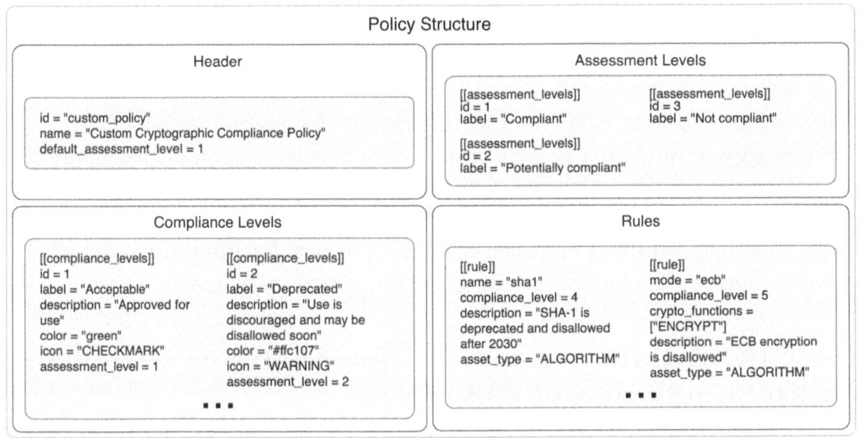

Fig. 2. Compliance Creation Structure.

3.2 Policies and Rule Matching

A policy is a container for a set of rules, with a header with metadata and a default assessment level to be used if no matching rules are found. This is a common pattern for e.g., access control policy languages like XACML.

Each rule contains:

- `name`: An optional string used to match the name of the cryptographic asset.

- `compliance_level`: The compliance level to assign if the rule matches.
- `description`: A human-readable explanation of the rule's purpose.
- `asset_type`: The type of asset this rule applies to (see Sect. 2.4); determines the set of attributes to be matched with the properties of cryptographic assets in a CBOM.
- One or more matching fields from the asset's property structure.

See Sect. A for examples of rules.

During policy evaluation, an asset in a given CBOM matches a rule in a policy if *all* non-null fields specified in the rule exactly match the corresponding properties of the asset.

In cases where multiple rules apply to the same asset, *CBOMkit* resolves conflicts by giving precedence to the rule with the highest *specificity* i.e., the rule that defines the greatest number of matching constraints on the asset's properties. If two rules have equal specificity, the one with the higher compliance level i.e., severity is chosen. After per-asset evaluations are completed, the engine aggregates these individual compliance levels into an overall assessment that reflects the system's conformity with the policy's defined levels. The assessment level is chosen among the ones defined in the policy (see Sect. 3.3).

To support parameter range conditions – e.g., key length $l \geq 128$, or $128 \leq k < 256$ – in addition to simple equality checks, we also modify the compliance engine, which previously could only verify whether an asset's parameter exactly matched the value defined in a rule.

3.3 Assessment Levels

Assessment levels are defined by the engine as one of three possible values:

1: **Compliant.** All assets conform to the defined mandatory rules.
2: **Potentially not compliant.** Some assets fall under discretionary rules recommending against—deprecated or unknown; all other assets are compliant with mandatory rules.
3: **Non-compliant.** One or more assets use algorithms or configurations explicitly disallowed by the policy.

Each assessment level may be referenced by multiple compliance levels, allowing asset-specific classifications to be mapped into a single global indicator. The aggregation process thus translates specific per-asset findings into a unified compliance status, highlighting the most severe level of non-conformance detected within the analyzed system.

3.4 Policy Configuration Language

TOML (Tom's Obvious, Minimal Language) [34] is a configuration file format designed to be minimal, easy to read, and semantically unambiguous. It is designed to map to key–value pairs and support hierarchical data, making it suitable for a broad range of configuration use cases.

TOML was chosen to represent our policies to ensure that policies can be easily authored and maintained even by users without programming expertise. Its clear, human-readable syntax provides the flexibility required to accommodate the structural and semantic needs of the extended software. CSV or equivalent spreadsheet formats were discarded due to the redundancy they would introduce, as many rows would need to be repeated with minimal variation; and JSON was excluded on the basis that its syntax is less intuitive for non-technical users.

4 Evaluation

To evaluate the correctness of the evaluation logic and custom policy, we apply the extended CBOMkit compliance engine to two CBOMs: a synthetic test CBOM designed to include representative assets of every type and compliance level (Sect. 4.1), and the CBOM generated for Keycloak [16, 15], a widely used open-source identity and access management solution (Sect. 4.2).

4.1 Test CBOM

Figure 3 shows the frontend viewer result of the compliance analysis for the test CBOM. In addition to the *Deprecated* result corresponding to an instance of the SHA-1 hash function (Fig. 4), the analysis also identified several other cryptographic primitives of interest. Instances of `HMAC-SHA256` were detected and correctly categorized as *Acceptable*. The `SHA-224` function was labeled as *Deprecated*, consistent with its phase-out under the policy. Furthermore, the `AES128-ECB-PKCS5` construct was classified as *Disallowed*, as ECB mode is explicitly prohibited for encryption operations. Conversely, `AES128-CBC-PKCS5` was assessed as *Acceptable*, since both the AES algorithm and the CBC mode of operation are approved for use under the same standard.

Due to the presence of various *Disallowed* assets, the overall assessment level of the CBOM was successfully deemed *Not Compliant*.

4.2 Keycloak CBOM

Figure 5 shows the frontend viewer result of the compliance analysis for the Keycloak CBOM. Details of the *Deprecated* result, corresponding to an instance of the SHA-1 hash function, are shown in Fig. 6.

In addition to hash function findings, the analysis also identified instances of elliptic-curve–based key generation algorithms using the `P-384` and `P-521` curves. According to the recommendations outlined in NIST SP 800 186 [9], these curves are among the recommended elliptic curves for federal use. Consequently, the compliance engine classified these instances as *Acceptable*, confirming that the ECDSA key generation mechanisms employed in Keycloak conform to current NIST guidance for approved elliptic-curve parameters.

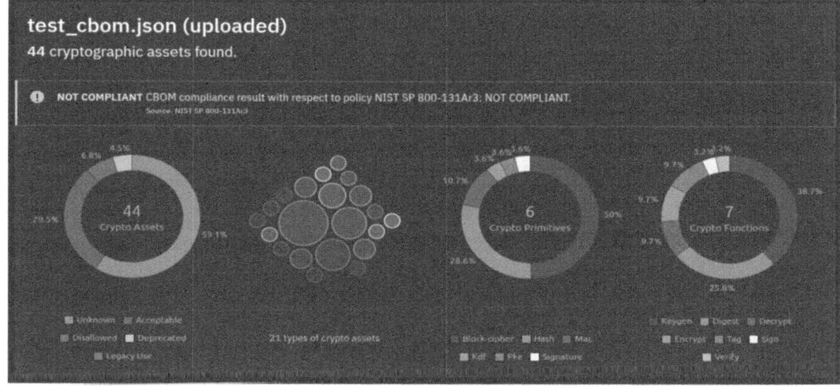

Fig. 3. Test CBOM stat screen.

List of all assets

Download CBOM

Cryptographic asset	Type	Primitive	Location
AES128-ECB-PKCS5	Algorithm	Block Cipher	SymmEncECB.java:19
SECRET-KEY	Related Crypto Material	*Unspecified*	NistRulesDemo.java:37
SHA1	Algorithm	Hash Function	NistRulesDemo.java:21
SECRET-KEY	Related Crypto Material	*Unspecified*	SymmEncECB.java:11
3DES	Algorithm	Block Cipher	NistRulesDemo.java:27
3DES	Algorithm	Block Cipher	NistRulesDemo.java:30

Fig. 4. Test CBOM asset list.

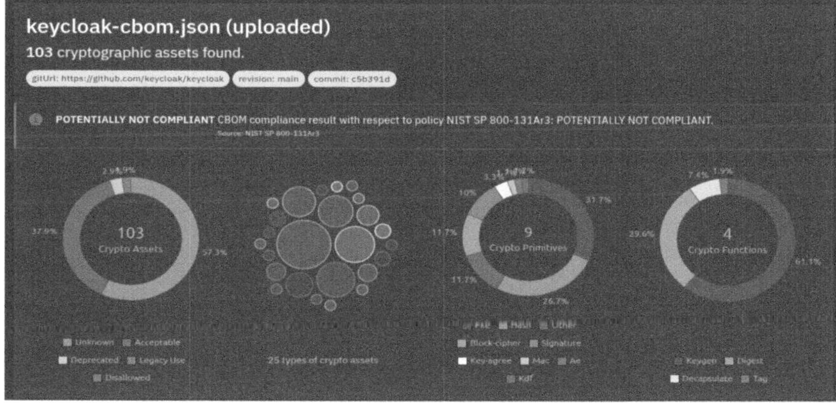

Fig. 5. Keycloak CBOM stat screen.

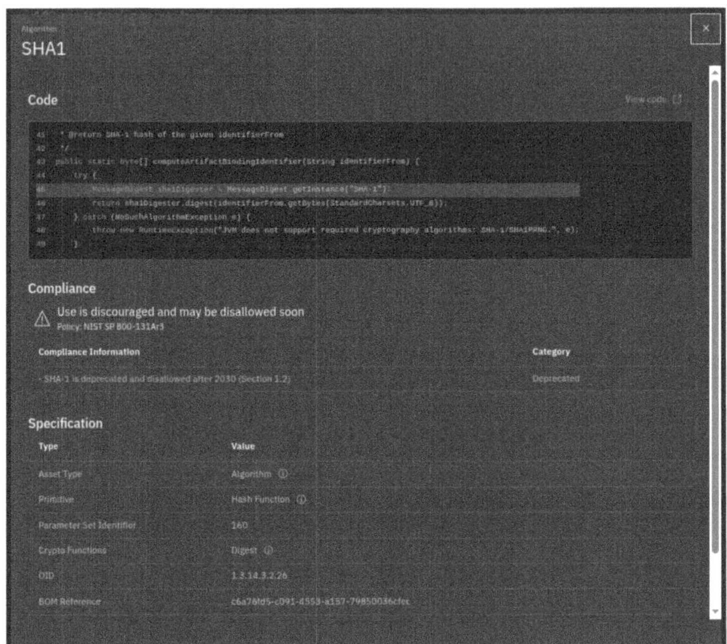

Fig. 6. Keycloak CBOM SHA-1 finding.

The SHA-1 finding is non-trivial to assess; see Sect. 4.3.

4.3 Benefits and Limitations

There are at least three criteria on which the framework here proposed could be assessed: whether it is possible and easy enough to write policies based on guidelines; how correct and complete the resulting assessment is; and how useful the assessment is to developers. All of these likely require expert assessment and trial, which we do not address here. Alternatively, automating the assessment of an automated assessment tool would be an interesting research question.

To the first and second point we provide remarks on the difficulties encountered in writing Elliptic Curve policies and in evaluating SHA-1 results, below. The effectiveness of TOML should be assessed in practice by others for an unbiased view; while it should not require IT-technical expertise, reading the recommendations and writing the rules still requires a certain degree of familiarity with cryptographic algorithms.

To the third point, one of the main limitations of *CBOMkit* is that currently very few libraries are available for analysis: python cryptography, JCA, and bouncycastle. This also limits the applications we can consider to evaluate our framework.

Evaluating Policy Writing for Elliptic Curve Cryptography.

Limitations of CBOMs based on CycloneDX 1.6. CBOMs produced using CycloneDX 1.6 exhibited several limitations that affected the accuracy and reliability of automated cryptographic compliance checking. Most notably, elliptic curves were represented using free-form text strings with no canonical vocabulary, meaning that a single curve could appear under multiple aliases—such as "B-233" and "Sect233r1"—depending on the library or naming convention in use. Determining the corresponding security strength therefore required manual cross-referencing with external sources such as [9,36]. Similar inconsistencies arose for primitives and algorithm families, which lacked a unified schema and had to be inferred from implementation details (e.g. Java class names), leading to incomplete or inconsistent detection. While integer-based schemes such as RSA could typically be evaluated from a single parameter, elliptic-curve assets often required custom mapping logic, and some curves listed in [9] were not detectable (see Table 2). These limitations made it difficult to express policies in a portable way or to ensure consistent and reproducible compliance evaluations.

Enhancements introduced with CycloneDX 1.7. The release of CycloneDX 1.7 is a substantial improvement through the introduction of a structured *Cryptography Registry* providing unique identifiers for elliptic curves, algorithm families, primitives, and parameter sets. This registry replaces the earlier reliance on ad hoc text labels and aligns nomenclature across NIST, SEC 2, Brainpool, and commonly used cryptographic implementations. Policies can now reference stable identifiers rather than implementation- specific strings, eliminating the need for custom mappings and increasing interoperability between CBOM producers and consumers. The registry also expands coverage and accuracy: curves or algorithms that previously appeared under ambiguous or deprecated aliases can now be identified consistently. Certain policy constraints remain inherently contextual—such as the allowance of Secp256k1 solely "for blockchain applications" in [9]—and thus require additional reasoning beyond CBOM metadata. Nevertheless, CycloneDX 1.7 provides a significantly stronger and more structured foundation for automated cryptographic evaluation, addressing many of the limitations observed in CBOMs based on version 1.6.

Evaluating SHA-1 Compliance. SHA-1 is a good example of the limitations of automated compliance testing. In revision 2 of SP 800-131A [5], currently still valid while revision 3 is in draft stage, SHA-1 is (our emphasis):

- **disallowed** for digital signature *generation* **except where specifically allowed** by NIST protocol-specific guidance;
- **allowed for legacy use** when used for digital signature *verification*;
- **acceptable** for non-digital signature applications that do not require collision resistance.

A concrete example of protocol-specific guidance explicitly allowing SHA-1 for signature generation are NIST TLS guidelines [22], where it is allowed for

TLS versions 1.0 and 1.1 ServerKeyExchange (Sect. 3.3.1.1.1 footnote 21) and CertificateVerify (Sect. 3.5 footnote 26) messages.

In the new draft revision 3, both exception and reference to collision resistance have been dropped; instead, the notion of "applying cryptographic protection". An excerpt of the two versions is shown side by side in Table 1.

Table 1. SHA-1 compliance in SP 800-131A Rev. 2 [5], Table 8 and Rev. 3 [6], Table 12.

Rev. 2		Rev. 3	
Use	Status	Use	Status
Digital signature generation	Disallowed, except where specifically allowed by NIST protocol-specific guidance.	Digital signature generation	Disallowed
Digital signature verification	Legacy use	Digital signature verification	Legacy use
Non-digital signature applications	Acceptable	Applying protection for non-digital signature applications	Deprecated through 2030 Disallowed after 2030
		Processing already protected information using non-digital signature applications	Acceptable through 2030 Legacy use after 2030

This presents the following challenges: in terms of compliance with [22], categorizing a finding of SHA-1 in a CBOM requires (a) checking whether it is being used for signature generation or verification; (b) checking which protocol it is being used in, and hence against other applicable guidelines published by NIST; and (c) making a judgement call as to whether the application does or does not require collision resistance, which requires a certain degree of security expertise and an evaluation of the context in which the primitive is being used.

(a) Checking against algorithm function can be addressed with CBOM by specifying a different compliance level for the two functions in relevant signature algorithms. This can be considered a success for CBOM. Rule definition is partially limited by the dictionary of algorithms – at the time of writing, the CycloneDX specification follows the JSON Signature Format (JSF) standard, which in turn

refers[1] to JWA [19] and JOSE [21]. This requires going beyond the github and RFC documents to the IANA registry [18], where SHA-1 algorithms (RS1, HS1) are listed – and explicitly prohibited.

(b) Checking against other guidelines on use in a specific protocol may be addressed by setting a default base value of Disallowed for the primitive in this guideline, then resolving conflicts with other guidelines. The resolution must be able to handle precedence in a way that is counter-intuitive to security, in the sense that the more permissive compliance level takes precedence if the guideline is protocol-specific. This likely requires further work to determine how to handle policy conflicts in general as it cannot be addressed by specifying a single guideline policy in isolation. Note that, even when an exception is not explicitly specified - such as its removal between revision 2 and 3 of [6] – conflicts may still arise and need to be resolved somehow; in other words, even though revision 3 does not specify that exceptions are acceptable, the permission to use SHA-1 in specific cases is not erased from [22].

(c) Expert discretion may be unavoidable in some cases. For instance, deciding whether an application of a hash function relies on the security property of collision resistance can hardly be automated. Collision resistance is one of several security properties of the primitive, as pointed out in the referenced publication [12]. Arguments could then be made about whether chosen prefix collisions might be undesirable in the specific application, such as defeating code signing or crafting a rogue CA certificate as demonstrated for MD5 [38], and to what extent that applies for a hash function with the same construction such as SHA-1 [20]. Fortunately in revision 3 the phrase "applying cryptographic protection" is defined as (our emphasis): "Depending on the algorithm, to encrypt or sign data, *generate a hash function* or message authentication code (MAC), or establish keys, including wrapping and deriving keys" [6, Appendix D]. While this clarifies that generating a new message digest is deprecated, there is no intrinsic distinction in calling a hash function to compute a digest for a new message or for the purpose of comparing the computed digest with an existing one, so an evaluation of the context is still necessary.

5 Conclusions

CBOMkit was extended with a structured, machine-readable policy format in TOML, capturing metadata, compliance levels, assessment levels, and rules. A Java evaluation framework was built, including a policy parser and an evaluation engine, which together allow both built-in and user-defined policies to be applied. Validation on a test CBOM and the CBOM of Keycloak, a real-world identity and access management platform, showed that the system correctly flags deprecated or disallowed algorithms and propagates these findings into a system-level compliance posture through assessment levels.

[1] https://github.com/IBM/CBOM/blob/main/jsf-0.82.schema.json.

While this establishes a solid foundation for cryptographic compliance evaluation, several opportunities for future work remain.

Future Work. Current analysis depends on CBOMs from static analyzers with limited language and library coverage, mainly Java and Python. Many cryptographic usages, especially in custom routines or niche libraries, may remain undetected by static approaches. Automating mapping from libraries to CBOM element detection at least in part would be highly beneficial, as it would both extend coverage to new libraries as well as ease the process of keeping support apace with library development – especially relevant given the expected integration of new PQC standard algorithms and hybrids. In addition to new algorithms being standardized and implemented, the computational assumptions of algorithms currently considered quantum resistant may turn out to be flawed, as in the case of SIKE; new algebraic attacks could reduce security, leading to frequent changes in security guidelines. Absent a common machine-readable format used by guideline-publishing authorities, automating the extraction of policies from guidelines would reduce the burden of keeping up with updates to technical documents.

Reference documents such as guidelines, standards and regulations may overlap and disagree on compliance levels of specific items. When dealing with multiple reference documents, analysts need guidance and tools able to identify such overlaps, prioritise them, and receive support towards fulfilling related requirements. Future work should address policy combining algorithms for multiple reference documents, and integrate support for developers as appropriate. Evaluation through interviews with developers and users on the usefulness of CBOM and compliance tool would also be desirable.

Disclosure of Interests. The authors have no competing interests to declare.

Appendix

A Example TOML Snippet Rules for Algorithms

This example defines two rules targeting cryptographic algorithms: one deprecating SHA-1, and one disallowing ECB mode for encryption.

```
[[rule]]
name = "sha1"
compliance_level = 4
description = "SHA-1 is deprecated and disallowed after 2030"
asset_type = "ALGORITHM"

[[rule]]
mode = "ecb"
compliance_level = 5
crypto_functions = ["ENCRYPT"]
```

```
description = "ECB encryption is disallowed"
asset_type = "ALGORITHM"
```

B Example CBOM Listing Signature Algorithm

Listing 1.1. CBOM example of signature. Source: [31].

```
{
  "name": "SHA512withRSA",
  "type": "cryptographic-asset",
  "cryptoProperties": {
    "assetType": "algorithm",
    "algorithmProperties": {
      "primitive": "signature",
      "parameterSetIdentifier": "512",
      "executionEnvironment": "software-plain-ram",
      "implementationPlatform": "x86_64",
      "certificationLevel": [
        "none"
      ],
      "cryptoFunctions": [
        "sign",
        "verify"
      ],
      "nistQuantumSecurityLevel": 0
    },
    "oid": "1.2.840.113549.1.1.13"
  }
}
```

C Elliptic Curve Mapping

Table 2. Elliptic Curve mapping between security strength, identifying strings, and recommendation for signature and key establishment (KE) [4] from [9,36], and *CBOMkit* in CycloneDX 1.6. Blank cells indicate no corresponding string is present in the source.

Security bits	SP 800–186 string	*CBOMkit* string	SP 800–186 recommendation
80		Sect163k1	
80		Sect163r2	
96		Secp192r1	
112	P-224	Secp224r1	Allowed for ECDSA, EC KE
112	K-233	Sect233k1	Deprecated
112	B-233	Sect233r1	Deprecated
112	brainpoolP224r1		Allowed for ECDSA, EC KE
128	P-256	Secp256r1	Allowed for ECDSA, EC KE
128	secp256k1	Secp256k1	Allowed to be used for blockchain-related applications
128	W-25519		Disallowed for ECDSA or EdDSA
128	Curve25519	Curve25519	Disallowed for ECDSA or EdDSA
128	Edwards25519	Edwards25519	Allowed for EdDSA
128	K-283	Sect283k1	Deprecated
128	B-283	Sect283r1	Deprecated
128	brainpoolP256r1	Brainpoolp256r1	Allowed for ECDSA, EC KE
160	brainpoolP320r1		Allowed for ECDSA, EC KE
194	P-384	Secp384r1	Allowed for ECDSA, EC KE
194	K-409	Sect409k1	Deprecated
194	B-409	Sect409r1	Deprecated
194	brainpoolP384r1	Brainpoolp384r1	Allowed for ECDSA, EC KE
224	W-448		Disallowed for ECDSA or EdDSA
224	Curve448	Curve448	Disallowed for ECDSA or EdDSA
224	Edwards448	Edwards448	Allowed for EdDSA
224	E448		Disallowed for ECDSA or EdDSA
256	brainpoolP512r1	Brainpoolp512r1	Allowed for ECDSA, EC KE
256	P-521	Secp521r1	Allowed for ECDSA, EC KE
256	K-571	Sect571k1	Deprecated
256	B-571	Sect571r1	Deprecated

References

1. ANSSI: Mécanismes cryptographiques: Règles et recommandations (2020), https://cyber.gouv.fr/publications/mecanismes-cryptographiques
2. Barker, E.: Guideline for using cryptographic standards in the federal government: cryptographic mechanisms (2020). https://doi.org/10.6028/NIST.SP.800-175Br1, https://csrc.nist.gov/pubs/sp/800/175/b/r1/final, NIST SP 800-175B Revision 1

3. Barker, E., et al.: Considerations for achieving crypto agility: strategies and practices (2025). https://doi.org/10.6028/NIST.CSWP.39.2pd, https://csrc.nist.gov/pubs/cswp/39/considerations-for-achieving-cryptographic-agility/2pd, NIST CSWP 39 (2pd)
4. Barker, E., Chen, L., Roginsky, A., Vassilev, A., Davis, R.: Recommendation for pair-wise key-establishment schemes using discrete logarithm cryptography (2018). https://doi.org/10.6028/NIST.SP.800-56Ar3, https://csrc.nist.gov/pubs/sp/800/56/a/r3/final , NIST SP 800-56A Revision 3
5. Barker, E., Roginsky, A.: Transitioning the use of cryptographic algorithms and key lengths (2019). https://doi.org/10.6028/NIST.SP.800-131Ar2, https://csrc.nist.gov/pubs/sp/800/131/a/r2/final, NIST SP 800-131A Rev. 2
6. Barker, E., Roginsky, A.: Transitioning the use of cryptographic algorithms and key lengths (2024). https://doi.org/10.6028/NIST.SP.800-131Ar3.ipd, https://csrc.nist.gov/pubs/sp/800/131/a/r3/ipd, NIST SP 800-131Ar3 ipd
7. Bradner, S.O.: Key words for use in RFCs to indicate requirement levels (RFC 2119). (1997). https://doi.org/10.17487/RFC2119, https://www.rfc-editor.org/info/rfc2119
8. BSI: Technical Guideline TR-02102 Cryptographic Mechanisms (2025). https://www.bsi.bund.de/EN/Themen/Unternehmen-und-Organisationen/Standards-und-Zertifizierung/Technische-Richtlinien/TR-nach-Thema-sortiert/tr02102/tr02102_node.html
9. Chen, L., Moody, D., Regenscheid, A., Robinson, A., Randall, K.: Recommendations for discrete logarithm-based cryptography: elliptic curve domain parameters (2023). https://doi.org/10.6028/NIST.SP.800-186, https://csrc.nist.gov/pubs/sp/800/186/final
10. CISA and the National Security Agency (NSA): A Shared Vision of Software Bill of Materials (SBOM) for Cybersecurity. https://www.cisa.gov/resources-tools/resources/shared-vision-software-bill-materials-sbom-cybersecurity, Accessed 07 Oct 2025
11. CycloneDX Project: `cdxgen`: Cyclonedx generator. https://github.com/CycloneDX/cdxgen
12. Dang, Q.: Recommendation for applications using approved hash algorithms. (2012). https://doi.org/10.6028/NIST.SP.800-107r1, https://csrc.nist.gov/pubs/sp/800/107/r1/final, NIST SP 800-107 Revision 1
13. EU: Cyber Resilience Act (CRA) (2024). https://eur-lex.europa.eu/legal-content/EN/TXT/?uri=CELEX
14. Germenia, R., Manfredi, S., Rizzi, M., Sciarretta, G., Tomasi, A., Ranise, S.: Automating compliance for improving TLS security postures: an assessment of public administration endpoints. In: SECRYPT, pp. 450–458. SciTePress (2024). https://doi.org/10.5220/0012764700003767
15. GitHub Advanced Security: CBOM action: Generate cryptography bill of materials with CodeQL. https://github.com/advanced-security/cbom-action
16. GitHub Security Lab: Addressing post-quantum cryptography with CodeQL (2023). https://github.blog/security/vulnerability-research/addressing-post-quantum-cryptography-with-codeql/
17. IANA: Transport Layer Security (TLS) parameters (2005). https://www.iana.org/assignments/tls-parameters/
18. IANA: JSON Object Signing and Encryption (JOSE) (2025). https://www.iana.org/assignments/jose/jose.xhtml
19. Jones, M.B.: JSON Web Algorithms (JWA). RFC 7518 (2015). https://doi.org/10.17487/RFC7518, https://www.rfc-editor.org/info/rfc7518

20. Leurent, G., Peyrin, T.: SHA-1 is a shambles: first chosen-prefix collision on SHA-1 and application to the PGP web of trust. In: 29th USENIX Security Symposium (USENIX Security 20), pp. 1839–1856. USENIX Association (2020). https://www.usenix.org/conference/usenixsecurity20/presentation/leurent
21. Liusvaara, I.: CFRG Elliptic Curve Diffie-Hellman (ECDH) and Signatures in JSON Object Signing and Encryption (JOSE). RFC 8037 (2017). https://doi.org/10.17487/RFC8037, https://www.rfc-editor.org/info/rfc8037
22. McKay, K.A., Cooper, D.A.: Guidelines for the selection, configuration, and use of transport layer security (TLS) implementations (2019). https://doi.org/10.6028/NIST.SP.800-52r2, https://nvlpubs.nist.gov/nistpubs/SpecialPublications/NIST.SP.800-52r2.pdf
23. Moody, D., Perlner, R., Regenscheid, A., Robinson, A., Cooper, D.: Transition to post-quantum cryptography standards (2024). https://doi.org/10.6028/NIST.IR.8547.ipd, https://csrc.nist.gov/pubs/ir/8547/ipd, NIST IR 8547 (IPD)
24. National Institute of Standards and Technology (NIST): National Vulnerability Database - CVE-2020-10148 (SolarWinds Orion API Vulnerability) . https://nvd.nist.gov/vuln/detail/CVE-2020-10148, Accessed 08 Oct 2025
25. National Institute of Standards and Technology (NIST): National Vulnerability Database - CVE-2021-44228 (Apache Log4j2 Vulnerability). https://nvd.nist.gov/vuln/detail/cve-2021-44228, Accessed 07 Oct 2025
26. National Institute of Standards and Technology (NIST): NIST interagency report (NIST IR) 8547: Cryptographic asset management. Tech. Rep. NIST IR 8547 (Initial Public Draft), National Institute of Standards and Technology (NIST) (2024). https://doi.org/10.6028/NIST.IR.8547.ipd
27. National Telecommunications and Information Administration (NTIA): The minimum elements for a software bill of materials (SBOM). https://www.ntia.doc.gov/files/ntia/publications/sbom_minimum_elements_report.pdf, Accessed 07 Oct 2025
28. Newhouse, W., Souppaya, M., Barker, W., Brown, C.: Migration to post-quantum cryptography: quantum readiness – cryptographic discovery (preliminary draft). Special Publication 1800-38B, National Institute of Standards and Technology (NCCoE), Gaithersburg (2023). https://www.nccoe.nist.gov/crypto-agility-considerations-migrating-post-quantum-cryptographic-algorithms, preliminary Draft; Released for public comment December 19, 2023
29. Newhouse, W., et al.: Migration to post-quantum cryptography: quantum readiness: cryptographic discovery (2023). https://www.nccoe.nist.gov/crypto-agility-considerations-migrating-post-quantum-cryptographic-algorithms, NIST SP 1800-38B (IPD)
30. OWASP Foundation: Cyclonedx (CDX). https://cyclonedx.org/, Accessed 7 Oct 2025
31. OWASP Foundation: Authoritative guide to cryptography bill of materials (CBOM) (2024). https://cyclonedx.org/guides/OWASP_CycloneDX-Authoritative-Guide-to-CBOM-en.pdf
32. Post-Quantum Cryptography Alliance: CBOMkit: an open-source toolkit for cryptography bills of materials. https://github.com/PQCA/cbomkit
33. Post-Quantum Cryptography Alliance: Sonar cryptography: Detection rule structure. https://github.com/PQCA/sonar-cryptography/blob/main/docs/DETECTION_RULE_STRUCTURE.md
34. Preston-Werner, T.: TOML: Tom's Obvious, Minimal Language (2021). https://github.com/toml-lang/toml, Accessed 29 Aug 2025

35. Santander Security Research: CryptoMon: Network cryptography monitor - using eBPF, written in python. https://github.com/Santandersecurityresearch/CryptoMon
36. SECG: Recommended elliptic curve domain parameters (2010). https://www.secg.org/sec2-v2.pdf, Standards for Efficient Cryptography (SEC) 2, Version 2.0
37. SOG-IS: SOG-IS crypto evaluation scheme: Agreed cryptographic mechanisms (2023). https://www.sogis.eu/uk/supporting_doc_en.html, version 1.3
38. Stevens, M.M., Lenstra, A.K., de Weger, B.M.M.: Chosen-prefix collisions for MD5 and applications. Int. J. Appl. Cryptography **2**(4), 322–359 (2012). https://doi.org/10.1504/IJACT.2012.048084, https://marc-stevens.nl/research/hashclash/
39. The Linux Foundation: The System Package Data Exchange (SPDX). https://spdx.dev/, Accessed 07 Oct 2025
40. US Government: President's Executive Order (EO) 14028 on Improving the Nation's Cybersecurity (2021). https://www.federalregister.gov/documents/2021/05/17/2021-10460/improving-the-nations-cybersecurity, Accessed 07 Oct 2025
41. Young, S.D.: Migrating to post-quantum cryptography. Memorandum M-23-02, Executive Office of the President, Office of Management and Budget (OMB), Washington, DC (2022). https://www.whitehouse.gov/wp-content/uploads/2022/11/M-23-02-M-Memo-on-Migrating-to-Post-Quantum-Cryptography.pdf

Author Index

A
Alnahawi, Nouri 181
Ansaroudi, Zahra Ebadi 69
Azouaoui, Melissa 181

B
Bormann, Christian 3
Bos, Joppe W. 181

D
Davies, Gareth T. 181
De Matteis, Pietro 202
Desmoulins, Nicolas 26
Dowling, Benjamin 111
Dumanois, Antoine 26

F
Foroncelli, Claudio 202
Fuchs, Jonathan D. 133

G
Golaszewski, Enis 133

H
Hale, Britta 89, 111
Hamer, Sophia 133

K
Kane, Seyni 26
Knob, Luis Augusto Dias 202

L
Lehmann, Anja 3, 46

M
Moon, SeoJeong 181

O
Onofri, Simone 69

P
Piras, Luca 202

R
Ranise, Silvio 69, 202

S
Saarinen, Markku-Juhani O. 162
Sciarretta, Giada 69
Sharif, Amir 69
Sherman, Alan T. 133
Sidorenko, Andrey 46

T
Tian, Xisen 89, 111
Tomasi, Alessandro 202
Traoré, Jacques 26

V
van Vredendaal, Christine 181

W
Wang, Lee 89
Wiesmaier, Alexander 181
Wimalasiri, Bhagya 111

Z
Zacharakis, Alexandros 46
Zieglar, Edward 133

H. C. Pöhls and C. J. Mitchell (Eds.): SSR 2025, LNCS 16466, p. 223, 2026.
https://doi.org/10.1007/978-3-032-19567-8

The manufacturer's authorised representative in the EU is Springer Nature Customer Service Centre GmbH, Europaplatz 3, 69115 Heidelberg, Germany. If you have any concerns regarding our products, please contact ProductSafety@springernature.com

Printed and bound by CPI Group (UK) Ltd, Croydon, CR0 4YY

07/07/2026

02160917-0005